Christian Ethics

Christian Ethics

Foundations and Practice

ROBERT BRUCE McLAREN

California State University
Fullerton

FOREWORD by
JOHN C. BENNETT

 PRENTICE HALL, Englewood Cliffs, NJ 07632

Library of Congress Cataloging-in-Publication Data

McLaren, Robert Bruce.
    Christian ethics : foundations and practice / Robert Bruce
McLaren.
        p.   cm.
    Includes index.
    ISBN 0-13-132804-2 (pbk.)
    1. Christian ethics.   I. Title.
BJ1251.M47   1994
241—dc20   91-40874
                                                                    CIP

Editorial/production supervision and interior design: *Margaret Antonini*
Cover design: *20/20 Services*
Prepress buyer: *Herb Klein*
Manufacturing buyer: *Robert Anderson*

© 1994 by Prentice-Hall, Inc.
A Simon & Schuster Company
Englewood Cliffs, New Jersey 07632

Printed in the United States of America
10 9 8 7 6 5 4 3 2 1

0-13-132804-2

Prentice-Hall International (UK) Limited, *London*
Prentice-Hall of Australia Pty. Limited, *Sydney*
Prentice-Hall Canada Inc., *Toronto*
Prentice-Hall Hispanoamericana, S.A., *Mexico*
Prentice-Hall of India Private Limited, *New Delhi*
Prentice-Hall of Japan, Inc., *Tokyo*
Simon & Schuster Asia Pte. Ltd., *Singapore*
Editora Prentice-Hall do Brasil, Ltda., *Rio de Janeiro*

To
ALTHEA
Ab Origine Fidus

CONTENTS

PREFACE

How can one speak or write of *foundations* (plural) of Christian ethics when the apostle Paul clearly declared, "No other foundation can anyone lay than that which is laid, which is Jesus Christ" (1 Corinthians 3:11)? You will note in the course of this book that the many varied practices among Christian people with respect to controversial issues in society reveal multiple origins in the mores and customs of diverse times and conditions, albeit weighed and judged by the biblical record of the teachings of Jesus, the Christ.

At a recent national conference on Christian ethics, a colleague who has authored half a dozen books in the field commented, "There really is no such thing as Christian ethics, you know. There is only ethics as an academic discipline. If you happen to be a Christian, you adapt its tools to your commitment to Christ." This evoked a considerable debate, which has continued via the mails for many months.

Is there such a thing as a distinctly Christian ethics that examines the issues of life in a multiplex world and reaches conclusions that would not be reached by any other path? It would be stating the obvious to note that Jesus was not, in any technical sense, an ethicist. He did make many pronouncements on the qualities of the good life, as even a cursory glance at his famous

Sermon on the Mount will reveal (a sermon that probably was a collection of sayings gathered from many of his public utterances). But while he utilized much of the Hebrew Scriptures and traditions in illustrating his moral position, he appears not to have been interested in the kind of detailed analysis of principles characteristic of the academic discipline we call ethics.

Most Christians, nevertheless, want to know how they should live *as Christians*, and study Jesus' life and teachings to find specific guidelines. Many call on "the Great Example" and books like Thomas à Kempis's *Imitation of Christ* (c. 1470) and almost countless books and novels written since, which suggest that if we could follow "in his steps" (the title of one such book) we would live the Christian life. Confusion arises when people discover that Jesus did not appeal to rules or principles or even the Ten Commandments (except in the case of one young man seeking a simple way to know if he qualified for eternal life; see Matthew 19:16f.). Jesus' emphasis was elsewhere: "A new commandment I give to you, that you love one another, even as I have loved you" (John 13:34). But there is wide divergence over definitions of love and how it applies to issues like abortion and birth control, capitalism and capital punishment, divorce, marriage, war, and a host of other urgent matters.

While Christians are seeking the Christian answer to these problems and specific ethical guidelines, they are charged by the non-Christian world that so-called Christian principles are inadequate or even defective; that Christianity may have caused many of the dilemmas of the modern world by unwise intervention (as in providing health care on mission fields, which prolongs life, and thus, according to this argument, extends poverty). It is also argued that Marxism has eclipsed Christianity in fighting for a just social and economic order, while churches have often sanctified a status quo which perpetuated slavery and kept the poor in subjection to kings, czars, and dictators, and to unjust political practices even in democratic societies. This book constitutes an effort to rediscover the different roots of the values by which Christians identify themselves, and the divergent paths taken to arrive where we are today *vis-à-vis* the problems and charges just noted.

The first chapter examines the background of the faith in which Jesus was nurtured, and the major themes of his teachings in light of his heritage. Chapter 2 traces the ideas promulgated by the early Christians, noting that many concepts thought to be orthodox by some were denounced as heretical by others, thus accounting for the plural foundations of Christian ethics encountered today. As the church gained secular power, its accommodation to non-Christian ideas and practices imported by converts evoked responses that led to further actions and reactions throughout the Middle Ages, the Reformation, and the Counter-Reformation. Subsequent changes in emphasis have produced the Protestant ethic, a variety of social gospels both Catholic and Protestant, and the liberal-conservative polarization, global missions, and the ecumenical movement. "New occasions teach new duties."

Chapter 3 invites the consideration of a number of criticisms of Christianity, and of a variety of responses to them. This is followed by a chapter on the nature of the Christian fellowship, and how its self-understanding has been shaped by movements and countermovements including what some people proclaim as a new reformation: liberation theology.

Just who is a Christian? Is he or she simply one who has adopted Christianity as the favored religion, or is there a sense in which the Christian, by identifying with Christ, becomes a new kind of person? Chapter 5, before addressing this question directly, takes a look at some major theories about the nature of human beings, especially those secular theories that many view as posing the most serious threats to a Christian understanding: the hypothesis of sheer organic evolution, the Freudian or psychoanalytic theories, behaviorism, and developmental theories. Some readers may find this digression confusing; "What has all this got to do with Christian ethics?" The contention here is that Christians must have their eyes open to secular alternatives to Christianity that threaten to make Christian ideas obsolete.

Beginning with Chapter 6, we focus on specific problems and issues that Christians will surely encounter in daily interaction with people and institutions, both Christian (with whom they may nevertheless sharply disagree) and non-Christian. The complex problems of sexuality are examined, including the much debated sexual revolution; private sexual concerns like masturbation; concerns of the institutional church with celibacy and the equality of men and women; and public policy as it relates to obscenity, abortion, and homosexuality. The family, as an institution undergoing severe changes, requires a separate chapter. The specifics of the marriage crisis, including divorce, are explored with a view to discovering as clear a Christian position as possible. The role of the Christian as citizen is plumbed, with special reference to politics and patriotism, justice, and the economic order.

Chapter 9 undertakes a study of the arts, education, science, and technology. The fact that, as Albert Einstein expressed it, these are all branches of the same tree has not prevented them from becoming separated and their practitioners at times mutually hostile. Each fosters ideas and actions with profound implications for Christian ethics.

Finally, in Chapter 10, we try to face objectively the many elements of Christianity that have become so enmeshed in purely secular ideas and practices as to be wholly un-Christian. Among the most flagrant is our attitude toward violence and our efforts to rationalize so-called just wars. Further, if Christians are to recover their essential nature as beings in Christ, they must ask what will be their relation to those who are not Christians, but nevertheless are highly moral, ethical persons belonging to other religious traditions, or to no religion.

Because of the very broad scope of such a book, I have been keenly aware of the danger of dilettantism. But the need for the Christian to develop an interdisciplinary habit of thinking, to relate faith to all areas of human experience is one that cannot be escaped. It has been my very great fortune over the years to teach on a number of university campuses where interaction with professors, artists, musicians, social scientists, and hard scientists has enriched my understanding of disciplines outside my own. It would be impossible to name them all. I must, however, express profound appreciation to some who have helped me quite directly with this undertaking, by reading portions of the manuscript and responding with criticisms and suggestions.

In particular I wish to thank John C. Bennett, former president of Union Theological Seminary, New York; Stanley Hauerwas, professor of theological ethics, Duke University, North Carolina; Brian Hebblethwaite, director of philosophy, theology, and religious studies, Queens College, Cambridge University; Edward LeRoy Long, former president of the American Society of Christian Ethics and professor emeritus of Drew University; June O'Connor, professor of religion, University of California, Riverside; John Polkinghorne, professor of mathematical physics and president of Queens College, Cambridge; Alan Suggate, professor of religion, University of Durham, U.K.; and Jan Womer, formerly principal at Manchester College, Oxford University, now pastor of St. Paul's Lutheran Church, Fullerton, California. I wish also to extend thanks to former president Jewel Plummer Cobb of California State University, Fullerton, for making possible a sabbatical and release time from teaching responsibilities for the writing of the book. Technical assistance with the manuscript was supplied by Rae Ann Rowley and by my daughter and typist, Christina McLaren Tardif

Finally, a special word of thanks goes to my wife Althea, portrait painter and sculptor, whose published writings in art and whose commissioned works in America, Europe, and elsewhere abroad have illumined my understanding of the discipline of the arts and their relation to faith and ethics.

FOREWORD

This book is a remarkable achievement. The range of subjects discussed is enormous. The writing is extremely well done, clear, forceful, interesting to read, sometimes eloquent. I looked forward to the reading from chapter to chapter.

Professor McLaren begins with the Biblical source of the central Christian commitment to the radical ethic of Jesus, radical in its emphasis on obedience to the will of God, and radical in its presentation of the commandment of love for all neighbors, including enemies. Jesus, his life and teachings, comes through to us through the New Testament as a whole against the background of the Hebraic faith inherited by Jesus.

The book then becomes an account of the story of the Christian life in the New Testament, and the early church, and in various phases of Christian history with emphasis for us on the current ecumenical community. All of this is seen in the context of the secular critics and rivals of Christianity, of great philosophers some of whom had distorted versions of Christianity, and some who were in sharp opposition to it. There is much emphasis on movements of psychological theory from Freudianism to psychologies of moral development. These are contrasted with Biblical approaches to the understanding of humanity as made in the divine image, and as both sinful and candidate for redemption.

The section on the various forms of liberation theology shows the author's concern for a transforming social and economic justice. Neither the religious right nor sophisticated neo-conservatives will find support in this book for their uncritical celebration of American capitalism, and it shows the author's rejection of racism and patriarchy. The chapter on sexuality is a systematic discussion of issues raised by pornography, abortion, and homosexuality and will be controversial. The chapter on the family which follows has a good chance of drawing out a very wide consensus.

The book extends the boundaries of what is often regarded as the scope of Christian ethics as it relates that discipline to science, art, education, and the relation between Christianity and other religions. The section on violence in the last chapter seems to me to be less discriminating than the excellent chapter on citizenship. Absolute pacifism seems to be taken for granted and this is not balanced by recognition of the claims in some situations for revolutionary violence, or of the claims for the historic criteria that have distinguished between just and unjust wars. Those criteria were used in the recent past as the basis on which many Christians opposed the Vietnam war, and they are now used as the basis for nuclear pacifism.

Such criticism in no way detracts from my admiration for the book as a whole, which is a great achievement in setting forth the grounds for and the development of the Christian life, inspired by the many-sided tradition of Christian faith, and responding to a secular world so full of ideas and commitments which deny the claims of Christian ethics, and so full of the most perplexing dilemmas calling for decisions by Christians.

John C. Bennett

CHAPTER ONE

Biblical Foundations

For a straightforward study of Christian ethics it would seem logical to begin with an examination of the social and ethical teachings of Jesus, and to determine how they were interpreted in the earliest Christian fellowship. The difficulty with this approach is that Jesus was not an ethicist. Ethics has to do with reflecting thoughtfully on moral customs and formulating principles that can be reduced to rules. A study of Jesus' teachings reveals that he had little or no interest in a theoretical examination of principles.

In fact, the term *Christian ethics* did not come into use until the fourth century, when Basil of Caesaria (330–379 A.D.) drew up a list of eighty rules for monastic life: *Principles of Christian Ethics*. Yet it is clear that the earliest disciples were concerned about what behavior was implied in being Christian. *Ethics* comes from a Greek verb *eiotha* "to be conventional"; the most characteristic ethical question was, "How are things done where you come from?" Caesar's admonition, "When in Rome, do as the Romans do," was an unacceptable option among Christians for whom the essential question was, "What would Christ have us do?" More important: What would he have us be?

Jesus' teachings were based on certain moral and spiritual presuppositions that he applied directly to problems at hand. He said nothing, for example,

1

about the principles of capitalism or of the right of individuals to own property. Indeed, when asked for a judgment on a related matter he retorted, "Who made me a judge or divider over you?" (Luke 12:14). He did, however, tell a parable in which he scorned the attitude of a landowner who hoarded great wealth in his barns and then built bigger barns to store his bumper crop without a thought for his starving neighbors. In that situation (Luke 12:13–21), as well as in other parables like the prodigal son (Luke 15:11–32) and the rich man and Lazarus (Luke 16:19–31), Jesus took a clear moral position on the relation of property ownership and greed, but did not seek Confuciuslike to delineate principles that could be reduced to law. Indeed, he devoted a great portion of his teachings to pointing out the futility of simply following rules, including the laws of Hebrew tradition, unless fulfilling the spirit of the law was the real motivation. His complaint against the law enforcers was that "they bind heavy burdens and grievous to be born" (Matthew 23:4); by contrast his own way was liberation (see Matthew 11:30). "It might be," as Oliver Johnson writes, "that had he had such an interest [in theoretical principles], he probably would have been far less successful as a moral reformer."[1] Paul Ramsey puts it this way: "It is as if in every one of his strenuous teachings Jesus were uttering the challenge, 'Try to make a law out of this if you can! Try to make this customary, conventional or habitual.' "[2]

Another reason we cannot simply begin with the teachings of Jesus is that they cannot be fully understood without comprehending their Hebrew background. Many Jewish rabbis today contend that Jesus' teachings contain nothing new, all his ethical concerns are essentially Jewish, and therefore Christian ethics should always be expressed in hyphenated form as Judeo-Christian. We explore this later in more depth, but for now we must simply acknowledge Jesus' Jewishness if we are to understand his ethical position. Even Jewish ethics does not stand alone, but shows evidences of Greek and Roman influence. While Jesus' teachings are rooted in the Old Testament, we must also consider the possibility of non-Jewish foundations that may undergird his teachings.

Again, we must recognize that the fellowship Jesus called into being did not initially formulate a body of ethical teachings, and that what gradually evolved was at least partly influenced by the selection of the books which make up the New Testament. These were not finally limited to the body of Scripture we know today until 367 A.D., when Athanasius enumerated the collection of twenty-seven books in his famous Easter Letter.

Finally, it is imperative that we discern the many nonbiblical and indeed non-Christian influences which have crept into the body of principles we call Christian ethics today, and which account for so much variety in defining what Christian behavior entails. Whatever fundamentals we may apply to given problems like abortion, birth control, civil rights, capital punishment, disarmament, or other complex issues facing us today, the Christian finds a ready argument with fellow Christians, each convinced of the biblical authenticity of his or her position. Charges of liberal and conservative or even leftist and fascist are hurled back and forth, and Christendom finds itself increasingly polarized. To our discomfort we must acknowledge that Christian churches remain among the most racially segregated groups in society, and some church members are as vigorously hawkish on military policies as any secular munitions maker. On the other hand, most of the energy for the civil rights movement comes from the churches, and peace initiatives are coming forth from the major Christian denominations in greater strength than ever before.

What are the foundations for such divergence? How often are Christian ethics a mere amalgam of biblical ideas and racial or regional pride, bearing a Christian label that is almost indistinguishable from the most secular of tags?

THE JEWISH BACKGROUND

It is of crucial importance that we recognize Jesus as one born into the Jewish heritage. Obvious as this may seem to historians, many Christians find it offensive to suggest the Son of God could have been influenced by the Jewish or any other system of thought. This notion gained prominence in the second century among the Marcionites who tried to purify Christianity from all contact with Judaism. It was revived by certain German theologians in the nineteenth century, and still prevails today among some ultraconservative Christian groups.

The ethics in which Jesus was raised can be summed up in the word *halakhah*, "walking is obedience." It was both law and ethics; as Leo Trepp puts it, "Judaism, as a religion of action, has always seen the law as an instrument of ethics, and as an ethical ideal to be pursued."[3] Beginning each day with the *Shema Israel* (Hear, O Israel), the faithful Jew took up "the yoke of the kingdom" and began his *halakhah*, his obedient journey on the highway of the kingdom.

Simeon the Righteous, a Jewish rabbi in the pre-Christian world, declared that civilization is based on three foundations: the Law (meaning the Torah), worship, and deeds of kindness. Jesus, for whom the holy Torah was authoritative, intended to fulfill it every "jot and tittle" (see Matthew 5:17f.). So central was the Law to Jewish thought that it was virtually synonymous with the word of God. From Psalms, Proverbs, and Ecclesiasticus, we understand that God's Law existed before the creation of the world, and daily study of this Law confers blessings greater than all other benefits one might desire.

A further source of Jewish ethics is the extensive Talmudic literature, and the Midrash incorporated in the Mishna. Midrashim were commentaries on the Law and on books of the Hebrew Scripture. This literature interpreted and expanded upon the Law. For example, although the Law forbids doing wrong to a neighbor in a business transaction, specific degrees of deception or wrongdoing and their penalties are left unstated (see Leviticus 25:14). The sages eventually fixed the amount that constitutes a fraudulent deal as being one-sixth of the worth of the object or the price paid. The injured party must be paid the difference.[4]

Rabbi Waxman insists that the ancient Hebrews were not only the first monotheists,[5] but found in the conception of God as One an inescapable moral corollary that underlay all subsequent ethical regulations. "The very essence of God is activity," he notes, so providence can be taken for granted: God must logically care for his creation, including humankind.[6] The election of Israel as a chosen people follows: ". . . for when in a world of nations sunk in idolatry there arises only one small group possessing the unique idea of the universal God, it has full right to conclude that it was elected by divine providence for that task."[7]

Election was not for power or material advantage, however, but for a noble and moral purpose: to "be a light to the Gentiles." So, lest the Jews fall into the idolatry of their neighbors, the Law was given and throughout successive centuries of tribulation, bondage, freedom, prosperity, and persecution, the Law has remained the ultimate frame of reference for all moral and ethical consideration.

Certain Greco-Roman influences became incorporated in Jewish thought, significantly influencing its development. Commerce with the Greeks brought Plato's call for a universal system of public education to Jewish attention. While Plato's dream was never completely fulfilled among the Greeks, the idea was adopted among the Jews and fully implemented. The Mishnah thus says that even if people must survive on the barest essentials for life, their education must not be neglected, particularly the study of the Torah.[8] Philo, the great Jewish scholar who lived in Egypt during the century before Jesus' birth, not only spoke and wrote in Greek, but conducted his life in much the spirit of the Stoics.[9] Further, under the influence of Hellenism the sect called the Sadducees developed among the wealthy class of Jews. Caiphas, the high priest appointed by Pilate and remembered among early Christians for his condemnation of Jesus, was one of these.

Rabbi Leo Baeck, in *The Essence of Judaism,* described the faith as inherently optimistic because even though mankind often violates the Law, mankind also received the revelation of the One God, whose nature made the moral law inevitable. As the Creator whose goodness could not tolerate the triumph of evil, God binds all mankind into a family, so it is possible to remain hopeful even in seemingly hopeless situations. "The distinctiveness of Judaism, which it has passed to the rest of mankind, is its ethical affirmation of the world: Judaism is the religion of ethical optimism."[10]

Did Jesus have anything new to add to this? No, claims Rabbi Nathan Rotenstreich. "Judaism looks upon Christianity as a daughter religion, but realizes at the same time that this added nothing new to the fundamental principles of Judaism. From the Jewish point of view, Jesus accomplished what he did because he was born a Jew, studied the Law and the Prophets, and strove to be what a Jew should be."[11]

In similar fashion, Leo Baeck insists that the practice of Jesus, when quoting a Jewish law or custom saying, ". . . You have heard it said . . . but I say unto you . . ." (see Matthew 5:21, 27, 33, 43, etc.) was not an innovation at all. The famous phrase, " 'But I say unto you,' is not the product of a later period; it is already found in the prophets and the Psalms. . . . One hears the same note ringing again and again in the Talmud, if only a corresponding formulation is given to the teachings: 'Ye have heard it was said to them of old time: thou shalt not commit adultery. But I say unto you: he who glances in his lust even at the corner of a woman's heel is as if he had committed adultery with her.' "[12] (see Matthew 5:27–28). Joseph Klausner goes so far as to claim, "Throughout the gospels there is not one item of ethical teaching which cannot be paralleled either in the Old Testament, the Apocrypha, or in the Talmudic and Midrashic literature of the period near the time of Jesus."[13]

If this contention is true, we must ask what it was about Christianity that enabled it to survive centuries of persecution and to become the dominant religion while Judaism went into decline and was almost annihilated. The Jews suffered persecution in 70 A.D., and were dispersed at a time when Christianity had hardly yet formed. Indeed, Christendom's formation was almost nipped in the bud; not only were Christians persecuted by Rome, but they were also persecuted by the Jews wherever the latter could organize opposition. The record of such persecution comprises much of the content of the Book of Acts and the Letters of the Apostles. For three centuries Christians were hounded almost to extinction by the Romans, being falsely blamed for the burning of Rome, falsely accused of cannibalism, tortured en masse for both "crimes" and herded by the hundreds into arenas for slaughter.

What was so distinctive about Christianity that it could not only survive, but eventually overcome the powers that sought its extermination? The answer is complex, and much of it is outside the scope of a book on ethics. Perhaps Will Durant put his finger on it when he wrote, "They turned from Caesar preaching war, to Christ preaching peace; from incredible brutality to unprecedented charity; from a life without hope or dignity to a faith that honored their humanity."[14] Beyond this was the good news that when we identify with Christ, his life becomes ours and ours his ("For me to live *is Christ* [italics mine]," as Paul wrote to the Philippians), so that no power on earth, not even death itself can separate us from the love of God, nor revoke the promise of eternal life.

JESUS' POSITION VIS-À-VIS JUDAISM

It is clear from the Gospels that Jesus was raised by Jewish parents with every expectation that he would be an obedient son of the Law. Luke tells us Jesus was circumcised "according to the Law of Moses" on the eighth day (Luke 2:21–22); he was taken to the temple at age twelve, then returned with his parents to Nazareth, "and was obedient to them" (Luke 2:51). His baptism was a Jewish ceremony observed among certain Jewish sects (Luke 4:16). Jesus' teachings contained much that was already familiar to his Jewish listeners. Yet the demand of Jesus for righteousness was more exacting than they were used to even from the most strict Pharisees: "I tell you, unless your righteousness exceeds that of the scribes and Pharisees, you will never enter the Kingdom of Heaven" (Matthew 5:20).

On this point it is worth noting that Jesus' opposition to the Pharisees has often been overstated. Rabbi Trepp notes, "There hardly exists any group in history that has been treated so unjustly by posterity. They maintained that service of God calls for the human heart. Love for Him and fellow man must undergird all our actions."[15] It is impossible for us to reconstruct the nature of Phariseeism today, for the reason that Jacob Neusner points out, "The only reliable information derives from Josephus, the Gospels, and rabbinic literature. . . . As is clear, none of these gives an accurate account of Pharisaic theology before 70 A.D."[16] It is clear from the Gospel records that the Pharisees were perceived by Jesus as making compliance with Jewish law a stifling affair with no freedom for the spirit, yet many of the Pharisees themselves took such liberties with it that Jesus denounced them (see Matthew 23:13, 14, 23, 24, 25–27; Luke 18:11, etc.).

Jesus did not, however, denounce all Pharisees and indeed may have been considered in the Pharisaic line himself, as many rabbis were. Jesus' attacks may have been prompted by the fact that the Pharisees had become Hellenized, and as such had imposed a very un-Jewish philosophical strictness on the interpretation of Mosaic law. "Palestinian Judaism," as Neusner points out, "and the Pharisaic sect in particular, are to be seen as Jewish modes of a common, international cultural 'style' known as Hellenism. . . . Some of the most important terms of rabbinic biblical exegesis have been borrowed from the Greek. This is basic. . . . The existence of such borrowing can be explained only by a period of profound Hellenization."[17]

It is a particularly Hellenistic trait to require precise, logical formulations in argument, adherence to exact wording of references being a hallmark of Greek discourse. It was against this almost obsessive preoccupation with the letter of the Law among the Hellenized Pharisees that Jesus fought, not against Phariseeism per se. One may, for example, consider Jesus' liberal interpretation of the laws against working on the Sabbath, when he plucks grain with his disciples (Luke 6:1). Technically they were guilty of breaking two of the thirty-nine laws governing behavior on the Sabbath. Jesus did not try to justify the action on grounds that they were starving (although his reference to the episode of David and his soldiers fleeing from Saul might seem to be such a plea). Paul Ramsey interprets the action of Jesus on this occasion:

> Jesus went wide of the law for the sake of an increase of the simple pleasures of taste and conviviality, the freedom of men to nibble grain when strolling through the fields without hindrance from those who consider themselves moral and religious authorities. His position was as far without the law as could be, and he

came to take this position, not on account of any consciously adopted antinomian program, but by preoccupation with concrete human needs, even casual and unimportant ones.[18]

This interpretation actually places Jesus closer to the older Jewish rabbinical tradition than were his contemporaries, and certainly highlights his statement "I have come that they might have life, and that they might have it more abundantly" (John 10:10).

A paradox is immediately apparent. Jesus liberalized the law, yet declared "one jot nor one tittle shall in no wise pass away from the law, till all things be accomplished" (Matthew 5:18). By healing on the Sabbath, for example, he did in fact breach certain literal details of the Law. Yet in a larger sense he was complying with the spirit behind the law of the Sabbath, which was to provide for emotional and spiritual renewal on a regular basis. Jesus' actions provided an example of presenting the Law in its obverse formulas, showing how to fulfill it more truly than by slavish conformity to the words. Another instance is in his offering the Golden Rule. This rule is exactly the obverse of the one that the Jewish sage Hillel called "the foundation of Judaism": "Do not do unto others what would be hateful to you were it done to you." Jesus put the emphasis on the affirmative side: "Whatever you wish that men would do to you, do so to them" (Matthew 7:12). The implications of this reversal in the practical life are extensive, as Jesus illustrated in his parable of the good Samaritan (Luke 10:30ff.). The priest and Levite are observed to have fulfilled the older dictum, by simply doing nothing, by not getting involved. Jesus' requirement was that we must become involved on behalf of suffering people, even as we would wish others to offer aid if we were the victims.

There is no warrant for concluding that Jewish ethics is in any way deficient in concern for one's neighbor; Leviticus 19:18 commands love for the neighbor equal to one's love for one's self. Nor did the Jews confine their love to fellow Jews, refusing to acknowledge Gentiles as neighbors (as they have wrongly been accused of doing). They were also commanded to love "the foreigner (*Ha-Ger*) who sojourns among you."[19] The shock of Jesus' parable was that he made a Samaritan the hero of the story at the expense of both priest and Levite. The Samaritan was not simply a foreigner, but a member of a despised sect of heathens who pretended to be Jews. Jesus swept aside this historic feud and laid the groundwork for two genuinely original teachings: His disciples must love not only neighbors and strangers, but also enemies (Luke 6:27); they must become perfect in their loving, as God is perfect in his love.

The command "You, therefore, must be perfect as your heavenly father is perfect" (Matthew 5:48) lays upon the Christian seemingly impossible obligations. As God loves the whole human family, so we must love each other with perfect, unselfish, and reconciling love. In his farewell discourse, Jesus, who had already declared, "the Father and I are one," says to his disciples, "This is my commandment, that you love one another as I have loved you" (John

15:12). To remove all doubt that by one another he meant not just the little band of friends, but the whole of mankind, he sent them out to "make disciples of all nations . . ." (see Matthew 28:19; Acts 1:18).

Behind and beneath Jesus' teaching there is a unique self-understanding. He was bar mitzvah, "son of the Torah," the Law of God and of Israel, but he also felt himself to be something more. The term *Son of man*, as used in Psalms 8:4 and in Ezekiel 2:1, 3:1, 3:10, and in many other passages from that book is tantamount to "mortal man." Jesus' reference to Isaiah 53, however, when appropriating the term for himself, suggests a distinctly messianic meaning. The title as it appears in apocalyptic literature (see Enoch and 2 Esdras) implies the judgeship of a being from heaven. This is clearly reflected in Matthew 25:31–46, "when the son of man comes in his glory" and will sit on his glorious throne and is referred to as "the King."

It is significant that Jesus did not identify with the traditional Davidic kingship. Jesus seems to deny that being a son of David is of importance to messiahship (see Matthew 22:41f.; Mark 12:35f.; Luke 20.41f.). While Rudolph Bultmann questions the authenticity of these passages,[20] it would seem odd that words so damaging to the prophetic hope concerning the Davidic line would have been included in three of the Gospels if they were not authentic. What is perhaps of greatest importance is that Jesus was "designated son of God in power according to the Spirit of holiness by his resurrection from the dead" (Romans 1:4). It is this that gives authority and force to his ethical teachings.

Major Themes in Jesus' Teaching

At least five emphases can be identified in Jesus' ethical position that clearly challenge the established order and clarify for us the special quality of his ethical concern. These include his focus on the sovereign will of God, the sinfulness of mankind, the reconciling love of God, the urgency of practical service, and the establishment of God's kingdom worldwide.

The Sovereignty of God

While classical philosophers sought the ultimate good in a transcendent realm of impersonal absolutes, and others sought it in nature or in the will of a national ruler, Jesus declared, "None is good save one, even God" (Mark 10:18). However we may wish to interpret the postbiblical doctrine of the holy Trinity, it is evident that Jesus rejected the adjective *good* as applied to himself, and made a clear distinction between himself and the Father: "Not my will, but thine be done" (Luke 22:42). He said, "I do nothing on my own authority, but speak thus as the Father taught me" (John 8:28). For Jesus, the sovereign will of God was the context, the absolute and only frame of reference for moral and ethical decisions. It is true Jesus declared, "The Father and I are one" (John

10:30). This has profound implications for "the ethics of the atonement" that we discuss later. But it is also true, as Paul observed, "Jesus . . . did not count equality with God a thing to be grasped, but emptied himself, taking the form of a servant" (Philippians 2:6–7).

Jesus' many references to the kingdom of God throughout the Gospels and his stress on "seeking" and "receiving" the kingdom clearly imply acceptance of God's sovereignty. The instruction on prayer that contains what we know as the Lord's Prayer includes the injunction that we should pray for God's will to be done.

Jesus' willingness that God's will be fulfilled is revealed in his acceptance of that will even though it would lead to his crucifixion. This is not the spirit of resignation of a soldier in battle because soldiers do not really accept death, but would avoid it if they could. Nor is it like Socrates's acceptance of the hemlock; Socrates believed that in teaching and challenging, he was fulfilling God's command "to search into myself and other men . . . exhorting . . . reproaching. For this is the command of God."[21] Yet Socrates urged the court not to condemn him, so that he could go on serving the state as its "gadfly." For Jesus, there was no pleading with the court for leniency; he believed that somehow the very salvation of the world lay in his identifying with mankind, as well as with God, so that the sins of mankind might be resolved in his death. Given this self-understanding, it was a risk unlike that taken by any other person. He anticipated that the mode of death would be the most painful (as in the sacrifice of the Paschal lamb) and most ignominious of all deaths, and that if he faltered, God's plan for the world's redemption would have been betrayed by him.

Throughout his career, this quality of at-one-ness with God instructed Jesus' every act, from the healing of people's ills and blindness to feeding their hungry bodies and souls. His confidence was that God's will would ultimately triumph, not despite but *through* the seeming tragedy of his life.

Another implication of God's sovereignty for Christian ethics lies in the realm of teleology, the study of ends or consequences. In biblical thought, all things exist because of God's creative will, and all things have a purpose. Aristotle, to be sure, developed such a view into a whole philosophical concept, one that Thomas Aquinas would adapt to his purposes as a philosophical support for his arguments in the *Summa,* as we note later. But Aristotle's teleology was naturalistic, rather than distinctly theological. He detailed the purpose of almost countless features in nature, all of which tended toward some goal or end, observing that one cannot understand fully a seed without knowing the flower it was destined to become.

Biblical thought extended the teleological concept beyond the realm of things to the world of events. Not only does every aspect of nature fit logically together from the smallest natural detail to the vast wheeling galaxies (as in the Eighth Psalm, and God's contention with Job), but God knew us and formed us in our mother's wombs (Psalm 139:13–16), and every hair of our heads is numbered (Matthew 10:30). Not only is nothing in nature haphazard, an insight reflected in Albert Einstein's argument against the indeterminancy theory ("Der Herr Gott furwelt nicht," The Lord God doesn't gamble), but every historic event is under God's supervision and judgment. This is not to say every occurrence is predetermined. This is not a doctrine of fatalism, which robs humans of free and responsible choice. But it is congruent with the apostle's concept of predestination (Acts 4:28; Romans 8:29–30, 13:1–5). In God's sovereignty, there is a plan; for each of us there is a *telos*, a destiny, which we must seek to fulfill. We ignore or reject it at our peril.

Sin and the Human Condition

Jesus does not propose a doctrine of sin, nor for that matter does the Hebrew literature in which he was nurtured. The writers of Scripture mainly addressed specific sins and faults (the most common Hebrew root is *Chet*: to miss or fail), or acts of revolting against God's laws (*Chataah*: to revolt or transgress),[22] or spoke of wickedness in general (*Chattath*). It is in Jeremiah that we come closest to an identification of sin as arising from the inner nature of mankind: "The heart is deceitful above all things, and desperately corrupt" (Jeremiah 17:9). And the author of Psalm 14 tells us, "There is none that is good . . . they are all alike corrupt." The Old Testament is replete with descriptions both of the Jewish people and of their enemies as "stiff-necked" and "hard-hearted"; their constant disobedience reduces even their little righteousness to "filthy rags" (Isaiah 64:6).

A comparison of Jeremiah (7:24, 11:8, 16:12) with Mark 7:21–23 makes it clear that Jesus stood in a direct line with the prophets of Israel in taking sin with utmost seriousness. His first word when he began his ministry was, "Repent, for the kingdom of heaven is at hand" (Matthew 4:17). Seldom does any Old Testament figure rival Jesus' scathing denunciation of contemporaries (and fellow religionists at that): "You brood of vipers, how can you speak good when you are evil?" (Matthew 12:34). The call to repentance (the verb "repent" comes from *metanoia*, requiring a radical alteration of mind) was a challenge not merely to change one's thinking, but to change one's way of being. "From within, out of the heart of men, evil thoughts proceed, fornications, thefts, murders, adulteries, covetings, wickedness, deceit, lasciviousness, and evil eye, railing, pride, foolishness: all these evil things proceed from within, and defile the man" (Mark 7:21–23). Neither nature nor the environment has warped us and made us something other than God intended; we are ontologically altered by our own perverse wills.

To speak of ourselves as ontological deviates is to confess that God has created us as beings intended to be persons of a specific nature, that is, bearers of God's image. Our *ontos*, our essential being, has been distorted by our willful rejection of his lordship, so that we have disfigured that image of God in ourselves. Our dilemma as ontological deviates is that we, on our own, can do nothing about it except to respond in faith to God's offer to restore that image through the reconciling work of Christ. That recovered image is contained in the biblical concept of "The new creation in Christ" (2 Corinthians 5:17).

Sin as ontological deviation is a condition of our being. We are creatures intended for a destiny of fellowship with God, but that condition has been so distorted that we have lost all hope of achieving that destiny. This is the meaning of those dreadful words in Jesus' parable: "I do not know where you come from; depart from me" (Luke 13:27). It is not simply that we have done evil deeds; we *are* evil. That is our condition, which makes it difficult for us even to perceive the distinction between the sacred and the profane. As Paul Tillich expresses it, sin is "the unreconciled duality of the secular and the holy. It is the state in which God is not 'all in all' but is understood by the secularized mind as simply something added to other things to which we give a sentimental nod now and then."[23]

Sin is also acknowledged to have a force all its own. Thus Houlden noted, ". . . sin is a religious category before it is a moral category. It is a force which beguiles and enslaves."[24] Jesus said it explicitly, "Truly . . . everyone who commits sin is a slave to sin" (John 8:34). Paul echoes this theme over and over, ". . . sin, finding opportunity . . ." and "sin, working death in me . . ." and again, ". . . making me captive to the law of sin" (Romans 7:11–25). As a natural consequence, sin issues in those behaviors we commonly refer to by the general term *sin*, such as lying, cheating, killing, and perhaps worst of all, tempting others to sin with us. Jesus reserved a special condemnation for the latter: "Temptations to sin are sure to come, but woe to him by whom they come! It would be better for him if a millstone were hung around his neck and he were cast into the sea, than that he should cause one of these little ones to sin" (Luke 17:1–2). Tempting others to sin by making unlawful or immoral behavior seem attractive is thus singled out by Jesus as particularly reprehensible.

Perhaps the most painful aspect of this understanding of sin is the recognition that we are creatures who, given freedom of mind and will with capacity unknown elsewhere in nature, have used that freedom to become alienated from God who gave us life, and apart from whom is death. God laments, "This people draw near to me with their mouth and honor me with their lips while their hearts are far from me" (Isaiah 29:13). Even in worship we can sin.

If "the wages of sin is death" as Paul tells us, his question must also be ours: "The good which I would I do not; but the evil which I would not, that I practice. Who shall deliver me out of the body of this death?" (Romans 7:24).

The body of this death is not merely *sarkos*, or biological flesh, but *somatos*, our whole human nature prone to worldliness rather than godliness. Although many regard our world as having been created good by God (after all, does not Genesis tell us God made the world "and saw that it was good"?), the Gospel of John insists that "the world" accepts neither Jesus (John 1:10) nor God (17:25). Jesus was not of the world, as were his disciples (8:2). His mission was to save them from the world (17:6, 14), so he could return them to the world to redeem it (17:18–23). Paul later cautioned, "Be not conformed to this world" (Romans 12:2), and James urged the new Christians to "keep . . . unstained from the world" (James 1:27). This flies in the face of much liberal theology in our own recent history, but as Paul Tillich noted, "The Kingdom of God stands against the kingdoms of this world, namely, the demonic power-structures which rule history and personal life."[25] No one who has lived through our world's holocausts, from Nazi Germany to the slaughter of populations in Uganda, Cambodia, and elsewhere, and witnessed the multibillions of dollars spent on military buildups while the hungry billions of the nations have nowhere to go but to the grave, can doubt the existence of "the demonic power-structures."

In such tragic times, it is well to recall Emil Brunner's caveat: "The first step toward true righteousness is the sincere confession that we are sinners."[26]

Reconciling Love

As the righteousness of God was the context for Jesus' understanding "the good" from which morality and ethics derive, so the acknowledgment of our sinful condition, our ontological apartness from God, was the setting for perceiving God's reconciling love.

God's love, however, comes to us as a two-edged sword, bringing a requirement that we too must love and be reconciled to those who have sinned against us (Matthew 6:12). Jesus' command "Thou shalt love" reaches a new level above that of the Hebrew Scripture which he quotes (Leviticus 19:18) concerning love of neighbor or even love of "the stranger who sojourns with you" (19:34). The Hebrew writers never included the enemy, especially enemies of God: "Do I not hate them that hate thee, O God?" (Psalm 139:21). Jesus reminded his disciples of this: "You have heard that it was said, love your neighbor and hate your enemy, but I say to you, love your enemies and pray for those who persecute you" (Matthew 5:43f.).

Love as *eros*, or passion, was of course well known in the ancient world, as was *philos*, or brotherly love (Plato even called love of wisdom *philos*). But love as *agape* is a self-sacrificing love inspired by God as revealed in Christ, which extends even to the enemy. This is new with Christianity. The agape phenomenon represents a new breakthrough in ethical thought and action. We explore its implications for family and social life, treatment of criminals, and acts of war in later chapters.

Paradoxically it is our sinful condition, even as we rejoice in God's *agape*, that makes our perception and understanding of love so difficult. If God were a god of justice only, meting out punishment as we are prone to do with each other, we would be without hope. Hebrew Scripture underscores this: "If thou, O Lord, shouldst mark iniquities, Lord who could stand? But there is forgiveness with thee, that thou mayst be feared" (Psalm 130:3–4).

Again we find in the teaching of Jesus and his immediate followers a departure from the prior Jewish attitude toward sin. Within Judaism, membership in the covenant community was a sign of chosenness, and to be among the chosen of God was to receive an invitation to holiness: "Ye shall be holy; for I Jehovah your God am holy" (Leviticus 19:2). This implied a state of grace in which one was forgiven, cleansed, and set apart: "The taking away of barriers of sin and guilt in order that many may again enter the divine presence and experience God's blessing in his life."[27] But among Christians, sin was regarded with greater forboding. They had witnessed the utter destructiveness of their alienation from God in the crucifixion, and had seen sin as mankind's willingness that even God be destroyed in order for human pride to be victorious. Jesus interpreted God's love as forgiveness in a correspondingly dramatic way. Repentance and sorrow for one's sins were not enough to merit forgiveness. A contrite heart must find practical expression: "Bear fruits that befit repentance . . . He who has two coats, let him share with him who has none; and he who has food, let him do likewise" (Luke 3:8, 11). But lest this become a mere penance by which one could think he had thereby earned forgiveness, Jesus asserted one cannot be forgiven unless he or she is also a forgiving person (see Matthew 6:14; Mark 11:25; Luke 11:4, 17:3). This is more radical than it may seem at first thought. We often find those who think confession and charitable deeds are sufficient to merit forgiveness while they continue to nurse grudges against those who have offended them. Jesus' stark warning in his parable of the unmerciful servant (Matthew 18:23–35) is that, as that man was delivered over for punishment, "so also my heavenly Father will do to every one of you, if you do not forgive your brother from your heart."

The refusal of God to forgive those who are unforgiving raises a painful question: Have Christians come to take salvation too lightly, as if "everyone who calls upon the name of the Lord will be saved" (Romans 10:13), and nothing else is required? Jesus flatly contradicts the notion (Matthew 7:21), and every student of Paul's writings knows that for him sin was no mere transgression which God could easily dismiss: "The wages of sin is death" (Romans 6:23). This death was not simply physical demise, but a sundering of all relationship with God, who is life. For his Jewish compatriots who had assumed that belonging to the covenant community gave special advantage, Paul had startling news: "There will be tribulation and distress for every human being who does evil, the Jew first, and also the Greek" (Romans 2:9). In fact, being one of the chosen put one in a more precarious position, not less, if he or she transgressed the law. But ultimately it must be seen that *any* thought or deed which is not the conscious product of faith is sinful (Romans 14:23).

How then can anyone expect anything but condemnation? We all know that most of our daily thoughts and actions are prompted by a myriad of trivial and wholly secular impulses. Jesus' response to the disciples' question "Who then can be saved?" went straight to the point: "With men this is impossible, but with God all things are possible" (Matthew 19:25–26). God's love for the world is freely extended. The key to any understanding of the Gospel is in Paul's proclamation to the Corinthians, written before the Gospels were compiled into official Scripture: "God was in Christ, reconciling the world to himself" (Corinthians 5:19). But this reconciliation, while offered freely, is not unconditional. Herein lies what we may call the ethics of atonement.

Ethics of Atonement

Jesus did not teach about or even mention the word *atonement*, so it may be questioned whether it is appropriate to discuss it in this section. Yet the concept is so central to the Christian life, that one of the first questions raised by those seeking to understand Christianity is, "How can the death of a man two thousand years ago affect people's salvation today?" If our redemption is, as affirmed in the preceding section, contingent upon "bearing fruit," in a moral life, what is the relevance of Jesus' atonement for our sins? Would it be ethical for God to require Jesus' death as a condition of other people's salvation?

It is important to keep before us the fact that the word *atonement*, though familiar in Hebrew Scripture, appears nowhere in the New Testament. The word *kaphar* was used to describe Jacob's gift to Esau, to atone for Jacob's theft of the birthright (Genesis 32:20). It was later employed to describe the "sin offering" to atone for the transgressions of the people (Exodus 29:36; Leviticus 16:19). Where it appears, a sacrificial system is usually required to fulfill it. The Greek equivalent for *kaphar* is *exilasmos*, but this word never appears in New Testament writings.[28] How then are we to understand the many metaphors used to convey the idea that Jesus' death was in some sense akin to the sacrifices of Hebrew Testament times?

It is not surprising that the early Christians would employ familiar analogies to the Hebrew sacrificial system, which was their own background. If Jesus' death somehow cancels the effects of sin as a barrier to salvation, they might see him as a scapegoat driven alive into the wilderness bearing the sins of the people (Leviticus 16:10), although Jesus was not driven out alive. Or they might see him as "the [Paschal] lamb of God" (John 1:29; 1 Corinthians 5:7), although the Paschal lamb was never a sin offering.

The uniqueness of the concept as Paul employs it has been almost obliterated by centuries of argument based on false analogies with "mystery religions" of the East, or with "dying gods" who save mankind by death and springtime resurrections. The reconciliation between God and estranged humankind is not achieved by a simple cycle of seasons.

The substitutionary atonement theory has also obscured what the Scripture writers were trying to convey. The idea that Jesus was sent by God to substitute himself at the punishment block for mankind's sins (as C. S. Lewis put it, "to take the rap" for us), impugns God's justice as righteousness. It reduces him to a petty tyrant demanding blood punishment, then letting us off after his bloodlust has been satisfied. We should never forget that the Hebrew thought in which Jesus and Paul were nurtured presents God as extending "loving kindness," *Hesed,* twenty-three times in the book of Psalms alone, but also elsewhere throughout the Old Testament as an integral part of his justice and righteousness. Paul Ramsey observes that "the righteousness of God actually borders on the meaning of loving kindness, or God's keeping troth, his unwavering faithfulness in keeping the covenant."[29]

A more powerful metaphor is attributed to Jesus, who is reported as saying, "The Son of man came . . . to give his life as a ransom for many" (Mark 10:45). This is echoed in 1 Timothy 2:6 and in Revelation 5:9. The ransom theory of atonement had numerous supporters during the Middle Ages (Origen, Athanasius, Augustine), but it was never made clear to whom the ransom was to be paid. Paul, too, writing to the Corinthian church, said, "You are not your own; you were bought with a price" (1 Corinthians 6:20). But to whom was the price paid? If, as a common tradition has it, the ransom (or price) was paid to Satan who holds mortal souls in bondage, surely God's justice is impugned. If his justice is so implacable that God must have a sacrifice (as in the substitutionary theory), he is only satisfying himself. But if God is depicted as bargaining with Satan, sacrificing Jesus as a ransom knowing he is going to raise Jesus from the dead (and thus deprive Satan of the prize), surely God is portrayed in a dishonest act.[30]

Close inspection of the passage in Mark (and its parallel in Matthew 20:28) has raised questions about whether the statement can be reliably attributed to Jesus. The episode in which it is "quoted" begins with a serious discrepancy, wherein Matthew reports that "the mother of the sons of Zebedee" came to Jesus asking a special favor for her sons, whereas in Mark, the two sons make the request on their own. Luke, reporting the same episode, makes no reference to Jesus' statement about giving his life "a ransom for many" and H. D. A. Major observes, "Luke's account . . . seems to indicate that he did not share the Jewish Christian view of the death of Jesus as a propitiary sacrifice."[31] Each of the Gospel writers reflects a particular understanding of the meaning of Jesus' death, and they do not all concur. As Rudolph Bultmann points out, "Whatever the origin of these passages, the thought of Jesus' death as an atonement for sin has no place in John, and if it should turn out that he took it over from the tradition of the church, it would still be a foreign element in this work."[32] It is not Jesus' death per se that is the focus for John's Gospel, but the Incarnation, in which the full life and ministry of Jesus, including his death and resurrection, must be seen in totum. "You are made clean," Jesus proclaimed, "by the word which I have spoken to you" (John 15:3).

On the other hand, we need not challenge the reporting skills (or integrity) of the writers of Mark and Matthew in order to deal creatively with the word *ransom*. The word *lutron* in the Greek might be better translated "price."[33] William Barclay suggests, "Suppose we say, 'Sorrow is the price of love.' We mean that love cannot exist without the possibility of sorrow, but we never think of trying to explain to whom that price is paid."[34] Similarly it is said that freedom is bought at the price of blood, sweat, and tears, without any intention that the question be raised about from whom it was bought or to whom the price was paid. Jesus made a beautiful statement of the extent to which his love would go in personal sacrifice; the effort to force the words into a cold theological mold does violence to the spirit of the statement.

The inadequacy of theories of atonement in satisfying the demands of God's righteousness and love should not dismay us. They simply demonstrate that Paul and the other New Testament writers were struggling with the limitations of the human vocabulary to say the unsayable. In much the same way Jesus strained the language to express the nature of the kingdom of God, likening it to "a grain of mustard seed" and "a pearl of great price" or again to "a thief in the night" or "a man [who] went forth to sow. . . ." Not one of these metaphors tells us what the kingdom is like if we insist on taking it literally. Jesus had to rely on the intelligence of his listeners to understand what he was saying beyond the words he used.

Jesus does, however, give us insight into his own understanding of the meaning of his life, death, and resurrection for our salvation in what we might describe as double identification. *Double identification* is not so much a theory of atonement as a proclamation of God's resolution for the enmity that mankind had created. Jesus portrayed this enmity with great pathos in Mark 12, where he told the parable of the husbandmen entrusted with the keeping of a lord's vineyard who brutally mistreated the messengers the lord sent for an accounting. In the end they killed the messengers, and even the lord's son, in order to gain control of the vineyard. Jesus' ending to the parable contained a warning of great retribution. But while addressing the disciples on his last night with them before the crucifixion, Jesus proclaimed his unity with God that was the means by which the enmity and retribution were resolvable. Thus his prayer: ". . . that they may all be one; even as thou, Father, art in me, and I in thee, that they also may be in us . . . I in them, and thou in me, that they may be perfected into one" (John 16:21–23). As Christ identifies with God, so he invites us to identify with him, that in our unity we share his life, death, and resurrection, and are thus brought to at-one-ment with God, the Father. This is the ultimate victory to which we are called in the Gospels and that enabled Paul to write, "Thanks be to God, who giveth us the victory through our Lord, Jesus Christ" (1 Corinthians 15:57).

We become one with Christ through the power of faith working in us, which is also the gift of God. This is why prayer for strengthened faith is always "in his name," and prayer for the vision and courage to do his will is also "in his name." Faith must always issue in good works, or it becomes empty piety. Many may claim to be Christians, but Jesus said, "By this shall all men know that you are my disciples, if you have love one to another" (John 13:35). A disciple later echoed this: "By this we know that we abide in him and he in us, because he has given us of his own Spirit. And we have seen and testify that the Father has sent his Son as the Savior of the world. . . . We love because he first loved us." Then the disciple added a clincher that could hardly have been more blunt: "If anyone says 'I love God,' and hates his brother, he is a liar" (1 John 4:13–20).

Perhaps nowhere has the ethics of the atonement been more clearly delineated in all its practicality than in the letter of James to the early Christians who, knowing themselves to have been reconciled to God, wanted a new definition of what the religion of the redeemed might entail: "Pure religion and undefiled before our God and Father is this: to visit the fatherless and widows in their affliction and to keep oneself unspotted from the world" (James 1:27). This intent to remain unspotted from the world strikes a discordant note in our generation that has accommodated itself to everything secular. We have forgotten that Jesus clearly told his disciples, "I chose you *out* of the world, therefore the world hated you. If they persecuted me, they will also persecute you" (John 15:19–20).

If the preceding is valid as an interpretation of the atoning event, what are we to make of the concept that Jesus died for our sins? In one sense he died, as he indicated all Christians must be prepared to die, because of the world's hatred of messages of peace and love, while profits are to be made from exploitation of the weak and from war. But in a deeper sense, he came into this world to accept the full brunt of mankind's hostility to God (despite our protestations of piety), because only in so doing could he identify fully with mankind, and effect the at-one-ment between mankind and God necessary for reconciliation. Double identification cuts both ways; death is the only corridor between life and Life.

The most essential feature of any concept of atonement must be that the atoning process is initiated by God. As Paul Tillich observes, the justice of God is seen in the fact that

> He lets the self-destructive consequences of existential estrangement go their way. The divine removal of guilt and punishment is not an act of overlooking the reality and depth of existential estrangement . . . but he can take them upon himself by identifying with them and by transforming them for those who share in his participation. In the cross of Christ the participation becomes manifest. Through participation in the New Being, which is the being of Jesus as the Christ, [the faithful] also participate in the manifestation of the atoning act of God . . . producing the state which Paul called "being *in* Christ."[35]

Being in Christ is clearly made possible for us only by the grace of God, but requires a response on our part, and that identification carries with it the most surprising of ethical demands: "If I then, your Lord and Teacher, have washed your feet, you also ought to wash one another's feet" (John 13:14).

The Kingdoms and the Kingdom

Jesus began his ministry with a call to repentance, "for the kingdom of heaven is at hand" (Matthew 4:17). He urged his disciples to make the quest for God's kingdom their top priority: "Seek first his kingdom and his righteousness . . ." (Matthew 6:33). Mortimer Arias, a Methodist bishop in Brazil, notes the centrality of the kingdom concept to Christian ethics, especially relating it to Jesus' great evangelistic commission in Matthew 28:19. "Might it be that the Biblical vision and the theological foundation of the Kingdom of God is the rallying center where Evangelization and Christian social Ethics come together where they belong?"[36] This line of thought had been affirmed by Wolfhart Pannenberg and Carl Braaten in the 1970s, both of whom he quotes appreciatively.[37, 38] Still earlier, T. W. Manson urged that "The ethic of the Bible from beginning to end is the ethic of the kingdom of God."[39]

But just how is the kingdom of God to be understood? Jesus strained the vocabulary to evoke imagery that would make the kingdom comprehensible. He likened it to a pearl of great price and to hidden treasure; he compared it to the activity of seeds planted in varying qualities of soils; he told stories of reclaimed prodigals and rich fools and compassion for strangers on the road. They were flashing facets of a rare gem, but they also made it clear that the kingdom of God had less to do with a place than with relationships. But they left us with intriguing questions like whether the kingdom is soon to break upon us "like a thief in the night" and if so whether this means that Jesus actually expected the kingdom to be fulfilled in his generation, or whether it was just a little way off or perhaps a future state "when all time shall cease." At the turn of the century, Albert Schweitzer expressed his belief that Jesus expected the end of this present world to come in his lifetime, a conclusion shared by others like Rudolph Bultmann and Gunther Bornkamm. Did not Jesus promise the thief on the cross "Today you will be with me in paradise"? (Luke 23:43); yet the Book of Revelation seems to point to a great cosmic confrontation in some future millennium.

Whatever eschatological, future-oriented interpretations of the kingdom we might devise, Jesus seemed to have little patience with those who speculated on just when the kingdom would come. There was work to be done among God's hungry, lonely, and abused people, and the practical service among them determined how Jesus' listeners would be judged: "when the Son of man comes in his glory, and all the angels with him" (Matthew 25:31f.).

The kingdom emphasis in his teaching brought with it a description of the ethical life of the disciples in three engaging metaphors: (a) "You are the salt of the earth," (b) "You are the light of the world," and (c) "I send you forth as sheep in the midst of wolves."[40] *Salt*, as everyone knows, is not only a seasoning and a preservative but, as Jacques Ellul reminds us, contains a specific reference to the covenant between God and Israel (see Leviticus 2:13). "Thus," writes Ellul, "in sight of men and in the reality of this world, the Christian is a visible sign of the new covenant which God has made with this world in Jesus Christ."[41] *Light* not only dispels darkness, but gives security and direction to those who possess it, and enables them to lead others through and out of darkness. *Sheep*, in Jesus' simile, are those who live by sacrifice, as does the Lamb of God, and never ally themselves with the wolves who would seek their lives.

The concept of a coming kingdom brings with it a challenge to a new kind of life. In fact, Jesus' prayer "Thy kingdom come" must be coupled with his caution for preparedness; it is not simply that the kingdom is coming, but we must be prepared to enter it, to be a part of it. " 'The kingdom of God' referred not only to the reign or power of God, but also life lived in response to God as king. The phrase pointed to the Spirit of God (God's kingly power) active in this world, and to the way of life engendered by the Spirit (life in the Kingdom)."[42] That new life is radically different from our familiar patterns of behavior, conditioned as these patterns are by the insistence that our first obligation is to the kingdoms of this world with, perhaps, a bit of religion added on. Our culture's "conventional wisdom," as Marcus Borg has pointed out, is dominated by collections of rules and regulations by which security and general tranquillity are safeguarded. "Do this and all will be well" is the conventional wisdom in all cultures. "Jesus," notes Borg, "was actually a subversive . . . calling into question their understanding and loyalties."[43]

If we take seriously Jesus' vision of life under God's kingship, in contrast to the loyalties we are required to pledge to cultural norms—to familial, ethnic, and racial ties, to military preparedness at any cost, to foreign policy strategies for the preservation of the American (or British, French, German, or other) way of life—we can see the radical nature of Jesus' call to leave behind the conventional wisdom: ". . . You cannot serve God and Mammon" (Matthew 6:24).

Some Christians, rejecting as too harsh that "the cares of the world choke the word" (Matthew 13:22), appeal to the romantic era's return to nature and the theme of the popular hymn, "This Is My Father's World." This is a way of agreeing with Wordsworth's poem: "The world is too much with us," turning away from the affairs of worldly commerce and politics, and retaining the Christian posture of reverence. Nature may indeed give us the illusion of closeness to God. An old bit of doggerel has it: "One is nearer God's heart in a garden than anywhere else on earth," but as Paul Ramsey reminds us, "When with the poet men turn from brooks and blackbirds . . . from physical nature where in general 'every prospect pleases and only man is vile,' when instead they begin to consider the happenings in human history, the tyrannical, embattled kingdoms of this world, if then men are not to be overcome by anxiety there must be some other ground for faith than God's love in nature."[44] The kingdom of nature is an inadequate match for the kingdom of God.

Still others follow a more recent trend to return to the kingdom of this world, with the affirmation that there is no real distinction between the sacred and the secular because God is Lord of all. The secular city, they declare, is the proper setting for encountering God's redeeming love and for our expressing it to each other. But the secular city theology popularized in the 1960s by Harvey Cox[45] tended to downplay the problem of sin. "It celebrated the joys of the secular city in which human beings are becoming progressively more free. However, in this same secular city society was imprisoning two-thirds of the world in hunger, misery, and poverty."[46]

Stanley Hauerwas echoes the concern, pointing out the inadequacy of the secularists' theology that claimed "all you need is love." Writes Hauerwas, "It is my conviction that this emphasis on love is bad theology which results in bad ethics. If 'God is love' is assumed to be a sufficient presupposition for the Christian moral life, then it can be shown that such a God is preferably 'no being' or, if existent, ethically unworthy of our respect or obedience." This is true, he affirms, because what passes for love even among Christians is mostly a sentimentalism unable to confront the massive assault against human values mounted by a largely atheistic world (whether communist or success-at-any-cost capitalist). "Modern atheism is not the clenched fist that dares God to exist in a world of suffering, but it is the shrug of the shoulders."[47]

There are indeed certain dangers in seeking the kingdom of God, whether in nature or in the context of our earthly kingdoms. Amos anticipated this when he warned, "Woe unto you that desire the Day of the Lord! Wherefore would you have the Day of the Lord? It is darkness and not light" (Amos 5:18). God's judgment upon the kingdoms of this world, ruled as they are by what Martin Luther later called "The Prince of Darkness," with reference to St. Paul's "Prince of this world" (see John 14:30; 1 Corinthians 2:6, 8; Ephesians 2:2) will bring into blinding focus the contrast between the two kingdoms. Thus Jesus' coming among us was appropriately described in Phillips Brooks's familiar Christmas carol "O Little Town of Bethlehem": "The hopes and fears of all the years/Are met in thee tonight." Jesus' advent brought both aspects of the kingdom into our midst, its judgments and its joys. The warning of Amos is balanced by the angels' song of "tidings of great joy." The perennial miracle of Christmas is that it renews our orientation to the kingdom, and reminds us of its judgments as well as its rewards planned "from the foundations of the world" (Matthew 25:34). But before the rejoicing is justified, we must hear the injunction of the Lord: "Repent, for the kingdom of heaven is at hand."

Focus on the coming kingdom, a study technically called eschatology, brings with it another peculiar danger in our own time, as we witness the abuse of Scripture by certain sects. Foretellings of the Second Coming and the Rapture have become popular among some evangelists asserting to know more about the kingdom and its imminent arrival than even Jesus claimed to know. Jesus declared no one but God could know this: ". . . not even the Son" (Matthew 24:36). Hal Lindsay's *The Late Great Planet Earth,* as just one example, is advertised as having sold over 15 million copies. Ignoring the fact that biblical prophets were primarily spokesmen for God's demand for justice, not crystal-gazing fortune-tellers, some religious writers have created a timetable for Final Judgment. All manner of signs and portents, earthquakes, and military troop movements today are purported to have been prophesied in the Bible. The "Gog" of Ezekiel is said to be the ruler of modern Russia, and "Meshek" is identified with Moscow.[48] Such use of Scripture not only flies in the face of biblical scholarship, but forces mistranslations and out-of-context passages to fit a comic book scenario wholly unrelated to Jesus' references to the kingdom. Meshak, for example, could not have meant Moscow; it was simply an ancient country in Asia Minor.[49] Such perversion of Scripture deserves Jesus' warning: "An evil and adulterous generation seeks for a sign, but no sign shall be given it except the sign of Jonah" (Matthew 12:39).

In selecting these five emphases in Jesus' teachings, as providing the basis for understanding his ethical position, what has been omitted is what we might call practical ethics. Surely Jesus taught a great deal about doing good, loving one's neighbor, turning the other cheek, walking the extra mile, feeding the hungry, clothing the naked, and so on. Yet it is noteworthy that when Jesus was asked, "What good deed must I do, to have eternal life?" Jesus' blunt response was, "Why do you ask me about what is good?" and pointed the man first to God ("One there is who is good"), and then to the Commandments (Matthew 19:16). It must be reiterated that Jesus was not an ethicist, and while he did give many examples of ways to lead the good life, these were for the most part good deeds that any decent citizen of almost any nation or religion might find familiar. The one exception to this might be with regard to the theme of liberation, which appears not so much as a distinct emphasis in Jesus' teaching as an underlying leitmotif. It was central to what he felt himself called to fulfill in the famous scene (Luke 4:18, 19) where Jesus read aloud the passage from Isaiah 61:1–2 and applied it to himself. Contemporary proponents of liberation theology make much of this, as will be noted in Chapter Four.

CHAPTER TWO

Cultural Foundations

An understanding of the relation of Jesus' ethical position to what is commonly called Christian ethics requires a prior confession of certain limitations. Jesus left no original writings. We can know of his teachings only through the writings of others, writings which influenced the understanding of the early Church and were in turn influenced by those church groups that meditated on the growing treasury of manuscripts. Wayne Meeks reminds us, "Christianity, even in its earliest decades, was already a complex of movements in several directions," reflecting the fact that there were also diversity and rapid changes within both Judaism and the Roman culture in which it was embedded.[1] The writers and the churches modified each other's understanding of the mind and teachings of the historical Jesus. "Jesus is to be found at the end, not at the beginning of the inquiry."[2] Paul's letters were written before the Gospels, but were not widely circulated until after 90 A.D., after the first three Gospels were in wide use. "Because Matthew stresses the continuity between Judaism and Christianity and makes the new law even more strenuous than the old, this may also account for some of the legalistic tendencies in second-century Christianity that seem so contrary to Paul's emphasis on the Christian's freedom from the law."[3]

On the other hand, much as the early understanding of Jesus' viewpoint came from the writings and deliberations of the apostles and congregations, it was also claimed that a more direct access to Jesus' mind and heart was available. Had not Jesus said to Peter, "Flesh and blood has not revealed this . . . but my Father who is in heaven" (Matthew 16:17)? Indeed much of Paul's understanding of the nature and ministry of Christ he claimed to have derived not from other people: "For I did not receive it, nor was I taught it, but it came through a direct, first-person revelation of Jesus Christ" (Galatians 1:2).

Another problem we must confess, however, if we are to be honest with the Scriptures, is that while the writers may indeed have been inspired by Christ and the Holy Spirit, the language and vocabulary they used was often freighted with meanings conditioned by their culture. The writers were trying to understand Jesus' ethical teachings and put them into contemporary Greek. We have the problem today of trying to understand precisely what the writers meant by the words they used, a special study technically called *hermeneutics*.[4] This is by no means easy; even if we can read the Greek words of their day, meanings have changed. Those who must depend on English translations are twice removed from the original language and many times removed from the cultural thought frame of two thousand years ago. Thus the study of hermeneutics is of critical importance.

Without becoming sidetracked in technical analysis, we can return to a problem closer to the source having to do with the struggle of the early Christians to keep their understanding of Jesus' ethical teachings uncontaminated from outside influences. "Scarcely had the course of events made it clear that Christianity was not to lose its distinctive message by absorption into the parent Judaism, when the faith confronted an even greater menace. As it moved out into the non-Jewish world, it was in danger of so far conforming to that environment that it would sacrifice essential features of the Gospel."[5] Some elements in that environment were religious, and many of them were considered quite orthodox until eventually seen as aberrations of the faith and denounced as heresies. Other elements were secular, such as the natural law concept of the Stoics, never officially denounced and to remain as a powerful undercurrent within Christian tradition.

CONFLICTING VIEWS IN THE EARLY CHURCH

Gnosticism

Gnosticism was a pre-Christian amalgam of Jewish, Persian, Egyptian, and perhaps other Oriental mysticisms that proposed a dualism between the material world and the mental or spiritual world. It is possible that the mystical identification of God as the Word, which the Gospel of John employs with such powerful effect, would not have arisen outside the Hellenistic context. John portrays Jesus as not praying for the world, but only for those whom God has given him "out of the world" (John 17:21–23). This segregation of those who are of the world from those who belong to the kingdom of mind and spirit is characteristically Gnostic (see John 6:63, "The spirit gives life, the flesh is of no avail"). "It is hard to believe that such a work as this is not to be rightly identified as Gnostic in tendency."[6] On the other hand, we need to remind ourselves that those Christians who embraced Gnosticism believed they were closer to Jesus' position than anyone else. "Christian Gnosticism emerged as a reaffirmation, though in somewhat different terms, of the original stance central to the very beginnings of Christianity. Such Gnostic Christians surely considered themselves the faithful continuation, under changing circumstances, of that original stance which made Christians Christian."[7]

The origins of Gnosticism are somewhat cloudy, and for many centuries it was regarded as simply the first chapter in the history of Christian heresies. One of its many tenets, that matter is evil and only pure spirit is good, is sharply at variance with Jesus' point of view. By contrast, Jesus seems almost materialistic, sparing no effort to feed hungry bodies, cure diseased flesh and crippled bone, and even clean his disciples' trail-worn and dirty feet. Yet the ascetic tendency in Gnosticism can be found in much of Paul's writing and certainly controlled the monastic ethic that later arose to condemn and punish the flesh as an aid to purifying the spirit.

Gnosticism (from the word *gnosis*, knowledge) was clearly a salvation-oriented philosophy, but one which contained a peculiar paradox that provided one of the reasons for its being ultimately condemned. Salvation came through knowledge of God, the wholly Transcendent One, so there was an implied obligation to avoid contamination by the world. Because the world and its laws, being material (and therefore evil), could not have been created by a wholly transcendent and perfect God, Gnostics believed there must be a *demiurge*, a secondary creator whom we must defy. Defiance of this demiurge's power by virtue of freedom from the law (Paul, it will be recalled, insisted "You are not under the law, but under grace," Romans 6:14) suggested to some Gnostics that they had permission to perform every kind of action without restraint. This libertine attitude eventually became virtually a mandate to leave no possibility of freedom unrealized. Students of the medieval story of Dr. Faustus will recognize this line of argument in Mephistopheles's reasoning away of Faust's Christian scruples. That such contention is at variance with original Gnostic asceticism is clear, but also helps elucidate why Gnosticism was denounced by Irenaeus circa 200 A.D., lest Christianity become just another Oriental mystery cult. Not only did it contain many internal contradictions, but challenged Scriptures at such crucial points as the humanity of Jesus (claiming the Christ could not have had a real, material body, so his death was an illusion) and the authenticity of the resurrection.

The discovery in 1945 by Muhammad Khalifah of the *Nag Hammadi Library*, fifty-two Coptic Gnostic gospels and tracts from about the third or early fourth century A.D. (with such titles as *The Gospel of Thomas, The Exegesis of the Soul, The Apocalypse of Adam,* etc.) has helped show that Gnostics did not view themselves as presenting an alternative form of Christianity to the orthodox position. Rather, they were offering a release from the grip of worldliness that held mankind in thrall. The association of this library with Christian monasticism is significant. Robinson points out, "It may be no coincidence that the *Nag Hammadi Library* was discovered in sight of the Basilica of Saint Pachomas, the founder of Christian Monasticism."[8]

Other Movements

The movement toward withdrawal from entanglements with the world was not confined to Gnostic Christians. A group of Jewish Christians called *Ebionites* rejected Paul as a heathen and, adhering strictly to the Torah and to the Gospel of Matthew (though rejecting the virgin birth story of Matthew), exalted poverty as a way to salvation. Meanwhile, the *Marcionites*, in an effort to purify Christianity from Jewish influences, arose in the second century to agree with the Gnostics on the notion of a demiurge as a virtual co-creator with God. The benevolent Father, revealed by Jesus, opposed this wrathful demiurge, and made love the core of the good news of salvation. This love, however, was not to be expressed sexually, since the body and all earthly desires are from the demiurge; chastity, celibacy, and poverty were required.

Montanism represented another second-century movement within the Church to renounce worldliness, urge celibacy and fasting, and also to proclaim the imminent return of Christ to bring the Final Judgment. One convert, a prominent bishop, declared the Coming to be within two years; his followers ceased to cultivate their fields and even sold their houses and possessions so as to be unencumbered when Christ would appear. The most prominent convert was Tertullian, who denounced all forms of accommodation to Jewish, Greek, or Roman thought, and wrote extensively against Marcionism.

During the third century, a Babylonian scholar, Mani (215–275), introduced an extreme form of dualism into Christianity. He proposed that an aboriginal Kingdom of Darkness waged war against the Kingdom of Light (an obvious borrowing from Zoroastrianism). The latter, incapable of using the weapons of darkness (violence, bloodshed, etc.), launched a strategy of purification of the world by love, thus restoring the primal goodness of God's creation. In what amounts to a vast cosmic drama, *Manicheism* viewed Christ as central to this plot, and the impact of it captured the imaginations of thousands of early Christians, including St. Augustine.

Other movements within the church, like *Apollinarianism, Arianism,* and *Nestorianism,* had their day, but with minimal impact on the ethics of the Church (with the exception of Arianism, which had a strong humanistic flavor in its three factions).[9] But *Pelagianism* is a different matter.

Pelagius (360–431 A.D.) was said to have been British by birth, and was well versed in current languages as well as those of Scripture. Augustine, while disagreeing with Pelagius's theology, called him "a saintly man" of highest ethical character. A prolific writer, he wrote against the doctrine of "original sin," and insisted that all people everywhere have complete freedom of will to choose good or evil. He was placed on trial in 411 A.D. by the Council of Carthage for devaluing the doctrine of grace, and was excommunicated. Later that year he was acquitted at Diospolis, fervently denying he was heretical, but insisting that divine grace is the natural condition of mankind's experience with God. Forgiveness from sin is available to all because of the love of Christ, but we must take the initiative. Freedom, wrote Pelagius, is the inescapable fact of our experience. In this he stands close to the position of modern Christian existentialism. Indeed, the importance of Pelagius to Christian ethics is precisely in the emphasis he places on autonomy; we are free agents and each ethical decision must be authentically our own. God may help us in our deliberations through the grace and discipline of his spirit, but ultimately we must take responsibility. No special grace or dispensation handed down from above is necessary for achieving the virtuous life.

Each of the movements just noted, though condemned at some point in the early Church as heresy, has left its mark. The Unitarian church, though many members do not adopt the title Christian today, was avowedly Christian when it began in Transylvania in the sixteenth century, and traces its humanistic teachings directly to Arianism.[10] The emphasis of Pelagius on freedom of will, dismissing of original sin, and proclaiming free grace are all themes that surface from time to time in liberal Christianity, and his emphasis on good works is close to the heart of the social gospel.

Meanwhile, influences from Greek and Roman thought very quickly made their impact felt in the shaping of Christian ethics.

SECULAR INFLUENCES

A strong moralistic theme runs through the writings of the early fathers like Clement, Polycarp, and the Shepherd of Hermas, some with Gnostic and Stoic overtones. We find Clement using Aristotelian references along with biblical ones in the refutation of Gnosticism.[11] Doctrinal disputes over the nature of Jesus as God's son, Messiah, and Redeemer detracted from the study of ethics as a discipline uniquely transformed by Christ's coming. Thus while heated arguments raged among proponents of the many movements we noted (some of which resulted in excommunication and even death), elements of Stoic and Neoplatonic ethics and the concept of natural law became amalgamated with Christian teachings.

Stoicism had been a popular philosophy for three centuries before the advent of Christianity. Begun by Zeno, in a world of turmoil, his followers (called Stoics after the word *stoa*, for the "porch" where they met) sought inner calm through cultivation of the virtues and an unruffled endurance of a troubled life. They believed there can be no degrees of virtue; one either is good, rational, and calm, or is not. Mankind's basic condition is depravity, so the effort to achieve virtue must be 100 percent, or all is lost. To be sure, there are daily duties one must perform, which have degrees of importance, but an uncompromising sense of the absolute good is the only guide to ultimate inner peace. Many early Christians, especially when faced with martyrdom, found solace in Stoicism. Yet its highest goal, *ataraxia* (aloofness and apathy), was diametrically opposed to an essential ingredient of Christian ethics: compassion. Jesus would never have gone to the cross had he been a Stoic. Indeed, self-sacrifice on behalf of others would have been regarded by Stoics as a neurotic aberration. The nineteenth-century Goethe, thinking himself a Christian maintaining Olympic calm, responded as a Stoic when he replied to an appeal to aid a humanitarian cause, *Nein, ich denke an meine ruhe* ("No, I concentrate on my tranquility").

Meanwhile *Neoplatonism*, a revisitation of the philosophy of Plato, made a bid for Christian allegiance. Given formal structure about 230 A.D. by Plotinus, it proposed that all things began in the mind of God, God being the ultimate idea of the good (bearing close resemblance to the Word of John's Gospel, thus making its appeal to many Christians). All things emanate like rays of light from this ultimate one, infusing all reality with its wisdom, purity, and goodness. There is a moral order in the universes; evil is only "error," which can be corrected, but punishment, when necessary, sets the cosmic scale back in balance. Ultimately good and evil are aspects of the cosmic drama. Clearly this philosophy would have appeal to many Christians living under torment, and we find its contentions reflected in Boethius as late as the sixth century. But again, a philosophy that fails to take sin with utmost seriousness, and particularly one which proposes a solution to the general problem of evil being the device of reincarnation, had no place in New Testament thought. Neoplatonism, nevertheless, was to have great appeal from time to time, and may be found even in the twentieth century woven into the fantasies of certain Christian cults.

Natural law made perhaps the most enduring impact on Christian thought of all the secular influences. We deal more extensively with it in a later chapter, but note at this juncture simply that among many philosophers of the ancient world as far apart as Plato the Idealist and Zeno the Stoic, nature was viewed as somehow rational. Goodness and virtue are grounded in something more enduring than the changing affairs of mankind and societies: Look to nature to find the basis for morals and the foundation on which ethics and law can be built. The concept that the whole universe is governed by laws which exhibit rationality can be found among many early Christian scholars down through the works of Aquinas, Montesquieu, Blackstone, and modern jurists. Indeed, it almost appears that nature has been set up as an alternate authority, as when it was made apparent at Vatican II that the primary argument against birth control put forth by the Roman Catholic church cited Ulpian's judgments more than those of biblical writers. Ulpian was not a Christian, but a third-century (d. 228 A.D.) Roman jurist and leading proponent of natural law.

We have already noted Clement's use of Aristotle's arguments to refute Gnosticism. Clement's administrative duties occupied so much of his time, he had little opportunity to study or publish on Christian ethics. Toward the end of the first century (c. 98 A.D.), he addressed a number of doctrinal disputes among certain presbyters and rebellious laypeople, but his moral admonitions were largely legalistic appeals to obey the rules of the Christian community.

To be sure there were those who resisted the incursion of secular influences, but we note a peculiar withdrawal from the secular world into piety and limited good works. The Shepherd of Hermas (97–140 A.D.?) urged Christians to go beyond expected rules; Bishop Polycarp of Smyrna wrote about the life of practical service as opposed to mere ritual: "Alms have the power to release from death." Barnabas (identity lost to history) wrote, "Work with thy hands for the ransom of thy sins"; Clement noted, "Fasting is better than prayer, but almsgiving is better than either." For the most part it seems that those who wished to engage in doctrinal dispute claimed the major pulpits and administrative reigns; those concerned deeply about the moral dilemma of mankind withdrew.[12] Edwin Hatch notes a similar tendency among secular philosophers at the time, and draws this analogy: "Just as ordinary philosophers had sometimes found life in society to be intolerable and had gone into 'retreat,' so Christian philosophers began to withdraw altogether from the world."[13] In time their retirement would be into places of structured solitude, the monasteries.

It is something of a paradox that so many in early Christendom, with the urgent message of Jesus to address human need so clearly before them, would detach themselves from the common life of their brethren. The "deterioration in the average moral conceptions of the Christian Churches," Edwin Hatch insists, "was due largely to Greek influences. For the average members of churches were now average citizens of the empire, educated by Greek methods, impregnated with the dominant ethical ideas."[14] He contends that Ambrose of Milan (340–397) set forth propositions that became the basis for moral philosophy during the Middle Ages, and that the writing is more Stoic than Christian. It is, he claims, "a *rechauffé* of the book which Cicero compiled more than three centuries before, chiefly from Panaetius. . . . Its ideal life is happiness: it holds that a happy life is a life according to nature. The ethics of the Sermon on the Mount . . . have been transmuted into the ethics of Roman law."[15] Charles Cochrane, writing on the impact of classical culture, also notes that Ambrose's book *De Officiis* is "consciously and deliberately Ciceronian."[16] But he also points out that it makes reverence for God, rather than self-realization, basic to ethical behavior, and further stresses the role of divine grace in determining the will of believers. "It is this fact, rather than any disposition to compromise with secularism, which accounts for the existence of the so-called 'double standard' of morality in Ambrosian ethics."[17] Nor should it be forgotten that Ambrose's practical application of Christian ethics is one of the most dramatic in ancient times, when he barred the Emperor Theodosius from attending Mass because of the latter's massacre of Thessalonica. In begging to be forgiven, the emperor prostrated himself before the altar, wearing a shroud, and cried, "My soul cleaves to the dust. O God, quicken me according to Thy word."[18] The Greco-Roman influence was strong in Ambrose, nevertheless, and the effect of it would be felt for centuries to follow.

The power of the secular infusions becomes strikingly clear in the fact that Augustine (354–430), after baptism by Ambrose, devoted considerable attention to refuting Neoplatonism and other secular philosophies with which he had aligned himself prior to his conversion to Christianity in 386 A.D. That experience gave him the light to perceive the deficiencies of classicism. His work resulted in a more thorough explication of mankind's nature and predicament than anything of which classicism had proved capable. Yet, while honoring Augustine by the founding of an order in his name, the Church continued to be guided by those same secular ideas, and Augustine's teachings were devalued in the enthusiasm of later Scholasticism. Not until the Reformation would Augustine's careful refutations of them be reexamined, when his *Retractations, Confessions,* and *The City of God* were regarded second only to the books of the Bible among Luther, Calvin, Melanchthon, and other reformers. In terms of Christian ethics, perhaps nothing of Augustine's was more helpful than his contention that "the old gods and the old religions had no concern with right and wrong, with 'justice,' with moral values, nor any teaching to guide men to attain a future life; a successful pagan empire without justice had nothing to commend it: without justice, what were kingdoms but great robberies *(remota iustitia, quid sunt regna nisi magna latrocinia)?"*[19] Righteousness, not success, is what God demands of us.

Yet Augustine did not reject all he had gained from Greek and Roman philosophy. His work *On the Morals of the Catholic Church* was a conscious effort to wed New Testament ethics to classical thought. To the "four cardinal virtues" that formed the foundation of secular moral life: wisdom, fortitude, temperance, and justice (justice here in the limited sense of "natural fairness"), Augustine added St. Paul's "abiding essences" of faith, hope, and love (see 1 Corinthians 13:13)

MEDIEVAL INNOVATIONS

With the collapse of Rome, Christianity, now established in many parts of Europe, found itself engaged in a task for which it was ill suited: civilizing the vast expanse of the Western world with its almost countless warring tribes and kingdoms. Leo the Great, who was pope from 440 to 461, tried to weld the pieces of the broken empire together with strong central government. Because Roman roads were still in good repair, communications were relatively easy in the

West. Christianity made progress eastward only slowly. Gregory the Great, Leo's most important successor, came to the papacy in 590, when famine, plague, and invasions all but destroyed every previous gain. His ethical writings were compared to Augustine's (by Gregory himself), as "bran to wheat," and indeed they are so filled with mythological allusions, superstitions, and functionary concerns of the priesthood to provide little guidance. On the practical level, however, he performed better than he wrote; he organized collections of food and clothing with such administrative skill, the Church was aptly described as "an open granary." He negotiated peace with the Lombards and began educational missions among the barbarian tribes.

The Dark Ages were descending, however, and a whole new ethical structure was soon to be encountered (and in part assimilated) among the Muslims. In 632 A.D., Muhammed died, and his followers began a spectacular advance conquering Palestine, Syria, Mesopotamia, Persia, and most of Egypt in a single generation. By 715 they had moved into Spain and were threatening to overwhelm all Europe. Most leaders of the Church abandoned the traditional stand against the use of military force in the face of continual harassment from European tribes (particularly Germanic and Norse), and from this new religion, Islam. Despite the devising of canon law to provide a semblance of order and humanitarian concern, and the Lateran Council's "laws of chivalry," the Church seemed unable to communicate a viable ethic for its people in so violent a time. In tragic fact, even so-called Christian communities were not infrequently at each other's collective throats in disputes over land and political control, and often sang *Te Deums* to the same God in the same Latin tongue at the altars of their slaughtered enemies.

Charlemagne had established amicable relations between his newly formed Holy Roman Empire and the Muslim leaders of Jerusalem early in the ninth century. Travelers began bringing back to him accounts of astonishing educational advances wherever the Muslims settled. Tuition-free schools and colleges were established in Baghdad, Mecca, Damascus, Cairo, Cordova, Seville, Granada, and Toledo. In Christian Europe at that same time, there was little education outside the monasteries, and Charlemagne himself was illiterate at the time he became emperor. The names of al-Kindī, al-Fārābī (called "the second Aristotle"), Avicenna, and al-Ghazālī became familiar among Christian scholars for their breadth of learning in the arts and sciences. Translations were made into Arabic of the mathematics of Euclid and the astronomy of Ptolemy. Some Muslim scholars speculated (perhaps on the basis of Aristarchus's heliocentric theory from the third century B.C.) that the earth was round and rotated around the sun. Ibn al-Haytham (965–1020 A.D.) did advanced work in optics, including the magnifying capacity of lenses. It is important to realize that for such Muslims, as was the case for Copernicus, Kepler, and Newton centuries later, science was as much a spiritual discipline as more obvious acts of faith, with clear ethical implications in the service of God and mankind.

Scientific developments within Islam caused a considerable stir in the early Christian universities and was one cause of the intellectual revolution that led to the Renaissance and the Reformation. Other lesser importations of Islamic thought and practice were the rosary, votive candles, and the swinging of incense burners during holy celebrations. Minor innovations as they seem, anything that alters behavior patterns and carries the weight of sanction: "This you ought to do" (e.g., say a prayer for each bead on the string) has ethical importance. They often determine who may be included or excluded from orthodox fellowship, who will be regarded as sheep and who the goats.

It was Averroës (1126–1198) who gained the greatest admiration as a Muslim among Christians. His encyclopedia of medicine became a standard text in Europe as soon as it was translated into Latin. He further clarified the study of optics, wrote of the function of the retina, and was the first to discover the possibilities of smallpox innoculation. His knowledge of international codes of law brought him the position of chief justice in Seville. He was the greatest authority on Plato and Aristotle of his day, so that Christians and Jews as well as Muslims would refer to him for many generations simply as "The Commentator."[20] Aristotle's Nichomacaean *Ethics* was hardly known among Christians until they read Averroës, and the Aristotelian assumption of mankind's inherent goodness was to affect Christian ethics profoundly. An ethic which starts with the contention that humankind is sinful, in need of God's grace even to discern the good, will be dramatically different from an ethic which starts from a point of view that mankind is already good and needs only encouragement. This latter belief is precisely what we find in Thomas Aquinas, shifting the ground for ethics in the whole of Western Christianity for centuries to follow.

Francis of Assisi (1182–1226) represents a brief return to an effort to bring New Testament ethics to light in the scholastic era. Popularly associated with the quiet life and having "the heart of a saint, but also of a troubador,"[21] he was in fact a controversial figure whose turbulent career was a constant worry to the pope. Born to wealth, he took literally Christ's admonition to the "rich young ruler" (Mark 10:17–25), renounced all his possessions, and walked to the Holy Land to beg forgiveness from the Muslims for the Christian atrocities in the Crusades. It is one of the bitterest ironies of history that the order founded by this loving man should have become the order which Pope Gregory IX pressed into service in the dreaded Inquisition, one year after Francis's death.

"The Angelic Doctor" Thomas Aquinas (1224–1274) was doubtless the most influential in developing the foundations for Christians ethics as they would be acknowledged prior to the sixteenth century. His primary focus was on "the common good," and he declared that a man might expose himself and his family to danger if the success of the enterprise should benefit the community. In words reminiscent of the Stoics he admired, Aquinas frequently referred to God as the unifying principle of nature. In this he also drew upon Aristotle's concept of teleology, in which he believed he found a fore-echo of the doctrine of the sovereignty of God, whose providence encompasses all things that are and all ends toward which they move (*Summa*, Part I, Q XL IV, with references to Aristotle's *Physics* and *Metaphysics*). For his treatment of ethics, the most cogent fact is that the Christian's vision of God is not confined to mystical experience nor to some future life (though the vision may be clarified and perfected there), but began in acts of participation in the world of nature and social experience.

Three brief examples of Aquinas's position may illustrate the way his theology directly influenced the ethical stance of the Roman Catholic church.

1. Ownership of private property was contrary to nature, and therefore disruptive and potentially destructive in social life.[22]
2. Money ought never be regarded as more than a medium of exchange, and never used therefore to gain more money at interest.[23]
3. Warfare is abhorrent to God, contrary to nature (Aquinas was aware that most animals do not war on their own species), and inevitably counterproductive in society.[24]

To be sure, Aquinas rationalized these tenets in terms of the society of his day. While private ownership was considered contrary to nature, Aquinas conceded that through efficiency in society and government some people are better able than others to put property to good use. Money ought never be lent for interest, but might be borrowed at interest if it was to be employed for good purposes. Wars take place because mankind has a sinful tendency (not a sinful nature), and recourse to war might be justified if it were the only means of securing the safety of the greatest number of people in the cause of justice and lasting peace. Such modifications in what Aquinas started with as basic biblical ethics shows clearly his admiration for Stoic accommodation.

Meanwhile, the ethical situation *outside* the books and treatises on morals and ethics of the period was in stark contrast with the popular portrayal of the "Age of Chivalry." Thomas à Kempis's book *Imitation of Christ* (the authorship of which has been in some dispute) has been called "the noblest product of this simple, mystical churchly piety,"[25] but the ecclesiastical hierarchy was living denial of the ethical ideal. Officially, private ownership of property might be denounced, but bishops often became the largest property owners in their realms. It was a time of growing papal wealth, absolution for sale, and general neglect of the poor. Popes spent more money on their private armies than on missions, and launched wars and crusades that decimated cities, spread slaughter, famine, and pestilence in a way reminiscent of the horsemen of the apocalypse. One pope, to be certain he had exterminated all his enemies in a city known to contain more Christians than pagans, ordered, "Kill them all; God will know his own."[26] The Inquisition was designed to search out and destroy all who opposed or even questioned the absolute authority of the Church. In marked contrast to Christ's forgiving those who sought to destroy him, the popes executed by the thousand those who even murmured against them. A three-volume documentary, *Le Registre d'Inquisition de Jacques Fournier*, details the way trials were conducted, with not a single acquittal recorded during the entire reign of Fournier as Pope Benedict XII.[27] This must be seen, however, not as an indictment of the Roman Catholic church per se, but of human nature when virtually unlimited power is available.

EMERGENCE OF THE PROTESTANT ETHIC

It has sometimes been debated whether Protestantism was a mutation in the evolution of Christianity or whether it represented a genuine return to the New Testament concept of faith and life. It is certain that many of the forerunners like John Wycliffe, John Hus, William Tyndale, and others sought vigorously to achieve what they thought was true reforming of the church along biblical lines. Many paid for their efforts with their lives: Hus, Tyndale, and Savonarola were burned at the stake, and the mere possession of Wycliffe's writings was punishable by death. Of all efforts at thought control from ancient times down through Nazi Germany, probably none have been so vigorously pursued as that of the Inquisition; all have ultimately failed.

In any case, a genuinely new approach to Christian ethics was born with Martin Luther's challenge to the Church of 1517. The Church, he maintained, had forsaken Christ, and merely used his name to sanction its return to the ethical sterilities of ancient Pharisaism. Indeed it was, as in the title of one of Luther's writings, under "Babylonian Captivity" to pagan aggrandizement. It was as though Christ had never come to set mankind free from sin and from ecclesiastical impediments for direct communion with God. But if people were to be liberated from churchly rules to live the free, Christian life, they must accept the infinitely more difficult challenge of Christ: "You must therefore be perfect, as your heavenly Father is perfect" (Matthew 5:48). This impossible obligation rules out "works of supererogation," which supposed anyone could accomplish more than God requires and thus have "merit" left over; no one can do more than 100 percent of what God requires. At the same time, Luther insisted in faithful Augustinian fashion that because of mankind's sinful condition all our supposed righteousness is "filthy rags" (Isaiah 64:6). Jesus' counsel to perfection would leave us in total despair were it not for his redeeming work within us. Because Christ's identification with us sets us free from the need for ecclesiastical intervention, we are to live as fully liberated men and women. In freedom we may err; indeed, living in a sinful world many of our actions of civil necessity (lending at interest, going to war) may cause us to sin. But if sin we must, "then let us sin boldly," in the knowledge that God will judge us according to his gracious understanding of our predicament and graciously forgive.

Needless to say, Luther's logic could be mistaken for encouragement to license, and this is what did in fact happen. He found himself having to denounce the peasants for revolting against landlords, thinking they were following Luther. While his Christocentric zeal set him apart from both the church of Rome and the humanist movement of his day, he was a conservative in his favoring of the landed aristocracy. He further believed that church and state should be separate in their functions, with the church playing the role of servant to those whom God has endowed with the power of civil authority. The key to Luther's ethic, however, is acknowledgment that good works follow, without compulsion, from union with God; as a good tree must bear fruits, love must gush from the heart freely. "What one must do (*das Gesollte*), must be what one in freedom desires to do (*das Gewollte*)."

It was John Calvin (1509–1564) who gave systematic content to Jesus' command to perfection, providing instructions on almost countless social relations. The third book of his *Institutes of the Christian Religion* reveals the theological foundations of his ethics, which led to his many social reforms. He cleared Geneva of the rampant immorality that made it one of Europe's most vice-ridden cities, and transformed it into such a model of Christian community life that mayors and administrators came from hundreds of miles to study and emulate its renewal. While residing in that small city-state, Calvin began to exercise a worldwide ministry. "His correspondence with princes, statesmen, theologians, church leaders and fellow religionists must have been exceedingly large. Through his letters with people all over Europe he directed the cause of the Reformed churches."[28] The entire Puritan movement drew from Calvin its own brand of ethics, and although maligned in later generations, succeeded in correcting much of the gross sensuality that characterized European and British life. Against fierce opposition from merchants and political leaders, which brought Calvin temporary banishment (until relapse set in, and the townspeople realized how much his reforms had been needed), he launched a moral crusade that reached halfway around the world. Thus the German historian Leopold Ranke called Calvin "the virtual founder of America," and the nineteenth-century French skeptic Ernest Renan wrote, "He succeeded simply because he was the most Christian man of his century."

Persuaded that only an educated laity, armed with the Bible, could translate the demands of the Gospel into effective measures for personal and social righteousness, Calvin's educational reforms were as remarkable and far reaching as his political influence. He organized a complete school system from primary grades through the university level. More than six hundred scholars were on hand for the opening of his academy, arriving from all over Europe, many at peril for their lives. The American historian George Bancroft referred to Calvin as "the father of popular education, the inventor of the system of free schools" and ". . . the boldest reformer of his day."[29]

Protestant ethics steered a course at variance from Rome (where ethics had always been subordinate to theology) as well as from humanism. It tended to find expression in bibliocracies wherever it flourished. In Puritan communities the Bible, rather than the church institution, was the frame of reference for ethics. Their principle of individualism, however, and the right of private interpretation under the Holy Spirit prevented the development of a body of definitive rules. Ethics remained freer to "blow where it listeth" than was the case in the Roman church. Missionaries on the American frontier tended to forge the Gospel into a weapon to fend off the temptations of the world, the flesh, and the devil; a host of social evils like drinking, gambling, and dancing, became targets for attack. Calvin's stress on the virtues and rewards of diligent labor has been described by some as the virtual source of the rise of capitalism, though this is an oversimplification.[30] The Calvinist-Puritan contention that a person must demonstrate his relation to Christ by the quality of his life did indeed produce a hardworking, industrious, and often prosperous individual. But the service motive of the Christian was the exact opposite of the capitalist spirit of competition and acquisition. It is service of one's neighbor that Christ requires, not rivalry with him. Indeed, as Emil Brunner points out, "It is not the Calvinist faith but . . . the decline of this faith, and progressive secularism which led to the greediness which one has in mind when speaking in a critical sense about capitalism."[31]

The era of history often called the Age of Reason is remarkable for a number of things, among them that many leading intellectuals at its beginning (c. 1564, the birth of Galileo) were churchmen whose commitment to Christian principles showed in their work. Copernicus was a canon in the Roman Catholic church; Galileo was convinced his science glorified God; Kepler was dubbed "the God seeker" by his associates; Newton said he would rather be remembered for his theological writings than for his mathematics. Tragically, some of these men were persecuted by the churches in which they served (think of the trials of Galileo; Bruno being burned at the stake in Italy; Thomas More, beheaded in England). Some fled to Protestant Holland, which invited Galileo after his condemnation by the Inquisition and hosted both René Descartes and John Locke. Holland's universities were thus enriched, and those at Leiden, Utrecht, and Groningen became the finest on the continent. In countries where the churches were closely allied with the state, leaders of both tended to acquire increasing power while the masses of the population suffered deepening poverty.

The Age of Reason may, because of these remarkable phenomena, also be remembered for the fact that it ended in an explosion of revolutions. The importance of this for a study of Christian ethics becomes clear as we examine certain features of the age. In England, it was the Puritans who toppled the government and beheaded a despotic king. In France, where intellectuals like Voltaire, Robespierre, and Danton became disenchanted with organized religion, not only was the government eventually overthrown and the king (and countless others) beheaded, but the Roman Catholic church itself was outlawed for a time. It was not that the church lacked a genuine Christian

ethic; its formalized ethic was impeccable. But it failed to teach and imple-
ment that ethic during the extravagant reigns of Louis XIV and of his son
and grandson in the face of massive poverty and human misery among the
people of France. Louis XV, in fact, anticipated the revolution to come: *"Après
moi le déluge."*

Meanwhile, in America, a vigorous Protestant ethic was at work where
the distance between clergy and laity was lessened by the concept of "the
priesthood of all believers," and where the drive for individual liberty was vigorous. A different kind of revolution was launched. As Norman Cousins expressed it, "Calvinism was more than a series of fixed points on a compass; it
was a way of life that embraced or affected politics, economics, social outlook
and . . . individual behaviors. . . ."[32] Most of the American Founding Fathers, while not all were Calvinist, shared a heritage steeped in Puritanism,
and most were Protestant. "To the extent they can be regarded as a group [they]
believed deeply in the ability of a human being to learn enough to take part in
self-government."[33] The result was a revolution against "fat King George" (as
John Hancock called him), and issued in a declaration that all people are "endowed by their Creator with certain inalienable rights."

If there are any lessons of history to be garnered from this, one of them
surely is that where congregational life is more characterized by an ethic practically and creatively implemented on behalf of liberty and human rights,
churches can be forces for good. Where churches are too closely linked with
governmental structures and remain silent in the presence of exploitation and
the denial of human rights, the churches may be swept away when the secular
structures fall. Examination of the reigns of terror that often accompany revolutions, as in our own century in Russia, China, Cuba, Iran, and El Salvador,
are not reassuring. In each situation organized religion tended to side with the
ruling class. Significantly, since Vatican II, the Roman Catholic church has
shifted more toward what has traditionally been identified as the Protestant position, literally *protesting* on behalf of the poor and disfranchised, advocating
greater self-direction and freedom for individuals and communities, and granting greater freedom of worship than ever before. Some fear, meanwhile, that
the Protestant ethic is weakest among some traditionally Protestant groups
which have equated piety with patriotism and have relinquished the prophetic
criticism that once gave the Protestant ethic its character and power. This
point is made with particular clarity, including its existential risks, by Paul Tillich in his *Political Expectations.* The risk is evident when we recall how prophets have frequently been rejected in their own generation for stepping outside
the accepted boundaries of both social standards and institutional religion, appealing to "a transcendent frame of reference."[34] This point is suggested by Alfred North Whitehead, who as a mathematician and philosopher perceived the
necessity for religious vision of "something which stands beyond, behind, and
within the passing flux of immediate things . . . the ultimate ideal, and the
hopeless quest . . . our one ground for optimism."[35]

THE SOCIAL GOSPEL: CATHOLIC AND PROTESTANT

While the term *social gospel* is often narrowly identified with late nineteenth-century efforts of Walter Rauschenbusch, William Booth, and others to address the problems of social disruptions brought by expanding populations, the industrial revolution, and economic competition, it would be an error to overlook the dynamic thrust of ethical concern in the whole of the Christian churches. The Franciscans and Jesuits had brought Christianity to the New World long before the Pilgrims landed at Plymouth Rock, and had already confronted Shinto ethics with Christian ethics in Japan in the sixteenth century. Father Bartolomé de las Casas blazed out against the barbarities enacted against natives of the Caribbeans by seekers of gold and other natural resources. Abbé de Saint-Pierre and Saint Vincent de Paul were both outspoken Catholics for social reform in seventeenth- and eighteenth-century France. Perhaps the greatest strides in the development of the state as the custodian of public welfare took place in Catholic Austria in the nineteenth century. In 1891, Pope Leo XIII wrote his endorsement of the welfare state into his great encyclical on labor, *Rerum Novarum*.

The presence of the churches, however, with whatever social strategies they may have envisioned, was inadequate to stem the dehumanizing influences of the march of progress in the nineteenth century. To be sure there were Christians like Carlyle, Rakes, and Kingsley who spoke out against the violation of human rights in the sweatshops, factories, and mines in the industrial cities. Today Hershey and Lugo remind us of conditions where "Children hauled tubs of coal up subterranean roads for twelve to sixteen hours a day. It was not unusual to find children of four or five years of age working in these conditions—conditions so terrible that criminals today would certainly choose the death penalty rather than be forced to endure them."[36] In response to these conditions in 1849, one-third of the Methodist clergy in England left their pulpits to join labor unions and

> they took with them their Christian ideology. Methodism was one among a few forces preventing England from having a Communist revolution. In countries where such revolution was feared, Fascism imposed cooperation between labor and capital at the hands of the State. This was understandable in Germany and Italy, where the industrial proletariat was Marxist. It was not so in England, where labor and capital could still converse in a Christian vocabulary.[37]

Karl Marx might rail against religion as the "opiate of the people" with some justification, for in too many situations the churches were supported and maintained by the wealthy families who oppressed the overworked and underpaid poor. But the fact remains that the Christian churches were the only organizations openly opposed to child abuse, prostitution, polygamy, cannibalism, and head-hunting on the mission frontiers, and the only voices (even when not united) against slavery, child labor, poverty, maltreatment of the insane and of criminals, and of warring nationalisms on the home front.

It is worth remembering that the Baptists, as early as 1787, officially condemned slavery; Anglicans, Catholics, Methodists, Presbyterians, and Quakers all set up underground railways for the freeing of slaves, and many clergymen lost their lives for it. Anglicans reformed the penal system of England during an incredible period of population growth and concomitant crime (England's population grew from 12 million to 21 million in the four decades prior to 1850). Yet by 1890, in London alone, conditions were so bad that 2,157 people were "found dead"; 2,297 committed suicide; 30,000 were living in prostitution; 900,000 were classed as paupers.[38] Perhaps the most dramatic single response to this was the formation of the Salvation Army by William Booth. Indeed, Booth was already at work as early as 1864, preaching on the streets, in pulpits, in factories—anywhere he could get a hearing on behalf of God's poor. His success was phenomenal even by today's standards, as he forged Christian ethics into a strategy that gathered and dispensed in one year (1889) 192 tons of bread, 140 tons of potatoes, 25 tons of sugar, 46 tons of flour, 12 tons of rice, 15 tons of meat, 15 tons of jam, and similar large amounts of other staples.[39]

But it was Walter Rauschenbusch who gave the social gospel its most articulate form. A German Baptist, Rauschenbusch spent most of his adult life as a pastor and professor in America. His book *Christianity and the Social Crisis* pointed out Jesus' indifference to ritual in favor of concern for the common needs of mankind. He demanded,

> Why has Christianity never undertaken the work of social reconstruction? The Church is to be the incarnation of the Christian spirit on earth, the organized conscience of Christendom. It should be swiftest to awaken to every undeserved suffering, bravest to speak to every wrong, and strongest to rally the moral forces of the community against everything that threatens the better life among men.[40]

It was not enough to gather food for the poor; Christian ethics must be made effective in nothing less than the total reconstruction of society.

Opposing capitalism because it divides society into antagonistic classes, Rauschenbusch proposed a system that would prevent the tendency of management to get laborers at cheap rates and force work from them beyond management's willingness to pay. "Here enters socialism. It proposes to abolish the division . . . and to give the whole body of workers [labor and management] the ownership of these vast instruments of production and to distribute among them all the proceeds of their common labor." The role of the Church, he believed, was to enroll itself on the side of the laborers until sufficient political power could be achieved to bring this relationship about. "Just as the Protestant principle of religious liberty rose to victory by an alliance with the middle class which was then rising to power, so the new Christian principle of brotherly association must ally itself with the working class if both are to conquer."[41]

There are many who would argue that the social gospel does not reflect a gospel ethic in the strict sense, inasmuch as so many of the problems to which the social gospel responded did not exist, or at least were not explicitly addressed, in the New Testament. Yet our point in this chapter has been to indicate how Christian ethics has been kneaded and molded by changing circumstances, social and political no less than ideological, from the time of the first-century Church. Christian ethics is by necessity dynamic, not static, and while we continue to examine the biblical sources about the mission and teachings of Christ, the way we perceive the direction of Jesus' ethic in contemporary problem solving requires our thinking amphibiously; Christians are creatures of two worlds who must found their faith on Christ alone, but their ethics on many foundations. Charles Curran, of Catholic University, claims that one of the failings of Catholic moral theology in the past was its inability to maintain this dichotomy in the name of theological precision. "Specifically in the area of moral theology, Catholic teaching has tried to avoid the tension created by the ethics of Jesus."[42] He suggests that the deficiency might be laid to the fact that natural law theories inherited from secular Rome have been too influential.

The natural law theory provided no real eschatology, no view of the future by which many social problems might be judged and rectified.[43] Consider, for example, the problem of slavery. No solution was provided by Aristotle or by Roman jurists who entertained a concept of natural law, because in their view some people are born, in the natural course of things, to be subservient to others. To be sure, if we were to look to the teachings of Jesus on slavery, no specific word would be found either because he did not address the matter. But Jesus' message about the kingdom of God, Christians' *eschaton*, proclaims their ultimate oneness as the family of God. Because Jesus affirmed all people, "even the least of these" to be his brothers, the way Christians treat them reflects their treatment of him (Matthew 25:31f.). On the basis of this, the Baptists in the eighteenth century condemned slavery a century before civil law did so, and only after a civil war. The eschatological principle rendered slavery intolerable. "The ethics of Jesus," as Curran points out, "involves a creative tension between the present and the final stage of the reign of God,"[44] but it is a tension that in itself provides hope of resolution.

Meanwhile, as Christians entered the twentieth century, many challenges to their ethical position, and indeed to the survival of Christianity, had yet to be faced.

CHAPTER THREE

Contemporary Background: Challenge and Response

A commonplace observation is that the twentieth century was born on a wave of optimism which gradually gave way to dismay over World War I, a global depression, a second world war, a succession of smaller wars, and heightened international tensions. Our era was heralded with countless inventions like horseless carriages, telephones, movies, and powered flight to sustain the impression that we were on an escalator to utopia. It was easy to echo the song of Swinburne "Glory to man in the highest / For man is the master of things."

To be sure, not everyone was so sanguine even in the early days about our "century of progress" (ironically the theme of the 1939 World's Fair, the year World War II began). Writers both religious and secular warned that our culture's moral development was still primitive, incapable of guiding the onward rush of technology. The industrial revolution had caused great poverty as well as great wealth, damaged family unity, and made slavery so attractive that a bloody civil war was required to scrub America's economy free of it. A warning against exploitive capitalism, written in the middle of the nineteenth century by Frederick Maurice, a Unitarian convert to Anglicanism, was avidly read as an antidote to both the threat of communism and the naïveté of secular humanism. He denounced unrestricted competition as "the folly of expecting universal selfishness to do the work of universal love."[1] Other churchmen, like Charles Kingsley, chaplain to Queen Victoria, and Brook Wescott, bishop of Durham, protested degrading social conditions that rendered spiritual as well as physical cleanliness almost impossible for the poor. "In an age which Mammon rules," wrote George Herron in 1894, "when property is protected at the expense of humanity, when the state regards material things more sacred than human beings, the gospel of the Kingdom of God . . . needs to be preached as the judgement of love to the brutal cynicism of the market, to the industrial despotisms."[2]

The dismay that followed the wars and depression of the first half of the century and deepened with the cold war and the nuclear arms race has been accompanied by sharp criticism of organized Christianity. While it is true that Christianity has always had its detractors, what is new is not the attacks against its doctrines or its inability to influence social, economic, or political affairs more effectively. Instead, the criticism is directed at its fundamental values. Some have charged that such historic horrors as the Crusades, the Inquisition, and religious wars have been the inevitable consequence of Christianity as promulgated by the churches.

It is important for Christians today to take seriously such judgments and to understand how they have arisen. It is fruitless to blame godless humanism or the failures of liberals, conservatives, or any other group within Christendom, when the roots of such disaffection lie at a deeper historical level. Brian Hebblethwaite of Cambridge University urges us to look at least as far back as the eighteenth century, an era we call the Enlightenment, to the influence of such philosophers as Hume, Kant, and Hegel, and keep searching through the nineteenth century of Nietzsche, Marx, Freud, and others.[3] If we are fully to understand the weakened position of Christian ethics today, of course, we cannot blame such individual writers either, nor does Hebblethwaite suggest we should; instead we recognize them as spokesmen who may well have reflected attitudes and insights already being felt but unexpressed in a formal way. A brief examination of these and other historical figures here may equip us to understand more clearly the situation in our time.

Many Christians have sought to respond with new ways of conveying the adequacy of the historic message. Some of these come to us with such titles as neoorthodoxy, situation ethics, death of God, and liberation theology. We explore some of these challenges and responses en route to engaging what for many is the ultimate question: Are we now living in a post-Christian era?

CRITICS OF CHRISTIANITY

David Hume

The rationalistic humanism of the eighteenth-century Enlightenment spawned, paradoxically, philosophers who extolled the adequacy of human reason as well as some who denied it. David Hume of Scotland (1711–1776) was one of the latter. He wrote vigorously against a tradition within Christendom since Thomas Aquinas that held reason to be humankind's most distinctive characteristic. Hume insisted that moral distinctions cannot be derived from reason. Rather, when we understand human nature we discover that choices of good and evil arise from our feelings of approval and disapproval. Our feelings, rather than our cognitive activity, govern our choices. Human beings, Hume believed, have an inherent tendency to altruism, so that "morals excite passions and produce or prevent actions. Reason itself is utterly impotent in this particular. The rules of morality, therefore, are not conclusions of reason."[4]

Born a little more than a century after England and Scotland had suffered their bloodiest religious wars, Hume concluded that intolerance and fanaticism, rather than ethics, are characteristic of the religious life. His caustic attacks on Christianity cost him an appointment to a professorship at the University of Edinburgh. Yet he was not an aggressive atheist. He simply insisted that our preference for ethical behavior arises from our own human nature rather than from religious inspiration. That argument provided the basis for many subsequent criticisms of Christian ethics. A thorough skeptic, Hume went even further in his attack on reason, pointing to the superstitious and violent actions of those in the past who used logic to justify religious or political positions. Self-interest, he believed, is the key to human nature; when faith and logic cease to serve our self-interest, they are quickly abandoned.

Immanuel Kant

In Germany, Immanuel Kant (1724–1804) took a position directly at odds with Hume's, contending that morality based on anything other than reason is unreliable, and claiming to find moral law fully embodied in historical Christianity. For moral law to have any force, he wrote, it must carry with it absolute necessity: "The basis of obligation must not be sought in the nature of man, or in the circumstances in the world in which he is placed, but *a priori* simply in the conception of pure reason."[5]

Kant's proposal represents a thoroughgoing idealism, in which right and wrong, good and evil stand independent of any examples we might use to exemplify them; they are part of the very fabric of the universe we inhabit and are perceived by reason. Kant rejected any idea of "heteronomous" ethics (i.e., imposed from outside ourselves). Even the Ten Commandments were not thus imposed. They were perceived by Moses as the logical expression of what is eternally right. It is important to note the difference here between Hume's and Kant's position. Hume would contend that the Ten Commandments came from within our own self-serving nature. Kant argued that they came *through* our reason, but not *from* our reason; reason perceived what is ultimately and eternally right: "No moral principle is based on any feeling," because feelings are always physical in nature, rather than rational.[6] Once the right is perceived, it is not imposed heteronomously from outside, but obeyed as a matter of moral obligation.

Identifying himself as a religious man, and as a Christian, Kant's position nevertheless serves to undermine the foundations of Christian ethics no less than did Hume's. Indeed, Brian Hebblethwaite insists,

> Kant's challenge is a more insidious one. The moral law or categorical impera-
> tive, as Kant calls it, is a law of our own rational nature. It is imposed upon us,
> quite autonomously from within. All that matters—and it matters uncondition-
> ally—is the good will, according to which I act only on those maxims which I
> can rationally will to be a universal law. Since, for Kant, morality is a matter of
> reason, the historical elements in Christianity are quite superfluous.[7]

In fact, God is also superfluous if one takes Kant's argument to its logical conclusion, as Johann Fichte did a generation later in formally rejecting any personal concept of deity.

Georg Friedrich Hegel

An even more serious undermining of Christian ethics arises in the writings of another eighteenth-century philosopher, Georg Friedrich Hegel, whose
life and work carried over to the third decade of the nineteenth century. Hegel
(1770–1831) published a life of Christ in which he presented Jesus as a teacher
of the inner moral law. Rejecting the traditional Christian view of a transcendent Father God, who is in a sense "over against" and distinct from us, Hegel
wrote in favor of an immanent "God within." In his celebrated *Philosophy of
Right* (published in 1821), he described right and conscience in terms of each
person's becoming self-aware when participating in the universal, or Absolute
World Spirit. His unified worldview incorporated the idea that "the basis of
right is, in general, mind; its precise place and point of origin is the will. The
will is free, so that freedom is both the substance of right and its goal."[8] Our
knowledge of the World Soul derives from a dialectical process of thought, by
which every proposition (thesis) evokes its opposite (antithesis); the interaction of the two forms a new concept (synthesis). Nothing is ever static. Persons, states, and the universe itself are in a constant process of becoming
something else, something greater and more refined.

Each of us, according to Hegel, participates in the universal Spirit, which
is essentially subjective (as opposed to the traditional Christian view of God as
objectively "there," over against us). Goodness is necessarily an abstraction, as
is rightness. Hegel titles Part I of *The Philosophy of Right* "Abstract Right," and
notes that our ability to perceive what is right is dependent on our ability to
recognize that "right" is "the embodiment of the absolute concept."[9] Hegel
states further that "the particular subject is related to the good as to the essence
of his will. Because of the abstract characterization of the good . . . subjectivity is the determining and decisive element in him, his conscience."[10]

Hegel's opposition to the objectifying of a Father God, as in traditional Christianity, was so intense that he attributed to it the corruption and slavery of humanity. Having so objectified God in this fashion, making it a matter of creed, Christians launched religious wars, fought, denounced, and murdered each other. Such horrific consequences, Hegel believed, were not accidental but inevitable.

Karl Marx

In the nineteenth century, Karl Marx (1818–1883) adopted the dialectical method of Hegel, but rejected the latter's concept of universal Idea, or World Spirit. At twenty-five, Marx identified himself as a Communist, and by twenty-nine had written the *Communist Manifesto* with Frederick Engels (1820–1895). Out of a profound concern for the plight of the millions of people impoverished and domestically disrupted by the industrial revolution, he revealed the imprint of his Judeo-Christian heritage in the primary value of his system. His famous dictum, "from each according to his ability, to each according to his need," is virtually a paraphrase of Acts 4:32–33. Marx understood firsthand the ravages of poverty, suffering the loss of three of his six children while living in cold privation in London. Shortly before his death, Marx wrote to Engels of his desperate eagerness to complete his book *Capital*: "If one wants to be an ox one can easily turn one's back on human suffering and look after one's own skin. But I should have regarded myself as really impractical had I died without finishing my book."

The oft-quoted judgment of Marx against religion as the "opiate of the people" is not so much a criticism of faith as an indictment of the economic situation. Religion, he wrote, is the heart's cry of alienated people. Out of his Jewish background, flavored with the scorn of Israel's prophets against exploiters of the poor, he saw religion as an illusion that eased the pangs of poverty. What he found detestable was the uses and abuses of religion by the bourgeois class, who maintained their churches to keep the poor compliant.[11]

Marx's challenge to Christianity was twofold. His thoroughgoing materialism denied the biblical account of Creation, as well as any notion that the cosmos shows evidence of plan or purpose or being presided over by a deity. Second, the sheer earnestness of his plea for justice, equal rights for all, free education, and abolishing class distinctions appeared to preempt any claim of Christianity to achieve such goals in the face of its history of failures. The concluding lines of his *Manifesto* are both an invitation and a challenge: "The proletarians have nothing to lose but their chains. They have a world to win."[12]

Charles Darwin

Charles Darwin (1809–1882) had a powerful influence in forcing a reevaluation of the biblical accounts of Creation and of the role of humans in biological history. But he was not an atheist, nor did he seriously challenge the ethical precepts of Christianity. In his youth, Darwin was quite orthodox, but perhaps at least in part as a reaction to the attacks against him from certain religious quarters, he let his interest in religious matters wane, stating only in his *Descent of Man* (1871) that he noted a continuity between certain behaviors of lower animals and religious practices of humans. In his *Origin of Species* (1859), he had admitted that the whole lawful system of nature might indeed have a Creator, a "First Cause," but that such a hypothesis added nothing to our knowledge of nature itself, which was his own goal as a man of science. He was thus an agnostic in the double sense of neither affirming a personal God nor finding it necessary to refute the idea. He nevertheless approved generally of the contribution of the religious impulse to moral behavior, and noted in Chapter 21 of *Descent of Man* that the moral faculties are of higher value than intellectual powers. He added that because the mind is a fundamental (even though secondary) basis of conscience, "this affords the strongest argument for educating the intellectual faculties of every human being."

Herbert Spencer

Herbert Spencer (1820–1903), on the other hand, proposing a "social Darwinism," coined the phrase "survival of the fittest." He flatly denied the reality of God, except as the synonym for nature. His scorn for altruism expressed itself in his advocacy of economic laissez-faire, unrestrained competition. Those people at the bottom of the social ladder were there, he declared, because they were inferior; to aid them would only perpetuate inferiority and retard progress. So insistent was he on this that Spencer devoted a whole chapter to it in his book *The Data of Ethics* (1879).

The popularity of Spencer's philosophy among strict free enterprise capitalists was almost immediate. Churches in capitalist nations often tend to favor a conservative status quo position, but many Christian ethicists saw in Spencer's ideology a threat to the Gospel, Jesus' "good news to the poor" (Luke 4:19). It was also seen to undermine economic opportunity for the poor, the hardworking people whose wages were so low they could not provide for their families or their own old age; the involuntarily unemployed, those laid off to protect the profits of those at the top; workers felled by illness of industrial accidents and without insurance or compensation; unmarried women; and widows with children to feed with no income unless they turned to prostitution.

Friedrich Nietzsche

On the continent, more threatening still were the writings of Friedrich Nietzsche (1844–1900), who not merely denied God, but accused the churches of coddling the weak, as did Spencer. He charged that Christianity preached a crippling morality, which "sided with all that is weak and base, with all failures;

it has made an ideal of whatever contradicts the instinct of the strong."[13] Nietzsche declared that anyone should be ashamed to be called a Christian.

Many Christians who know of Nietzsche only secondhand, from his famous proclamation, "God is dead . . . we have murdered God" (from his *Joyful Wisdom*, published in 1882), have concluded that Nietzsche was an immoralist. This is not the case. Nietzsche was actually telling a parable to affirm that we create religions and deities because we need them to stabilize our world. Yet, he wrote, we also sin against our creation and ultimately kill God and pervert the religion. Once this is done, nothing, not our individual lives nor our society or civilization, can ever be the same again. Indeed, if God is dead, nothing is true and anything is permissible. Nihilism rules: All existing structures are destroyed. Nietzsche saw with a prophet's eye the coming disruptions in Western culture, its ideological wars and moral decadence, the decline of education into mere training of minds to live in a mechanized society bent on sheer acquisition of wealth and on mindless pleasures. In its place he wanted to create a new morality, to inspire a new generation of elite supermen, with the prowess and intelligence of Napoleon and Goethe. Traditional (or Judeo-Christian) morality, which panders to the weak and powerless, must be swept away. He viewed Jesus as "the only Christian," and perhaps one to be admired for his courage, but rejected as a simple fool. The only person to receive humanity's applause should be one whose affirmation of life is expressed in the "will to power," in passionate individualism.

That this intense individualism has caught the imagination and won the allegiance of many of our contemporaries even within Christianity is a dilemma for Christian ethics. It is a theme popular in a pragmatic age of self-made individuals, but can lead to a self-righteousness seriously at odds with the spirit of Christ.

Sigmund Freud

Still another figure of monumental proportions whose work confronts Christian ethics with one of its greatest challenges is Sigmund Freud (1856–1939). During his counseling sessions, Freud discovered what he termed a libidinal substratum of bestial powers in all his patients, which if unchecked or somehow sublimated could erupt with inhuman violence. Extrapolating to the whole human scene, Freud declared we also are born with a superego, a kind of repository for all the moral teachings and conventions of society. This is not a static entity, however, but has energy with which to engage the libido on the battleground of the ego. The personality is thus shaped in the midst of ongoing battles. As children grow and discovers that the parents on whom they rely for protection and guidance are not infallible, the yearning for security prompts the creation of a Father God, the product of wish fulfillment. "Psychoanalysis concludes that he really is the father, clothed in the grandeur in which he once appeared to the small child."[14]

Freud acknowledged the value of the solace religion provides people in times when life overwhelms them with a sense of helplessness. Yet he resented religion for keeping people in this state of dependence on an illusion. Ultimately, he viewed belief in God as dangerous to mental health and the enemy of an intelligent view of reality. "Of the forces which dispute the position of science," he wrote, "religion alone is a really serious enemy."[15]

In declaring religion the enemy of science, Freud posed a dichotomy that was a more serious problem for Christians than had been presented by others who had previously challenged the faith. It was not merely the threat of atheism. Religious people have always encountered those who denied the existence of God and have dismissed them with greater or lesser degrees of impatience. The Psalmist declared, "The fool says in his heart 'there is no God' " (Psalm 14:1). But many Christians have believed there is no serious conflict between science and religion; some prominent scientists, including Nobel laureates like Robert Millikan and Arthur Holly Compton, have been convinced Christians. When so formidable a scholar as Freud claims not only that religion is the enemy of science but that the source of the God figure has been revealed to be nothing more than a projected illusion of one's own parent, neurotically clung to out of emotional desperation, the believer may feel spiritually denuded. Coping with this problem deserves special attention in a later section.

With the twentieth century, the challenges to Christianity came increasingly, not only from individuals, but from schools of thought or whole movements. There would still be individual critics like Bertrand Russell (1872–1970), who in a book titled *Why I Am Not a Christian* rehearsed Christendom's often sorry record of persecuting dissenters, blocking scientific progress, and denying equality to women and racial minorities. But most thoughtful Christians have been equally dismayed by such aberrations, following Jesus' injunctions to love and care for fellow human beings. If Russell's charges were the whole truth about Christianity, no one would wish to be a Christian. His lament simply is not the whole truth, but a caricature about a fraction of Christianity's history.

What we witness in our own century, however, has been the development of whole philosophical movements that have treated Christianity and Christian ethics, if they regarded them at all, either with mild disdain or complete disregard. Freud's writings, for example, launched *psychoanalysis* which, having discounted God and religion, interprets sin as a misnomer for subconscious and completely natural drives of the libido. Control of these instinctive urges is exercised by the superego, which is not a God-given conscience, but a natural protective counterbalance to the libido, comprised of the social safeguards learned from family and community. The self, or ego replaces the soul as the battleground on which the libido and superego contend for dominance. An elaborate system of defense mechanisms has been proposed by which the personality survives and shapes itself. Critics of psychoanalysis, both religious and secular, have accused its founders of having gone far afield from science to create a substitute religion no less exotic and mystic than the Freudians attacked.[16]

August Comte

Another set of challenges to Christianity and its ethics has come from *positivism*. This movement began in the late nineteenth century, based on the work of August Comte (1798–1857), called the father of sociology. Comte rejected metaphysics and all suggestions of purpose in nature, limiting "belief" to the acceptance of data that can be verified by the senses. Philosophically a descendant of Protagoras (fifth century B.C.), the Sophist who proclaimed "man is the measure of all things," Comte insisted that societies create their own values. Religion and ethics arise from the purely natural impulse to establish organization and social cohesion. He rejected Aristotle's concept of God as "first cause," along with other religious or philosophical notions of causation: "Our business is . . . seeing how vain is any research into what are called causes, whether first or final . . . to analyze accurately the circumstances of phenomena, and to connect them by natural relations of succession and resemblance."[17] Belief systems betray us by forcing conclusions without adequate support. "It is always and everywhere wrong to believe anything on insufficient evidence." What constitutes sufficient evidence is empirically verified data, expressed in logically stated propositions.[18]

The key to the positivist position is the insistence that all statements which can be judged as true must belong to one of two mutually exclusive kinds; they must be either analytic or synthetic. Analytic statements are those that are necessarily true, such as "a triangle has three sides." They are a priori; the truth of the statement does not depend on its being observed or demonstrated; it simply is so. The problem here is that true statements of this kind do not necessarily yield useful information. One might say, for example, "It is either raining or it is not raining." That is certainly a valid statement, but fails to tell us which is the case: Is it raining or not? Synthetic statements, on the other hand, are those whose truth or falsity is determined a posteriori, and that do contain factual information. "The Pacific Ocean lies west of here" is a synthetic statement, put together by bits and pieces of verifiable data.

The problem for Christian ethics, posed by positivism, becomes clear when we submit such a statement as "God is good, and demands justice for all his people." God is not subject to empirical verification like a triangle or the location of an ocean. The statement is thus neither analytic nor synthetic and thus, according to the positivists, is a nonsense proposition: literally nonsense. Statements about sin, goodness, morality, or the spiritual life must simply be dismissed on the same grounds. A. J. Ayer put it quite bluntly: "It is impossible to find a criterion for determining the validity of ethical judgements . . . because they have no objective validity whatever."[19]

If, as William Clifford insisted, "it is wrong to believe anything on insufficient evidence," and God is merely a projection of our earthly father's image, and the most urgent questions of the Christian life cannot even be asked because "they have no objective validity," has the ground been completely removed from beneath our feet?

William James

William James (1842–1910), one of the fathers of *pragmatism*, gave encouragement to Christians bewildered by the assaults on ethics and morality by the positivists. His book *The Will to Believe* affirmed, contrary to Clifford's claim, that many practical situations require that we act on beliefs for which we have very little evidence. If a child is drowning 200 yards from shore, and the boy's father has never been more than a casual swimmer with no empirical evidence that he can swim the necessary 400 yards round trip to save the child, his will to believe in his ability may actually make the rescue possible. Indeed there are countless incidences of such "impossible" rescues. "There are cases," James insisted, "where a fact cannot come at all unless a preliminary faith exists in its coming."[20]

A proposition, according to James, can only be validated through experience: The truth of an idea depends on whether it works. Thus if faith works for a person, if it makes that person more honest and more compassionate toward others, then it can be said that person's faith has been validated. James found corroboration for his pragmatic interpretation that "true" religion is ethics in practice in the New Testament epistle of James (1:27), and his writings were a source of inspiration in many liberal pulpits for decades to follow.

John Dewey

Some pragmatists were not satisfied with James's personalist validation of faith and showed their positivist sympathies in declaring that terms like *God, truth,* and *immorality* can be said to have value only to the community where those words are acceptable. They sought norms of convenience and utility. But John Dewey (1859–1952) found even those norms inadequate, fearing that religious values, when objectified by churches or states, lead to tyranny and dehumanization. "The habit of identifying moral characteristics with external conformity to authoritative prescriptions . . . tends to reduce morals to dead and machine-like routine; the results are morally undesirable."[21] Growth in ethical understanding can only derive from experiences of tension being worked out in life situations, in light of the needs of society. Dewey's emphasis on experience, tension, and growth appear at first glance to have much in common with Hegel's position, except that Dewey firmly insisted there is no separate entity as "mind." Thinking is merely a biological function, and mind is the system of meanings we acquire in the process of adjusting to and growing within our environment. Consciousness is the awareness of these meanings. God is a term that refers to the unifying experience of ends toward which we grow. There is no absolute, or universal mind with Dewey.

As presented in Dewey's book *A Common Faith*, pragmatism opposes all forms of supernaturalism, and provides instead a naturalistic humanism, in which the role of religion is to bring the actual and the ideal into harmony with each other.[22] The difficulty with this for Christian ethics is that for pragmatists, the "ideal" is never considered to be an end in itself, something to pursue for its own sake. Traditionally we have understood that there are two kinds of values: end values and means values. We employ certain ways and means to achieve desired ends. But for the pragmatist, all values turn out to be means values, or instrumental values. We work to earn a paycheck, to buy food and clothing, to live well, to impress our neighbors. "And so life goes," writes Ernest Bayles, "one quest after another in such a continuing succession that we are almost convinced that the questing itself is where the fun lies. This is what is meant by the ends-means continuum."[23] But on what basis are we to determine the merit or justification for the means? If there are no ultimate values, no transcendent standard of right or wrong, how can we be sure we are justified in using one set of means as opposed to another? Bayles's only response (and that of most pragmatists) is: ". . . means values—also called instrumental—are perforce dependent for their own value on the service they render toward achievement of the end-in-view."[24]

"Values," according to the pragmatist, "are only tentative and temporary statements of what ought to be done. They are never to be considered universal. They always apply to this or that situation. If I ask 'What should I do?' the only sensible answer is the familiar qualifying counter, 'It all depends.' "[25] All values are relative to the society they serve, and societies are in a constant state of change.

Pragmatism has received a resounding rebuke from certain morally sensitive persons who recall, as does Robert Conot, its implementation during the Nazi era in Germany. "The great numbers of Germans who hailed Hitler were not psychopaths or natural killers," he notes. "They accepted his leadership in a time of devastating economic depression because he stabilized the economy, created jobs, and promised to restore their place in the world." In a time of food shortages, he began to eliminate "useless eaters": the mentally defective, the physically handicapped, the very elderly . . . then turned his attention to such "enemies of the state" as dissident Christians, Gypsies, and Jews. The erosion of ethics and morality was gradual and secretive at first. Objections were quickly and ruthlessly silenced. "The entire history of Nazi Germany could be summarized as the triumph of pragmatism over principle, of utilitarianism and expediency over humanity and justice."[26]

Pragmatism continues to be the guiding principle in much of life in the Western world. Tragically, after the fall of Naziism, when the Nuremberg trials supposedly ended the reign of their philosophy, "the nations of the world went right back to policies governed by few considerations other than pragmatism and self-interest."[27] Clearly there is no room in pragmatism for Christian ethics, which insists that societies and the values they espouse come under the judgment of a transcendent God. Nor is there any acknowledgment of the need for the reconciling work of Christ and his church.

J. B. Watson and B. F. Skinner

Another movement to challenge Christian ethics in our century is *behaviorism*. Arising from the field of psychology through the early work of J. B. Watson (1878–1958), this movement was promoted with missionary zeal as a way of understanding human nature. Renouncing not only metaphysics, but also the notion that there are such entities as "minds," Watson developed what came to be known as stimulus-response or, simply, S-R psychology. Human personality and character, he declared, are the product of experience. If the environment of a child could be artificially controlled, all stimuli strategically provided, the child's every response, word, and action could be predicted. There is no such thing as free will, or even, in the strictest sense, responsibility because all behaviors are conditioned.[28]

The determinism of Watson's model of human behavior was somewhat modified by Harvard psychologist B. F. Skinner, who proposes that behaviors are not so mechanically elicited, but rather "emitted" by the responding subject in a voluntary manner. By way of illustration, Skinner described a setting using an experimental rat:

> A hungry rat [is placed in an] experimental space which contains a food dispenser. A horizontal bar projects from one wall. Depression of the lever operates a switch. When the switch is connected with the food dispenser, any behavior on the part of the rat which depresses the lever is, as we say, "reinforced with food." The apparatus simply makes the appearance of food contingent upon the occurrence of a arbitrary bit of behavior. Under such circumstances, the probability that a response to the lever will occur again is increased.[29]

It would not be accurate to describe the "reinforcer" (in this case food), as a reward for behaviors, nor as a bribe to elicit a repeat of the behaviors, though it is clear that the use of them tends to cause those activities to be repeated. To employ words like *bribe* or *reward* would imply that the animal (or person) is thinking about them, and Skinner is reluctant to use terms like *thought* and *reason*. It is more scientific, Skinner believes, simply to talk about stimuli and responses. Further, as reinforcers stimulate desired behaviors, withholding them serves to reduce undesired behaviors, more effectively, Skinner affirms, than old-fashioned punishment. Shaping behavior may at times require "negative reinforcers," however, by which the subject associates an unpleasant experience with behaviors that the "behavioral engineer" (teacher, or other director) wishes to "reduce to extinction."

Critics of behaviorism have pointed to its effort to be scientific as a major flaw. Psychologist Gordon Allport notes that it has

> imitated the billiard-ball model of physics, now of course outmoded. [It has] delivered into our hands a psychology of an empty organism, pushed by drives and molded by environmental circumstances. But the theory of democracy requires that man possess a measure of rationality, a portion of freedom, a generic conscience, appropriate ideals, and unique value.[30]

For the Christian ethicist, no less than for a psychologist like Allport, there is a requirement that humankind, created "in God's image," be understood as free and responsible. Behaviorist B. F. Skinner insists, "The hypothesis that man is not free, is essential to the application of scientific method to the study of human behavior."[31] The obvious conflict between behaviorism's essential hypothesis that man is not free and the Christian insistence that humankind is free, leaves Christianity with yet another challenge to address.

Søren Kierkegaard

A final challenge to consider arises from *existentialism*, a movement that began in the middle of the nineteenth century, but came to have its greatest impact on Christianity after World War II. It originated in the writings of the Danish philosopher Søren Kierkegaard (1813–1855), who was a Christian, but was critical of both the Church and of idealism, the dominant philosophy of his day. Both of these, he wrote, try to make life easy by providing either creeds or philosophical formulations (in the case of Hegel's idealism, the thesis-antithesis-synthesis principle) by which life's complicated and often tragic events can be interpreted.

The distinguishing idea in Kierkegaard's thought is in the immeasurable difference between finite and infinite; between time and eternity; between man and God. He did not attempt to develop an ontological argument that would aid in understanding the nature of man as opposed to the nature of God. To do so would have been to make God an objective reality, a being among other beings. Instead Kierkegaard stressed that God is "wholly other." As eternity is "over against" time, so God is "over against" all creation, absolutely unique. God is infinite, pure being, eternal. By contrast, we are finite, existing, and always in a state of *becoming* in a time-bound, space-hedged world. Because of this gulf between ourselves and God, and because we cannot conceive of God in any objective fashion, we cannot possibly know his will for our lives in an objective way. Yet we know ourselves to be wholly dependent on God if our lives are to have ultimate meaning. Our effort to live the Christian life is thus a passionate leap of faith, a great spiritual risk, and as impossible an effort as trying to comply with Jesus' challenge: "You must be perfect as your heavenly Father is perfect." It would be impossible to create a "Christian ethic" because each person must make that leap of faith alone, without formulations or ethical guidelines. For Kierkegaard, Christianity was essentially subjective, and in his *Concluding Unscientific Postscript*, he insisted that "an objective acceptance of Christianity is paganism or thoughtlessness."

We have already noted that Friedrich Nietzsche maintained a similar subjectivity, and, while denying God and the transcendent altogether in order to make room for humankind to create our own values, Nietzsche strongly influenced the development of the atheistic existentialism that was to become so prominent in the twentieth century. Indeed, as Hebblethwaite points out, "This is the source of the atheistic existentialism of Jean-Paul Sartre and [has] been very influential on the development of existentialism generally."[32]

Martin Heidegger

Atheistic existentialism was given a new form in the writings of Martin Heidegger, whose work also influenced Jean-Paul Sartre. Heidegger (1889–1976) sought to overcome the dichotomy of being and existence proposed by Kierkegaard, by offering his conception of *Dasein*: human existence rooted not in god, but in itself. Being, paradoxically, contains within itself the possibility of nonbeing, so it is inseparable from nothingness. In death we see the prospect of not being, so death in a sense defines our existence. It also imposes on us the freedom to choose the quality of our lives. One characteristic of *Dasein* is caring (*Sorge*), that is, concern for its own being. This is more than a mere survival instinct; it is a painfully conscious dread (*Angst*) of nonbeing, while also defending itself against the world, which is being-toward-death.

> *Nothing* is that which makes the revelation of what-is as such, possible for our human existence. *Nothing* not merely provides the conceptual opposite of what-is, but is also an original part of essence (*Wesen*). It is in the being (*Sein*) of what-is (*Seiendes*) that the nihilation of nothing (*das Nichten des Nichts*) occurs.[33]

If all this seems somewhat surrealistic or too abstract to have any relevance to Christian ethics, remember that a century earlier, Hegel pondered the question of being and nonbeing and concluded that "pure being and pure nothing are one and the same." The apparent contradiction was resolved (for Hegel) in the concept of becoming, or process. The importance for Christian theology is seen in Heidegger's reference to Creation, where he takes *creatio ex nihilo* to mean that God created the universe out of no thing. This is not to say Heidegger believes the biblical account, but he uses the reference to show how the problem has persisted throughout the history of metaphysical argument.[34]

Significantly, even in his agnosticism, Heidegger does not close the door on the possibility of a realm of the holy, as a quality of Being. In his letter on

"Humanism," he declares that humankind stands open to the lighting up of being, and exists "in the neighborhood of being," where the dimension of the "holy" is disclosed.[35] Ultimately, he dissociates himself from atheism.

Jean-Paul Sartre

Jean-Paul Sartre (1905–1980), while gaining much from Heidegger's dissolving the dichotomy of being and existence in *Dasein*, being-rooted-in-itself, refuses any hint that there may be a realm of the holy, or anything rational outside man himself. "Existence precedes essence" was, in effect, Sartre's battle cry. There is no God, so there is no preset human nature. "First of all man exists, turns up, appears on the scene, and only afterward defines himself."[36] Our responsibility is to make of ourselves what we will, without divine aid (or blame). "Such is the first principle of existentialism. . . . Man is at the start of a plan which is aware of itself . . . nothing exists prior to this plan; nothing in heaven; man will be what he will have planned to be."[37]

If existence precedes essence, and nothing is predetermined, we must take responsibility for our own thoughts and actions, according to Sartre. Further, because our decisions inevitably involve other people, we are responsible for the effects our decisions may have on them. Therein lies our ethics, and the Golden Rule quite appropriately reminds us of this even if it cannot be called a rule in the strict sense (inasmuch as we must follow our own inner dictates and not external rules).

If there is no God, and no rule external to the self, critics of existentialism raise the question: Why must we take responsibility for our actions and their impact on others? What is to prevent the existentialist from throwing in the towel, so to speak, and just do whatever pleases? There is an implicit "ought" in Sartre's writings that seems not to follow logically from his argument. Sartre himself worked diligently for the resistance movement against Naziism in France. What prompted this self-sacrifice? Surely not the mere fact that he existed? Yet Sartre's writings, his essays, books, and plays, hold a fascination for millions of people, and Karl Jaspers, a fellow existentialist of considerable stature in his own right, declared, "Sartre's existentialism . . . has conquered the world."[38] If people can be courageous, as Sartre certainly was, and even benevolent without believing in God, what advantage is there to Christian faith and ethics?

SOME CHRISTIANS' RESPONSES

In full view of the individual criticisms of Christianity noted, and those of philosophical movements that have claimed our generation's attention, we must ask whether Christian ethics can provide a persuasive rebuttal. Many Christians, perhaps even a majority, have chosen to ignore the attacks. They proceed to worship and carry out the ethical requirements of the faith to feed the hungry, care for the sick, love their neighbors, and maintain a Christian family life to the best of their ability as if none of the assaults had taken place. Others have responded either by positing irreducible tenets or "fundamentals" of the faith beyond the reach of attack, or by reinterpreting the faith in light of scientific and cultural advances. We examine a few of these here.

Conservative Christians have traditionally taken the Bible as the authoritative word of God, free from error in providing answers to scientific as well as moral and spiritual questions. Paleontologist L. S. B. Leaky, whose work at the Olduvai Gorge in East Africa added much to our understanding of evolution, observed somewhat bitterly that despite all the evidence, many if not most churches in the nineteenth and twentieth century accept the date 4004 B.C. as the year of the earth's creation.[39]

To be sure, not all conservative Christians support so literal an interpretation of the Bible, and many regret the infamous monkey trial of John Scopes, in 1923, when a ban on teaching evolution was upheld.[40] A more positive response to the seeming threat of science to faith was the 1912 publication of twelve pamphlets called *The Fundamentals*, which served to identify what should characterize Christian faith and life. Thus *fundamentalism* was born.

It is impossible to do justice to fundamentalism in so brief a space as we have here, but it is helpful to note some of its key points, as foils to the attacks just noted. "The heart of fundamentalism," it has been said, "is in its concern for salvation. The only really important question is, 'Have you been saved?' "[41] To sustain the integrity of their position, fundamentalists claim the infallibility of the Bible as the literal word of God. One fundamentalist writer went so far as to claim that even the punctuation of the Bible was inspired and hence without error.[42] Because all humans live in sin and apart from God, our only hope of salvation is in God's having sent his son, Jesus Christ, to take our sin on himself, and pay the penalty of death (since Paul said, "the wages of sin is death"). By confessing our sinfulness and accepting Christ's substitution of himself in our place, we are saved. The perfect society, "heaven on earth," awaits Christ's return, a time when history will end in catastrophe, and Christ will set up his kingdom and rule for a thousand years. At the end of that era, a final battle will be fought between the forces of God and Satan, and in the victory of God all those saved will enter heaven, and the rest will descend to hell forever.

Liberal Christians have long believed that such a reading of the biblical message, to say nothing of the understanding of natural and human history, offers only a simplistic scenario, and fails to answer the troublesome charges registered against Christendom since the Enlightenment.

Friedrich Schleiermacher (1768–1834), himself a product of the Enlightenment, agreed with Hume's position that the heart of religion is not in rational proofs, but in feelings and intuition. He differed from Hume's declaration that religion is essentially ethical because religion invokes a sense of our interdependence as children of God's family. He wrote that Christ's uniqueness was not in his divine birth or working of miracles, but in having a sense of God consciousness to a supreme degree, which gave rise to his ethical standards. The church Jesus established provides the setting in which we come close to each other and to God by emulating Jesus, both in his faith and in his righteous acts.

Later in the nineteenth century, Albrecht Ritchl (1822–1889) advanced Schleiermacher's views, declaring that faith in Christ rests not on doctrines, however logically argued, but on the fact that Jesus, as the Christ, became the founder of a value-creating movement. Jesus was the embodiment of the highest ethical values. Our response is to strive to live as he did, and therein achieve salvation.

By the beginning of the twentieth century, Christendom appeared to be divided into two camps, conservative and liberal (or fundamentalist and modernist, as they were often identified). The liberal attitude was to be open to scientific interpretations of nature (including evolution), and to use scientific methods to gain a clearer understanding of the origins of the Bible. Liberals also maintained that human nature is basically good, and that a major task of religion lies in the realm of social ethics. They often accused conservatives of anti-intellectualism (for ignoring or fighting against scientific evidence), and for having reduced Christianity to a salvation religion at the expense of social concern. Further, they have generally regarded themselves as optimistic and conservatives as either naive about the human condition or (with their emphasis on sin) as pessimistic. While many liberals denied the doctrine of original sin, they claimed to take more seriously than fundamentalists the actual facts of sin, as experienced in political corruption, exploitive economics, racial discrimination, and other manifestations.

Ethics clearly was a central concern of liberal Christians, and the term *social gospel* was perhaps their most evident banner. The Christian could not simply await the Second Coming of Christ to establish righteousness on earth while all around people were suffering poverty, disease, and political oppression. The kingdom of God must be brought into the present world. Not all liberals agreed as to what this kingdom is, some having so humanized the Bible and the person of Jesus as to prefer (as Leroy Waterman did) calling it instead "the kingdom of Man."[43]

Conservatives countercharged that liberalism has lost both the Bible and the essence of Jesus as God's messiah. Liberal ethics was no longer Christian, but merely humanist and indistinguishable from the most secular philosophy. Moreover, conservatives were able to demonstrate that their own ethic was more active and practical than anything the liberals could boast of, as witness their record of benevolence giving, their building of hospitals, schools, and agricultural stations on mission fields around the world. (This has in fact been substantiated by the National Council of Churches' *Journal of Stewardship* for nearly every year since its founding.)

The events of the twentieth century have overclouded the conflict between liberalism and conservatism. Since World War II, Western culture has been in the grips of what French author Francois Duchene calls "the endless crisis," forcing a reexamination of Christianity and its ethics.[44]

What is noted by many theologians is that neither conservatism nor liberalism dealt adequately with the challenges of Christendom's important critics. Conservatives appeared either to have ignored them, or as in the case of Darwin and Spencer, responded with invective and retreated to a literal reading of Genesis 1 (ignoring the fact that Genesis 2 contradicts the order of creation in Genesis 1). Liberalism, on the other hand, seemed to have accommodated the Gospel to Kant's rationalism, Hegel's concept of the immanent "God within us," Marx's decrying the evils of capitalism, and Freud's denial of human sinfulness, while replacing sin with powerful natural urges that may yet wreck one's social adjustment.

Significantly it was among some of the leading liberals that the call for reassessment was heard most urgently. Harry Emerson Fosdick (1878–1969), who became a liberal theologian and preacher after having been raised in strict orthodoxy, declared in a 1935 sermon, "The church must go beyond modernism." Liberals, he declared, had been preoccupied with intellectualism to the neglect of the deep spiritual crises to be found everywhere. At the same time, liberalism had been too sentimental about human "goodness," and about the supposed inevitability of social progress. Also, liberalism had diluted the concept of deity, making God "a kind of chairman of the board of sponsors of our highly successful human enterprise." Finally, and most ironically, despite modernism's avowed concern for social ethics, it actually failed to provide any antidote for the dark side of nationalism (like that in Germany or Russia), or capitalism, or racism, or a host of other evils plaguing society.[45]

Unquestionably the most popular preacher of his day, and perhaps the most respected liberal Christian, Fosdick's words sounded a new challenge: Modernism had "lost its ethical standing ground and its power of moral attack." Ours was not the kind of world God intended, and liberalism as then constituted was incapable of changing it. Many fellow liberals, particularly among the younger ones agreed: Henry Pitt Van Dusen, later to become president of Union Theological Seminary in New York; John C. Bennett, his successor; Walter Marshall Horton and D. E. Roberts, co-editors of *Liberal Theology*; Eugene Carson Blake, later to become a president of the World Council of Churches; D. Elton Trueblood, founder of the international Yokefellows movement, who began his reappraisal of liberalism with the brief but potent study, *The Predicament of Modern Man*, at the outset of World War II. Gone was the earlier optimism about the efficacy of humanistic ethics and, in place of the earlier insistence that "man is basically good," there developed a confessional mood. Humankind was still seen as rational and responsible, but for whom repentance before God is a constant requirement.

But from Europe, where people had suffered the ravages of war, depression, and state terrorism in a measure incomprehensible to most Americans, came voices saying that both fundamentalism and liberalism failed their theological mission. Chief among these Europeans, often identified as representing a new movement called *neoorthodoxy*, were Karl Barth and Emil Brunner. Their American counterpart was Reinhold Niebuhr, and although none of them felt quite at ease with the term, neoorthodoxy describes fairly accurately what they stood for: a rediscovery and restatement of orthodox themes, though with new understanding gained from modern science and other intellectual developments.

Karl Barth

Like many of his fellow neoorthodox theologians, Karl Barth (1886–1968) began as a liberal in pre–World War I Germany, hoping the kingdom of God might be ushered in by the essential goodness of mankind and the aid of socialism. The orgy of destruction he witnessed in that war shattered his confidence in human nature, and drove him back to the prophets of the Old Testament and to God's mighty presence in the life, death, and resurrection of Christ.

For Barth, there could be no ethics without theology, and no theology without ethics. Modern civilization was in the grips of a crisis, and if Christianity was to provide an adequate ethic it must dissociate itself from the dying culture in which it had nested. God's Word must be heard again, as coming from one who is "wholly other," unlike any being who can be known by reason or by natural analogy. God can be known only through his self-disclosure, and on his own terms. "God is the unknown God . . . therefore the power of God can be detected neither in the world of nature, nor in the souls of men. It must not be confounded with any high, exalted force, known or knowable."[46]

These words, from Barth's commentary on Paul's *Epistle to the Romans*, in 1919, were not meant to imply that God is unreachable or unknowable, or that his Word has nothing to say about human affairs. God has much to say to us, but all communication has its origin with God, not with mankind. At a conference of ministers in 1922, at Wiesbaden, he insisted that the roots of the ethical question, "What must I do . . . ?" reached beyond all temporal situations, and by that question we demonstrate our relation to God. We are not simply animals living out instinctual patterns, but rational creatures seeking from the depths of our beings to know whether our actions are worthy.[47] Twenty-five years later, with a depression and the Nazi holocaust between, Barth was still assuring that God's otherness does not imply his remoteness in the spiritual sense: "God in the highest, does not mean someone quite other, who has nothing to do with us, who does not concern us."[48]

The seeming contradiction is clarified in Barth's discussion on human sin. Our efforts to find and understand God always fail, not because God wishes to be remote, but because our reason, by which we try to comprehend God, has been clouded by our sinful condition, our spiritual alienation from our Creator. When we make God an object of study we are actually, no matter how subtly, trying to bring him under our power. This is why most religious or philosophical thought about God leads to idolatry. Barth agrees with Kierkegaard that there is a gulf between man and God, between time and eternity, but Barth insists this chasm has been bridged by God in Christ.

Barth is clearly at odds here with Christian liberals, who taught that God was immanent, and that mankind's inherent goodness enables us to find our way to God and salvation by our own, albeit inspired effort. But Barth is also critical of fundamentalists for failing to realize that Christ, not the pages and words of the Bible, is the living Word of God. The Word does indeed come alive for us as we read the Bible, but Barth warns against making the Scriptures "a paper Pope," self-sufficient and infallible. The Bible enables us to perceive the Word, but the Bible itself is not the Word; the Word of God transcends all words, as God transcends all things and all history.

Barth makes much of the human capacity for reason, but takes issue with Emmanuel Kant that pure reason establishes the validity of faith, and is the essence of true religion. No person's reason remains pure and objective; all our thought processes are colored by affections and loyalties (and hates). Reason can justify the actions of a tyrant as well as those of a saint.

Our knowledge of God arises from God's gracious self-disclosure. Such knowledge is therefore not a priori. God addresses us, and if we are faithful, we may receive his Word. Most importantly for Christian ethics, God's Word comes to us as invitation and command. The address is not abstract but always specific and concrete. Here again Barth shows the influence of Kierkegaard. He stresses that we must be attuned to hear God's orders in each moment, in each existential situation. Always we must check our impression of God's demands against the background of the Bible and the Church, but then we must decide for ourselves and take that leap of faith in the response of obedient action.

True to his convictions, Barth became a leader, at great personal risk, in the Evangelical churches' opposition to Hitler's tyranny. This led to the publishing of the great *Barmen Declaration* in 1934, which also led to his having to flee to Switzerland.[49] Yet Barth remained adamant that Christianity must never be identified with any political system, nor allow itself to be defined merely by what it opposes. For this reason, though he personally opposed communism, he refused to sign himself as an anti-Communist.

Barth's conviction that an uncompromising faithfulness to the God and Father of Jesus Christ is the only basis for discussing the position of other philosophers and theologians, established the vantage point from which he dealt with writers like Kant, Nietzsche, Marx, and others. "There was a time," he wrote, "when with Kant . . . people took the ethical problem to be the expression and witness of the peculiar greatness and dignity of man." Such a conclusion today is untenable as we witness the savagery and immorality of so-called moral people.[50] Kant, he decided, erred when declaring that human morality must be self-generated to be authentic; no one can claim total credit for one's own moral standards because they are the product of so many familial, societal, and cultural crosscurrents. But unless there is some ultimate standard by which they can be judged, they have no staying power. Even Kant's "categorical imperative" begs the question: "By what compulsion must I obey this sense of duty?" Kant's idealism leans too heavily on a highly questionable individualism. Nietzsche also erred, according to Barth, in his effort to proclaim total self-sufficiency for his superman. "No man is an island," as John Donne expressed it; we are all interrelated, and we all need the support and restraint of laws to govern the unruly among us. So Barth speaks of "the fulminations of Nietzsche" against law, and against the very existence of governments that are indispensable to civilized life.[51] Nevertheless, in his treatment of the Christian doctrine of man (in a massive multivolume *Church Dogmatics* that remained unfinished at the time of his death), Barth does find occasion for gratitude to Nietzsche. Christ, Barth declares, was quintessentially "the man for others," and in Nietzsche's utter rejection of the concept of humble service to one's fellow men, considering such service debasing, Nietzsche clarifies the essence of Christianity by sheer contrast. We are all, says Barth, by virtue of our oneness in Christ, to discover our common humanity precisely in service one to another, and particularly to the weak and the needy.[52]

Emil Brunner

A contemporary and leading disciple of Barth in his early years, Emil Brunner (1880–1966) was ordained in the Swiss Reformed Church and served as a pastor from 1916 to 1924. He joined the theological faculty at the University of Zurich in 1924, and began a career of teaching, writing, and extensive lecturing throughout Europe, America, and Asia. In his early books, like *The Mediator, Theology of Crisis,* and especially *The Divine Imperative,* he sought to establish an understanding of the theological basis for Christian ethics. This was important because Western culture had transformed Christianity into a mere social designation, so that most Christians were unaware of the way secular ideas (like "the dignity of man," individualism, and capitalism) had become identified as Christian. These ideas are considered "good," and therefore must be Christian. But Brunner insisted, "The true Good lies only in the power of God and not in that of man; no other human goodness and conduct exists save that which is based on the free gift of God."[53]

By this Brunner did not imply that ethics cannot exist without God. Historically, systems of ethics may have existed even before the time of Hammurabi. While many subsequent systems developed within a religious context, some have been declared to exist "on their own," or rooted in nature, in society, in the state, or simply within each person's individual psyche. This is why Brunner could say, "There is no general conception of ethics which would also include the Christian ethics."[54] The Christian conception of "the Good" differs from other conceptions in that it cannot be defined in terms of "principles," but only in terms of the Will of God, which cannot be summed up under any principle. "The will of God is not at our disposal, but is absolutely free. The Christian is therefore 'a free **lord** over all things' (as Luther declared), because he stands directly under the personal orders of the free Sovereign God. This is why genuine 'Christian' conduct is so unaccountable, so unwelcome to the moral rigorist and to the hedonist alike."[55]

The moral rigorist would insist that the Christian must abide by "eternal principles" or by rules derived from natural law or the state; the hedonist would have the Christian live for self-fulfillment, or perhaps "the good of society." But Brunner insists that "human conduct can only be considered 'good' when, and in so far as, God Himself acts in it, through the Holy Spirit."[56]

Brunner, however, did not take the extreme position of Karl Barth that the image of God, in which mankind was created, has been so completely lost because of sin that there can be no knowledge of God apart from the Bible. At this point Brunner may appear to be casting Barth in the role of a fundamentalist, which of course would not have been accurate, as Brunner was well aware. But in his book *Man in Revolt*, Brunner notes that there is such a thing as "natural knowledge," which is different from thought not necessarily excluded by the knowledge of faith.[57] But all human knowledge, whether "natural" or that derived from the insights of faith, is blurred and distorted by our sinful condition.

Brunner's assessment of the origins and effects of sin is more penetrating than that of fundamentalism, which tends to create a scenario of its genesis as literal history. For Brunner, original sin was more than the disobedience of some primal ancestor of the human race; it was an act of rebellion in which we all participate. The first thing the Bible tells us about primal sin is that it is the revolt of the creature against the Creator; thus it is not something negative, it is a "positive negation." . . . "And this is the very origin of sin: the assertion of human independence over against God.[58] Yet the pathos of our situation is that there is nothing heroic about this insurgency. "Man does not sin like Satan himself, purely out of defiance and rebellion. He is led astray by sin." It was our glory to become masters of the realm of nature, but it was our weakness and arrogance to want complete mastery over everything including our own destiny. Yet "man never sins purely out of weakness but also in the fact that he 'lets himself go' in weakness. Even in the dullest sinner there is still a spark of decision."[59]

In his *Divine-Human Encounter*, Brunner emphasizes the grace by which we are redeemed. "Undoubtedly man is a sinner, he is unfaithful, he denies; but God is compassionate and forgives sin."[60] He parts company, however, with those fundamentalists who claim "once saved, always saved." "The covenant is conditional, as Psalm 103 shows us: He is 'compassionate to those who sustain

His covenant and remember His commandments, to do them.' "[61] To those who do not sustain the covenant, or turn their hearts away from God: "Ye shall surely perish" (Deuteronomy 30:15f.). Sin is the destruction of personal communion with God and, as such, is a fact that we ourselves cannot alter. But if God planned to forgive our sins and restore the bond of communication, why did he not simply do it? "Why Christ after all? Why not simply God? How can we understand faith in a mediator as the expression of personal correspondence?"[62] Here Brunner dares to raise the question that has not only divided Christians and Jews, but which has been a stumbling block even to many Christians. The answer, as Brunner provides it, is contained in the prologue of the Fourth Gospel: "No one has seen God at any time." God, apart from his revelation in the form of a human being, is a mystery. God can only be known in personal self-disclosure. "His personal revelation is the Incarnation . . . unveiling His quality of being Person, and hence at the same time His will to fellowship. . . . [This] . . . is therefore at the same time revelation of Himself as Love. Jesus Christ not only reveals, He at once fulfills and realizes the Will of God."[63]

From this flows Brunner's theological ethics. In a succinct phrase he presents the Gospel and the Gospel's ethics: "We may not talk about God without at the same time talking about His Will, and what is meant by His Will can be stated briefly: The Kingdom of God, revealed and grounded in the incarnate Son."[64] In Christ we hear the "Thou shalt" of God, but spoken now not so much as command, as invitation. How can one command "Thou shalt love thy neighbor as thyself," as does the Book of Leviticus? But in Christ, who is the incarnation of Love, we discover the meaning of what is given freely rather than under compulsion. Here is no Kantian "categorical imperative," but a gracious invitation to share the life we have as Christ shares his life with us.

True to his contention that Christian ethics is not grounded in rules or principles, but in the will of God revealed in Jesus Christ, Brunner states, "In every case in which the individual has to act, the one essential is that— through faith—and taking his neighbor into account—he should be able to perceive the Will of God in the work which has to be done."[65] Society is organized in certain "orders of creation," which are God given: the family, the church, the state. There are also special communities established within these orders like art, education, science, and the like. Throughout his writings Brunner is in quest of dialogue between theology and culture, with Christian ethics as the point of contact. Simply to read through his endnotes and appendices is to immerse oneself in a vast array of literary and philosophical, as well as theological allusions, wherein he undertakes to answer the challenges of Christendom's critics. He notes, for example, a confusion of thought in Hume, Bentham, and J. S. Mill between the effect of well-being and the motive of happiness. Mill, and the pragmatists who follow his initial utilitarianism, summon us to choose "higher" forms of pleasure as against "lower" forms, without realizing that they are "slopping into the imperative type of ethic" which presumably they earlier rejected. He also points to logical inconsistencies in Kant's appeal to logic for, having refused to see the content of ethics anywhere else than in reason, he is obliged to become a legalistic moralist, secretly appealing to natural law. The essential themes of Spencer, Marx, and Freud he traces to the skepticism characteristic of ancient philosophers like Pyrrho and Carneades in their cultural era of decline, echoed again in the era of Montaigne and Rochefoucauld. Nietzsche he notes to have been a prophet of this deadening skepticism in our own day, and "once again in the case of Freud, it becomes plain that naturalistic psychology inevitably ends in skepticism. The response of the Christian is to live by God's Word . . . in the midst of the world with one's face to the world to come, drawing life from that future world. Therein lies hope. This hope, by which and for which the Church exists [the hidden Church of faith] is the motive power for the Christian life."[66]

Reinhold Niebuhr

While both Barth and Brunner lay great stress on the redemptive work of Christ, and the relation of each individual to Christ as Lord, they were thought by some to have neglected the nitty-gritty of actual social problems. The reverse criticism was sometimes made of Reinhold Niebuhr (1892–1971). Niebuhr, who began his career as did Barth with a strong liberal persuasion, learned through his pastoral experience in Detroit that Western culture, and industrial America in particular, had exacted a terrible cost in human suffering and the destruction of humane values for its vast profit making. He accused Christian fundamentalism of inattention to urgent social problems in favor of a salvation religion; he found liberal Christianity hopelessly naive about the dark side of human nature that could exploit the weak, starve the poor, and launch fratricidal wars.

Niebuhr's evangelical-reformed background caused him to reexamine the older orthodox faith, and there he found what to him was a more realistic appraisal of the human condition. Shocked no less than Barth and Brunner by the carnage of World War I, he became a pacifist. His direct encounters with the callousness of big business toward decent working conditions and even basic safety for laborers, and corporations' often brutal ways of discouraging the formation of labor unions prompted Niebuhr to become a socialist. In the 1930s he broke with the Socialist party, but it is important to recognize that he had not come to the socialist position out of a radical mind-set, but from a careful reflection on the biblical message from Amos to the Gospels, to the Book of Acts (especially the second and fourth chapters), with their emphasis on justice for the poor and compassion for the oppressed. His *Leaves from the Notebook of a Tamed Cynic*, published in 1929, traces his pilgrimage from liberal optimist to disillusioned socialist to "Christian realist," at the time he left the parish ministry to become a professor at Union Theological Seminary in New York.

Within three years of joining the faculty, Niebuhr's book *Moral Man and Immoral Society* was published, which in one sense set the tone for much of his sociotheological work to follow. As a theologian he does not begin with a doctrine of God and develop extensive creedal themes as theologians often do. Instead, he sounds his warning that man is a self-betrayed sinner, and though individual Christians may repent and seek to be moral, the societies they create never do. "The nation is a corporate unity," he notes, "held together much more by force and emotion, than by mind." The public, by and large, is uncritical and self-serving, representing a "least-common-denominator," both intellectually and morally. "So nations crucify their moral rebels upon the same Golgotha, not being able to distinguish between the moral idealism which surpasses, and the antisocial conduct which falls below that moral mediocrity, on the level of which every society unifies its life."[67] Thus it was with the prophets, and Christ, and countless martyrs who have sought to bring moral judgment into the arena of national affairs. On the other hand, the individual Christian must be aware that however clear his or her judgments seems, any ethic of perfection will be suspect as long as that person remains identified within those social structures.

Moral tension is a theme that dominates much of Niebuhr's work, showing the influence of Kierkegaard. Man (Niebuhr used the generic term before it was considered sexist) experiences this tension between himself and the absolute, between what is and what ought to be, as an evidence of his transcendence over the natural order. He makes this point in *An Interpretation of Christian Ethics* (1935) and again in *Does Civilization Need Religion?* (1941), and stresses that Jesus' perfectionist love ethics ("Thou shalt love") opens up the vertical dimension of our lives, but is an impossible obligation in our horizontal relationships. "Every truly moral act seeks to establish what ought to be because the agent feels obligated to the ideals . . . as being the order of life in its more essential reality."[68] This is one of the chief values of religion to society, but also one of its more disturbing aspects. "The value of religion in composing the conflict with which the inner life of man is torn, is that it identifies man's highest values about which he would center his life, with realities in the universe itself, and teaches him how to bring his momentary impulses under the domination of his will by subjecting his will to the guidance of a absolute will."[69]

This was no exercise in abstraction for Niebuhr. Out of the tension he felt in his own religious experience, he turned from his outspoken pacifism to a strong opposition to pacifism, and urged that we had no choice as a nation but to oppose Hitler and the Nazi movement. He opposed communism too, but with less overt vigor because he said communism was a Christian heresy pledged to the relief of human suffering and the liberation of the laboring class, as should have been the Christian concern. Communism was still to be opposed for its utopian pretensions and its record of cruelty in trying to fulfill them. But Hitler's movement was altogether different; it was openly and aggressively anti-Christian and virtually antihumanity except for those whom it could control.

By all measures, Niebuhr's most important book was *The Nature and Destiny of Man* (1947), comprised of the first and second 1943 Gifford lectures ("Human Nature" and "Human Destiny"). Here he notes that whereas lower animals are submerged in the herd or flock, leaving no records to instruct the next generation, man alone creates science, writes books and music, and leaves a chain of cultural monuments. "Man's freedom to transcend the natural flux . . . enables him to change, reorder and transmute the causal sequences of nature, and thereby to make history."[70]

As a creative spirit, bearing the image of God, a human is at his best . . . except for the one fact that freedom to create must inevitably carry within itself freedom to pervert and destroy. "The tragedy of history consists precisely in the fact that human life cannot be creative without being destructive . . ." and our downfall derives from pride in the ability to make the choice whether to be creative or destructive. This was Adam's dilemma. (Niebuhr uses the term *myth* to describe Adam's taking the forbidden fruit, myth not as fairy tale or lie, but as a literary device for portraying a profound truth about the human condition.) Adam thought that being able to make such a choice would make him like God (Genesis 3:5), and this has always been mankind's greatest temptation; it is the sin of pride. "Man falls into pride, when he seeks to raise his contingent existence to unconditioned significance."[71] The inclination to emulate or usurp the prerogatives of God is a basic element in sin, and Niebuhr notes that tyrants always imagine their position somehow exempts them from the erosions of mortality. To ensure their maintenance of such superiority over the other mortals, they go to extreme lengths. "Thus the greatest monarchs of the ancient world, the Pharaohs of Egypt, exhausted the resources of their realm to build pyramids, which were intended to establish or to prove their immortality."[72]

Niebuhr details other forms of pride, such as that of intellect, morals, spirituality, and sensuality, all of which transgress the will of God. He then shows how these become incorporated in social life and are then institutionally justified. Then, he notes, because groups and especially states can go beyond the limits which an individual might dare: "The group is more arrogant, hypocritical, self-centered and more ruthless in the pursuit of its ends than any individual."[73]

It is here that Niebuhr's Christian social ethics catches fire and burns with special brilliance. He is impatient with Christian fundamentalism for assuming that a gospel directed at the individual is sufficient simply because the goal is to "save a soul." But he is equally impatient with liberals for having failed to deal with either the individual or the society in terms of sin in all its ugly ramifications.

When invited to address the World Council of Churches, at its formation in 1948, Niebuhr issued a challenge to all Christendom to take politics and economics seriously as a realm in which humankind most clearly exposes itself in all its potentials for good or evil. But he also challenged the churches to recognize their own complicity in much of the world's evil. "There is no social evil, no form of injustice whether of the feudal or the capitalistic order which has not been sanctified in some way or other by religious sentiment, and thereby rendered more impervious to change."[74] But the church ill serves people and societies if it merely persuades them to acknowledge their sin.

> Everywhere life is delivered unto death because it is ensnared in self-delusion, and practices every evasion rather than meet the true God. And everywhere the Church is caught in this dance of death because it allows the accents of national pride and of racial prejudice, the notes of self-esteem and complacency to color its message. The new life which we require collectively in our age is a community wide enough to make the worldwide interdependence of nations in a technical age sufferable; and a justice carefully enough balanced to make the dynamic forces of a technical society yield a tolerable justice rather than an alienation of intolerable anarchy and intolerable tyranny. To accomplish this purpose some of our own preconceptions must go, and the same law of love which is no simple possibility for man or society, must be enthroned as yet the final standard of every institution, structure, and system of justice.[75]

In his many books and in the many journals he edited (*The World Tomorrow, Christianity and Crisis, Christianity and Society,* etc.) Niebuhr often took the opportunity to respond to the critics of Christianity past and present, noting logical inconsistencies in Hume; the implicit idolatry in Hegel's identification of Absolute Spirit with nationalism; and the mindless determinism in Freud's reduction of human impulses to the libido, which Freud declared has "no organization and no unified will, only an impulsion to obtain satisfaction."

Before the end of his life in June 1971, Niebuhr was a frequently sought adviser by members of the State Department. He was an early advocate of diplomatic relations with mainland China, and an outspoken opponent of U.S. military involvement in Vietnam. His influence on policy planners in both the World Council of Churches and in secular government was so great as to evoke from an eminent social scientist, Hans J. Morgenthau, the description of Niebuhr as "the greatest living political philosopher of America."

In retrospect, it may be questioned whether the movements discussed here, or their individual representatives, adequately answered the challenges leveled against Christianity and its ethics since the Enlightenment. A secular referee like self-proclaimed humanist Walter Lippman might argue that neither fundamentalism nor liberalism measured up to the task. The former failed because it avoided argumentation by retreating to "primitive Christianity." The most articulate fundamentalist of the 1920s to the 1940s, J. Gresham Machen of Princeton, had indeed insisted that questions of defining and defending Christianity can only be resolved by studying its beginning in the New Testament.[76] Lippman admitted this was a bit arcane, but noted that the liberals had tried so hard to accommodate the philosophers and scientists, they had abandoned the Bible, and were therefore not representing Christianity at all.[77] Another humanist, Charles Potter, declared that if confronted with the alternative: "Better a clear-cut Fundamentalism than this sadly inadequate Modernism. The Modernists have fallen between two stools in trying to sit on both."[78]

The neoorthodox movement appears to have fared better, both in answering the charges of the critics and in presenting a more clearly articulated and searching Christian ethics. Reinhold Niebuhr gave due respect to the contribution of the critics in forcing Christians to reexamine their own history and practices with honesty. But he also noted that "the rationalistic and naturalistic rebellion against religion in the eighteenth century must be appreciated as being partly a rebellion of the ethical spirit against religious confusion." Correcting this confusion is what systematic theology is all about. While Niebuhr did not write a systematic theology as such, his monumental *Nature and Destiny of Man* serves the purpose and provides the foundation for the application of Christian ethics in virtually all fields. Even more so did *The Divine Imperative* of Emil Brunner serve such a purpose, and it is noteworthy that the concluding chapter of Karl Barth's *Church Dogmatics* is titled "The Battle for Human Justice." Yet by the end of the 1950s, it was evident that neoorthodoxy, too, was fading as a theological force. New directions were being sought by young Christians to help them through the clamorous confusion in the secular society and within Christianity itself.

NEW DIRECTIONS

A profound secularism overtook Western culture in the 1950s and beyond, due in part to the new nationalistic spirit among emerging third world countries involved in the United Nations, a defensive response among older societies that felt threatened, and to a host of other factors including a general questioning of the adequacy of traditional religious values. The old arguments between liberals and fundamentalists, the great neoorthodox themes of anxiety, sin, faith, and the wholly-otherness of God seemed irrelevant to the thunder on the right of national politics, the strident demands for civil rights and racial equality, the emergence of the death of God theology, situation ethics, and liberation theology. Meanwhile, as a kind of backdrop to all this, the ecumenical movement in Christianity, seen in both the World Council of Churches (and their national counterparts) and in Vatican II, forced a rethinking of older assumptions in Christian ethics. Three theologians whose work received special attention in this period were Paul Tillich, Dietrich Bonhoeffer, and Harvey Cox.

Paul Tillich

Paul Tillich (1886–1965) was a contemporary of Barth and Brunner, and once described himself as "the last liberal." Reflecting more than these others the influence of existentialism, Tillich defined religion in terms of "ultimate concern." Religion is not a separate function that can be set aside for special occasions, nor is it a special faculty to be identified along with others like the moral, intellectual, and esthetic faculties. It is what he calls the depth-dimension, which undergirds and orients everything else we are and do to that which is ultimate and unconditional. "Man is ultimately concerned about his being and meaning. 'To be or not to be' in this sense is a matter of ultimate, unconditional total and infinite concern."[79] Kierkegaard, he notes, stressed that the object of religious faith, whether one uses the term God or not, is always of overwhelming concern and passionate devotion. This is what gives religion, and indeed life itself, its existential character. While not everything we think or do has the quality of ultimate concern (in domestic decisions, for example, whether to buy a new house), it is remarkable to note the degree of sheer idolatry involved even in trivial matters. We make possessions, social position, racial superiority, or patriotism our ultimate value so they, in effect, become the god we worship. "The extreme nationalisms of our century are laboratories for the study of what ultimate concern means in all aspects of human existence. . . . Everything is centered in the only god, the nation—a god who certainly proves to be a demon, but who shows clearly the unconditional character of an ultimate concern."[80]

Tillich's existentialism made him a popular figure in the 1950s and 1960s when existentialism was being widely discussed on college and university campuses, as well as in theater and literary groups and in more sophisticated congregations. Existentialism, Tillich said, was the "good luck" of Christian theology, contributing to its rediscovery of mankind's self-estrangement, anxiety, and sin. We are self-estranged, ironically, because we are essentially free.

> Man is free, insofar as he has the power of contradicting himself and his essential nature. Man is free even from his freedom; that is, he can surrender his humanity. . . . Symbolically speaking, it is the image of God in man which gives the possibility of the Fall. Only he who is the image of God has the power of separating himself from God.[81]

Tillich notes that there are three traditional systems of thought behind the ethical assumptions of modern society, and finding that each falls short, proposes what he holds to be the basis of Christian ethics. First among the traditional systems is the static supernaturalism represented by the Roman Catholic church, and expressed in the ethics of Thomas Aquinas. "The world is conceived as a system of eternal structures, preformed in the divine mind, which are substance and essence of everything and which establish the norms and laws for man's personal and social practice."[82] This worked well as long as the Roman church could successfully fend off rival systems. But Protestantism and the Enlightenment created new systems of ethics so that when the Holy See issued pronouncements on social or political problems, it found itself ineffectual as a determining influence.

Quite an opposite ethical stance is found in the second system of thought, represented by the continental vitalistic philosophy and by Anglo-American positivism and pragmatism, "the latter being only a different form of the vitalistic philosophy." While there are differences among them, "it is important to make it clear that [they] belong to the same type of ethical dynamism."[83] According to this position ethics must be expressed in terms of changing forms and trends. Here Tillich notes the same theme in Nietzsche, for whom "Truth is that lie which is useful for a particular species of being." This, Tillich holds, is untenable, because when its proponents find themselves victims of such relativism, "they take refuge in an 'ethical instinct' that is supposed to lead to an ethical common sense." It does not, as is clear when we listen to the conflicting ethical demands of dissatisfied groups and nations with different histories and values.

The third alternative Tillich finds is the rationalistic-progressive position, born of the Enlightenment. The assumption had been that there are certain ethical imperatives which, once discovered, will never disappear again. Its optimism withered in the face of the dynamic irrationalism of the fascist ideologies that erupted in our century.

Tillich's solution to the ethical problem is "implied in the basis of Christian ethics, namely, in the principle of love in the sense of the Greek word *agape*. Love, *agape*, offers a principle of ethics that maintains an eternal, unchangeable element, but makes its realization dependent on continuous acts of a creative intuition."[84] Embodying and acting out that principle requires being alive to every situation, being free to respond to every existential requirement without coercion or restraint from institutions like church or state, and above all to be responsible for the results of one's decisions.

Dietrich Bonhoeffer

Dietrich Bonhoeffer (1906–1945) assessed the progressive secularization of society as a sign of our emerging from dependence on religion. He abandoned his earlier pacifism as he witnessed the atrocities of the Nazi movement, and wrote some of his most penetrating insights while in prison awaiting execution for his part in an assassination plot against Hitler. Bonhoeffer believed the time had come for the end of organized religion. He was not an iconoclast: "God is teaching us that we must live as men who can get along without him. The God who makes us live in this world without using him as a hypothesis, is the God before whom we are ever standing. God allows himself to be edged out of the world and onto the cross."[85]

Bonhoeffer's ethics stems from this concept that God in Christ, suffering for others, suffering even for those who nailed him to the cross, is our paradigm. "Our relation to God is not a religious relationship to a supreme Being, absolute in power and goodness, which is a spurious conception of transcendence, but a new life for others, through participation in the Being of God."[86]

Bonhoeffer's contribution to Christian ethics cut deep into the assumptions long held among some Christians that there is always a reward of some kind for "doing good," even if only a warm inner feeling and peace of mind. Bonhoeffer, who was soon to be hanged knew better, and wrote from his prison cell, "When Christ calls a man, he bids him come and die." He affirmed in his book *The Cost of Discipleship* that Christians must be prepared to die if they are faithful to their Lord, but also that the churches, the fellowship of Christians, would die if they were not faithful. Indeed, the death of the church was almost at hand: "The price we are having to pay today in the shape of the collapse of the organized church is only the inevitable consequence of our policy of making grace available at too low a cost. We gave away the word and sacraments wholesale, we baptized, confirmed and absolved a whole nation unasked and without condition. But the call to follow Jesus in the narrow way was hardly ever heard."[87]

If Bonhoeffer's prediction of the death of the church was startling in the 1940s, what emerged in the 1960s was more so. In 1961, *The Death of God* was published by Gabriel Vahanian, followed by *Honest to God* (declaring as fanciful some of the tenets of the creeds of Christendom) by Bishop J. A. T. Robinson (1963); *The Secular Meaning of the Gospel* by Paul Van Buren (1963); and *Radical Theology and the Death of God* by Thomas J. J. Altizer and William Hamilton (1966). While their messages differed, their mood was the same: The secular culture in which we do our daily work and raise our families constitutes the only arena worthy of concern for Christians. All our ethical norms derive from that realm, and honest reading of the Bible reveals that Jesus, too, was decidedly "this worldly" in his ministry of feeding the hungry, healing the sick, and liberating the human spirit. Above all they insisted we must recognize that the God of our classical creeds is dead; God has been "eclipsed" (to use the metaphor of Martin Buber) by the clamor of this world, and even more by the church itself, so God is no longer available to us in a genuine I-Thou relationship. Nietzsche was right: "God is dead, and we have killed Him." Freud, too, was correct: The God to whom we pray for comfort and safety is a projection of our earthly father figure, and such a God is dead.

Harvey Cox

With or without the living god, our world has been thoroughly secularized, according to Harvey Cox whose book *The Secular City* was published in 1965. One major contribution of the Bible, wrote Cox, was the desacrilizing of nature. No longer was nature to be viewed as mystical or pervaded by spirits. Life was not "an unfathomable mystery," but a set of problems better solved by science than by intuition or mystical contemplation. Modern man, he wrote, "brackets off the things that cannot be dealt with and deals with those that can. He wastes little time thinking about 'ultimate' or 'religious' questions. And he can live with highly provisional solutions."[88] Cox's emphasis on the efficacy of the pragmatic and his apparent confidence in the ability of secular urban humanity to solve its problems was a welcome note in the gloom-laden aftermath of the assassinations of President John Kennedy, Bobby Kennedy, Martin Luther King, Jr., race riots and civil rights marches, and the escalating Vietnam War.

While Cox did not subscribe to the death of God movement, he described himself as a "radical theologian" in the sense that he identified the Gospel with the faith of the "losers," the poor and outcast people to whom Jesus directed so much of his ministry, and which is seen emerging today in the third world. Today, after more than a quarter of a century, Cox's *Secular City* remains a metaphor for humankind's greatest creative potential.

Just as the Book of Revelation envisions the City of God as a place where churches are not needed precisely because everyone relates to God and to each other in love and service (as in Augustine, John Bunyan, and William Penn), so with Cox. In *The Seduction of the Spirit,* he notes that Christianity was born at just that period in history when the foundations for our global-urban civilization were being laid. Nature was no longer the focus for understanding God's plan for us; our social setting with its poverty and wealth, political power struggles, and economic promise provide the matrix wherein we discover what kind of creatures we are, and what God's commands require of us. "Christianity centers mainly on man's powers and temptations in the personal and political realms."[89]

But has Christianity provided an ethic sufficient to deal with the issues of power and temptation? Cox believes it can, but has not. There has always been a certain sentimentalizing of nature to the discredit of urban life, and Cox notes that even Marx and Nietzsche, who stood against Christianity, were influenced by the tradition to offer a Promethian paradigm for fighting against the enslavement which they believed awaits urban man. The "Prometheus complex" is countered by some who call for the "Epimethean Man," who quietly, unassertively husbands the earth and refuses power. "Christian theology, instead of holding human creativity and creatureliness together, has falsely emphasized the *contrast* between exercising power and accepting the will of God. . . . The frenzied soul-saver and the frightened recluse represent Christian versions of Prometheus and Epimetheus."[90] The contrast is false; the two must be melded.

Cox urges that we dare not be naive about the city's ability to crush and dehumanize, but argues against the idea that the city is a symbol of a world without God (as with Thomas Merton), or that the city is the incarnation of total depravity (Jacques Ellul). It is true that cities offer every opportunity for human sinfulness to express itself, but cities do not cause the sin. We struggle not against flesh and blood or the technical and social products of flesh and blood. The Christian is called to struggle against "principalities and powers" in the realm of the spirit, against "powers of darkness," which foster the sins of pride and greed. Taking the Christian doctrine of sin with utmost seriousness, Cox also calls us to embrace the Gospel of Grace, and reminds us that "Biblical religion celebrates the vision of a city as man's ultimate destination. Man's destiny is not to return as a drop to the great sea but to find himself and his fellow man in the New City."[91]

What makes Cox's position radical is not any form of iconoclasm as in the death of God movement, but in rebellion against the sterile forms of Churchianity with its accommodations to the worst in secular life, its culture-bound bureaucracy and elitism. His radicalism calls us to the immediate problems of God's people in the social and political situations where they are being made to suffer. The summons, he insists, is always specific, never vague or mystic.

Situation Ethics

In *situation ethics*, another radical movement of the 1960s, the summons is also presented as specific, forcing us to ask how Jesus' command "Thou shalt love . . ." applies in each given instance. The term is most familiarly associated with Joseph Fletcher, whose 1966 book by that title became one of the most controversial religious writings of the decade. A lecturer on medical ethics as well as theology, Fletcher contended that Christians must steer between old authoritarianisms, whether biblical or ecclesiastical, and the unstructured posture of existentialism. "Judaism, Catholicism, Protestantism—all major Western religious traditions have been legalistic . . . encumbered with a whole apparatus of prefabricated rules and regulations. Any web thus woven sooner or later chokes its weavers."[92]

At least three primary characteristics can be identified in situation ethics. There is first of all an emphasis on individual responsibility in decision making, so we cannot hide behind some institution or social custom and say "my family," or my state, my church, or other agency "made me do it." Secondly, there is a rejection of legalism, or "rule ethics," in favor of responding to each situation with love as our guide. "New occasions teach new duties," and each occasion calls for a fresh response: "What does the love of Christ require right now?" This is not an unfamiliar idea to those who recall how Jesus sometimes suspended rules in order to serve human need. We find it in Karl Barth's actualism, and in Dietrich Bonhoeffer's decisive response to Hitler's tyranny. We can even find it in Reinhold Niebuhr's appeal to the perfectionist love ethic of Jesus, though he also warns against trying to employ it in all situations.

A third characteristic of situation ethics is its inevitable relativism, inasmuch as love may require different things of us at different times. It may even require that we tell a lie, as in a situation where a criminal known to have a grudge against his father demands to know the father's whereabouts. Love then justifies breaking the rule against bearing false witness, despite the Bible's command. Fletcher thus insists, "We are commanded to love people, not principles."[93]

Critics of situation ethics have been numerous, their objections usually focusing on its emphasis on individualism and the consequent dangers of anarchy. No person, it is claimed, has enough insight to understand all the ramifications of all situations or to know how love applies in all cases. Pope Paul VI opposed it, thinking it to be a substantive ethic, and as such a threat to the authority of the Church. Dubbed "the new morality," it was banned from all seminaries by the Supreme Sacred Congregation of the Holy Office.

In response, Fletcher points out that the situationist does not reject all rules and mores, but enters each experience fully armed with ethical rules of his community and his heritage. "He treats them with respect as illuminators of his problems. Just the same, he is prepared in any situation to compromise them or set them aside if love seems better served by doing so."[94] Further, it is not a substantive ethic, in the sense of being a self-contained ethical system. It is rather a method for decision making, and thus no threat to the Roman Catholic or any other system. Another supporter of situationism, Paul Lehman, wrote that Christians never really act as isolated individuals. One is nurtured by the Church and by centuries of Christian consensus as well as by the Holy Spirit. "It makes all the difference in the world, in what context your ethical insights and practices are nourished."[95] The situationist simply learns to trust his conscience rather than rule books; one struggles free of social, racial, nationalistic, and even religious conditioning, in order to affirm what Christian love requires.

The charge of naïveté arises at this point. Breaking rules for the sake of exceptional cases, writes Brian Hebblethwaite, can lead to empty and even dangerous romanticism. "It is naive to think that one can always appeal straight to love, or pile up exception upon exception." He points to Fletcher's own field of medical ethics, "where the complexity and seriousness of the issues of life and death, which are part of the day to day work of doctors and nurses in a large hospital, preclude the possibility of referring each decision directly to the love principle."[96] He further notes the judgment expressed in ecumenical circles that, with its emphasis on circumstances deciding cases, situation ethics is "in danger of being manipulated and controlled by circumstances and events." Furthermore, "love as justice is too structureless a concept to guide action in social and political conflict,"[97] and certainly, one might add, in most police action and military conflict where the preservation of whole populations might be at stake.

We must now extend our investigation of the response of Christians to the many secular and religious challenges of the past. This can best be undertaken by examining those areas of Christian life that were the subject of those attacks: the institutional church itself, interpretations of human nature, the meaning of our sexuality, the sources of ethics and law, the role of religion and culture, and so forth. Amid unprecedented ecumenical efforts of the churches in the past two decades, new voices and movements have evoked a whole new dynamic that has moved beyond simply responding to earlier criticism and has created unexpected innovations. Liberation theology, one of the most important of these movements, was itself not simply a product of ecumenism, but has commanded the attention of ecumenists and ethicists alike. We examine liberation theology in some detail in the next chapter.

CHAPTER FOUR

The Church and the Churches

Ethics, as noted in Chapter 1, has to do with how things are done acceptably in the framework of society's customs and demands. What distinguishes Christian ethics from philosophical ethics is that the Christian does not look to society in general for clues to behavior, but seeks to understand how the Church, the community of faith, lives and works as (to use the apostle Paul's powerful metaphor) "the body of Christ." Paul's welcome to new Christians contains this striking figure of speech: "Now you are the body of Christ, and severally members of it" (1 Corinthians 12:27). This imagery proclaims that the Church is a radically different reality from other organizations, even from other religious institutions. No other, whether Jewish, Muslim, or Buddhist calls its members so to identify with the person of the founder as to become one with him: "I am in my Father, and you [are] in me, and I in you" (John 14:20, 17:20–23). The ontological bond with Christ, established by faith, gives Christ sovereignty in all decision making. "Whatever does not proceed from faith," Paul tells us, "is sin" (Romans 14:23), so that outside this relationship all loyalties are secondary and even rivals of the faith. Political, monetary, and nationalistic concerns are at the root of much of the violence and chaos characterizing our world. They are often the most serious compromisers of the

Church where concern for losing members (and financial support) causes the leaders to refrain from speaking and acting against injustice.

It is obvious that the churches in which people hold memberships are often, perhaps necessarily, involved in affairs of the secular world, holding stock in commercial companies, for example, or supporting ideologies that seem to many members contrary to their understanding of "the body of Christ." It was this condition to which a trenchant set of essays was addressed at the close of World War II on "The Shame and Glory of the Church." In this first major publication of the World Council of Churches, in 1948, H. Richard Niebuhr wrote of "The Disorder of Man in the Church of God," pointing to the Church's many divisions and debilitating quarrels, as it appeased the secular world's demands that it be "liberal," or "capitalist," or accept some other popular designation.[1]

Historically, the Church has witnessed its Scriptures being quoted to justify slavery, to bless the profit motive, and to exclude racial minorities from equal participation in society and even in worship. It has observed the trivializing of its message and function. We have already noted Dietrich Bonhoeffer's charge that the organized Church is collapsing because "We gave away the word and sacraments wholesale, . . . baptized, confirmed and absolved a whole nation unasked."[2] But if these aberrations have evoked skepticism about the Church in the past, what can be said of more recent misrepresentations of its practices and the scandals that have stained its reputation? Canon William Rauscher documented such distortions of the Church's services as a bridal party dressed in white G-strings; comedian Jimmy Durante, being buried from a Catholic church while the organist played "Inka Dinka Doo"; and worshipers being led blindfold through a New York church to a bathroom where "a smiling individual with toilet paper draped around his neck flushed his sins away in a symbolic declaration of absolution."[3] The moral and fiscal scandals of certain television evangelists have had an even more crippling effect.

Such offenses have outraged many sensitive Christians while giving ammunition to enemies of Christianity. The situation is not without precedent. During the post-Reformation Pietist movement, the phrase *ecclesiola in ecclesia* was coined to distinguish "the little church within the church," that is, the body of the truly faithful people within the larger organization (to which St. Augustine, as early as the fifth century had given the name *corpus permixtum*). A contemporary theologian expressed his concern: "Christianity has no meaning for me apart from the Church, but I sometimes feel as though the Church as it actually exists is the source of all my doubts and difficulties."[4] There is a hunger among certain Christians to be identified in some way distinct from the corruptible organization, to be truly one with Christ and not simply be churchgoers. Yet most understand that the "body of Christ" cannot be divorced from its earthly incorporation, and that apart from the latter we probably cannot realize the former.

How are we to understand the nature of the Church as Christ intended it while acknowledging the value of what it is empirically, as it actually exists? How does it serve as a community fostering debate and timely deliberation while preserving moral tradition and shaping Christian identity? What are the ethical implications of the ecumenical efforts of Christian denominations that seek opportunities for dialogue and cooperation not only among themselves, but with non-Christian religions as well? Is the new liberation theology an invitation to anarchy or a movement to recreate the Church as Christ intended it to be, and thus to equip it for greater service to humanity in the spirit of Christ? These are the questions central to this chapter.

THE CHURCH AS ETHICAL CONTEXT

From the biblical point of view the Church is best understood as beginning at Pentecost, not as an institutional endeavor but as the Holy Spirit's creation. It was an unprecedented event that dissolved all barriers of race and nationality, and even of tongues: "They were amazed, saying, How is it we hear everyone in our own language?" (Acts 2:7–8). This phenomenon reversed the trend toward racial and cultural divisions symbolized in the story of the Tower of Babel (Genesis 11). The Church came into being as the *ecclesia*, the fellowship of those "called out" of the rest of society with all its contractual organizations and that often serve to perpetuate separations. The Church began its work under Christ's instruction to "go into all the world" proclaiming the good news of release to all who are in bondage of any sort, whether institutional, political, or spiritual (Matthew 28:19–20). His delegation to baptize, teach, and heal is best seen in conjunction with the charge that Jesus imposed on himself, when he first stood before the congregation at Nazareth and read to them from the Isaiah scroll (Luke 4:18). The Church as his body, his earthly incorporation, is to continue to fulfill that commission in the world.

A great temptation within the Church has been for individual leaders to interpret Jesus' commission as a mandate to arrogate to themselves the prerogatives that belong only to the Christ. Thus as early as 258 A.D., Bishop Cyprian declared, "The Bishop is in the Church, and the Church is in the Bishop. If anyone is not with the Bishop, he is not in the Church." The subsequent setting up of institutional regulations and a hierarchy of authorities led to the monolithic structure of the medieval church, which proclaimed itself collectively *Omnium Priorum Mater*. Individual members were absolutely beholden to the officials for salvation.

During the Reformation, Martin Luther avoided the word "Church" (*Die Kirche*) in his biblical translations, using instead "congregation" (*Die Gemeinde*). As our ethical context, the congregation provided a *gestalt of grace*, that spiritual setting wherein God's love and guidance were experienced. Luther's focus was on "the congregation of all believers in which the Gospel is rightly taught and the sacraments rightly administered" (*Augsburg Confession,* Article VII). This gave rise to the expression for which Luther is perhaps best remembered, "The priesthood of all believers," wherein we are "as Christ to one another."

Luther's doctrine of the Church was one of his most important tools in the struggle with the pope on one side and a certain radical element among reformers on the other. "Against both sides he defined the Church as the holy Christian people: the crowd, community or assembly of those who have received the gift of faith in Jesus Christ. No institutional form of the church can claim to be the true church, [which is] something internal, an assembly of faith not a collection of bodies."[5] More significantly, the true Church which is "hidden" can be recognized by its "possession of the cross" (in the way the Roman Catholic church insisted on possession of sacred relics for a church to be consecrated). Possession of the cross means sharing in the afflictions of Christ. Luther had a low view of institutional prosperity, noting in his *Dictata Super Psalerium* that prosperity produces smugness, whereas if the Church is doing its job it will incur the wrath of the world by exposing greed and exploitation in the marketplace and the cruel oppression of the poor by governments.

John Calvin could also write of the "hidden church," *ecclesia invisibilis:* "The Church refers not only to the visible church . . . but likewise to all the elect of God, including the dead as well as the living."[6] This has its origin in Hebrews 12:1, where the writer tells us "we are surrounded by a great cloud of witnesses," reminding us of the timelessness of him whose body we are as the living Church.

The rigorous emphasis of the Reformation on the Church as the embodiment of Christ was seriously challenged by the critical philosophers of the seventeenth and eighteenth centuries, as we noted in Chapter 3. Efforts at rebuttal by churchmen and theologians were only marginally successful, and the nineteenth century witnessed a rallying cry: "Back to Kant." The neo-Kantians (especially Hermann Cohen and Paul Natorp, at Marburg) insisted that every human being is endowed by nature with a consciousness of moral duty. Ethics, then, is autonomous, and has no need of either religion or church, except as the latter forms a place for social and esthetic enrichment. Among the most articulate of the group was Albrecht Ritschl (1822–1889), who strove to eliminate everything mystical and metaphysical from religious experience, and described the Christian experience solely from the practical view of applied ethics (see *Rechtfertigung und Versoehnung*, 3rd ed., II, p. 55).

In reaction, Ernst Troeltsch (1865–1923) insisted that the Church is that context in which "we are conscious of the father of Jesus Christ as a living presence in our daily conflicts, labors, hopes and sufferings, and when we arm ourselves, in the power of the Christian spirit, for the weightiest decision in the world: the final victory of all eternal and personal values of the soul" (see *Religionsphilosophie und Ethik*, 1913, p. 440). Troeltsch declared that the central concern of the Church should not be salvation, but teaching people how to love again as Jesus loved. Christology must be subordinated to bringing cultural life into union with God. He identified three manifestations of Church life: the inclusive Church possessing a quality of holiness to the degree it administers graciousness, the exclusive sect, and the isolated religious mystics. These are practical designations, rather than classical definitions, which may help clarify why Troeltsch favored Calvinism for its vigorous social reforms, and held a position in the revolutionary government of post–World War I Berlin.

Emil Brunner reminds us that there are at least three classical definitions of the Church, and "our choice of definitions is decisive for every system of theological ethics." The first is that the Church is *coetus electorum*, the community of those whom God has called. In this understanding, "The sole foundation of the Church is the will and choice of God; God, not man, is the *auctor ecclesiae*." Secondly, the Church is the *communio sanctorum*, the community which, though grounded in the eternal, is realized within history. This is the Church that we see, in which we hold memberships, and where decisions of faith are made. And "faith means being united not only with God, but with our fellowmen." Thirdly, "the union between this invisible 'other worldly' church, and the visible 'this worldly' congregation is expressed in the metaphor which is both spiritual and natural, of the *Corpus Christi*."[7]

Brunner calls us to remember, though, that however we define the Church, "it is the community of those who are still sinners; therefore the Church is always an imperfect community, permeated with sin. This is not due to the corruption which has entered into it incidentally, in the course of history, but belongs to its very nature; when we see this we have found the key to the understanding of the relation between the Church of faith and the Church as an institution."[8] The question deserves to be raised how the Church can be "permeated with sin" and be at the same time "the body of Christ." Karl Barth warned against any facile equation: "We must eliminate all ideas of other human assemblies and societies. The Christian congregation arises not by human decision but as a *divine convocatio*. Those called together by the work of the Holy Spirit, assemble at the summons of their King."[9] Dietrich Bonhoeffer, too, insisted, "The Church is not a religious community of worshippers of Christ, but is Christ himself who has taken form among men."[10]

No one can fault the earnestness of Barth, Bonhoeffer, and others who have wished to safeguard the concept of the sacredness of the Church. Yet those who have worked within its corporate structures, and particularly with the training of its personnel, know that neither clergy, elders, nor deacons spring forth fully mature like Minerva from the forehead of Zeus. Their schooling is mundane, whether in theology, church administration, or Christian ethics. The imagery of the Church as "the messianic community" in Suzanne de Dietrich's work is helpful at this point. She notes that as the vocation of God's Old Testament people was transferred to Christ as the Paschal Lamb, so Jesus transferred the responsibility to the disciples: "As He is the light of the world, we are to be the light of the world and the salt of the earth. It is to the immediate disciples, and through them to the whole Church as a body that Christ speaks. . . . The responsibility of representing Him and speaking in His name lies on the fellowship of believers."[11] This fellowship is comprised not of saints but sinners; it can hardly be otherwise, as every board member of any local parish church can attest: There are no emeritus sinners.

This community of sinners is nevertheless the bearer of a moral tradition, hewn on Sinai, confirmed on Calvary, and transmitted generation after generation to the present time. The value for each of us in being part of a tradition is that belonging keeps us mindful of our place in the scheme of things. "For moral development, as for personality development in general, it is axiomatic that we know, or at least deeply sense, who we are. Our moral growth and maturity thus requires being part of a moral history and being aware of it as a part of us. Lack of such a tradition . . . results in a moral drift, a values-limbo that leaves the person bewildered and incoherent in the moral life."[12]

The consequences of this "values-limbo" are more serious than might seem to be the case on first reflection. During World War II, Dorothy Sayres, better known at the time as a writer of mysteries, published a stern warning titled *Creed or Chaos*. In it she contrasted the burning enthusiasm of the Nazi youth with the uncertain and lackluster commitment of the British to a vaguely understood Christianity. "We on our side have been trying to uphold a particular standard of ethical values which derives from Christian dogma, while gradually dispensing with the very dogma which is the sole rational foundation for those values. . . . 'Never mind about theology,' we observe in kindly tones, 'if we just go on being brotherly it doesn't matter what we believe about God.' "[13] Elsewhere, she commented on the current condition in England: ". . . particularly in the matter of Christian doctrine, a great part of the nation subsists in an ignorance more barbarous than that of the dark ages."[14]

The Church's gift of moral tradition is not a settled and static affair, and it may be argued that the sorry condition of moral commitment which Sayres lamented was due at least in part to the fact that the Church presented it as if it were set in concrete to be accepted uncritically. But the tradition, properly understood, was developed through generations of changing circumstances. It provides each generation with tools for fashioning fresh responses to the ethical demands of the times. In this sense the Church is not simply a repository of ethical rules, but a stimulator of new patterns of thought and action. As the "salt of the earth," the Church does indeed preserve the tradition, but as "the light of the world," it is the illuminator of new possibilities (Matthew 5:13–14). Historically this has brought its pioneers and prophets into conflict with those who cherish only what is established and comfortably fixed, but that too is part of the dynamic of the Church as a living organism. The war protests of the 1960s; the civil rights marches of the 1970s; and the new ferment called liberation theology emerging in South America, Africa, and in many parts of Asia have drawn much of their motive power from this aspect of Church life. It is not mere happenstance that Albert Schweitzer, Martin Luther King, Jr.,

Mother Teresa, and Bishop Desmond Tutu, who have received applause from the secular world and been awarded the Nobel Peace Prize, are members of the Christian tradition.

Yet beyond preserving and transmitting the tradition, and stimulating creative change, the Church serves as a community of moral discourse, in which each member's moral identity is shaped. Few of us can claim to be guardians of tradition in any significant way, and still fewer strive to be pioneers and shapers of history after the manner of a William Carey, Father Damien, or Frank Laubach. But within our congregational experience, all of us have known the correcting and shaping influence of both tradition and challenge. This has been true since the founding of the Church, wherein the community of faith, just as it had been for ancient Israel, was the starting point for determining conduct. "The self-understanding of those who came together owing to their common involvement in the claims of Jesus Christ upon their way of looking at life is plain. According to the New Testament, the Church is a historic reality which, as it were, comes upon the historical scene as the answer of disciples to that which God during the earthly life of Jesus, had done in and through him."[15] Knowing themselves to be the *ecclesia,* the "called" people of God in Christ, they asked what specific actions were in keeping with who they were. "Doing flowed from being, and being was defined by the nature of the community."[16] Paul urged the people in the Roman *Koinonia* (a word used more often for the Christian fellowship than *ecclesia*) to encourage each other (Romans 1:12), and to "pursue what makes for mutual upbuilding" (Romans 14:19). As the Scriptures establish and maintain the Church's corporate identity, so the Church itself establishes and shapes individual identity: "Part of what it means to be the 'Church' normatively speaking, is to shape individual lives in keeping with the Church's own moral identity."[17]

Shaping individual lives is achieved in numerous ways, from direct instruction to a host of more subtle influences. Stanley Hauerwas, in his insightful book *A Community of Character,* points out that Martin Luther began the Reformation by posting ninety-five theses that were meant to reform the Church. Once underway with his reforms, Luther wrote a catechism and used both it and the Bible for direct instruction, the effects of which were literally to change the lives, the commitment, and behavior of hosts of people for generations to follow. Despite the oft-repeated disclaimer that "Christianity is caught, not taught," a great deal of direct teaching went into the shaping of Christian personalities in every era of history.[18]

It is also true, of course, that much of Christian character is "caught" through the influence of stories told, hymns sung, dreams and aspirations shared. Many a child has been impressed by the singing of such a simple gospel song as "I would be true, for there are those who trust me/I would be pure, for there are those who care,"[19] and later as an adult found the faith and certain behavior affirmed in the hymns, anthems, and oratorios, as well as in the sermons and discussions sponsored by the Church. "For the Church to be, rather than to have a social ethic means we must recapture the social significance of common behavior, such as acts of kindness, friendship, and the formation of families."[20] One of the most important contributions of the Church to individuals and to society as a whole is to provide a setting in which we learn to trust and depend on each other. This is no small achievement in a world where people and nations spend untold billions of dollars on weapons of war, simply because they do not trust each other enough to be mutually dependent.

THE ETHICS OF ECUMENICITY

The ecumenical movement that seemed to burst upon the Christian scene after World War II in the creation of the World Council of Churches is actually centuries old. As an action directed toward bringing unity to a diverse Christendom, it has been alive since at least the fourth century A.D., but its roots are biblical. Its ethical significance is incalculable because it runs counter to an exclusiveness and particularity common to many religious denominations. It requires a global perspective that is transnational and transracial, and even transreligious. It requires loyalty to the whole family of God.

The Old Testament community viewed itself as being uniquely the people of God, brought together by God's election; so also the New Testament fellowship celebrated a continuity in having "one Lord, one faith, one baptism" (Ephesians 4:5). But their mission differed markedly from that of the older Israel, in that they were to reach out to the gentile world and not spurn it. "Other sheep have I that are not of this fold; them also must I bring" (John 10:16). To be sure there were those even in the brief period after Jesus' resurrection who wanted to proclaim their exclusiveness, arguing about the superiority of their baptism over that of others, depending on who performed it. Paul denounced such divisiveness: "There is quarreling among you . . . each one of you says 'I belong to Paul,' or 'I belong to Apollos,' or I belong to Cephas,' or 'I belong to Christ.' Is Christ divided? Was Paul crucified for you? Or were you baptized in the name of Paul?" (1 Corinthians 1:11–13).

Unity was considered a given among the apostles. The clue to the biblical approach is that in the New Testament, oneness in Christ is invariably discussed in light of the incarnation, death, and resurrection of the Lord. This rules out any view of unity as merely an optional benefit on one hand, or any effort to achieve it by adopting a superficial friendliness, as so often characterizes interfaith activities in our own day. These latter do in fact serve an important social function in lessening frictions and animosities that fester in some communities. But the real issue is that "unity is given to us in Christ, and in this sense the Church is already one, but lives as if this were not true."[21]

The concept of *oikumene*, literally "the inhabited world," was potentially identified with the "household of faith" for the first time in 325 A.D., when the first Ecumenical Council was held (often referred to as Nicea I, because a second was held in Nicea in 787 A.D.).[22] Seeing the large number of contenders for orthodox interpretation of Scriptures and the nature of Jesus as the Christ, Constantine ordered the leaders of the churches to establish a creedal statement that would settle once and for all what Christians should believe. The Arian controversy was the primary cause of the mandate, and out of the conference emerged the Nicene Creed. Other ecumenical councils followed; one was held in Constantinople fifty-six years later to clarify the role of the Holy Spirit; Chalcedon was the scene of another in 451 A.D. to identify Christ's two natures. Today many Protestants disregard the fifteen or so councils that followed; even Nicea I is seldom held as binding. The single exception concerns Vatican II (1962), which is recognized as having opened the door for the first time for a rapprochement between Roman Catholic and Protestant Christians. This is what the World Council of Churches had encouraged since 1948.

During the nineteenth century, the proliferation of missionary societies around the world began to trouble many leaders of Protestant Christianity. A unification of missionary efforts seemed appropriate to avoid wasteful duplication and, more importantly, to clarify in the minds of people in whose lands the missionaries worked that the Gospel is indeed one. Membership in the body of Christ required articulation of all people and programs despite denominational labels. Many of the leaders of this cooperative endeavor had been part of the Student Volunteer Movement, which, since 1886, had sent thousands of young people from England and the United States into foreign missionary service as educators, physicians, and agriculturalists, as well as evangelists.

In 1910, the meeting of the World Missionary Conference gave birth to the International Missionary Council, which in turn attracted growing numbers of representatives from Africa and the Orient, as well as from Europe and America. A generation later, meeting at Madras in 1938, 470 delegates came from 70 nations: The modern ecumenical movement was underway.

The Second World War had a disastrous effect on missions, and temporarily at least had a stifling influence on ecumenics. Yet within three years of its end, in 1948, the World Council of Churches was born in Amsterdam.

In full acknowledgment of the wretchedness of the human condition that could blast civilization at its very roots, and had wrought a holocaust on a scale unknown to human history, the World Council selected as its theme "Man's Disorder and God's Design."[23] One hundred and fifty church bodies from all over the world affirmed their determination to create a council wherein Christians of widely diverse creedal and ethnic backgrounds could cooperate in the healing of mankind's self-inflicted wounds. It was in no sense a superchurch, since it had no power to legislate for member churches or to make any effort to enforce conformity.

The ethics of ecumenicity came sharply into focus when delegates to Amsterdam were reminded that ecumenical means "the whole inhabited world." Christ had sent his apostles into the world, not just into Jerusalem or even to

Israel. Wherever people suffer hunger, despair, or bondage of any sort, there Christ intended to live and work through his *ecclesia*.

The scores of denominations that affiliated with the World Council, and with many national and regional councils of churches formed shortly thereafter, found they were able to do together far more than they had ever done individually in terms of sheer practical service to the world's people. Beyond all their denominational missionary efforts, through the World Council they aided over 150,000 refugees from devastated countries by mid-1950, and distributed more than 150,000 tons of food, clothing, and other commodities (including medicine) per year thereafter in over fifty nations. They helped war-torn lands improve their agricultural programs with shipments of poultry and livestock, and even bridged the Iron Curtain to supply medicine and other forms of aid to suffering people in communist lands.

By 1983, the National Council of Churches of Christ, in the United States, responding to Jesus' injunction in Matthew 25:31f., was working with churches in more than ninety countries around the world to meet human need and to address the underlying causes of poverty and injustice. Church World Service, an affiliate of the World Council of Churches, resettled 69,150 Indochinese refugees, nearly 56,000 Cuban refugees, and arranged visits with Christian communities in the People's Republic of China, Russia, Poland, and other communist countries. This represents a characteristic of the ecumenical ethic: to strengthen the Body of Christ throughout the world, where political strife feeds on fear and dissention and encourages violent solutions to problems instead of reconciliation. "The kingdoms of this world derive their being from fear of one another; the rule of God means that a community can exist where trust rules, trust made possible by the knowledge that our existence is bounded by truth."[24]

The theme of the World Council of Churches, meeting in Vancouver in 1983, expressed the ethical commitment of the delegates from more than a hundred nations in its theme "Jesus Christ—The Life of the World." The life of every person on the planet was seen to have a claim on the "response-ability" of every Christian, and corporately of every congregation, in order that justice and peace might be secured for all. But a significant caveat was issued: "Many of those who are attracted to Christ are put off by what they see in the churches. Thus the call to conversion should begin with the repentance of those who do the calling."[25]

The ecumenical movement is by no means confined to Protestant Christianity, as became clear in the statement of Pope John Paul II, February 2, 1986, when he met at New Delhi with Tibet's leading Buddhist, the Dalai Lama. Indeed he went far beyond the call of his predecessor, Pope John XXIII, who had called upon Protestants and Catholics to seek harmony twenty years earlier. John Paul II called for "all the religions of the world to collaborate in the cause of humanity." In a later address to some ten thousand Indians of various faiths, he spoke of the need to cooperate to "eliminate hunger, poverty, ignorance, persecution, discrimination and every form of enslavement of the human spirit."[26]

Students of world religions have long known that there are many similarities among the many faiths. This is not to say all religions are alike, for it simply is not true that Buddhists believe in the Fatherhood of God, or that the Hindu caste system would affirm the equality and brotherhood of all humankind. Yet as Harvey Cox has noted, "We live during a historical period in which a new religious sensibility is struggling to be born. . . . As men and women of faith we have available to our spirits rich veins of religious wealth hardly imagined before." Cox writes of the need for greater sharing of this religious wealth: ". . . we need a universal church that will correspond to our growing awareness that the only adequately inclusive religious community is humankind itself."[27] He is not advocating a homogenized religion that ignores significant differences, but is urging a willingness to worship together in the faith that God can use our diversities of belief as well as talents to create a more vital moral and ethical climate for successive generations. In the same vein, Brian Hebblethwaite observes,

> All the great religions of the world, despite their differences, have some claim . . . to be fostering love and compassion, service of the neighbor and a concern for the right ordering of society. How should exponents of Christian ethics view these facts? On both human and theological grounds, it seems that they should welcome these facts as signs of the universal Spirit of God at work in human religion.[28]

Meanwhile, arising from many of the third world countries, unbidden by any formal ecumenical movement, a new theological ethic is being heard that is responding to the cry of oppressed people for liberation from many forms of oppression. Liberation theology may prove to be the most vital single phenomenon of our time. Indeed, Harvey Cox has expressed what many feel: "For me, the touchstone by which I respond to religious phenomena is summed up by the single word, 'liberation.' . . . The liberation of humankind is the purpose of Christianity."[29] Liberation theology is not systematic in the classical sense, but provides a new hermeneutic, a new way of understanding and interpreting the Scriptures in light of the social and political conditions under which people live, suffer, and struggle for freedom.

LIBERATION THEOLOGY: A NEW REFORMATION?

With its roots in the Hebrew concept of liberty (*Daror*) as freedom from spiritual as well as political bondage,[30] and its New Testament equivalents (*Aphesis* and *Eleutheria*),[31] liberation theology is perhaps the oldest "new" theological movement since the Reformation. Its antiquity, however, should not diminish for us its radical impact as a new force. It is a movement still in the process of discovering itself and its mission, as it emerges in a number of different social and political settings: among the blacks of North America, the Hispanics of South America, the victims of apartheid in South Africa, the Minjung of Korea, and among women of all nations where the Gospel has been heard.

Some extol liberation theology as "a new Reformation";[32] others view it with extreme caution, suspecting it of using "in an insufficiently critical manner, concepts borrowed from various currents of Marxist thought."[33] Still others from a more moderate view would agree that it is "an attempt to spell out the social and political implications of the Christian gospel, in terms of the liberation of men and women from oppression and injustice."[34] Some question the theology of the movement, suggesting it is simply another point of view within Christian ethics, equating redemption with liberation, and "neglecting the fact that a man can be redeemed even though he remains in political bondage."[35] However, their self-designation as theologies rather than as ethical systems reveals that "they are concerned with the change of an entire world view, rather than with the formulation of different norms within an existing framework."[36] Not yet a systematic theology, it nevertheless provides clear statements on sin, salvation, and eschatology, all of which have profound implications for Christian ethics.

Advocates insist that liberation theology is rooted more surely in the biblical faith than traditional Western theologies; that it presents different "faces" (American, African, Asian, feminist, etc.) precisely because they represent actual historic settings in which Christ is at work ministering *to* his people *through* his people. In countries where murder, torture, rape, and assassination are standard techniques by which governments control their people, Christ's ministry focuses on emancipating the people from their oppression, and provides a sociopolitical hermeneutic by which to reinterpret both the Bible and the claims of faith on our lives.

The Biblical Foundation

The proposition that liberation theologies are more authentically biblical than most traditional forms arises from the recognition that quite early in Christian history, Platonic and Neoplatonic influences introduced a metaphysic that was more Hellenistic than biblical. Gustavo Gutierrez notes that while "theology in the earliest centuries was meditations on the Bible," it became increasingly to be called a science, "an intellectual discipline born of the meeting of faith and reason."[37] Scant attention is accorded among major theologians from the twelfth century on to issues of political and economic injustice and their relation to poverty and human suffering.

Anyone who has read much in the theological classics (Augustine, Luther, Calvin, Barth, Berkouer, et al.), will recognize that the theme of oppression has received little or no attention there. One might think the Bible says little about oppression. However, when we strike the rock of a complete Bible concordance, to our great surprise we hit a gusher of texts and terms that deal with oppression. In short, we find a basic structural category of biblical theology.[38]

It is significant that from Abraham, who entered Canaan as an immigrant, to Moses, who was called to liberate his people from Egypt, through the days of Joshua, Judges, and the prophets, the biblical story is one of God's concern for his oppressed people. The latter suffered under a succession of dominating powers: Egypt, Assyria, Babylon, Persia, Greece, and Syria. The entire New Testament was written with God's people under the boot heel of the Roman Empire. Jesus' impending birth was heralded by Mary's declaration that the advent of the Messiah should be characterized:

> He has put down the mighty from their thrones, and
> exalted those of low degree;
> he has filled the hungry with good things,
> and the rich he has sent empty away. (Luke 1:52–53)

The theme of deliverance from oppression is again sounded by the father of John the Baptist, when he prophesied, "Blessed be the Lord God of Israel, for he has visited and redeemed his people, for he has raised up a horn of salvation . . . that we should be saved from our enemies" (Luke 1:68f.). Throughout his ministry, Jesus addressed himself to the physical as well as the spiritual needs of the people, and identified his whole purpose as fulfilling the prophesy of Isaiah 61:1–2.

> The spirit of the Lord is upon me,
> because he has anointed me to preach
>   good news to the poor.
> He has sent me to proclaim release to the captives and
> recovering of sight to the blind
> to set at liberty those who are oppressed. (Luke 4:18, 19)

"When Jesus describes the life of the poor, he calls attention to the role of oppression. He does not here deal with sin primarily in individualistic or pietistic terms [sex, alcohol, drugs], but in socio-economic terms of oppression, the brutal crushing of personalities and human bodies—things that the rich do to the poor, that the strong do to the weak."[39]

The utter seriousness with which the biblical writers took the matter of oppression is revealed in the many words that are used to describe its meaning for society, and the great many times the words are used: *ashaq* for injustice, which appears in one or more forms 59 times; *yanah*, enslavement, 20 times; *nagas*, to dehumanize (literally to "overwhelm with work" as with an animal),

23 times; *daka*, to crush (literally to pulverize, with fatal consequences), 31 times; *anah*, to humiliate (expressing the devastating psychological impact of oppression), 82 times![40] Given the abundance of references to such experiences, and the corresponding emphasis of biblical writers on the need of the people of God for deliverance from sociopolitical oppression, it is all the more surprising that so little attention has been given the themes by traditional theologians since the days of Constantine. One is tempted to suggest that the reason lies in the virtual captivity of institutional Christianity since those days by the power structures, both clerical and secular, which have so often been the instruments of oppression.

Methodology

The methodology of liberation theologies, which sets them apart from traditional forms, is essentially inductive, rather than deductive. Instead of erecting logical propositions about God, his nature, and commandments, and deducing ethical implications from them, liberation theologians take their example from the biblical Habakkuk, who declared, "I will stand upon my watch and will wait to see what [God] will say to me" (Habakkuk 2:1). In each situation, the person of faith will seek not a formula for action drawn from logical precepts or rules, but rather for what God, at that moment in time, has to say.

This approach has much in common with existential, or situation ethics that was popular in the 1960s and 1970s, as liberation theology seeks to understand and interpret God's will for each crisis as it arises. But whereas situation ethics made love its ultimate guide and justification, often without biblical reference, liberation theologies seek to relate the Scriptures to the problems at hand. The historical precedent for this is the practice of the early Christian church. "In the early centuries of the Church," Father Gutierrez reminds us, "what we now term theology was closely linked to the spiritual life. It was essentially a meditation on the Bible, geared toward spiritual growth."[41] What resulted was a theology useful for the time and place in which the early Christian lived. It was both contemporary and practical. Reflecting this methodology in our time, Cyris Moon of Korea notes, "We are convinced that the sociopolitical framework can be our frame of reference for the formulation of our theology of Minjung. Thus it is an *inductive* methodology working toward the central message of a liberating gospel to the Minjung, who will become the subjects of their own history and destiny."[42]

One consequence of this is that liberation theologies are predominantly represented by ethnic and racial groups, often characterized by distinctive features not common to their counterparts elsewhere. While this seems a weakness to many critics,[43] those who proclaim their differences insist it is both inevitable and its strength that it should be so. Thus Kosuke Koyama of Thailand calls his brand "Waterbuffalo Theology," and tells of his ministry:

I decided to subordinate great theological thoughts, like those of Thomas Aquinas and Karl Barth, to the intellectual and spiritual needs of farmers. God has called me to work here in northern Thailand, not in Italy or Switzerland. The theology that serves Jesus Christ in northern Thailand, will surely come into being when we dare to make this decision.[44]

Varieties of Emphasis

The different faces of liberation theology do present certain inconsistencies among its national and even regional forms. In his book A Black Theology and Black Power, James H. Cone tells us, "The goal of Black Theology is to prepare the minds of blacks for freedom. God's revelation in Christ can be made supreme only by affirming Christ as he is alive in black people today."[45] In a later book, Cone becomes more explicit: "Unlike white theology which tends to make the Christ-event an abstract, intellectual idea, Black Theology believes that the black community itself is precisely where Christ is at work. The Christ event in twentieth-century America is a black event."[46] Jesus is, in fact, conceived in specifically black racial terms: "The norm of all God-talk which seeks to be black talk, is the manifestation of Jesus as the Black Christ, who provides the necessary soul for black liberation."[47]

Not all black theologians agree with such a racially centered theology, fearing that it simply reflects the same oppressive posture of which traditional white theology has been guilty. Charles Long argues that theology itself may become a mode of domination, and writes, "We must not allow Black Theology to reduce itself to ethnic particularism."[48] In fairness, it should be noted that Cone's extensive travels have caused him to modify his position, recognizing other colors than black and white.

Out of Africa, where apartheid continues to hold blacks in the grip of white tyranny, comes a warning from Alan Boesak, elected president of the World Alliance of Reformed Churches in 1982. "In the aftermath of the deaths of Malcolm X and Martin Luther King, Jr., of the riots and the Black Panthers, Black Power has become a thoroughly obscure concept. [It] means discovering that the white power structure defines the reality of black life. The strongest ally of the oppressor is the mind of the oppressed."[49] Boesak agrees with Cone that "white people with their sorry record of violence at every level, are not morally equipped to preach the gospel of non-violence to black people."[50] But he insists that nonviolence is not a white issue or a black option, it is simply the way of Christ. "Black Theology therefore finds itself in intention and theological methodology, and certainly in its passion for liberation, not only alongside African theology, but also alongside the expressions of liberation theology in Latin America and Asia."[51]

Urging a nonviolent response to oppression, the African form of liberation theology has its counterpart in Korea, where the sufferings of the Minjung is expressed in the word Han.

Han is the hallmark of the Korean Minjung. Koreans have a troubled social biography which stretches back for centuries. For 36 years they endured humiliation under Japanese colonial rule. National liberation in 1945 did not improve the situation at all. The nation was divided into two hostile parts by two superpowers for their own selfish interests. The tragedies brought about by the national division are beyond description. *Han*, however, is the starting point for a new human history. In *Han* we encounter God who comes down to the *Han*-ridden people.[52]

In the Bible, the Minjung find the familiar pattern of oppression, when the Egyptians heaped heavy burdens on the Hebrews, and discovered that when the *Han*-ridden people cried out, their cries were answered with liberation. National tragedies followed, however, because the Israelites adopted the same oppressive tactics when they were victorious; liberated slaves often make the worst tyrants. The experience of the Minjung in Korea has been that a loveless, careless, and greedy people perpetuate oppressions. The essential teaching of Choi Je-oo, who initiated the Tonghak Rebellion of 1895, was love of people, care of one's body, and purging of greed, called *Dan*.

> In order to release the power of Han, one must cut oneself off from greed. To the oppressors it means they should stop being greedy and oppressive. To the oppressed it means they should stop wishing to be like their masters, and wanting to take revenge. Our hopes turn to the arrival of a Messiah, to undertake this necessary exorcism. Jesus is clearly the liberator. He was from Galilee, the lower depths of society. He suffered with the Minjung, and learned of their Han. He taught his followers to take the act of *Dan*, sharing bread, serving one another. The mighty exorcism, the glowing *koinonia*, and the unsparing attack on evil brought him to a horrible end on the cross. But the subsequent resurrection reversed the picture and completed the exorcism. Through his death and resurrection the Minjung were liberated from the spell of the evil spirit and transformed into a Jesus-movement that ultimately transformed the whole world.[53]

There are many parallels between the liberation theology of Korea and that of Central and South America. The primary difference lies in the fact that the oppression suffered in Korea is viewed as being best overcome through a spiritual purging, *"Dan"* self-denial,[54] "inviting God in the heart," and "overcoming the vicious circle of Minjung Han revenge."[55] In Latin America, on the other hand, the focus is on the sociopolitical and economic conditions which have created such grinding poverty that suggestions of further deprivation and self-denial would fall on deaf ears. As Father Gutierrez stoutly affirms, Latin American liberation theology is primarily addressed to liberating the poor.[56] Richard Shaull puts it succinctly: "The poor always knew they were poor; now they know why. They once accepted poverty as their fate; now they know that their suffering is produced by a social order that they can change, and they are determined to change it."[57]

Still another form of liberation theology has been emerging for several generations, which arises not from oppressed races or impoverished populations, but from that one-half of the world's population which is female. Feminism appears from one perspective to be a limited concern to end male domination, rather than representing a new theology. Yet it can hardly be denied that the dominant role of men in society has historically had the sanction of many religious traditions. It is implicit in Hebrew Scriptures and explicit in the Qur-an and in the writing of Confucius. Today "women comprise roughly half of the world's population. They work two thirds of the hours worked, but receive only one tenth of the income, and own less than a hundredth of the world's property. It's hardly surprising that the World Health Organization has found that the most widespread illness affecting women is exhaustion."[58]

From a biblical perspective, requiring women to take a subservient role is unjustified. References to Eve being created to serve as Adam's helper abound in the literature, but an examination of the Genesis passage reveals that the word translated as "helper" or "helpmeet" is *ezer*, which does not imply an inferior, but one who is equal to or superior; God himself is spoken of as *ezer* (Psalm 33:20, 70:5, 115:9–11, 121:2, 124:8, 145:5). How the role of woman was later interpreted as subordinate to man can only be attributed to social custom, not to theology.[59] Certainly the New Testament provides much encouragement for women to see their social and religious roles in a positive light. The Gospel of Luke affords a special place to women: Jesus' birth is told from Mary's point of view; in Luke we read of Elizabeth, and Ana, and the woman who anointed Jesus' feet; in Luke we find vivid pictures of Mary and Martha, and of Mary Magdalene. Further, although Paul reveals the influence of his Jewish upbringing in early statements about women keeping silent in the Church, he later addresses specific greetings to women who held important roles in young congregations (Romans 16:3; 2 Corinthians 16:19; 2 Timothy 4:19), and openly declared that in Christ "there is neither male nor female," but all are one (Galatians 3:28).

In a real sense, the New Testament provides a prima facie case for a theology of women's liberation. In subsequent Christian history, women sometimes made the issue of faith and freedom central to their theology, and when forced to a choice, made faith paramount. This was the key to the martyrdom of Vivia Perpetua (181–203), who chose death rather than renounce her faith: "I cannot forsake my faith for freedom."[60] In our own generation the choice is seldom if ever Christian faith (and death) or freedom. But Christian faith provides a vision of a new humanity, in which broken relationships are restored to wholeness by the power of Christ working through us. In her book *The Future of Partnership*, Letty Russell espouses "a new revolution of consciousness," in which humankind breaks from thinking that is dominated by power and authority, and embraces an eschatology in which the "new order" in Revelation can be achieved within our own human history.[61] This new order would succeed in achieving freedom from exploitation in the marketplace, equality in pay and employment practices, an end to sexual exploitation, and more creative family life. In short, liberation means a holistic salvation, touching and transforming all relationships because they are seen as partnerships established in Christ.

Implications

All theology is contextual, deriving hermeneutical principles from history and experience. The prophets of the Old Testament were "doing theology" as they reflected on the way Yahweh was perceived to be working through Israel toward divine ends. They anticipated the future, and uttered warnings and encouragements as they gained insight into the human condition and its destiny. "The prophet," as Oscar Cullman pointed out, "does not limit himself as does the fortune teller . . . but his prophesy becomes preaching, proclamation."[62] In this way contemporary black theology, identifying with the Exodus experience of the Bible, and drawing on black's experience upward from slavery, has derived its hermeneutical principles by which to interpret the Bible's message appropriate to their need. In the case of the prophets, as well as both American and African blacks, the issues of injustice and oppression led to a politicized hermeneutics. That such may be a necessary and inevitable consequence should be no surprise to American whites, whose Puritan, Moravian, and Quaker ancestors all viewed the political arena as the appropriate place to work out plans for America to become, in William Penn's words, "a holy experiment in government." Father Gutierrez calls the liberation movement in Central and South America "a political hermeneutic of the Gospel,"[63] and A. Sung Park asserts quite plainly that in Korea, "Minjung theology is a socio-political hermeneutics of the Christian Gospel."[64]

This does not mean that liberation theologies are simply efforts to make the Gospel message conform to the needs of different groups of people suffering one or another form of oppression. The basic hermeneutical task of Minjung theology, for example, is not to interpret the Bible in light of the Korean situation, but rather to interpret the suffering experience of the Korean Minjung in the light of the Bible.[65]

The implications of this hermeneutics for Christian ethics are extensive and profound. In the past, a compassionate reading of human suffering has usually brought forth strategies for helping the poor and oppressed with gifts of money, food, medical and agricultural aid, and the sending of missionaries. This seemed a viable response to the biblical injunction to care for the needy and oppressed. The deficiency at the heart of such strategy was that it failed to provide any means of altering the structures of politics and economics which promoted and perpetuated the conditions of oppression and poverty. These structures of violence remained untouched. As long as a few people control most of the wealth at the expense of the exhaustion and starvation of the rest of the populace, a morally intolerable situation exists that must be overcome. The traditional Christian response, based on a nonpolitical hermeneutic, led to a relationship of paternalism, which was barely an improvement on earlier colonialism. Further, it has come to be an accepted fact that "when economic aid is given to needy countries, it tends to shore up the repressive and totalitarian regimes. Such aid is often accompanied by military aid, to ensure that 'subversive' or left wing elements do not gain sufficient strength to challenge the corrupt regime in power."[66]

Liberation theology challenges us to reexamine the human condition in the light of the Bible. Theology, as Father Gutierrez defines it, is "the critical reflection on the liberating praxis of Christians." Praxis is the dynamic interaction between theory and practice, which points us to the command of the Bible, not merely to contemplate, but to act. To know God, according to the prophets, is to *do justly*, to *love mercy*, and to *walk humbly* with God (see Hosea 4:1-6, 6:6). Jesus did not command orthodox belief as a condition of discipleship, but said those who enter the kingdom will be those who *do* the will of the Father (Matthew 7:21). The doing implied specific care for the poor and hungry (Matthew 25:31f.).

Liberation theology challenges us to a new worldview, in which we see (and feel) the pain and broken condition of God's people under social, political, and economic conditions for which, in some measure, the capitalist system is responsible and from which many of us (including our Christian churches) have prospered.[67] It provides a new approach to biblical understanding of the intention of God in sending Jesus Christ to liberate us from sin—not simply from the "popular" sins of sensuality, but from the sins of willing participation in political systems that are at the root of injustice and oppression.[68] It speaks to us of understanding that Christ came to set us free by binding us to the plight of our fellow human beings in their struggle for freedom, that together we may enjoy that liberation which can never again be ensnared in the yoke of bondage.

BEYOND LIBERATION THEOLOGY

As powerful as is the appeal to view the primary mission of the Church as the fulfillment of Jesus' claim concerning an aspect of his own ministry: ". . . to set at liberty those that are downtrodden" (Luke 4:18), many Christians remain uneasy. This surely is not the whole ministry of the whole Church, the tasks of which are complex and range from fostering private prayer and public worship to financing overseas medical and agricultural stations.

Jacques Ellul, writing in *The Subversion of Christianity*, warns that throughout nearly two thousand years of Christian history, the Church has allowed itself to be diverted from its intended nature and function as the community of the faithful to become whatever the dominant culture demanded of it: "monarchist under monarchy, republican under republic, socialist under communism. Everything goes."[69] Christianity, he concludes, "becomes an empty bottle that successive cultures fill with all kinds of things."[70] The current liberation theme is perhaps another such bit of filling. It may be demanded by temporary exigency, but is it truly "of the Gospel"? This is not to suggest, and Ellul does not say it, that liberation theology is merely an "ism," or novel trend. It does appear, as he notes, "a popular movement that expresses in history the ongoing action of the Holy Spirit. But it is not theology; it is pastoralia."[71] Besides all this, suggests John Pottenger," one wonders if the project itself—however noble and sincere—is too late." The vastness of the task in the face of so much human alienation, timid congregations, and lack of specifics, places it all in doubt.[72]

The themes and strategies of liberation thought seem, unfortunately, to have had little practical effect in the mainline churches. "It is rare," writes Ephraim Radner, "to come across material dealing with the practical tasks of reforming communities."[73] Just how, he asks, are churches to eradicate poverty in their neighborhoods or states without a specific set of programs for dismantling or at least redirecting the agencies, industries, cartels, and their political support systems that created the poverty? One can decry the mismanaged and often cruel prison systems from which we wish we might liberate prisoners. But what strategies are to be implemented for changing the violent culture that precipitates the need for prisons? "This," he charges, "is rhetoric posturing on a grand scale. In fact a liberationist outlook obscures rather than clarifies the practical imperatives of Christian ministry."[74]

Radner's alternative is for the Church to recover its identity and its mission as "a Fellowship in Exile." The early Christian church, he reminds us, was defined as a community "called out" (*ekklesia*) of existing social and alternate religious conditions. Being thus disentangled from worldly alliances it was often scorned, vilified, and persecuted. But to what degree are modern Christians willing to be divorced from their familiar ecclesiastical settings?

> The notion of exile is poorly understood by Americans even though immigration and assimilation [of exiles] are the basis of our vigorous commonwealth. The image of exile returns North American churches to one of the central strands of New Testament ecclesiology. By maintaining the integrity of the Christian community in the face of the dominant culture, churches can rediscover the means to embrace new members from the margins of their culture, forming a commonwealth in exile, a distinct and enticing place of renewal.[75]

Engaging as the image of a church in exile might be to some, its proposal leaves unanswered just how many traditional Christians, comfortable with the status quo, would be enticed by the prospect of exile. Further, Radner's concept suffers the same lack of specificity as the liberationism he rejects. It offers no clear program for the churches to follow as they struggle for a meaningful role in society while presumably being exiled from it.

In the first decade after World War II, the mainline denominations enjoyed a brief rebirth from the malaise they had experienced during the Great

Depression. But beginning with the 1960s until now, a sharp decline set in, in terms of both membership and church building. The Presbyterians, for example, have lost a third of their membership in the past thirty years, and other mainline denominations have witnessed comparable decline.[76]

Enrollment losses are not the key issue here, however, because, in fact, gains in membership may mean only that the churches have accommodated themselves to the secularism that Jacques Ellul decries. The point would seem to be not whether the exile model should replace the liberation mode, but whether each of them represents a way in which the churches may fulfill their calling, providing they do not mistake their contribution for the whole mission and character of the Church.

The Church as a designation of the churches that earnestly seek to respond to the summons of Christ to "feed my sheep" has been on a centuries-long journey, the destiny of which has often been obscured by the many short-range goals it has set for itself. But as Oliver O'Donovan has expressed it, "Only as the pilgrimage reaches the end which God has destined for it can the faith and hope of the church be validated."[77] It was with careful forethought, he notes, that the apostle Paul grouped faith, hope, and love separately from the "spiritual gifts" of speaking with the tongues of men and angels, prophesy, knowledge of secret things, and the courage of martyrs. (1 Corinthians 13:1–3). These do indeed have their own intelligibility and without them the Church would be little but a pious social club. But all together without love, they are nothing, as Paul insisted. They are what have made liberation theology possible. But the Church is more than these, more than public gatherings however religious, more than education, missions, and social projects. "The true moral life of the Christian community is its love, and its love is unintelligible except as participation in the life of One who reveals himself to us as love, except that is, as the entry of mankind and of restored creation upon its supernatural end."[78]

If The Church is to be known by its participation in the life of Christ, who is revealed as love, the question remains how it is to express that love in the communities of the world. One of the most important, surely, has been its preservation and transmission of the Bible. Philip Wogaman is quite right to insist that "the canonization of scripture by the church is one of its most important exercises of moral teaching . . . it represents the faith of the community of faith in its deepest form."[79] The Church also has countless ways to express its love through interaction with the world without subverting itself as Jacques Ellul fears. Nor should it be overly concerned with those declines in membership that tend to reflect on an anxiety for popularity. This is not to lull evangelistic efforts that are the lifeblood of necessary growth and community outreach. Yet it may be that if the churches were truly "the salt of the earth" (Matthew 5:13), they would lose more than popularity. Speaking and acting against injustice, like the antiapartheid churches have done in South Africa, has been costly in terms far more painful than mere membership loss. If the churches were faithful to the Christ in their midst, they might suffer such persecution as Christ anticipated yet receive it with joy (Matthew 5:11f., 10:16–25).

It is not only difficult but probably futile to predict what the churches in the future will be like. If they are seen primarily as organizational structures in which professional clergy increasingly imitate secular executives, they may succeed only in a temporal sense, trivializing the Church's role in society and eventually collapse. But the degree to which they are successful in interpreting Scripture in the light of contemporary issues and making their impact felt on the morals and ethical practices of society will be in proportion to their nurturing faith through worship; hope through a focus on the *eskaton,* the coming fulfillment of God's redeeming work through Christ; and love for God and our companions. The latter must of course include our nonhuman companions in environmental responsibility and stewardship, for "the earth is the Lord's, and the fulness thereof" (Psalm 24:1). Almost everything else we might speculate on concerning the future of the Church must have to do with the way it addresses such concerns as we explore in the next chapters. All else would be polity and architecture.

CHAPTER FIVE

Human Nature and the Christian Person

The study of ethics focuses on human behavior and on rules for evaluating such behavior. Yet as Paul Lehmann reminds us, everything in the study of ethics depends on what we mean by the term *human*.[1] Throughout nature different creatures function in ways that biologists call species specific. We do not expect dogs to act like spiders, nor birds like fish. What kind of creatures are we as humans? Is our nature limited to our genetic predisposition, so that virtually every action is determined by biological necessity as sociobiologists propose?[2] Some theorists would venture so far as to suggest we are no more than animals destined to claw and fight our way to whatever level of dominance we can achieve.

We noted in Chapter 3 that behavioral psychologists (in contrast to the sociobiologists) insist that our responses to life's demands are conditioned by environmental forces. Few would go so far as to suggest that we are merely machines to be programmed, though B. F. Skinner's behavioral conditioning sometimes leaves this impression. Where sociobiology or behaviorism prevails, the human is portrayed with no real freedom of choice, without which the study of ethics is impossible; it presumably does not occur to a spider or a tiger, much less to a mechanical contrivance, to inquire how it "ought" to behave. This was a point made with considerable force by a group of Russian scientists at the World Congress of Philosophy in 1988, when they insisted (to the surprise of many present) that "man's essence is not his species," and that we must reconsider the "spiritual dimensions" if we are to understand human nature.[3]

Historically, most people have concluded that while we do in fact share many characteristics of lower animals, we also exhibit qualities not found elsewhere in nature, and freedom of ethical determination is one of them. We can decide which of several courses of action is more noble or virtuous, and while some may choose the Buddhist Eightfold Way as preferable to the Ten Commandments, and admit that cultural conditioning played a strong role in the choice, it was nevertheless a choice. Clearly it will be of great importance whether we elect to believe we are creatures made "in God's image," as in biblical parlance, or merely a species of evolved primate. If it is further concluded that, as beings created in God's image, our choices have been so selfish as to distort that image to the degree we have become estranged from God, further questions must be addressed as to how we can restore the relationship, or whether God alone can effect the restoration. The belief that the latter is the case underlies the messianic theme of Judaism and Christianity. The faith of the Christian that the Messiah has come in the person of Jesus Christ is at the heart of Christian ethics.

When we turn to the Bible for insight into human nature, we find seemingly contradictory claims, some of which offer little to counter the scientific (or at least naturalist) position. On the one hand, we are told "all flesh is grass" (Isaiah 40:6); "Man is like the beasts that perish . . . their graves are their homes forever" (Psalm 49:11–12). On the other hand, we are assured that we have been created "in the image of God" (Genesis 1:27), are indeed only a little lower than God (Psalms 8:5), and our graves are *not* our destiny (John 14:1–3; Romans 8:11, 31–39; 1 Corinthians 15:20–58).

Yet the Bible tells us something more serious about ourselves. The Scriptures are filled with tales of our warfare, our perversities, and self-defeating lust, and charge, "there is not a truly good man on earth" (Ecclesiastes 7:20). In the New Testament, Jesus refers to the disciples as "the salt of the earth" and "the light of the world" (Matthew 5:13–15). Yet he appears to take their evil nature for granted: "If you then, who are evil, know how to give good gifts to your children, how much more will your father who is in heaven give good gifts to those who ask him?" (Matthew 7:11). He understands the potential for human callousness, violence, and hypocrisy, and fully expects persecution and suffering for himself and his disciples (Matthew 10:16, 20:17–19).

Reinhold Niebuhr suggested, "All modern views of human nature are adaptation, transformations and varying compounds of two distinctive views of man: (a) the view of classical antiquity, that is of the Graeco-Roman world, and (b) the Biblical view."[4] This distinction must be amplified, to be sure, to allow for the very real differences between, for example, Plato's contention that we are born with an innate knowledge of the good, and Aristotle's naturalism wherein knowledge of the good is gained "developmentally." We must also make room for the materialism of Democritus (later expounded by Epicurus and Lucretius), which Aristotle denounced; it posited that nothing is inherently right or wrong, but only instrumentally useful or destructive. By the same token we must acknowledge that there is not one biblical view of human nature that runs coherently through the Bible, but a many-faceted understanding of the human condition for which, nevertheless, God has a redeeming word. In this chapter we explore some of the many views of nature, and of humankind's place in it as proposed by the ancients, as well as by people of the medieval and later periods including the modern. Special attention is given to some contemporary theories of the Greco-Romans among us in biology and psychology. Without at least a minimal acquaintance with their work, the Christian is seriously unprepared to contend.

Next we try to recover a biblical perspective on the nature of humankind as created, fallen, and redeemed by God's reconciling work through Jesus, the Christ. With this background we discuss how the "natural man," becoming one with Christ (justified and sanctified, to use the ancient terms), becomes the Christian person.

A final section provides clues for the necessary interaction of the Christian with non-Christians. In our shrinking pluralistic world, encounters with believers in other religious traditions and with nonbelievers must surely increase with the expansion of trade and travel. Opportunities for dialogue and fellowship may provide our generation's most creative human experience.

NATURE AND HUMAN NATURE

Speculation on the nature of nature and of humankind's place in the natural order began long centuries before an Aristotle, Augustine, or Spinoza attempted to put the puzzle of life together.[5] Even before there was any literature as such, primitive people were trying to make sense of the chaos of natural disasters, plagues, and tribal warfare that left whole populations in shambles. One evidence is in the funeral praxis of Neanderthal people, 100,000 years ago, who buried their dead with weapons, tools, and food placed along with flowers in their graves. This suggests something of their concept of human life as transcending the raw powers of nature and of death itself.

Philosophic Inquiry

Philosophies of history, and even the form of naturalism that disavows concern for metaphysics, may nevertheless have their roots in the religious impulse. "Philosophy developed religion's first intuitions and poetic interpretations of the nature of the world and man, into a systematic pattern of thought."[6] It is also possible, on the other hand, that the first efforts to comprehend the natural order and humankind's role in it began as early attempts at science. Samuel Stumpf makes the flat statement, "It is a fact of the history of thought that science and philosophy were the same thing in the beginning, and only later did various specific disciplines separate themselves from the field of philosophy, medicine being the first to do so."[7] Perhaps, taking a more inclusive view, we may find useful Einstein's observation that "all religions, arts and sciences are branches of the same tree. All these aspirations are directed toward ennobling man's life, lifting it from the sphere of mere physical existence and leading the individual toward freedom."[8]

A number of different lines of thought concerning nature developed during the score of centuries before the Christian era. Among these, the biblical concept of the natural order as being directly established by a single Creator is in vivid contrast to those found among the many forms of animism and polytheism to the time. "All Egyptian cosmogenies were basically concerned with divinities of nature: the sky, the earth, the wind, the sun, the moon and the stars."[9] The *Vedas*, of the Indo-European immigrants to India (c. second millennium B.C.), personify the many aspects of nature such as fire (*Agni*), the dawn (*Usas*), storms (the *Maruts*), rain (*Indra*), and so on. In the folk religion of the Greeks, made famous by Homer, the natural world was the playground and battlefield of the gods.

The classical philosophers of Greece ignored the myths (Plato sought to forbid the use of Homer's writings among youth, believing that so much sex and violence was harmful), and proposed instead that reality is dual: material nature and the realm of mind or idea. These are set in opposition, with the material world presented as transitory and therefore not fully "real," while the world of mind is eternally real and good. In his *Timaeus*, Plato describes the nature of these two worlds, the first being the realm of perfect order and containing the models of ideas that are in turn reflected in the second world. The first world is real; the second, our natural world is only an imitation of the ideal realities. We humans belong spiritually to that first world, but are distracted by our sensual experience in the material world. The latter is evil, in that it entices us away from our real home and destiny.[10] Plato and Aristotle, despite important differences, shared a common conviction that the human soul's best and preferred state was to be free from the material encumbrances of nature. Indeed, it was Aristotle who contended that the major virtues of courage, temperance, and prudence are achieved by our will to overcome nature, that is, the natural impulses to indulgence, fear, and the quest for easy answers. This exaltation of mind and spirit over body has provided the classical doctrine of man, which has influenced all subsequent rationalistic and dualistic philosophies since, including Neoplatonism, which strongly impressed itself on Christian thought in the first centuries.

A very different view of nature emerged from the writings of Democritus (c. 500 B.C.), who proposed the first theory of atomic particles. Here all reality, which for him included mind and spirit, is composed of tiny solid particles falling endlessly through space, constantly colliding, linking to form the familiar objects of our natural world, and then disengaging to continue their random careers. Epicurus, two centuries later, drew the clear ethical implications from this: If all reality is composed of lifeless atoms in a purposeless universe, there are no rights and wrongs, only behaviors which tend to yield pleasure or pain. The good is therefore whatever yields well-being; evil is whatever upsets the peaceful, tranquil order of things. Somewhere about 55 B.C., the Roman poet Lucretius based his treatise *The Nature of Things* on Democritus's and Epicurus's writings to provide a thoroughgoing materialistic philosophy. It can hardly be described as an "objective" view, inasmuch as it reveals his almost virulent hatred of religion. Nevertheless, its implications are clear: If nature is a *danse macabre* of dead particles, practical reason must conclude that altruism and other ethical concerns are irrelevant except as they are required to preserve friendships and one's own peace of mind.[11]

Aristotle, as just noted, rejected the materialism of Democritus, on the ground that it leaves no room for understanding the complexity of human experience, including not only mind and spirit, but such practical problems as the nature of governments, the sciences, and the arts. Later writers like Augustine, the medieval scholastics, and Aquinas stressed that our human nature prompts the acquisition of knowledge, the quest for justice, and the yearning for love and beauty. The hunger for such values shows our nature to be set within the larger framework of God's created realm, but still distinct from the mechanical processes of the natural order.

A fundamental question for philosophy has related to just this issue. If mankind were no more than a natural entity, and if all human activities can be seen to stem from natural conditions and impulses, why then do not our arts, education, science, and other aspects of civilization just fade back into nature? There have been those romantics like Rousseau who believed our wandering away from nature into civilization has resulted in a loss of our humanity, rather than a gain. His treatise in 1749, "Has the Progress of the Arts and Sciences Contributed More to the Corruption or Purification of Morals?" was answered on the side of corruption. Yet Rousseau was not fully persuaded by the back to nature theme so often attributed to him. He insisted that children should be treated with kindly persuasion and given freedom, but within carefully constructed boundaries. While he believed human nature to be inherently good, he feared that untamed natural impulses would lead to anarchy, a contradiction of which he was either unaware or chose not to address. The idealists, following Plato's lead, would of course have provided at least one possible answer: The anarchic impulses arise from the carnal side of our nature whereas the capacity to see the danger and guard against them come from the mind or soul. In his doctrine of *eros*, Plato presents the natural vitalities as being sublimated, or redirected by reason.

Most of the philosophers during the Age of Reason (roughly between the birth of Galileo, 1564, and the American Revolution) stood within the Christian tradition, and sought to resolve the philosophical questions of the relation of God to nature and of nature to humankind in keeping with theology. This was no small undertaking, and yielded at least three quite different views First, René Descartes (1596–1650) suggested that once God had created the natural order and given the physical world its own laws, he set the process in motion and left it to run itself. Descartes maintained a strict dualism between matter and mind, so the mind is free from natural causation to comprehend nature and commune with God. Second, and in contradiction, George Berkeley (1685–1753) insisted that God is not only the Creator, but that nothing in nature happens without God's direct involvement. "Nature," he declared, "is a vain chimera, introduced by those heathens who had not just notions of the omnipresence and infinite perfection of God."

The third position to emerge was expressed by Baruch Spinoza (1632–1677), a convert from Judaism, who held that God and nature are virtually synonymous, encompassing all. "For man, whether guided by reason or desire, does nothing save in accordance with the laws of nature." Spinoza had less confidence than Descartes in the capacity of reason to control passion, but his quasi-pantheism alleviated his uneasiness, and he pronounced humankind more likely to do good than evil.

Nineteenth-century science departed sharply from earlier efforts to harmonize with theology, and naturalism came of age. The biological sciences began to represent the human species as simply one of the many populating the animal kingdom. Our spiritual qualities were seen as merely transformed impulse and sense perception. The evolutionary theories of Pierre Laplace (1749–1827), who also developed the nebular hypothesis in astronomy, and of Charles Darwin (1809–1892) placed humankind squarely in the natural order. The hypothesis of natural evolution proposes to comprehend the whole of life in terms of processes which, beginning with the most rudimentary particles or forces, have produced the complex life forms of our familiar world. These present species have evolved from earlier, primitive forms. Long before *Homo sapiens* appeared, according to this hypothesis, there were humanoid creatures now assigned names like Pithecanthropus, Neanderthal, and Cro-Magnon. The question of molecular biologist Jacob Bronowski is, "At what point can we say that the precursors of man become man himself?"[12] Anthropologists may be correct in suggesting that the human race emerged not from a single line of progenitors, but from many "Adams" who developed during approximately the same period of evolution at different places on the globe. Thus Ramapithecus, found in Kenya and India, and Australopithecus, in Tanzania, may qualify as different forebears. A *Christian Century* editorial, in light of Louis Leaky's research at the Oldevai Gorge, noted, "The monogenism-polygenism controversy will not be settled by appeals to the Bible or to Christian doctrine, however threatening the multiple-origins theory may be to traditional Christian thought. This is a scientific question, and scientific questions are eventually settled by science."[13] Emil Brunner, the Swiss Protestant theologian, and

Teilhard Chardin, a French Catholic paleontologist and priest, concurred that in the light of science, "We can no longer teach that man, as created by God, is descended from Adam in Paradise and the primitive state."[14] Chardin, who was instrumental in the discovery of Peking man (perhaps the first "true man," who used fire), argued not for Genesis versus evolution, but for the proposition that the increasingly complex life forms culminating in rational and loving human beings bespeak an intelligent Planner, whom we may rightly call God and Father. Brunner insisted that the man of Genesis, created in God's image, "is not the Neanderthal man, nor the Peking man, nor *Homo sapiens,* but simply 'man in general' "; responsible, self-determined man, aware of having deviated from the self God intended.[15]

Opposition to naturalistic evolution was neither as widespread nor as intense in the nineteenth century as it was to become in the twentieth. Indeed, "the major journals of the day greeted [Darwin's] *Origin of the Species* with a respect bordering on reverence. The author was uniformly praised for his previous accomplishments and for that genius of observation so evident in this."[16] Most of the progressive philosophers of the eighteenth-century Enlightenment proposed theories of social and economic history containing evolutionary ideas, some of them even anticipating a survival of the fittest motif. So in a sense, the nineteenth century was prepared for Darwin's hypothesis.

The ethical implications of the evolutionary hypothesis were developed by Herbert Spencer (1820–1903), who scorned any idea of the spiritual life as a vestige of primitive imagination. He maintained not only that the fittest alone survive, but that whatever functions enable individuals and societies to survive and prosper are morally obligatory: "Strange as the conclusion looks it is nevertheless a conclusion to be here drawn, that the performance of every function is, in a sense, a moral obligation."[17]

The study of sociology was developed during this time, based primarily on the work of August Comte (1798–1857), also a thoroughgoing naturalist. Comte insisted on abandoning all notions of purpose in nature and of moral obligation, seeking only to understand the natural laws that govern the actions of persons and societies. It is an engaging paradox that Comte and Spencer, both committed to evolutionary naturalism, arrived at contrary conclusions about purpose and moral obligation within the framework of nature.

It remains the hallmark of naturalism to insist on certain basic tenets: The knowable universe is composed of natural objects; the natural order is a system of processes involving these objects; the natural method of studying is (1) describing natural processes, (2) explaining the processes by way of stating hypotheses, then (3) testing the hypotheses. It is also basic to naturalism that nature be understood as intelligible, that is, its processes are regular and predictable; reason is the consistent application of method, and science is the purest example of reason, which is self-correcting; the only cognitive mode of experience is the scientific; outside science there is no real knowledge to be had; the universe as such has no moral character except for the presence of human beings who do have and pursue values.[18]

Among the most forceful contemporary writers insisting on a thorough-going naturalism for defining human nature has been anthropologist and social biologist Ashley Montague. "Human beings are not born with human nature," he insists, "they develop it. What human beings are born with is a complex of potentialities for being human."[19] He distinguishes our physical characteristics (which he calls *hominid*) from our mental capacities, which are truly human. The process by which we learn necessary social patterns is termed *humanization*. He insists we are born without instincts,[20] completely lacking psycho-physical predispositions that cause other animals to behave in certain ways. Yet he declares with equal fervor that "human beings are born with an already built-in system of values which have been biologically determined."[21] Among these is the drive toward goodness and toward the ultimate value, which is love. Having no place for God or spirituality in his scheme of things, Montague declares, "Love is God, *not* God is love. . . . If there is divinity in man, it is this innate drive toward goodness."[22] Are not built-in values predispositions? He demurs.

While Montague is not a systematic developmentalist, we may see his basic contentions reflected in some contemporary theorists who are. Four of these deserve special attention: Sigmund Freud, Erik Erikson, Jean Piaget, and Lawrence Kohlberg, all of whom define human nature in naturalistic terms, albeit with significant variations.

Sigmund Freud

Freud maintained that each person grows through five specific stages en route to becoming fully human.

1. From birth to about eighteen months, the child is an immature, dependent organism, making insatiable demands for mothering, which are expressed orally. Frustrations experienced during this *oral stage*, due to deprivation of satisfactions in nursing, are in later life manifested in excessive oral behaviors such as talking too much, compulsive eating, smoking, and nail biting.

2. The *anal stage* occurs from eighteen months to about three years, when the child can no longer be free for bowel and bladder elimination, and undergoes toilet training. If this training is thoughtless and severe, the frustrated child becomes a self-centered and abrasive personality, quick to take offense, but paradoxically preoccupied with rules and conformist behavior, compulsively neat, stingy, and authoritarian.

3. According to Freud, the *phallic stage* is reached about age three and continues through the seventh year, when the child discovers pleasure in the genital parts (which is often forbidden), and simultaneously develops unconscious sexual feelings for the parent of the opposite sex. The sense of

rivalry against the parent of the child's own gender evokes guilt feelings and fears of being punished by removal of the sex organs. Many problems of sexual adjustment in later life, including frigidity, impotence, and even homosexuality can be traced to this area of frustration.

4. Freud contended that most personality characteristics are formed by the sixth year of life. He identified a *latency stage*, between the sixth and twelfth year, when sexual feelings are suppressed and sublimated through sports and games.

5. The *genital stage* is awakened in adolescence, when romantic infatuations and emotional upheavals require new adjustments. These establish the character of the now fully human adult, albeit not always the perfectly adjusted adult.[23]

Human nature, according to Freud, must be understood in purely naturalistic terms—not only the organism with its nervous system, but also its instincts and mental processes.

> If now we apply ourselves to considering mental life from a biological point of view, an instinct appears to us as a borderland concept between the mental and the physical. By the *source* of an instinct is meant that somatic process in an organ or part of the body from which there results a stimulus represented in the mental life by an instinct.[24]

Even those qualities that Freud considered to be evidence of the best of human characteristics are biological in origin:

> Religion, morality, and the social sense—the chief elements of what is highest in man—were originally one and the same thing . . . they were acquired phylogenetically out of the father-complex. It seems that the male sex has taken the lead in developing all of these moral acquisitions, and that they have been transmitted to women by crossinheritance.[25]

Erikson

Some of Freud's early followers felt he had gone so far in his adherence to naturalism that he became a determinist. Among these is Erik Erikson, a Danish psychologist who contended that Freud's determinism was actually fatalistic, and did not do justice to the qualities of freedom and potential greatness in human experience. Coming to the United States in 1933, Erikson did not publish his first book until 1950, focusing on the psychosocial development of human beings rather than on the psychosexual as Freud had.

As compared with Freud's five stages, Erikson proposed eight, based on the *epigenetic principle* that development follows a ground plan, whereby each part of the personality is formed in response to "life's inner and outer dangers."

Of special importance to Erikson is that these stages must be met on schedule if the personality is to develop in a healthy fashion.

These stages can be summarized as follows:

1. *Infancy* (birth to one year: *basic trust vs. mistrust* in which infants' ability to trust themselves and other people depends on whether their basic needs are cared for, including their need for affection and for the confidence that their environment is safe and dependable.
2. *Early childhood* (two to three years): *autonomy vs. shame and doubt* during which children crawl, walk, and explore. If parents are patient and allow for this freedom, the child gains independence and competence. If parents stifle initiative in this stage, youngsters begins to doubt their own abilities and to feel ashamed.
3. *Fourth to fifth year: initiative vs. guilt* is a stage wherein children begin to shape their own behaviors, if encouraged to use a growing repertoire of motor and mental skills. If suppressed, they experience a sense of guilt for wanting to express themselves.
4. *From the sixth year to puberty* the child goes through the stage Erikson calls *industry vs. inferiority.* During elementary school years, the child discovers a world that rewards effort and achievement, but punishes or belittles failure. Children who encounter only scorn and harassment experience feelings of inferiority driven ever deeper.
5. During *Adolescence* (twelve to eighteen years), the period of *identity vs. role confusion* is underscored with such questions as "Why am I here?" and "What kind of creature am I?" Trying on new roles as they meet romantic opportunities, ponder vocational choices, and achieve emancipation from home, they either gain a sense of "centered" identity, or take on multiple roles of delinquent, deviate, or whatever seems to serve their confused purposes.
6. *Young adulthood* is an extended period characterized by *intimacy vs. isolation.* Hopefully it is a time for developing abiding friendships and learning to care deeply for other people. However, if close involvement brings rejection, withdrawal and isolation may result in a misanthropic personality.
7. *Middle adulthood* involves reaching beyond one's immediate social circle to the whole of society and to future generations. This stage Erikson calls *generativity vs. stagnation.* Those that fail to reach out are self-preoccupied persons who tend to become physically as well as mentally sluggish and are dull company.
8. In *old age* the final stage of *integrity vs. despair* is reached. Those who have nurtured a philosophy that enables them to survey their past with satisfaction achieve an integrated personality and are able to face the future unafraid. Despair characterizes those who view their lives as failures, realizing time may be too short to make amends.[26]

Many feel that Erikson's work provides a welcome alternative to Freud's. "He offers a more optimistic view; [he] holds open the prospect of healthy and positive resolutions of our identity crisis."[27] Others have criticized Erikson for merely replacing Freud's stages with his own, which are no less deterministic inasmuch as each must be encountered and lived through in sequence and at specific ages. Further, his stages are lacking in precision, and cannot be tested empirically.[28]

Jean Piaget

A third theorist to describe the stages by which *Homo sapiens* becomes "human," from the naturalistic vantage point, is Jean Piaget. Whereas Freud was concerned with psychosexual development and Erikson with psychosocial development as keys to humanization, Piaget focused on the cognitive aspects. Development, he wrote, is a matter of progressive adaptation to the challenges of the environment, beginning with the purely reflexive and then the instinctive responses, and upward through modifying one's own behaviors to meet the demands of the surroundings.

Piaget's stages parallel Freud's and Erikson's in interesting but distinctive ways. From birth to age two, he calls the *sensorimotor stage,* during which the child discovers the relation between sensations and the ability to decide how to deal with them. From two to seven years of age, the child is in the *preoperational stage,* learning to use symbols, especially language, to deal with objects or events. Children learn the words for "house" and "baseball," but always in the context of actions relating to them, and thereby creating mental images of them. In the *concrete operations* stage (ages seven to eleven), mastery of logical operations is achieved, such as understanding concepts like conservation of mass, number, weight, and the solving of mathematical problems. *Formal operations* begin about the time of puberty, and extend throughout the remainder of adult life. This stage involves the ability to form hypotheses about objects, events, and even concepts only concretely understood before. For example, a younger child may understand how a baseball behaves when hit by a bat, but at the formal stage, there develops an understanding how spheres in general might behave under hypothetical conditions; how a planet yet undiscovered might orbit our sun if found to exist at such-and-such a distance moving at a specific velocity.[29]

These three theorists portray the development of human nature in terms of naturally determined stages, which appears to leave little room for what a Christian ethicist seeks in trying to understand moral and spiritual development. Of the three, Freud asserted that moral development is rooted in the superego, which is somewhat akin to the notion of conscience, but is biologically, not spiritually derived. Erikson finds the conscience to originate during the basic trust vs. mistrust stage and to be developed during elementary school years amid the demands for mastering social and learning skills. Piaget provided a two-stage theory of moral development, the first that of "heteronomous morality," deriving from the authoritarian environment of the preschool and school-age child. During this period, morality is a matter of obeying rules imposed from outside the child. During adolescence, the youngster begins to develop an "autonomous morality," making rational decisions among the many possible ethical alternatives presented by peer group and society. Such decisions require that the person has arrived at the stage of formal operations.

Lawrence Kohlberg

Lawrence Kohlberg, a Harvard psychologist, has extended and refined Piaget's theory, and proposes that moral development occurs in six distinct and irreversible stages. Stages 1 and 2 he calls *preconventional* and divides them into obedience-and-punishment and hedonistic-instrumental. In these stages the child obeys to avoid punishment, and is motivated by a selfish desire to obtain rewards. Stages 3 and 4 are grouped together as the *conventional* stages of "good boy–nice girl," and an acceptance of social conventions in a law and order mentality. The *postconventional* stages include 5, the *social contract* orientation, wherein morality is based on agreements (largely pragmatic), and 6, the quest for a *universal ethical principle*. In this later, the most mature level, behavior is controlled by an internalized and highly personal set of values based on abstract concepts like universal fellowship, the equality of human rights, and some form of the Golden Rule. Kohlberg assumes these to be truly self-chosen, and not merely conditioned into us as the behaviorists would have us believe.[30] More recently he has suggested the possibility of a seventh stage, more clearly religious in substance, nothing that "indoctrinative" aspects may be required.[31]

A critic has noted that while "Kohlberg's higher stages of moral development reflect the ways in which Western conceptions of law have evolved . . . they do not necessarily hold across different cultural contexts."[32] Others have objected that even within Western culture, Kohlberg's observations are not as applicable to women as to men because of the differences in child-rearing practices for the genders.[33] Yet there is no quarrel with the contention that, however one structures the different stages, whether Kohlberg's or his predecessors, all arise within the process of nature, unaided by supernatural intervention. Even Kohlberg, who is free to acknowledge his sympathy with theism, denies that the Deity interferes with nature's processes.

The most rigorous insistence on defining human nature within the framework of biological processes comes today from *sociobiology*, which constitutes almost a new movement within the scientific community. Originally the title of a book by Edward Wilson of Harvard, sociobiology proposes that biology is the key to human nature. All behaviors are genetically determined. Neither courage nor altruism prompts our actions, not even the most (seemingly) generous impulse; all represent biologically evolved traits to ensure the survival of the species.[34]

Wilson based his theory on studies done almost entirely among insects and extrapolated to the human species. Another sociobiologist, Mary Batten, notes that some behaviors, though natural, are socially counterproductive, as in the example of rape. "Rape evolved as an adaptive strategy benefitting males who lost out in competition for mates," in which case survival-of-the-less-fit may prevail to the detriment of the fittest.[35] That such behaviors cannot be tolerated within human society is acknowledged: "Demonstrating a genetic bias toward a certain kind of behavior does not justify its perpetuation in society. The tendency toward rearing the maximum number of offspring could mean environmental disaster."[36]

Reducing ethics to sheer naturalistic descriptions leaves at least two major problems. Philip Wogaman notes that the first group places ethics solely within the framework of developmental psychology, leaving us without any normative position for making judgments. For Kohlberg to state that his stage 6 is morally preferable to stage 5 or even stage 1 begs the question: "On whose scale of value?" One cannot argue that old age is better than youth just because it is late and irrevocable. We may agree with Kohlberg, but our agreement has to come from some standard apart from the stages themselves.[37]

Secondly, Wogaman notes, the assumption that morality is essentially a cognitive matter, as Piaget in particular insists, omits the fact that one's ability to rationalize certain behaviors is no guarantee that such a person's character is of superior moral quality than someone less favored with intelligence. We have all known people who were brilliant but corrupt, or whose earlier idealism eroded while the person backslid in a distinctly reversible pattern of behavior. Further, people of highest moral character have often lamented their inability to sustain such standards: "Our moral conceptions may be considerably higher than our pattern of behavior. Did not Paul write, 'The evil I do not want is what I do' " (Romans 7:19)?[38]

Some transcendent court of appeal is needed if the contributions of psychology and biology to understanding human nature are to be evaluated. This is not because these fields are deemed incapable of making important statements of their own. Nor is it because the natural sciences are per se antithetical to a theistic view. Rather it is to note that the conclusions of these disciplines are based on observation, which itself is morally neutral, while the tacit implication (that either there is no God involved in these natural processes, or that if a deity exists, that fact is an irrelevance) is not a morally neutral position.

The Christian risks the charge of arrogance in suggesting that a biblical view provides a normative position from which to offer an evaluation. Yet it is an unavoidable risk if we are to make a case for Christian ethics. All Christians acknowledge the realms of nature to be God's handiwork, and include human nature and character within the natural framework. What they object to is the position that Nature (with a capital N) is "all there is," and that humankind is only one product among all others of purblind natural processes. Such a concept fails to do justice either to the potential greatness of humanity that strives to move beyond the confines of nature toward a moral perfection, or to the stubborn reality of humankind's willful self-violation throughout its bloody history.

RECOVERING A BIBLICAL PERSPECTIVE

The Genesis accounts of Creation have no parallel in any of the other great religions of the world in the sheer grandeur of the presentation of a Deity, whose providence establishes the relationships of all aspects of nature, then creates humankind "in his own image." It has often been pointed out that the two accounts in Genesis contradict each other on some important particulars.[39] The discrepancies notwithstanding, the primary message is clear: God is no mere "cosmic urge" or "primal cause," but a personal Deity whose command: "Let there be . . . " was one of conscious deliberation. The creation of humankind, both male and female "in our image" (note the plural) establishes that God transcends gender, but also clarifies humankind's unique relationship to the Creator.[40] Further, God's fashioning Adam from the dust of the earth (underscoring our affinity with elemental nature), and breathing into his nostrils the breath of life, clarifies that a human being is not essentially a soul inhabiting a body, but a body made alive by God. This eliminates the dualism of classical philosophy.

The story of Creation reminds us that we are defined not by our biological roots nor by the boundaries of our physical nature, but by God's summons. We are called into being and defined by our Creator, and this with specific reference to himself. Here we gain a theomorphic concept of man, rather than an anthropomorphic concept of God.

The conflict between those who insist on the historic accuracy of Genesis and those who embrace the view of natural science may be ameliorated by understanding Creation as "an Epiphany of God"[41] and evolution as a process guided by the Creator toward a fulfillment whereby humankind might enter into full, rational, and loving fellowship with God. To defend the literal message of Genesis, notes Lenn Goodman, is fraught with the irony that the believer, in the very act of testifying faith in Creation, might strip Creation of its significance as a manifestation of Deity. Creation may be a fact, but it is robbed of its full significance when reduced to a mere fact.[42] By the same token, defenders of evolution may overplay their position when they extrapolate from perhaps quite accurate descriptions of physiological origin and development to psychological, moral, and spiritual development. This point has been powerfully put forth by Nobel laureate Sir John Eccles.[43]

Curiously, the Hebrew Bible does very little with the "image of God" concept,[44] beyond inferring in the passages already quoted (and in Genesis 5:1–3; 9:1–7, and Psalm 8) the exceptional relationship of humans to God and to nature. Nor do Hebrew Scriptures suggest that the Fall destroyed that image in humanity.

The story of the Fall of Adam presents human nature in a profoundly neg-ative light. The writers of Genesis do not entertain the question of why God did not give Adam greater strength of character, probably because it was obvi-ous that to be fully human, freedom of choice is necessary. Did not God foresee that granting freedom entailed a risk that humankind might become estranged from God? The recognition of this is acknowledged in the New Testament con-cept that the Word of God, which created the world and later "became flesh and dwelt among us" (John 1:14), did indeed foresee the hazard, and planned ahead for the resolution of the problem: "The world was made through him, yet the world knew him not. . . . But to all who received him, who believed in his name, he gave the power to become the children of God, who were born not of blood nor of the will of the flesh nor of the will of man, but of God" (John 1:10–13).

It must be acknowledged, of course, that Hebrew Scriptures do not an-ticipate this Johannine interpretation. The story is told in picturesque simplic-ity of Adam's sin by which he forfeited his special relationship to God. But the sin does not appear to arise from rebelliousness, nor from an arrogant will-to-power as is usually proposed in Christian theology. Adam is no Promethian hero striving against God. In fact it is not Adam, but Eve, who first hears the seductive appeal of the serpent that to learn the distinction between good and evil would make them like God. Adam simply acquiesces.[45] Almost immedi-ately they become aware of their physical nakedness, a metaphor for spiritual exposure. Their reaction is to conceal their nakedness from each other, then try to hide from God.

An important clue to the Genesis author's understanding of the human condition is revealed in Adam's reply to God's summons: "Where are you?" God clearly knows where they are physically, but Adam's answer is existential: "I was afraid." Sin leads to alienation and alienation to fear; the response to "Where are you?" is "in fear." Greek mythology might show a Sisyphus hero-ically defying the gods, but Adam is merely pathetic. The God against whom he sins is not a tyrant, but a God of love and creativity, who desires and pro-vides the best for his creatures. Adam merely wants his own way. Apprehended, he blames first his wife, then tries to shift the blame to God himself: "The woman . . . whom thou gavest to be with me. . . ." Eve blames nature, in the form of the serpent. Only at last do they confess, and are exiled from Eden.

The story of humankind is thus sketched out for us: We were created to live in fellowship with God, but by free choice "all we like sheep have gone astray" (Isaiah 53:6), and we continue to blame it on each other, on nature, or on God. But nowhere in the Hebrew Scriptures do we find the Fall of Adam utterly destroying the image of God in humankind. God continually strives and even pleads with his people. "Come now, let us reason together . . ." (Isaiah 1:18). The Hebrew writers make clear their understanding of humankind's pro-clivities to sinful behavior, but there is lacking a real doctrine of sin. By the same token, there is no clear doctrine of immortality; the Pharisees believed in the resurrection of the dead, but the Sadducees did not. Further, the connection between sin and death, and the prospect of life for sinful humanity beyond the grave is vague.

In the New Testament, on the other hand, these concepts come into sharp relief. The connection between sin and death is made explicit (Romans 5:12, 6:23), and the loss of the *Imago Dei* appears central to understanding why Christ came to identify with sinful humanity, died, and was raised from the dead. Adam is seen as the prototype of humankind (*protos anthropos*); Christ is the "second Adam," with whom we are to be united: "As in Adam all die so also in Christ shall all be made alive" (1Corinthians 15:22). The concept *In Christ* is for Paul no mere figure of speech, but one of ontological union. Christ, as the true image of God, exchanged his form (*morphe*) of God for the likeness of humanity (again *morphe*, meaning mode of existence), in order to invite us to exchange our nature (as old Adams) for the new life, literally a "new being." This new nature "is being renewed in knowledge after the Image of its Creator" (Colossians 3:10).

While it is impossible (or certainly incorrect) to speak of *the* biblical view of human nature, certain themes emerge with great consistency. (1) *We are mortal;* "all flesh is grass . . . the grass withers and the flower fades . . ." (Isaiah 40:6–7). Part of Adam's temptation in Eden was to gain knowledge that would enable him to be like God, and live forever. Failing this he (we) sought to overcome mortality by creating things so enduring that we could sustain the illusion of our own permanence: a tower, a temple, a cathedral, a skyscraper, a family genealogy that spans generations. "The hope and belief is that the things man creates in society are of lasting worth and meaning, that they outlive or outshine death and decay, that man and his products count."[46] Among things we create there is also the cult of the hero, the figure whose wisdom or might conquers all, and successfully challenges fate and even the gods. But though we try to identify with this hero of our creation, we know he is our own creation, and while the hero has the power to inflict death, he cannot overcome it.

(2.) *We are sinful creatures*, prompted to oppose the will of God by pride, by passion, by the social institutions we have created and which we must serve. Whether we object or not, we must pay taxes to support wars, questionable government programs, sales of weapons to predator nations for profit, and policies many Christians would not tolerate in the private sector. The biblical writers do not equivocate on the sinful nature of humanity, the Psalmist declaring, "There is none that is good . . . all alike are corrupt" (14:1–3), and even a "twice born" Christian like Paul confessing, "I can will what is right, but I cannot do it" (Romans 7:18), and concluding "Whatever does not proceed from faith is sin" (Romans 14:23).

(3.) *We are ignorant creatures*, apparently unable to learn the lessons of history, or penetrate the future, or even to fathom the depths of our ignorance about ourselves.[47] God's challenge to Job: "Who is this that darkens counsel by words without knowledge?" is addressed to Everyman. The meaning of life eludes us today no less than it did the writer of Ecclesiastes, who pronounced "all is vanity," and it was neither sarcasm nor despair, but a searching honesty that compelled T. S. Eliot to ask:

> *Where is the Life we have lost in living?*
> *Where is the wisdom we have lost in knowledge?*
> *Where is the knowledge we have lost in information?*
> *The cycles of Heaven in twenty centuries*
> *Bring us farther from God and nearer to the dust.*[48]

Yet the Bible's estimate of humanity is by no means all negative. God's ultimate compliment in creating us in his image brings with it a special gift: (4) *We are, potentially at least, reasonable creatures.* We are invited in Psalms and Proverbs to "seek wisdom," and in Isaiah, to reason with the Lord. (5) *We are also creatures capable of love,* the highest quality of godly life, and with which Paul seems to suggest we can make our reason more effective: "Though I understand all mysteries and all knowledge . . . and have not love I am nothing" . . . but if we do have love, wisdom and reason can enable us to perceive our mortal, ignorant, and sinful state and turn in repentance to God. The promise is that, if we seek God with all our hearts, we shall find him (Jeremiah 29:13), and the Gospels make it clear that if we accept God's gift of forgiveness in Christ, and become one with him, we will share the victory of Christ over sin and death (John 17:20–26; Romans 8:1).

Scriptures tell us still more about the human condition. For example, they tell us that we are all one family, God being no less the Father of the Ethiopians, Philistines, and Syrians than of Israel (Amos 9:7; Isaiah 19:25). Furthermore, we are responsible for the well-being of all, because when we serve the needs (or neglect the needs) of "the least of these, my brethren," so we have treated Christ (Matthew 25:31f.).

Perhaps the most critical revelation is that humanity is completely dependent on God, not alone for life and all that sustains it, but for any hope of salvation. Humanity is unable to save itself from the consequences of its own folly, inasmuch as sin taints everything we attempt. Paul makes a unique triangle of the human self, in noting; "*I of myself* [i.e., through freedom of will] serve the law of God with my *mind,* but with my *flesh* (the worldly self), I serve the law of sin" (Romans 7:25). In crying out, "Who shall deliver me out of the body of this death?" Paul acknowledges that only an "outsider," that is, one sent from God, can effect our redemption. This in fact is Paul's whole Gospel: that Christ has come to liberate us from law, flesh, sin, and death (Galatians 2:19–21), and that this emancipation leads to sanctification, that is, to our transformation into the likeness of Christ (and the restoration of the image of God).

This is the eschatological hope, the future fulfillment for which our souls long, and that is promised to us in the Scriptures. It is not something that anyone can claim to have achieved as yet. Despite Christ's redeeming work, we mortals remain ignorant and sinful beings. Wars continue, and oppression festers on all parts of the globe. Even Paul confessed, "Not that I have already obtained this or am already perfect; but I press on to make it my own, because Christ Jesus has made me his own. . . . I press on toward the goal for the prize of the upward call of God in Christ Jesus" (Philippians 3:12f.).

What are the ethical implications of this? At the very least it means that Christians must acquire the grace to love, grace that dissolves all social, religious, and racial distinctions, and binds humankind into the family which God intended from the dawn of Creation. It also means much more, as we employ the gift of reason, disciplined by love, in the uses of the arts, education, economics, politics, science, and technology.

Meanwhile, we must still consider the problems encountered in achieving the Christian life.

BECOMING CHRISTIAN

The popular injunction that to become a Christian one must be "born again" will not withstand careful scrutiny. The words were not addressed to everyone who came to Jesus, but only to Nicodemus, and the latter had not come asking how to become a Christian. He had not even inquired about salvation (John 3:2f.). Jesus perhaps anticipated such a question, and gave the advice gratuitously, then chided Nicodemus for not understanding the words about being born again, traditionally used in addressing would-be converts to Judaism.

An important feature of Jesus' response to people who came to him was that he tailored his message to suit each person's private need. Thus to the "rich young ruler" who did come asking how to obtain eternal life (Luke 18:15f.), Jesus said nothing about being born again, but that the man must sell all his worldly possessions and distribute the proceeds to the poor. Perhaps the popular preference today for the advice to Nicodemus over the more stringent demand to the young ruler reveals something of our preference for spirituality over practical ethics.

Another popular slogan with reference to being a Christian is "all you need is love." This was a favorite phrase during the 1960s and 1970s, when situation ethics emerged on the American scene coincidental with the civil rights movement and anti–Vietnam War sentiments. It was also termed *the new morality* by those outside the Christian tradition, who concluded that the good life was one free from the strictures of organized religion. All we needed was love. The fact that the new morality may actually have begun as a Christian protest against rules/ethics and spilled over to the secular society is significant. It may demonstrate that what originates within Christianity still has relevance for non-Christians.

Nevertheless love as popularly understood is not sufficient either as a guarantor of the Christian life nor as a means of transforming the world from its violent and corrupting ways. It is one thing to affirm that God is love, and that the essence of Christian ethics is in our loving service to God and to our fellow humans in need. It is quite another matter to assume that confronting a warring world with love, and only love, is the full requirement of the Christian life. Stanley Hauerwas stresses this point in a most perceptive way: "The Gospel is not about love, but it is about this man, Jesus Christ. The ethic of the Gospel is not a love ethic, but it is an ethic of adherence to this man as he has bound our destiny to his, as he makes the story of our life his story.[49] Jesus, writes Hauerwas, did not come into the world "preaching platitudes about everybody loving everybody."

It may be argued that Hauerwas has overstressed his point; that inasmuch as "God is love," and Jesus said, "The Father and I are one," his gospel is about love. Of course he did not preach platitudes about everybody loving everybody. Nevertheless Jesus did say that love was *the* distinctive characteristic by which his disciples would be known (John 13:35). Hauerwas is correct in the recognition that most Christians have not understood the distinction between love as *eros* and love as *agape*. Eros is that natural form of bonding which arises from the life urge itself; it is necessarily defensive, egocentric, and life preserving; it may be identified with the procreative drive but also with the drive to protect one's home and offspring. It may even be considered "spiritual" in its hunger for immortal life (thus revealing most salvation religions as arising from *Eros*, who was in fact a Greek deity). What I call the *agape phenomenon* emerged as part of the Christian experience with Christ, who embodied God's love as transcending all earthly bonds, prepared to spend himself endlessly on behalf of friend and foe alike, even unto death. This is a love that most of the world rejects; indeed it is illegal to love one's enemy, especially in wartime (one definition of treason!). But it is the one quality of life that ultimately has the power to heal, unite, and build a new world.

Jesus calls us to become one with him in his mission of healing, of speaking the truth to a world fed on lies and diplomatic double-talk, and of establishing conditions of peace. But "not peace as the world gives peace" (John 14:27). Often it will be a controversial and even divisive peace, setting brother against brother (Matthew 10:21–34). Becoming Christian has its painful aspects.

The key to Jesus' invitation is that we are not merely to join a church but to join him, to become ontologically one with him. We are so to identify with him that we can say with Paul, "It is no longer I who live, but Christ who lives in me" (Galatians 2:20). This is the true atonement, at-one-ment, which requires no ritual or ceremony, but an emptying of one's self (as Christ emptied himself and took the form of a servant: Philippians 2:7), so that Christ might enter in, and become one with us and we with him, as he is one with the Father (John 17:21–23). Only then can love, which is God's love, not our own sentimentality, be effective in cleansing and redeeming the world. Only then can we become the "new creation," the old Adam made new in Christ.

Paul Tillich, who had a penchant for the trenchant, expressed this:

> If I were asked to sum up the Christian message for our time in two words, I would say with Paul: It is the message of a "New Creation." Let me repeat one of his sentences in the words of an exact translation: "If anyone is in union with Christ he is a new being; the old state of things has passed away; there is a new state of things." Christianity is the message of the New Creation, the New Being, the New Reality which has appeared with the appearance of Jesus who for this reason, and just for this reason, is called the Christ.[50]

All of us live in the "old state of things" until we are united with Christ, and even then we continue to participate in the evils of the "old" world. But persons justified (in the Pauline sense) and sanctified in Christ experience a transformation that equips them to relate to the old Creation in a new way, prepared to undertake Christ's work of cleansing, healing, and reconciling, and thus reveal the New Creation in the midst of the old.[51]

Sanctification, though it has its roots in the Hebrew concept of *Qadosh*, or "separateness" (as God's holiness makes him separate from his creation, wholly other), is more truly a New Testament term. In the Gospels and in other writings, it never implies taboo or untouchable (as was the Ark of the Covenant in 1 and 2 Samuel, to touch which was death), but saintliness: drawn apart from the contaminations of the world, and empowered with moral courage (see Acts 2:40f., 4:31–37, 9:13; Romans 1:7). In Hebrews 2:11, Christ is identified as the sanctifier (see 7:26–27).

But how does this come about? Christians are not born all of a sudden. Nor is there a formula by which one's union with Christ is to be achieved. If the experience of Nicodemus teaches us anything, it is that some kind of conversion is required, a turning around (the literal meaning of repentance). But more than that is needed if we are to become one with Christ, and as we have noted, the born again metaphor does not fit all cases, any more than does Jesus' advice to the rich young ruler. Paul's conversion on the Damascus Road is suggestive, inasmuch as it involved a background of religious growth and training, plus an encounter with Christ himself. Would the encounter have been as fruitful if Paul's background had been less well prepared by his active involvement in the religious life?

James Fowler, in a highly original contribution from developmental psychology, proposes that there are seven stages of faith by which we might become ready for such a conversion experience. As infants, he notes, we start with a *primal faith*, which involves bonding and attachment with parents or other caregivers. "The first symbols of faith are likely to take primitive form in the baby's hard-won memories of maternal and paternal presence."[52] At this point, Fowler is in accord with Freud, Erikson, and other developmentalists who have sought the origins of the religious experience in infantile attachments. Fowler then notes the introduction of language at about age two, and calls his second stage *initiative-projective faith*. The child, now able to move about and question everything, awakens to the mysteries of her surroundings, and especially of death, which she may experience in a pet or member of the family. This preschool child has now begun to symbolize internally and project subtle understandings onto the world.

The third stage is *mythic-literal faith* (which closely parallels Jean Piaget's concrete operational thinking of the early school-age child), and includes thinking about right and wrong, good and evil, and a sense of fairness based on reciprocity. Faith relies on stories and family values.[53] By adolescence, a significant alteration comes about which is not simply a "climbing the stairs to a higher stage." Fowler calls this a *synthetic conventional faith*, based on the use of formal reasoning and use of symbols to construct a synthesis of other people's wisdom and one's own. Fowler recalls St. Augustine's "Confession" of his own adolescence when he wrote, "I became a problem to myself." It is often a time of confusion and self-doubt, which finally emerges into the next stage: *individuative-reflective faith*. There is now an emergence of an "executive ego," a differentiation of the self behind the *personae* (masks) one wears and the roles one bears, from the composite of roles and relations through which the self is expressed. There is also now an objectification and choosing among the beliefs, values, and commitments identified in adolescence. There is an effort to achieve integrity of belief.

By mid-life, a new transition may be achieved, called *conjunctive faith*, evoked by the need to face and hold together certain "polar tensions" in life, such as awareness of being still young, yet growing old; of being curiously both constructive and destructive; of having both a conscious self and a "shadow self which recognizes the rights and validity of other people's faiths. Persons of Conjunctive faith are not likely to be 'true believers,' in the sense of an undialectical, single minded, uncritical devotion to a cause or ideology. They will not be protagonists of holy wars."[54]

The seventh and most mature level involves *universalizing faith*, a decentration from self and achieving a perspective no longer based on fears about one's own significance or worth, or even survival. One values above all the Creator, and the values loved by the Creator, including other persons, nature, and Creation itself. "From the paradoxical attachments and polar tensions of Conjunctive Faith, the person best described by universalizing faith has assented to a radical decentration from the self as an epistemological and valuational reference point for construing the world, and has begun to manifest the fruits of a powerful kind of *kenosis*, or emptying of one's self."[55]

Becoming a Christian, from Fowler's point of view, requires some such spiritual pilgrimage toward becoming a mature adult. It may be questioned whether *only* such persons can become Christian, but certainly one's readiness to achieve the conversion experience to the Christian life would be enhanced. Fowler does insist that in neither of the types of development represented by the psychosocial theorists or by faith development theory is development per se necessarily tied to the recentering of one's passion or restructuring of one's values or virtues. Yet

> conversion means a release from the burden of self-groundedness. It means accepting, at a depth of the heart that is truly liberating . . . the conviction that we are known, loved, supported and invited to partnership in being with One, who from all eternity intended us, and who desires our love and friendship. It means making an attachment to the passion of Jesus the Christ—a loving, committed, and ready-to-suffer passion for the in-breaking commonwealth of love.[56]

Thus, while it is true as Hauerwas pointed out that "Love's not all you need," love as *agape* remains the ultimate evidence of whether or not we have become one with Christ. The writer of 1 John put it succinctly:

> This is the message which you have heard from the beginning, that we should love one another. By this we know love, that He laid down His life for us; and we ought to lay down our lives for the brethren. Beloved, let us love one another for love is of God. Everyone who believes that Jesus is the Christ is a child of God. By this we know that we love the children of God, when we love God and obey his commandments. (1 John 3:11, 16, 4:7, 5:1,2)

THE CHRISTIAN VIS-À-VIS NON-CHRISTIANS

Despite the emphasis on love as an essential aspect of a Christian's relationship with others, there has also existed a certain reserve, a kind of exclusiveness that tempts Christians to regard non-Christians as being less worthy of fellowship or even of contact. We hardly need to be reminded that this attitude sometimes prevails even among Christians of different denominational loyalties. But the castigating of non-Christians as outsiders, as "unsaved" is at once more common and more blatant.

We think not simply of the smugness of ultraconservatives for whom their own tradition alone is virtuous. There appears to be some scriptural support for not being "unequally yoked together with unbelievers" (2 Corinthians 6:14) and keeping oneself "unspotted from the world" (i.e., from the world outside the Christian fellowship; see James 1:27). It should be noted, however, that Paul was not contrasting Christianity and other religions, but "righteousness and iniquity," or "light and darkness," or again "Christ and Belial" (the latter is a name for Satan). Some things are fundamentally incompatible, and Paul's concern was foreshadowed in his first letter to the Corinthians where (in 5:9ff.) he warns against associating with fornicators and idolaters. Even then, Paul says he cannot forbid all such contact, "since then, you would need to go out of the world." Paul not only does not restrict contact between Christians and non-Christians (as was the case between Jews and non-Jews); he does not forbid marriage with them either. Quite to the contrary, he declares, "The unbelieving husband is consecrated through his wife, and the unbelieving wife is consecrated through her husband" (1 Corinthians 7:14).

Until fairly recently in our history (c. early nineteenth century), the superiority of Christianity as an ethical system was assumed by most Christians. It was taken for granted that morality was inseparable from religion, and since religion meant Christianity (or at least the Judeo-Christian tradition), the ethics of nonbiblical philosophies was relegated to academics. During that century, the study of religion on a comparative basis revealed the implausibility of this view. "Theologians could no longer deny the fact of other systems of religious ethics. But even the highly sophisticated missionary theologian, Hendrik Kraemer, could still assert, "The Christian ethics is entirely incommensurate with all other ethics in the world."[57]

The origins of the collective egocentrism among Christians is itself something of a puzzle, given the world inclusiveness of Jesus' outlook (Matthew 28:19), and that expressed in John 3:16. But it can be traced to the earliest days of Christianity, and perhaps has its origins in the defensive posture against the Jews, who were their first persecutors. However that may be, it is still startling to read Eusebius's *Ecclesiastical History* (c. 324–325 A.D.), in which he describes "the fate which has beset the whole nation of the Jews from the moment of their plot against our Savior." It is more shocking still to read Origen's explanation of the anti-Semitism of his day: "Because of the crime of the Jews, the city [Jerusalem] perished utterly . . ." and Augustine's account: "The Jews who rejected him, and slew him, after that were miserably ruined by the Romans and were dispersed over the face of the whole earth."[58] But perhaps the most vitriolic attack against the Jews came from Chrysostum (John of Antioch, 347–407 A.D.), who having charged them with *deicide* (a word he coined) declared, "I hate the Jews because they violate the Law. It is the duty of all Christians to hate the Jews." Christians today can only be grateful that both the World Council of Churches and the Vatican have denounced Chrysostum's charge as false. At its organizing meeting in 1948, the World Council of Churches stated, "We call upon all the churches we represent to denounce anti-Semitism, no matter what its origin, as absolutely irreconcilable with the profession and practice of the Christian faith."[59]

It hardly needs documenting that prejudice among Christians has not been confined to rejection of the Jews. But we have entered a period of history when two powerful movements have begun not only to ameliorate animosity, but to establish positive links with the non-Christian world.

The first has been the missionary movement during and since the nineteenth century, which has been responsible for, among other things, expanded educational opportunity, medical and agricultural development in the third world, and the study of comparative religion. As already noted, this latter suffered some early mistakes including a paternalistic superiority complex. But as studies of other religions of the world advanced, a greater openness to diversity became characteristic. Further, similarities began to be noted in the tenets of Buddhism and Christianity (for example, an emphasis on compassion), and the fact that Judaism and virtually all the major religions contain some variant of the Golden Rule. These observations prompted for a time a new enthusiasm, that all religions are basically alike. In a spirit of misplaced generosity, many teachers of comparative religion sought a kind of homogenizing of the many faiths. This was unrealistic because in fact all religions are not alike, and we do not do them justice to minimize important differences.[60] Nevertheless, the new openness to people of non-Christian faiths has been a healthy corrective.

A second movement to create links with the non-Christian world has come from the reawakened concern for human rights. In much the way that justification by faith was the rallying cry of the sixteenth-century Reformation, liberation has emerged as perhaps the most powerful theme of our time. It is not a new motif in Christian history, but a recovery of a long-neglected Gospel emphasis. "Jesus came to bring liberation to the captives, freedom to the oppressed, good news to the poor. If liberation is meant for one, it is meant for all."[61] The realization has encouraged the transcending of boundaries of race and religion, and seeing all people everywhere in terms of the biblical call for extending justice and helpfulness to the whole human family precisely because we are God's family.

A chastening aspect of this recovery of a basic Christian concern is the discovery that it is not exclusively Christian. The U.N. Declaration on Human Rights is neither avowedly Christian nor even religious in the usual sense. It is arguable that such a declaration could only have arisen in a philosophical climate conditioned by religious concern, but it is also a reminder that God has often worked through secular channels to accomplish his will (Isaiah 10), when people of traditional faith have hardened their hearts. The rights of all people to life and liberty, to freedom from want (to say nothing of freedom from arbitrary arrest and torture), to freedom of movement, and a host of other liberties are sought on behalf of the world's oppressed people by many non-Christian organizations.

It nevertheless remains true that the Christian tradition, Catholic and Protestant, has been the most vigorous of agencies in enunciating the theoretical foundations for the rights of people to the many freedoms that make life human. This theoretical undergirding derives from the theological concept of the inner link, the *imago dei* that holds individual, social, and life-giving human rights together. Our shared humanity is a given because of belief in the Fatherhood of God, and because we all share the *imago dei*. It is not accidental that discussion of human rights has become central to the agenda of the entire ecumenical movement.

Nor is it accidental that so many in the secular world who work for securing human rights have been educated within the context of the Christian tradition. Neither is it altogether surprising that there has been a corresponding withdrawal from concerns about human rights among those who openly reject that tradition. Marxists, for example, in 1948 officially repudiated human rights as a "bourgeois ideology" for the veiling of capitalist exploitation.[62] This may shed some light on the paradoxical situation in which, despite their countless protestations of concern for the workers of the world to throw off their chains, Marxists built walls to prevent freedom of movement of those workers. The dismantling of those walls, which began in 1989, was not only a repudiation of the ideology that put them there, but evidence of a hunger to reassert the basic human need for free association within the human family. The Commission of the Churches for International Affairs (CCIA) of the World Council of Churches declared in its 1974 meeting, "All human rights, be they social, economic, religious, or political are interrelated. They must be taken as a whole."

The task of the Christian vis-à-vis non-Christians is to recognize in each human being the *imago dei*, and to accept each person as a member of God's family. Various lists of human rights have been drawn up by both Roman Catholic and Protestant councils, in an effort to clarify the parameters of Christians' responsibility. The 1974 Roman Synod of Bishops, for example, listed after the "right to life," the "right to nourishment," certain socioeconomic, cultural, and political rights, and the right to religious freedom. This closely resembles the list of the CCIA conference of that same year. Of crucial importance, as Jurgen Moltmann points out, is recognition that "the Christian faith has over and above the different rights and duties of humanity, to esteem the indivisible dignity of the human being in his or her life with God—without in doing so, excluding other religious or humanistic conceptions of human rights."[63]

Without sacrificing religious integrity, but indeed fulfilling its demands (when we recall the meaning of *re-ligio*: to bind back, or connect again), the Christian will seek opportunities for creative dialogue with both fellow Christians and non-Christians. Paul Tillich observed, "Religion and Christianity are under strong accusation that they have not brought reunion into human history." This, he noted, is because Christians, no less than the non-Christians, still live for the most part as creatures of the Old Being, the unredeemed Adam. "Nothing is more distinctive of the Old Being than the separation of man from man."[64] Many Christians still live on the wrong side of the resurrection, where the power of separation and death were nullified. The resurrection proclaims a new state of things, a new reality, a new way of understanding human nature. The Christian person is one who has known the risen Christ, responded to his summons to become one with him in being a channel of God's reconciling love to the world, welcoming every opportunity to serve as an agent of liberation among all people.

CHAPTER SIX

Sexuality and Christian Ethics

Most religious traditions, and monotheistic ones in particular, have agreed on the concept that human sexuality is a special gift by which we are granted the privilege of participating in the miracle of forming new life. This takes place not merely by urge or instinct, but in the context of loving and responsible decision. It is this that makes sexuality and procreation of ethical concern. How it finds a distinctively Christian expression is our focus here.

The Bible contains no specific word for sex,[1] yet its concern for the quality of sexual behavior, including judgment against abuses of sexual relations, is almost as insistent as its concern for faithfulness in love and the stability of marriage and family life. Chapter 7 examines familial issues and problems in greater detail, but a preliminary word is in order here as we explore sexual ethics in a Christian context.

In our contemporary situation with its much discussed sexual revolution, premarital sex, sexual harassment, sexual child abuse, and the transition away from the once prized nuclear family, considerations of the sex-love relationship (that now include homosexuality and serial marriage) seem not to be greatly influenced by appeals to the Bible or Christian tradition. Amid all the changes, Harvey Cox confesses to a "queasy" feeling about such sentimental celebrations as Christian Family Sunday because, he notes, the Scriptures do not present a consistent argument for the nuclear family, with a father and mother dutifully nurturing a close-knit brood of children.[2] Further, Jesus declared that his preferred family was not his parents and siblings, but rather those among whom he worked (Matthew 12:48) and who were even prepared to reject father and mother if necessary to serve the kingdom (Luke 14:26).

This is not to suggest that the Bible and Christian tradition are irrelevant or that Jesus was not interested in marriage and family life as important ways to respond to God's summons to a life of faith. Too much of Scripture can be cited to demonstrate the contrary. Indeed, James Gustafson laments the fact that ethicists have given so much attention to the *problems* of sexuality they have often neglected the *purposes*, which he takes to be the formation of families, a position also held by Stephen Post.[3] Yet Jesus' declaration just quoted reverses an old cliché about blood being thicker than water. In the community of faith the water of baptism is thicker than blood; baptized persons become members one of another as their bodies are "members of Christ" (1 Corinthians 6:15; Ephesians 4:25). Through baptism, a Christian transcends the sheer happenstance of being born into an organic, genetically related family.

Controversies to consider in the next two chapters include those particularly related to sexuality (not excluding the "maleness" of God), birth control, homosexuality, and abortion. We also examine some of the many interpretations of love and how they relate to sexuality, and yet are distinct from it. Finally, we have to face the present crisis in marriage, which Emil Brunner called "the most difficult problem with which a Christian ethic must deal. For not only are we here dealing with the very foundations of human existence, but here too all ethical problems are condensed into a complex at one point."[4] What an ethic has to say on these matters may be a measure of its value in dealing with others.

BIBLICAL PERSPECTIVE

It is clear from the Genesis account that God created us male and female for the purpose of procreation (Genesis 1:28; 2:15–25; 9:1, 7; 35:11). It is to this that Jesus appeals in his reference to marriage (Mark 10:6–9). Sexuality is a part of the established order. The words for man (*adam, gebar, ish*) have the implication of strength, Genesis 2:7 providing a bit of wordplay (*adam,* man and *adamah,* earth): Adam: "earthly man" (note Romans 5:12, where sin came into the world through this earth-man). *Gebar* specifies strength, even heroic qualities. Woman (*ishshah*) is the feminine of *ish*, and in later literature took on the attributes of softness and compassion that a male-dominated culture assigned. God's creation of humans "male and female in the image of God" (Genesis 1:27) reflects both the strength and compassion that were deemed to be part of God's nature. In the developing patriarchal culture of the Hebrews, the "Fatherhood" of God became the accustomed reference, and this is reflected in common names given to children: Eliab, "My God is Father" (*El,* a name for God, and *Ab,* the prefix for Abba or father), Abraham, Abimalech, Absalom, Abija, and so on. But the strict maleness of God was apparently not the intent of the earliest Hebrews, nor of the early Christians.[5] God, whose name *Jehovah* was not to be pronounced among the Hebrews (who verbally substituted *Adonoi,* The Lord), to avoid idolatrous objectification, was essentially Spirit, transcending anthropomorphic attributes including gender. Christians were later reminded that "in Christ there is neither male nor female" (Galatians 3:28). Gender designations are ultimately nullified as far as rank or value is concerned among Christians. The question remains how we are to accept our gender differences and live with them creatively to fulfill our mortal needs (and God's requirement) to "be fruitful and multiply."

For the Christian ethicist, there are numerous problem areas demanding attention. These range from private sexual acts and decisions (like masturbation and use of artificial methods of birth control, both condemned by the Roman Catholic church),[6] and questions of institutional sexual discipline, like celibacy and sexual equality, to matters of wider public concern such as obscenity and pornography, abortion, and homosexuality. Overarching this whole complex is the question whether we are in the midst of a so-called sexual revolution, or merely experiencing one of many recurring changes in mores that inevitably accompany social evolution. We address this general question before considering the more specific topics.

HAS THERE BEEN A SEXUAL REVOLUTION?

The much publicized sexual revolution, monitored by social psychologists and others since the Kinsey report of the late 1940s, is thought by some to be little more than the tendency of every generation to conclude that its youth have gone astray.[7] Great changes have nevertheless taken place in the past generation that have had more far-reaching consequences than anything seen in many generations before. We may consider, for example, that before 1915, 75 percent of first-time brides were virgins; in 1982 the figure was down to 43 percent. Of the 57 percent of unmarried women who engage in premarital sex, nearly one-third will become pregnant and only 35 percent of those will marry before the baby is born.[8] Since 1969, the number of out-of wedlock births among American teenagers has increased 139 percent, twice the rate in England and seven times higher than in the Netherlands.[9] A decade ago America recorded 430,000 teenage abortions each year, 240,000 illegitimate births, 12 million young Americans with sexually transmitted disease, and a rise in cervical cancer among sexually active women.[10] In 1992, a million teenagers became pregnant; 50 percent resorted to abortion. Teenage childbearing is judged to be one of the major sources of poverty in the United States, costing the federal government more than $16 billion annually in cash assistance, food stamps, and medical care.[11]

The current sexual situation, often portrayed as a new morality, appears to have its roots in the 1960s. "Between 1938 and the mid-1960s, incidence of pre-marital intercourse was fairly stable for college men and women: around 55 percent for men, and 25 percent for women."[12] In studies done after 1955, nine of fourteen studies showed coital incidence for females up to 40 percent and for males up to 60 percent. A 1989 text quotes a University of Georgia study placing the latter figure at 77 percent.[13] A study at an Ivy League college revealed that most students considered virginity to be a deviant condition rather than the norm, and a 1992 text states that "About 95 percent of men and 80 percent of women participate in sexual intercourse before marriage."[14]

The specter of sexually transmitted disease, which many had thought would diminish with easy access to prophylactics, has actually increased with 100,000 new cases of syphilis reported each year in the United States, a million new cases of gonorrhea, and 20 million cases of incurable herpes.[15] The most devastating consequence of the new sexual activism has been the emergence of acquired immune deficiency syndrome (AIDS). Deaths from AIDS in the United States rose from 644 in 1983 to 11,713 in 1986, and were expected to reach 179,000 by 1992. However, by September 1992, the figure had already approached 300,000.[16] The World Health Organization projects 40 million cases worldwide by the year 2000.

The causes of the sexual revolution are not clearly defined, and it appears that unwanted pregnancies and deadly disease have not been significant deterrents to its acceleration. It has been maintained that social class, education, and religion are correlated with the changes in mores. The famed Kinsey report of 1948 found that unmarried people in the lower social strata were more sexually experienced than those from middle and upper middle classes.[17] By the mid-1960s, such distinctions were fading,[18] but it was found that premarital intercourse was more common among youth who did not go beyond a high school education.[19] Some developmentalists have noted that "Adolescents who attend church are less likely to have had sexual intercourse than non-church goers."[20]

There is little question that the media have a profound effect on shaping public behavior, from hairstyles and clothing fads to taste in music and, according to many studies, morality. This latter was the major message of the Kefauver Subcommittee Report as early as the 1950s, the Eisenhower Commission study on "Mass Media and Violence" in the 1960s, the surgeon general's report in the 1970s, and the attorney general's report in the 1980s. People have always emulated their heroes and heroines, and when their favorite stars engage in premarital sex, adultery, and wife swapping, such role modeling is thought by many to encourage imitation.[21]

Sigmund Freud advanced the theory that civilization makes greater progress when sexual energies are restrained. Cambridge sociologist J. D. Unwin set out to disprove Freud's thesis, but after studying more than eighty ancient and modern primitive societies, he discovered an unvarying correlation between the degree of sexual restraint and the rate of social progress.[22] Pitrim Sorokin of Harvard came to the same conclusion independently: Sexually permissive cultures are less creative and intellectually vigorous than those that exercise moral restraints. With increased sexual freedom, a cultural decline follows.[23]

The implications of this for Christian ethics are numerous and challenging. If social class, education, church attendance, and the media are in some way correlated with public behavior, the Christian has some parameters within which to work. Since the beginning, Christianity sought to cross social barriers and unite people of all classes and races in a bond that their oneness in Christ provides. Education and worship have always been at the center of the Christian endeavor. As for the media, Christians may recall that (when not employing vindictive criticism or censorship), the Church historically has been a major patron of the arts and an agency for communicating the culture. The message that human sexuality is a gift of God, not to be misrepresented or abused for profit, has not been communicated effectively to those in charge of the entertainment media today. Yet significantly, the news media can generally be counted on to assist the churches in educating the public about their values and their contributions. Former Surgeon General C. Everett Koop was quoted in the *Los Angeles Times* (May 31, 1991) to the effect that while government spending for the care and treatment of AIDS sufferers has been declining, "some of the best social works aimed at the relief of the problems of AIDS have been organized by churches." With sensitive cultivation, other branches of the media primarily concerned with entertainment and information may follow.

PRIVATE SEXUAL CONCERNS

Private acts or decisions related to sexual expression, like masturbation and birth control, seem to many as rather quaint topics for controversy. The practices have become widely accepted as presenting few, if any, moral, medical, or psychiatric implications, except within the Roman Catholic church, which still condemns both.

Masturbation

Biblically, there is no objection (or even a reference) to masturbation. Onanism, or "the sin of Onan," in Genesis 38:8–9, is often misunderstood as synonymous with it, and in some states is the legal term for masturbation. But onanism refers instead to a situation in which Onan, brother of Er, refused to fulfill an ancient rule that if a man dies childless, the brother must impregnate the widow to perpetuate the family line. Onan's transgression was not masturbation, but coitus interruptus.

The Roman Catholic church has condemned the practice on the basis of its interpretation of natural law. In *The Sacred Congregation for the Doctrine of Faith,* it published a statement on January 15, 1976: "On the basis of the nature of the finality of the sexual faculty, masturbation is condemned as an intrinsically and seriously distorted act."[24] Protestant churches have as a rule taken the silence of Scripture as an indication that the practice has no theological significance. Medically it is of no interest unless overindulged and accompanied with pathological fantasies. "Masturbation engaged in during childhood and adolescence is not a sexual abnormality, and is considered by many authorities to be a necessary and desirable preliminary to adequate genitalization of the sexual drive as an adult."[25]

Catholic theologian Charles Curran, reacting to the strictures of the Church, observes: "The reality of masturbation always falls short of the ideal of human sexuality, and indicates a lack of total integration of sexuality in the life of the person, but such actions very frequently are not of grave moral significance or importance in themselves."[26] Protestant sex therapist Mary Mayo concurs, stating that as long as the practice does not become a neurotic fixation (which she identifies as a kind of idolatry), the Christian can take the silence of Scripture as evidence that "God apparently wasn't upset enough about (it) to be specific."[27]

Birth Control

On artificial birth control the Bible is silent, though it is probable that both Jews and Christians were aware that contraceptives were being used in Egypt; the oldest medical recipe for preventing conception is contained in the *Petri Papyrus,* dating back to 1850 B.C.

It is clear that the apostle Paul regarded sexual relations to be of benefit to married couples without expectation of pregnancy (1 Corinthians 7:5), though nothing is said about interfering with the natural process of conception. St. Augustine held that procreation was the natural consequence of intercourse, so contraception was a violation of natural law. In 1230 A.D., Pope Gregory was explicit in its condemnation, declaring it the equivalent of murder.[28] This may have stemmed from the fact that nothing was yet known about the ovum as the woman's contribution to the new life. The assumption was that the child was entirely from the father's "seed," any interference with which was tantamount to killing that father's lineage. Thomas Aquinas extended the prohibition against contraception on the grounds that enjoyment of sex without specific intention of creating new souls was inherently sinful.

Artificial birth control has traditionally been condemned by the Roman Catholic church, on the grounds that it contravenes the primary goal of human sexuality, which, for that church, is procreation. That conception is not the only purpose is clear from the fact that the Roman church permits the "rhythm method" by which intercourse may be avoided on "fertile days," all other bonds of affection being considered. This was reiterated at the Second Vatican Council and has been retained in official writings since 1962. The key for Roman Catholics is, and has always been, responsible parenthood.

The Protestant Reformers did not agree that the essential motive for marital relations must be procreation. By the eighteenth century Protestant churchmen were emphasizing "responsible parenthood," in recognition that some married couples should avoid parenthood until they were financially as well as spiritually prepared. The Anglican church, not considering itself Protestant, retained the dictum of the church of Rome against artificial birth control until the Lambeth Conference in 1920. In 1959, the Anglicans stated explicitly, "The responsibility for deciding upon the number and frequency of children has been laid by God upon the consciences of parents. . . . the means of family planning are in large measure matters of clinical and aesthetic choice (provided they are admissible to the Christian conscience)."[29]

In 1961, the National Council of Churches in the United States affirmed a similar position, reflecting the practice of many of its member churches, and in 1966, the World Council of Churches committed itself to a like stance in cooperation with the United Nation's demographic concerns. It stated that the ethics of today demand responsible parenthood, but stopped short of advocating specific means.

It is, of course, the *means* of responsible parenthood that remain the point of contention within some sectors of Christianity. By authorizing the rhythm method when the ovum is not in proper position for conception, the Catholic church has tacitly admitted, Aquinas to the contrary, that pregnancy is not only or even the primary justification for sexual activity. The rhythm method only avoids the stigma of "frustrating nature" mechanically or chemically. "Obviously," wrote Emil Brunner, "this means that the Catholic principle has broken down; sexual intercourse is permitted even when its aim is not that of procreation, but indeed when the latter is to be avoided."[30] In fact, states Catholic theologian James Burtchael, nothing could be more artificial than the rhythm method. "It inhibits not only conception, but the expression of affection. It is, in my opinion, a base theology that would want intercourse to harmonize with the involuntary endocrine rhythm of ovulation and menstruation, while forsaking the greater spiritual and emotional ebbs and flows which should govern sexual union."[31]

The Christian concept of love, based on an ontological union of persons wherein "the two shall become one flesh," as Jesus expressed it (Matthew 19:5), precludes the calculating use of each other merely for selfish pleasure. But it also puts to shame any prohibition of sexual freedom between married couples simply to accommodate the estrus cycle. Love is most richly experienced when two persons communicate with each other from the depths of their existence; when each can say to the other, "I give to you, and to you alone, my whole self from the center of my being."[32] Contraception can be the means by which a couple, dedicated to each other within the covenant of their God, share themselves wholly while awaiting the time when they can agree that their love and material resources have expanded to include the lives of children. When homes are thus lovingly planned, not only is private life fulfilled but the whole of society is thereby enriched. This would seem a superior ethical consequence to having families and society impoverished by irresponsibly begotten populations.

INSTITUTIONAL CONCERNS

Spiritual discipline sets boundaries to personal freedom. These limits to autonomy often create resentment in our individualistic age, but few who examine the situation carefully can disagree that giving free reign to every whim or desire would create anarchy. To cite a classic dictum, no one has the right to yell "fire" in a crowded theater when no such danger exists; the resulting panic and stampede might cost lives. To demand absolute freedom for all simply ignores the human weakness for ego expression that so often gives way to greed, oppression, and cruelty, a reality known even among those who deny the concept of sin. When, however, institutions like the Christian Church impose such stringent laws as celibacy, and deny equality to both sexes, ethical controversy is inevitable.

Celibacy was not unknown in biblical times; Jesus acknowledged that some people prefer to remain single for religious reasons (Matthew 19:2), and Paul preferred that single persons remain so (1 Corinthians 7:8), although this may have been due to his expectation of the imminent return of Christ. But at no point do the biblical writers require celibacy, because God's command to "be fruitful and multiply" had become integral to the life of faith. For Jews, it was unthinkable that people would avoid marriage; childlessness was regarded a great sorrow for a woman to endure (Judges 11:37). Marriage was "a duty to be performed for the sake of the law and for the preserving of the nation."[33] Thus it is difficult for Jews to understand why so many Christians insist that Mary, Jesus' mother, would remain the Virgin Mary throughout her life, in contradiction to her Jewish upbringing.

It is probable that most of Jesus' disciples were married, and it is certain that Peter, whom Rome calls "the first pope," was married (Luke 4:38). It is also known that Paul was not insensitive to the sexual needs of youth and, while he preferred the single life for himself, insisted that for most people "They should marry, for it is better to marry than to be aflame with passion" (1 Corinthians 7:9). Indeed there is great tenderness in Paul's encouragement of frequent sexual relations between husband and wife: "Do not refuse one another except perhaps by agreement for a season, that you may devote yourselves to prayer; but then come together again" (1 Corinthians 7:5–9).

The practice of celibacy entered Christianity through certain isolated aspects of Judaism, but primarily through Gnosticism, a philosophy later rejected as heretical. The Gnostics identified sex with the carnal world, which they believed was Satan's domain. This notion was augmented by Paul's concern that Christ's return to earth was drawing near, leaving no time for domestic commitments. The world had only a brief last hope to receive the Gospel (see Romans 8; 1 Corinthians 7; Galatians 5). Later, Chrysostom and Augustine would defend marriage as sacred, almost in opposition to the monastic life wherein celibacy was a useful rule for running the affairs of the order. By 692 A.D., a council declared that marriage might be acceptable before ordination for a deacon or priest, but not afterward; any married priest aspiring to rise to the post of bishop must give his wife up to a convent. By the Middle Ages, "celibacy was enforced upon clergy and upon monks, but lack of proper ethical principles led to appalling immorality."[34]

The leaders of the Protestant Reformation rejected enforced celibacy, not simply because of the difficulty of maintaining it or the frequent lapses that brought scandal to the Church. They contended that celibacy was wrong in principle, contrary to Scripture, and a distortion of God's gift of sexuality. It is true that under Henry VIII (who denounced papal rule, but not the Catholic church), enforced celibacy of the clergy was retained in 1539, but ten years later under Edward VI, marriage was allowed (then repealed in 1553, to be restored permanently in 1559). Martin Luther, in Germany, and John Calvin, in Geneva, were both married. Calvin pointed to the inconsistency in the Roman church's calling marriage a sacrament, then denying it to the very people who should set an example of the full Christian life.[35] Calvin also led the fight against the prevalent practice of treating women as chattel, whereby their every possession, and their own bodies, were regarded as the rightful property of the husband.

Roman Catholic theology never invoked celibacy as based on divine law, as sometimes inferred in Protestant writings, but acknowledges it to be a matter of ecclesiastical law and administration. Recognition of marriage among Eastern Orthodox clergy, and the granting since Pius XII and Paul VI of the ordination of former Lutheran pastors who are permitted to keep their homes intact, reflects a new ethos. It is clearly an ethical question that is being addressed in terms of both Scripture and social custom.

Sexual equality is another issue of major ethical concern. It is by no means a new one. It has been a point of contention ever since Paul insisted, "In Christ there is neither male nor female" (Galatians 3:28), against the background of Judaism's institutionalized inequality. For centuries, despite occasional celebrations of the memory of heroines like Deborah, Ruth, and Esther, women were officially of lower status than men. A daughter was always of lesser value than a son (Leviticus 12:1–5), and could in fact be sold for a debt by her father (Exodus 21:7), or even made a prostitute by her father (Judges 19:24). The word *wife* signified her role as "belonging to a man" (Genesis, 2:24f.), and though she might be the object of extravagant praise while young and beautiful (Songs of Solomon), and of great satisfaction when industrious and virtuous as a wife (Proverbs 31:10f.), she could be divorced easily (Deuteronomy 24:104; Isaiah 50:1; see Hosea 2:2).

It would be a misrepresentation to portray the lot of women in Hebrew society in wholly negative terms. A bridal price was usually exacted by the father before he would give a daughter in marriage, and once married her influence on the children gave her special honor. Sometimes she was of stronger character than her husband, and where there were other wives, the first was virtually queen of the harem, directing the affairs of the whole household (the dominance of Sarai in Abraham's house is a particularly striking example in Genesis 16; see also 1 Samuel 25; 2 Kings 4). Respect for one's mother was not only expected, but demanded on pain of severe reprimand (Exodus 20:12; Leviticus 20:9) and even a curse (Deuteronomy 27:16). Yet outside of marriage, a woman had little status and was at the mercy of relatives or charity. In a Jewish morning prayer, there was a thanksgiving in which the man thanked God that "Thou hast not made me a Gentile, a slave, or a woman."[36]

It is nevertheless probable that women held a stronger position in Hebrew society than elsewhere in the ancient world. Even in Greece, where Aristotle enunciated a "principle of equality," there was no compulsion for men to relinquish leadership to women. Men, according to Aristotle, have "by nature, a capacity to rule," which women do not; equality of skills (which he noted especially in mathematics) must be weighed against their capacity for "masculine-type" leadership. Unequal economic and political treatment of women is therefore required, according to Aristotle, by that very principle of equality! When the sanctions of male-dominated religious institutions are superimposed on such arrangements, it should not be surprising that unequal treatment of women would be perpetuated.

In the New Testament, a change in the status of women is immediately apparent. Women figure frequently and prominently in the ministry of Jesus, in all four Gospels but especially in Luke. The birth narrative is told from Mary's point of view. The names of Mary and Martha, of Mary Magdalene, and "the other Mary" (unidentified in Matthew 28:1, but possibly the mother of James, as suggested in Luke 24:10), and the unnamed "woman at the well" are inseparable from the accounts of Jesus' life. Later, in the post-Resurrection church, despite the early influence of his Jewish past causing Paul to urge that women should "keep silence in the churches" (1 Corinthians 14:34), women became deacons and exercised considerable leadership and influence. They were dragged into prison along with the men for their religious activities (see Acts 8:3, 9:2, 18:26; Romans 16:1; 2 Timothy 1:5). It was Paul who, despite his latent separatist attitude drawn from his Jewish background, made clear the equality of men and women by declaring their differences null and void "in Christ" (Galatians 3:28). Old distinctions were done away; in place of separation there is communion; all are one in Christ.

How, then, are we to account for the continuing denials of equal rights for women? In non-Christian parts of the world the question is seldom asked.

There, as noted previously, the World Health Organization has revealed that women comprise half the population as elsewhere, but do two-thirds of all the work, receive only one-tenth of the income, and own less than 1 percent of the property.[37] But the perpetuation of inequality between the sexes in Christian societies remains a paradox, if not a contradiction of Christianity's early promise.

One reason for this condition may lie in the fact that most Christians live on the wrong side of the Resurrection. We retain many vestiges of pre-Christian patriarchal tradition, not the least obvious of which is found in the male-dominated clergy. The developing hierarchy of the early Church emulated the Old Testament model to a significant degree. Women who sought the religious life were directed into convents or abbeys, often founded and effectively led by gifted and scholarly abbesses. But these latter had limited influence on the centers of ecclesiatical power where men gained increasing power and wealth. This is not to suggest that all the men were simply power hungry; Aquinas, Francis, Benedict, and Loyola had no such worldly aspirations. Yet, as noted earlier, great wealth was amassed and often protected with military vigor and inquisitorial thoroughness. For centuries women were not allowed to sing in church choirs. Boys were trained instead and castrated before puberty to provide the desired high soprano voices. This practice was made illegal in Protestant churches during the Reformation, where women were encouraged to contribute to the worship life of the congregation (but not as clergy, except among Unitarians).

What the Church decreed in terms of separation and subordination was reflected in society in general until the nineteenth century, when in 1848, the Seneca Falls Women's Convention issued a demand for equality with men, giving a new emphasis to what the U.S. Constitution presumably stood for: "We hold these truths to be self-evident: that all men *and women* [italics mine] are created equal. The history of mankind is a history of repeated injuries and usurpations on the part of man toward woman, having in direct object the establishment of absolute tyranny over her."[38]

This is not the place to rehearse the subsequent battles for equal rights, though it is not amiss to note that despite many gains from the suffragette movement to recurrent efforts to add an Equal Rights Amendment to the Constitution, women still receive only 83 percent of men's salary for equal work done (for black women the figure is even lower: 79 percent), and overall, women with a college degree are making about the same wage as men with an eighth grade education.[39]

The social movement broadly designated feminism has been called "the most profound and global shift in human relations of the modern era."[40] It has risen in specific response to the failure of both the churches and the secular world to fulfill a principle made explicit in the constitutions of both, the principle of genuine and full equality. One of the chief obstacles to the fulfillment has been ironically the very reverence that Western men have traditionally reserved for women.

The pained include priests in the middle and older years who cherish a senti-mental view of womanhood in the image of a recent Marian piety, but who never consciously harbored anti-feminist sentiment, and who indeed revere the virtue of women. It is this very sentimentalism which may be the hand of those deter-mined to see human rights respected in the Church.[41]

There are those who, despairing of finding the Church in the vanguard seeking equal rights (where they assumed it should be), have shifted the em-phasis to *sexual politics*. As they describe the relationship, sex is a status cate-gory with political implications. It is precisely because certain groups have no representation in a number of recognized political structures that their position tends to be so stable, their oppression so continuous. Yet if we read correctly the history of the overcoming of other inequities in society, notably the secur-ing of civil rights for America's minority populations in the days of Martin Luther King, Jr., politics is often purified and strengthened by religious com-mitment. In Christianity the ground for such commitment is already present. Either we achieve parity in Christ, or we remain separate and unequal accord-ing to the variety of readings of civil law, nature, or politics. Greater progress does seem to be found in some socialist societies, but where equality is main-tained by force of government in the absence of a deeper commitment, it is a tenuous and unstable phenomenon. Governments come and go. Our oneness and our equality in Christ is forever grounded ontologically.

Yet a word is needed on the issue of equality of the sexes as it relates to ordination to the professional ministry. Many mainline Protestant churches have admitted women to ordination, but there are still some that have denied this expression of equality. The arguments are many, but perhaps the most common are two: one is enunciated by the Roman Catholic church as "a defect in Natural resemblance," whereby a female cannot embody the sign-value of the Holy Sacrament that is the gift of God (the Father), and of Christ (the Son), both male. The second argument is that of an "unbroken tradition," which must not be cast aside after so many centuries.[42]

The objection to both arguments, as presented increasingly by Catholic writers, points to the fact that the first rests on Thomistic sacramental theol-ogy, which overlooks the nature of God as spirit (John 4:24), and as love (1 John 4:16), transcending gender. Further, "given the sign-value of feminine humanity as one might analyze it today, Thomas' theology of orders may indeed provide an argument for ordination of women from reasons of fittingness."[43] As to unbroken tradition having normative value, one Catholic theologian notes that tradition often differs from biblical precedent, and besides, "We must con-front the profound truth of the sinfulness of the Church."[44] If tradition was so persuasive an argument, could we make a brief for retaining the institutional sins from the Inquisition onward simply because they were traditions?

Somewhat ironically, the best argument for the ordination of women to the priesthood within the Roman Catholic church (and it would be no less an effective model for other denominations) comes from the magisterial teaching in *Gaudium et Spes:* "With respect to the fundamental rights of the person, every type of discrimination whether based on sex, race, color, social conditions, language, or religion is to be eradicated as contrary to God's intent."[45] It remains to be seen whether the institution that holds such convictions will fulfill them; the history of ideas and ideals would seem to favor a positive outcome.

PUBLIC POLICY

Public policy on matters of changing sexual mores often follows institutional precedent, as in theocratic societies where religious regulation becomes civil law. This was true in ancient Israel, in Puritan America, and persists in most Islamic countries today where the religious institutions have set the standard. It is far less the case today in most Western nations, where the prohibitions of institutional religion on matters of obscenity and pornography, abortion, and homosexuality appear largely ineffective.

Obscenity and pornography are not biblical terms. The word *obscene* comes from ancient Greek theater, where any act deemed too violent or sensual for public viewing like murder or rape always took place "offstage" (*obscenus*). The ancient Hebrews considered nakedness obscene (Leviticus 20:17–19), when to force someone to appear naked in public was a dire form of punishment.[46] Similarly, *pornography* is of Greek derivation, referring to the writings of prostitutes. Because the biblical writers condemned prostitution, we can assume they would have condemned any lewd writings or depictions that tempt one to violate the laws against illicit sexual behavior, or which "cause one of these little ones to stumble" (Luke 17:1,2).

The development of institutional concern for suppressing erotic works of literature, art, drama, and the like, has an uneven history. The famous sculpture *Venus of Willendorf* (c. 15,000–10,000 B.C.) is thought to have been a fertility fetish intended to stimulate sexuality.[47] It was erotic, but not pornographic, nor is there evidence that it was ever proscribed, as were the fertility figures of Hindu India under the rule of the British in the nineteenth century. But long before the establishment of the Roman Empire, "every acceptable and unacceptable sexual practice that we know today (with the exception of obscene phone calls) had been sketched, painted, carved, or sculpted countless times." In no such instance is there any record of official prohibition.[48]

In the New Testament, we find a case of book burning, when converts who had practiced "magic arts" came together and voluntarily burned their books (valued at some "fifty thousand pieces of silver," according to Acts 19:19), but there is no reference to destroying erotic art. Throughout the early centuries of Christendom, it appears that condemnation was limited to apocryphal Scriptures and to writings considered heretical, as in the 170 A.D. *Muratorian Canon* and at the Council of Nicaea, 325 A.D. The first catalog of forbidden books, called an *Index* by the Roman Catholic church, designed to prevent "the corruption of morals" and the dissemination of theological error, did not appear until 1559.

By the time of the Reformation, theologians were condemning erotic works on moral grounds. Exposure to sexual stimuli was expressly to be avoided because of the dangers involved in inciting impure thoughts, initiating improper desire, and motivating prurient behavior.[49]

During the Reformation, a counterforce was posed against the authority of both Roman and Protestant churches in a wave of uninhibited publications flaunting illicit sexual practices.

> This trend had originated in the Renaissance, during which time sexual license and violence had followed the fanatic attempt of the medieval church to suppress the natural instincts of man. The freedom of expression which the writers and poets of the Renaissance enjoyed, and which lasted well into the English Restoration period, has been unequalled ever since.[50]

For illustration we have only to look into the writings of Boccaccio, Poggio, Aretino, Brantome, and, of course, Casanova. One historian relates that obscenities were not confined to literature: "Even exhibitions of human intercourse for the entertainment of special guests were not at all rare occurrences from the time of the Renaissance, through part of the eighteenth century in France, and it is well to remember that these exhibitions took place before mixed audience of men and women."[51] Another writer notes, "It is quite likely that the upper classes in the days of Louis XV were far more dedicated to what is now called the 'new morality' than people are today. Moral cynicism and contempt of rules ran deep."[52] To be sure, the French Revolution overthrew the corrupt court and destroyed the aristocratic class, but it also outlawed the Catholic church, whose clergy were accused of being in league with both king and aristocracy. The deism of the day had little use for the biblical God or for the older moral standards. Amid the crosscurrents of ethical opinion the Marquis de Sade (1740–1814) represented the most extreme form of libertinism. Every sexual excess was justified in his writings as evidence of one's freedom from the tyranny of religion. Nature was God, and laissez-faire sexuality, no matter how sadomasochistic, was regarded natural and therefore normative.

The effort to derive ethical principles for bringing obscenity and pornography under control has always foundered at two levels. First, there is no definition of either term on which courts of law, legislators, or even moral philosophers can agree. Second, even when some consensus has been reached on the definitional level, there has been little agreement about how to handle the problem.

Historically, the most vocal opposition was taken within the Calvinist tradition (most characteristically among the Puritans), and through the Roman Catholic tradition of canon law. For the Calvinists, the Bible, interpreted under the discipline of the Holy Spirit, was normative. Because the Bible strongly asserts the sinful proclivity of human nature, and lays on us the command to love our neighbor, the Christian was always to be on guard against temptations to misuse the gift of sexuality, and to be diligent to protect the innocence and sensitivity of others. "Temptations to sin are sure to come" they could quote from Luke 17, "but woe to him by whom they come! It would be better for him if a millstone were hung around his neck and he were cast into the sea."

Canon law 1399 (numbers 8 and 9) lists general classes of forbidden literature that "professedly discuss, describe, or teach impure or obscene matters."[53] This was revised after the Second Vatican Council. It remains true, however, that neither the Protestants' use of the Bible nor canon law have been successful in providing a definition usable in a public court of law to guide jurists or the general populace. The task is to distinguish *sensual idealism* and *erotic realism* from *pornography*. The first includes works of art and literature that utilize the nude figure and sometimes references to sexual activity, intended to enrich our appreciation of human potential. These include everything from classical Greek sculptures and the biblical Songs of Solomon to numerous Renaissance depictions by Michelangelo, Raphael, Rubens, and others; many poems and operas of the Romantic era; and contemporary works including photographic studies.

Erotic realism is known for its explicit sexual content presented to evoke psychological responses ranging from humor to horror, but stopping short of intentional stimulation of lust or the *prurient interest* (a term traditionally reserved for pornography). Eberhard and Phyllis Kronhausen would include in this category such items as the bawdy wit of Samuel Pepys's *Diary*, *Tom Jones*, Joyce's *Ulysses*, and the writing of Henry Miller, "whom we have called 'the apostle of the gory detail,' (who) is as realistic about bedbugs and lice in cheap Paris hotel rooms as he is about the underwear of the girls he slept with."[54]

Pornography, on the other hand, is designed to entice, to stimulate, and to gain acceptance for an aggressively erotic life. The Supreme Court definition makes it clear that sexual portrayal per se does not constitute obscenity, but only that which "taken as a whole appeals to the prurient interest," with the term *prurient* reserved for "material having a tendency to incite lustful thoughts." A distinction was made in the American Society of Criminology between soft-core and hard-core sexual literature, with the former not revealing the erect penis or an actual act of copulation; with the latter, "anything goes" including sadism and bestiality.[55]

It is probable that most Christians have little difficulty accepting sensual idealism as a legitimate part of our artistic and literary heritage. While many object to erotic realism on aesthetic and, in some cases, moral grounds, censorship is seldom considered a viable response. Pornography is quite a different matter, for as John Court notes in his study on *Sex and Violence*, the gradual acceptance of such soft-core magazines as *Playboy*, *Oui*, and *Hustler* has made the transition to hard-core material easier. "It is clear that without a period of widely available soft pornography, the present genre of pornoviolence would never have gained the acceptance it has." The rise in availability of sex litera-ture may be illustrated by its growth as an industry from $537 million in 1968 to $4 billion in 1980, to $8 billion in 1986, and $10 billion in 1990.[56]

The National Coalition Against Pornography, coordinating the efforts of leaders from seventy Christian denominations, has stated, "If Americans know what obscenity is, and know that the key to law enforcement is contemporary community standards, and know that those standards are established by citi-zens, they will rise up en masse."[57] The fact that citizens, including Christian citizens, have not yet risen up en masse may be due in part to the long history of disclaimers quoted in the media to the effect that "there is no evidence" of a linkage between pornography and crime. The 1970 Presidential Commission, for example, published that pornography was not harmful. Further, a widely publicized removal of restrictions on pornography in Denmark was purportedly followed by a decrease in "crimes of passion." Subsequent studies, however, have refuted both claims. Indeed, great amounts of research have been under-taken in the past fifteen years that support more traditional contentions about the influence of sexual literature on behavior, particularly the kind that com-bines sex and violence. Studies in the United States, England and Wales, Den-mark, New Zealand, Australia, and Japan revealed dramatic increases in rape reports between 1964 and 1974 (139 percent in the United States, for example, and 160 percent in Australia) after pornography laws were "liberalized." In Ha-waii, from 1964 to 1974, rape reports rose by 900 percent, but when restrictions against pornography were again applied in 1974, a significant downturn oc-curred in rape reports.[58]

The 1986 Attorney General's Commission on Pornography contended that a direct link exists between sexually violent materials and "anti-social acts of sexual violence." In its 2,000-page report, ninety-two specific recommen-dations proposed a wide-ranging crackdown on pornography at the federal, state, and local levels, noting that people who immerse themselves in such ma-terials are more likely to commit acts of sexual violence.[59] Disapproval of the report was immediate from several quarters, including the American Civil Lib-erties Union, which published a critique that it was "little more than prudish-ness masquerading behind social science jargon."[60] Others objected that the report encouraged censorship and government big brotherism, invading pri-vacy. In an effort to test the popularity of the report, *Time* magazine engaged Yankelovich Clancey Shulman to conduct a poll, the primary result of which showed that "The Meese commission is fully in tune with most Americans: both consider pornography a worrisome problem . . . the proportion of people who want government to crack down harder on pornography has varied only slightly since 1974. It was 74% then; it is 72% now."[61]

A member of the Justice Department's American University project on pornography and delinquency, Laura J. Lederer describes interviews with 35 men, serial murderers convicted of sex crimes involving 118 victims, which revealed that among the interests they had in common, pornography led the list. Judith Reisman of American University examined the three most popular soft-core pornographic magazines (*Playboy, Penthouse,* and *Hustler* with combined annual sales of $200 million), and found 2,016 child-related cartoons, 75 percent of which involved sexually violent activities including gang rapes and child molestation.[62]

The Christian searching for an ethical position that is not simply a reflection of prevailing secular opinion looks to a number of considerations. First, one affirms, in accordance with both Scripture and church tradition, that humans are created according to God's ordination. As God is good, so the gift of sex is good. Second, the misuse of any gift from God is to be denounced, and especially the sexual gift, which in most instances involves the rights and dignity of other people. Any misuse of sex that injures, demeans, or reduces another person to a mere tool for one's own satisfaction is clearly contrary to the Christian concept of the sanctity of personhood. Third, the enticement to the misuse of sex appears to be the primary purpose of pornography. Even so-called benign obscenity, which does not depend on violence for its appeal, depreciates a relationship that Christians have always recognized as sacred. Divorce statistics reveal that people who engaged in illicit sex before marriage are at far greater risk of marital breakdown than those who had maintained chastity as a discipline.[63]

A fourth consideration has to do with whether or not pornography does in fact promote specific acts of sexual abuse inside or outside marriage, including the sexual abuse of children and outright rape. This problem is likely to continue to be a point of heated contention for a long time to come, but the words of many who study the issue increasingly affirm a dark view. "Pornography is virulent propaganda against women," writes Susan Brownmiller. "It promotes a climate in which the ideology of rape is not only tolerated but encouraged."[64] The assault against women in pornography has been likened to antiblack and anti-Semitic attacks in literature, which prompted feminist Gloria Steinem to comment that for a woman, reading *Playboy* was something akin to a Jew reading a Nazi manual. Former president of CBS, Arthur Taylor, finds a direct link between pornography, violence, and child abuse. From his years of experience in broadcasting, he speaks of a "universe of moral corrosion supported by advertising, through promotion, by employment and salaries, by ownership, by equity interest. It is deeply imbedded . . . in the economic realities of the nation."[65]

Inevitably, when one advocates curbing the proliferation of pornography, the issue of censorship and violation of the First Amendment to the Constitution is raised. This is appropriate. No Christian can argue against freedom of speech thus guaranteed. Obscenity laws, however, are already in place and have been tested in the courts. It is quite within the constitutional prerogative of every Christian to insist that the laws be enforced. Where freedom has become license to promote that which is unlawful and can be shown to be injurious to the public (as the link between pornography and violence, child abuse, and sexually illicit behavior would indicate), the same rationale can be used for creating additional laws to curb its spread as is employed in outlawing certain drugs.

It is helpful to recall that the New Testament church was set in a non-Christian culture, which was both as religiously and morally pluralistic as ours. The early Christians saw their responsibility as one not of moral coercion, but one of serving as "leaven," gradually permeating the "whole loaf" of society (Luke 13:21; 1 Corinthians 5:6–7; Galatians 5:9). This is essentially the recommendation of Arthur Taylor, who warns, however, that "It would be foolish to underestimate the strength of the opposition. The three great television networks with their affiliated record companies have made the problem worse, not better." Yet he, and the American Coalition Against Pornography, are optimistic that an educated public can curb the abuses of the First Amendment and demand and receive a positive response from the media and publishing industries.

Abortion is a second issue at the storm center of public policy, and over which there is perhaps even more heated contention than about pornography. Many argue that religious considerations are irrelevant, inasmuch as abortion is nowhere mentioned in the Bible or other ancient sacred literature.[66] Others would contend with anthropologist Margaret Mead that abortion *is* a religious issue, and one from which the state should remove itself, agreeing only "on laws that require no citizen to violate what he or she understands as the will of God."[67] A third group would concur with theologian Karl Barth that abortion is a religious issue, and that sanctions should be invoked to forbid it as an act of murder, *except* in certain extenuating circumstances wherein abortion may provide the only humane solution.[68] A fourth position is taken by many feminists and other prochoice advocates who deny that abortion is murder, insisting that every woman has a right to determine extenuating circumstances in making decisions about her own body and her right to privacy. Meanwhile, the development of the steroid RU-486, which acts both as a contraceptive and a very early abortifacient, may shift the ground of argument inasmuch as it prevents the implantation of the fertile ovum (and thus, according to the argument, interdicts the development of a truly individual human life).[69] Each of these positions deserves examination before deliberation begins on whether abortion should come under legislative control. Even then the Christian ethicist may demur on other grounds.

First, we should examine the argument that the absence of the word *abortion* in Scriptures rules it out as a religious issue. The biblical writers omitted many terms familiar to ethical concern, like embezzlement, bootlegging, pimping, gambling, and suicide. Yet the practices are clearly within the framework of biblical judgment. We have only to consider the words of the Psalmist: "Thou didst form my inward parts, Thou didst knit me together in my mother's womb" (Psalm 139:13), or God's declaration quoted by the prophet, "Before I formed you in the womb, I knew you" (Jeremiah 1:5) to recognize that prenatal life was considered sacred and not to be treated carelessly. It is significant that the same Greek word *Brephos* was used to describe the fetus (Luke 1:41), and to refer to a newly born baby (Luke 2:12). From the moment of conception, in the biblical view, we are dealing with a human life. Its *ontos*, its essential nature, has been established by providence and the laws of nature. It is not only the case in New Testament thought that God knew us before we were conceived, and guided our development, but also that "those whom He foreknew He also predestined to be conformed to the image of His Son" (Romans 8:29). Abortion cuts irrevocably across that predestined path.

The early church fathers understood the religious implications of abortion, Tertullian including it under the category of homicide, which he regarded as one of three irremissible sins.[70] The Council of Elvira (c. 300) delivered a similar judgment, denying a woman Holy Communion if she underwent an abortion. Augustine, two centuries later, was more lenient, simply assessing a fine for the first abortion, but treating a second abortion as an act of murder. In the Middle Ages, Aquinas condemned the practice on grounds that it violated natural law and like all sin springs from an immoderate self-love.[71]

Protestant ethicists did not deviate significantly from the position of the Roman church in denouncing abortion until our own century. The pronouncement of Pius IX (1869), in affirming the "ensoulment" of the embryo at conception, was viewed in all branches of Christendom as consistent with Scripture. The rigor of the Roman church's condemnation of abortion, however, was never quite equaled in Protestantism. The encyclical *Casti Connubi* of 1930, for example, forbid abortion on any grounds, and was so strictly enforced that nuns, raped when the Russians invaded Germany in 1945, were forbidden to abort the unwanted fetuses.[72]

What of the second argument, that as a religious issue the decision for or against abortion should be left to the individual conscience, free from legal interference? This is an idealist solution with paradoxical overtones of situation ethics. But to say this does not do justice to Margaret Mead's position, even though she made perhaps the strongest case for it. Mead was quite aware that moral discernment is largely conditioned by cultural experience, and those persons who have had only haphazard training in values, and have made no conscious commitment to a specific ethical tradition, have little basis on which to make so momentous a decision.[73] Indeed, they will probably fall back on an unexamined hedonism, deciding that a "good" choice is one that yields the least amount of personal discomfort. Mead's solution is to repeal laws governing abortion, and "place abortion under the medical profession and under the churches who may educate their own members and work to convert nonmembers to their point of view."[74]

The medical profession generally holds the preservation of life as the highest value, following the Hippocratic oath. The decision is often complicated by the question "whose life?" in a crisis where a choice must be made between saving the child or the mother. Physicians practicing in Roman Catholic hospitals have traditionally followed the dictum of that church in saving the life of the child. The decision in such cases obviously does not derive from the medical field itself. Other physicians have complied with the wishes of the family or relied on their own judgment, or (as in the case of physicians in Nazi Germany) acceded to the state. Since the *Roe vs. Wade* decision by the U.S. Supreme Court, in 1973, granting women the right to an abortion up to the sixth month of pregnancy, physicians have presided over an increasing number of abortions on demand, from 744,600 that year to 1.58 million in 1986, one-third of all pregnancies in the nation. In France and Germany, the figure is closer to 50 percent of all pregnancies.[75]

In a dramatic reversal of what had come to be seen by many as a policy of laissez-faire, one of the strongest counsels against abortion has come from a physician who founded the political action group to legalize abortion. Bernard Nathanson was director of an abortion clinic that performed 60,000 such procedures. Then suddenly he resigned. While still believing it should not be forbidden by law, he had grown uneasy over the fact that the fetus responds to pain, makes respiratory efforts, moves spontaneously, and exhibits electroencephalographic activity. The fetus, he concluded, is a human life. "The long-term effects of ending so many lives worries him. He fears that it will 'coarsen our sensitivities through common practice and brute denial.' "[76]

Another part of the question remains unanswered. Even granting that abortion is a religious issue, and the medical profession and the churches are the agencies best equipped to guide public decision, should the legal aspects be dismissed and no laws of any kind be created to regulate the practice?

Hidden within this question is another: If our concern is with the preservation of human life ("Thou shalt not kill" is a civil as well as a religious law), have we yet a clear definition of when human life begins? If it begins at conception, then clearly abortion is an act of killing a human being, and therefore comes under legal jurisdiction. But if it begins only when brain wave activity starts (as death is defined when it ceases), or when the fetus could exist outside the womb, then different criteria are called for in determining when abortion becomes a criminal act. If we look to science to determine the matter, the word of Jerome Le Jeune (the first to describe chromosomal disease in humans) may prove helpful: "When does a person begin? It is from the fertilization of the female cell (the ovum) by the male cell (the spermatozoon) that a new member of the species will emerge. Life has a very, very long history. But each individual has a very neat beginning, the moment of its conception."[77]

Congressman Henry Hyde, advocating prolife legislation, insists that "defining when human life begins is the sort of question Congress is designed to answer, competent to answer, must answer."[78] Opponents have argued that the Supreme Court has not demonstrated the competence to decide such matters, and point to the Dred Scott decision in 1857, when it could not even define accurately what is meant by "human." That Court excluded all black people from the human race, and consequently ruled they were not entitled to protection under the Constitution. It is an archaic example to be sure, but one which illustrates how courts, lacking expertise in a given area, may be swayed by special interests. Opponents of making abortion a legal issue also argue that if life is to be preserved through laws abolishing abortion, the quality of that life must also be guaranteed.

> To instill quality into the life of the pregnant, ghetto-raised teenager, the government should give assistance economically and in supportive counseling. This means providing a livable home situation, and job training and opportunity. It means making available affordable day care service, and opportunity for the growing child to receive an education that may help him or her break the cycle of desperation and violence that leads to early pregnancies. The government should bear responsibility for each pregnancy it forces to be brought to term. Is such an immense social program affordable, workable, or desirable?[79]

Inasmuch as government is not willing to assume such responsibility, the question of abortion should not, according to this view, be a matter for governmental determination.

The third position as represented by Karl Barth, but also advocated by many others, is that abortion should be subject to both religious and legal prohibition, but that under certain circumstances it may be required by humane considerations. It is well known that nature aborts some 58 percent of fertilized ova prior to implantation, and another 12 percent after implantation when biological conditions are unfavorable for a successful pregnancy.[80] If nature, in what is sometimes called "body wisdom," aborts unfortunate pregnancies, should not intelligence and compassion permit us to abort other fertilized ova that have no change for a decent or healthy life? These might well include the products of rape or incest and those in which gross physical deformity is anticipated or the probability of psychosis is high. Barth would also include situations where the mother's health or life is in jeopardy.

Daniel Calahan, writing as a Roman Catholic and former editor of *Commonwealth*, objects on principle. He acknowledges,

> Abortion is one way to solve the problem of unwanted or hazardous pregnancy, but it is rarely the only way, at least in affluent societies (I would be considerably less certain about making the statement in poorer societies). Even in most extreme cases . . . alternatives will usually be available and different choices open. It is not inevitable that every unwanted child is doomed to misery. It is not written in the essence of things that a woman cannot come to accept, love and be a good mother to a child unwanted. Nor is it a fixed law that she could not come to cherish a grossly deformed child.[81]

Protestant writer Marilyn Fanning would agree, noting that of the 15 million abortions performed in the dozen years between the *Roe vs. Wade* case in 1973 and 1985, only 3 to 5 percent fall into the category of such hardship cases. "Fifteen million abortions in twelve years averages 4,000 abortion-deaths a day, and 13.7 million more deaths than all the soldiers lost in our nation's history."[82]

The primary concern here appears to be the exploitation of the loophole, where almost any excuse to avoid the inconvenience of pregnancy and parenthood becomes license to use abortion as simply an alternate form of birth control. Barth was aware of "this possibility of deliberate killing, treated as if it were just another expedient and remedy in a moment of embarrassment, nothing more being at issue than an unfortunate operation." Yet the strict prohibition against abortion has always been made with reference to abstract rules and principles: "There can be no doubt that the abstract prohibition which was pronounced in the past, and which is still the only contribution of Roman Catholicism in this matter, is far too forbidding and sterile to promise any effective help."[83]

What Barth insists on is that we acknowledge God's sovereignty in matters of life and death.

> Human life, and therefore the life the unborn child, is not an absolute, so that while it can be protected by the commandment it can be so only within the limits of God, who issues it. It cannot claim to be preserved in all circumstances. In grace God can will to preserve the life that has been given, and in grace God can will to take it again. Either way, it is not lost.[84]

Barth is not suggesting that, since we are all in God's hands, it doesn't matter whether a child is aborted or not. He does affirm, however, that our very zeal to preserve all life at all costs is a reflection of our anxiety, which emerges from our faithlessness and therefore godlessness, and prompts us to set up standards by which to coerce others.

> What grounds have we for the absolute thesis that in no circumstances can God will anything but the preservation of a germinating life, or make any other demand from the mother, father, doctor, or others involved? If God can will that this germinating life should die in some other way, might God not occasionally do so in such a way as to involve the active participation of others? How, then, can we indict them in these circumstances?[85]

Such considerations may provide solace for those seeking to make a difficult choice on grounds of faith; after all, no one can presume to know what God "might not occasionally do." Others may find more helpful guidance in some principles offered by James Gustafson:

> Life is to be preserved rather than destroyed; those who cannot assert their own right to life are especially to be protected; (but) there are exceptions to these rules. Possible exceptions are: (a) medical indications make therapeutic abortion morally viable; (b) pregnancy has occurred as a result of sexual crime (I would grant this as a viable possible exception in every instance . . . if the woman her-

self were convinced that it was right); (c) the social and emotional conditions do not appear to be beneficial for the well-being of the mother and child.[86]

Of primary importance in Gustafson's recommendations is his recognition that the Christian moralist, giving advice, can never pontificate as a final authority. The counselor must continue to be responsibly involved in the life of the person who has been advised.

> He cannot dismiss her to engage in subsequent implications of the decision on her own and to accept the consequences of such implications on her own. First, he is obligated to assist, if necessary, in finding competent medical care. Second, financial resources are needed. To put her on her own in this regard would be to resign responsibility prematurely for a course of action in which the moralist concurred. Third, the woman needs continuing social and moral support in her efforts to achieve her aspirations for relief from anguish and for a better human future. Fourth, the moralist is under moral obligation . . . to seek reform of abortion regulation that would remove the unjust legal barrier to what he believes to be morally appropriate.[87]

Many feminists and other prochoice advocates hold to a point of view at variance with all three positions discussed thus far. Virtually sweeping away as irrelevant such arguments as whether abortion is a religious or legal issue, or whether exceptions might be granted, they assert the right of every woman to privacy in decision making and her right to determine what is best for her own body.

The first of these two points was made the cornerstone of the 1973 Supreme Court decision on the *Roe vs. Wade* case: A woman's right to privacy extends to her decision whether to continue or terminate an unwanted pregnancy. On the second of these points, concerning the right to determine what is best for her own body, Attorney Sarah Weddington expresses the resentment of many prochoice advocates over what is popularly set up as the alternative: prolife. "Those of us who favor the availability of alternatives are not 'for abortion.' We are for such things as preventing unwanted pregnancies."[88] In short, prochoice advocates are also prolife, but within the framework of the woman's right of private choice. What divides the two camps, she insists, are three specific issues: the definition of human life, the weighing of concerns for both the woman and the ovum, and the implications of constitutional law.

Concerning the definition of human life, Weddington is silent, but as we noted in previous discussion here, neither theology nor biological science has been silent. According to an ancient doctrine called *traducianism*, the unique human person comes into being at the moment of conception.[89] Medical practice teaches that the individual human life comes into being at the moment the ovum encounters and unites with a sperm cell out of some 200 or 300 million available at the time. "The embyologic age of the embryo-fetus is dated from the time of conception."[90] Thus is established the unique and never-to-be-repeated information unit that will be locked into every one of the cells that comprises the cytoblast, the embryo, the fetus, and ultimately the 15 trillion cells of the newborn child. Those who argue for the right to choose abortion may wish to shift the focus from what is human to what is personal and self-aware, but it is quite clear from genetics that the individual human being begins at conception.

The point at which the forming human being becomes a person, one who has rights independent of the mother, is of crucial importance to the argument about the right of the mother to her own body. The impregnated ovum may be a human object, yet still be so much a part of the mother's system as to have no true independence. Yet it is equally clear that *neither* the fertilized ovum *nor* the fetus it becomes is the *same as* the mother's body. The issue then focuses on this question: At what point do the mother's rights over her own body infringe on the rights of the newly formed human person within her? That point in the fetus's personal history may have to be decided medically, but if at that juncture we are dealing with a child of God, its own rights must not, at least within the purview of Christian ethics, be violated.

"The implications of constitutional law" to which Weddington referred present a peculiar twist to the argument. The contention is that pregnant women are often discriminated against in the job market; in some states they are denied employment altogether and forced to become economically dependent on family or on welfare; they may be barred from employment for several months after the child is delivered, and (especially in Texas, where the illegitimate father has no statutory responsibility for child support) be left with so heavy a responsibility as to be forced onto a cycle of poverty. This does not cover all the problems, such as being barred from education, exposed to humiliation, and losing most of her personal liberties.

These lamentable conditions are offered by prochoice advocates as reasons for liberalizing abortion laws. Yet prolife advocates argue that the issues have been confused. The key problem here, they contend, is the one of unfair legislation vis-à-vis educational and economic rights. These must be addressed independently of arguments about abortion.

A final point of debate has recently been raised with reference to RU-486, briefly alluded to earlier. This is a French antiprogestin drug (mifepristone) that acts both as a contraceptive and an abortifacient. Many acclaim this drug as radically transforming the abortion issue because it causes the fertile ovum to abort before it can be implanted in the uterus. Here again the argument arises as to just when the human being becomes a human person, with claims on the state for protection. For many prolife advocates the time when quickening is noted, that is, when the fetus is able to move on its own, has been taken as evidence that a human child with inalienable rights has been formed. Those who insist that a human person has been established at conception generally reject RU-486 on the grounds that the steroid is murdering the unborn. If, however, the substance is a true contraceptive, preventing conception from occurring in the first place, that argument must be referred to the debate on birth control.

A strong support for the acceptance of such contraceptive/abortifacients as the one just discussed may arise from an unexpected quarter, in research derived from the study of identical twins. Prior to implantation, the cytoblast is a unified mass. After implantation, a division may take place resulting in two completely independent beings, each with its own complete biological and personal identity. It would seem logical to assert, then, that although a human "being" is present prior to implantation, that "being" is only an existent, not yet a person. James Gaffney makes a special point of this, noting,

> The only line-drawing that seems not at all arbitrary is that which may be thought to separate a non-individuated embryo, e.g., one capable of twinning from one determinate individuality. To say "I was" something that could turn into both me and my brother seems to me no more literally correct than to say "I was" a pair of gametes that turned out to be the transmitters of my genetic heritage. Meanwhile, however, I see no reason to justify the treating of what may perfectly well be moral objects like ourselves as though they simply were nothing of the kind.[91]

There remains for the Christian ethicist a concern, even if RU-486 or an alternative drug should be adopted, or the Supreme Court legalized abortion right up to the time of delivery, that we not ignore the words Jeremiah wrote as from the Lord: "Before I formed thee in the belly I knew thee . . ." or the words of the Psalmist: "Thou hast searched me and known me . . . thou hast covered me in my mother's womb." When dealing with nonbelievers, who care nothing for biblical or theological argument, if our concern extends to their health and the stability of the society, we should not falter in making a case for the sanctity of life. As in other realms where technology outruns moral sensitivity, the very ease with which abortion has become just another form of birth control has made it clear that one of the greatest challenges for Christians is to seek opportunities for open dialogue with both fellow Christians and non-Christians. Dialogue, wherein the conflict of thought can be separated from a conflict of wills, enables the Christian to make biblical and theological positions clear in a context that avoids narrowing the argument to an exercise of religious authority, a process which historically has alienated those who might otherwise have benefited from Christian insight. Quest for a national dialogue on the abortion issue has been instigated by a number of denominations.[92] There are grounds for optimism beyond the apparent deadlock.

HOMOSEXUALITY

During the spring of 1992, the Roman Catholic church, and many of the mainline Protestant denominations, reaffirmed their historic reasons for rejecting homosexual behavior as inconsistent with Christian ethics. At their April meeting, the Disciples of Christ predicted a region-by-region ban on the ordination of practicing homosexuals, and the Anglican Church of Canada cancelled the license of a homosexual clergyman.[93] In May, the governing body of the United Methodist Church, through its 990 delegates, declared that the practice of homosexuality is "incompatible with Christian teaching."[94] The Southern Baptist Convention, representing 15 milion members, expelled two congregations for condoning homosexuality.[95] A Vatican document, promulgated by the Vatican Congregation for the Doctrine of the Faith, stated that denying civil rights (in the matter of housing and employment) may be justified to protect traditional family life, and, comparing restrictions on homosexuals to those placed on people with contagious diseases and "the objectively disordered" (e.g., the mentally ill), urged opposition to the notion that homosexual activity is morally acceptable."[96]

It should be noted that in most of these decisions there were voices of dissent. Within the United Presbyterian church (U.S.A.), a lesbian was approved on July 30, 1992, by her local judicatory for pastoral installation in a church in New York (she had been previously ordained before revealing her sexual preference).[97] But on November 3, 1992, the denomination's Permanent Judicial Commission voted 12–1 to reject her installation. Philip Wogaman, a member of the task force for the United Methodist Church's study on homosexuality, urged deleting the term *incompatible,* as too harsh and divisive. The American Baptist Churches in the United States narrowly rejected a call for an all-out condemnation of homosexual practice as a violation of God's plan. The vote was 91 to 88, with two abstentions.[98]

It is useful to consider some of the sources of the debate, including Scriptural tradition and ecclesiatical policy, and some contemporary arguments from the perspective of human development, sociobiology, and medical research. Some Christians may find such an array of sources bewildering, asking, "Aren't the teachings of the Bible sufficient?" The Bible, however, may not be, in all cases, as clear and explicit as we might wish, and we are always called to remember that Jesus himself did not hesitate to say "You have heard it said: . . . (and quote a biblical saying, then follow with): . . . "but I say unto you" . . . giving an unexpected, new point of view, sometimes at odds with the old (Matthew 5:21, 27, 31, 33, and especially 5:38–42 and 43–48.) Christian ethics is always engaged in an effort to understand God's will in the context of the world's wisdom as well as its folly.

The condemnation of homosexual behavior in the Bible appears to be unequivocal. The word *sodomy,* as a legal term for homosexualism, comes to us from the story in Genesis 19, where "the men of Sodom, both young and old" surrounded the house where Lot was staying, demanding that he send his two companions (angel visitors?) out to them for the crowd's sexual pleasure. Lot pleaded with the crowd not to commit such an abomination, even offering to send his daughters to them instead (which raises ethical questions quite apart from the sodomy issue). The angel visitors intervened, striking the crowd with blindness, then urging Lot to take his family and flee, so the city could be destroyed. Sherman Baily, in a book that tries to blunt the homosexual charge by translating the Hebrew verb *yadha* ("to know" in the sexual sense) to mean merely "to get acquainted with," insists that the story has been freighted with misunderstanding. But George R. Edwards, while making a strong case for a new hermeneutical study of Scripture, which may yield a more sympathetic view of the homosexual problem, asserts that Baily's argument is "not persuasive."[99] The context of the story makes it clear that a homosexual gang rape was being threatened, and according to the story the Lord's revenge was swift and devastating.

Elsewhere in Scripture, Leviticus 18:22 and 20:13 forbid homosexual practices as an abomination worthy of death. In the New Testament, Paul declares in his letters both to the Church at Corinth (1 Corinthians 6:9) and at Rome (Romans 1:27) that those who practice such behavior have no place in the kingdom of God. John Boswell, in a carefully-documented study of the original languages of the Bible, objects that the word *malakos*, used in both the Romans and Corinthians passages, need not be translated "homosexuals." It could, he states, just as easily mean "licentious" or "wanting in self-control."[100] He points out that Aristotle uses the word in the *Nicomachaean Ethics* to indicate "unrestrained" or "wanton." Closer examination of the passage, however, makes it clear that what Paul specifically describes in Romans 1:27 is "women consumed with passion for one another, men committing shameless acts with men and receiving in their own persons the due penalty for their error" (the latter figure of speech may refer to venereal disease). There is even less opportunity to misunderstand the word *arsenokoitai* in 1 Corinthians 6:9, which referred to male prostitutes frequented by men. Jude 7 reminds the early Christians how God punished the people of Sodom for their "unnatural lusts" with a holocaust.

Interestingly, secular Rome, while copying many other aspects of Greek culture, condemned homosexual practices, often prescribing the death penalty. But within the growing Christian Church the practice, while denounced, appears seldom to have been overtly punished except for imposing penances or, more rarely, excommunication. The medieval church preferred to handle cases "in house," rather than turn the offenders over to the civil magistrates.

In Thomas Aquinas's writings we find more pointed reference to the "sin of sodomy" in his *Summa Theologica*, where he rates it second only to bestiality in its degradation. Again, in his *Summa Contra Gentiles*, he condemns the practice along with prostitution, but primarily on the grounds that both fail to engage copulation for its natural and spiritual purposes.[101]

The Reformers did not deviate importantly from the position of the medieval church, except for basing their arguments primarily on the Bible (whereas Aquinas appealed to natural law and quoted Scripture only at the end of his argument). Most mainline Protestant churches today denounce the practice as we noted, but in cautious terms reflecting a greater exposure to the insights of medicine and psychiatry. Charles Curran notes that while the Roman Catholic church regards homosexual acts as sinful, there is now (as of Vatican II) a recognition that "there are some persons who are incurably and definitely homosexual" through no fault of their own.[102]

If Curran's contention is correct, that some homosexuals are incurably so, it would appear there must be degrees of homosexuality. This is a point made by many psychiatrists, who would agree that "Homosexuality is not an 'all or none' phenomenon . . . in many persons a latent tendency may never become overt."[103] The late Alfred Kinsey estimated that about 4 percent of American males were exclusively homosexual, but that as many as 37 percent may have had a homosexual experience at some time in their lives.[104] Sigmund Freud proposed that most boys and many girls go through a gang stage in youth, when sexual experiments are not uncommon, but that fixation at that stage lasting into adulthood represents a form of neurosis.[105] Hans Sachs, a proponent of Freud's views, was careful to distinguish between neuroses and "perversions," the latter being a popular though cruel misconception of the nature of homosexuality.[106] This view was widely accepted for a time, though clinicians noted that more than psychological aspects must be considered. It has been demonstrated that some homosexual men have "a high output of the estrogens of the opposite sex."[107] The American Psychiatric Association has stated that "For a mental or psychiatric condition to be considered a psychiatric disorder, it must either regularly cause subjective distress or regularly be associated with some general impairment of social effectiveness of functioning."[108] In our society, some conclude that homosexuals qualify for that description. But this is thought by others to be misperception, based on society's long nurtured prejudices. In fact, that statement was issued in 1973 as a rationale for removing homosexuality from the APA's list of mental disorders.

The debate whether homosexuality might be biologically based is of fairly recent origin. It is well known that among Greeks of the classical period homosexual behaviors were accepted as a natural relationship in settings like a school or military camp. Yet Aristotle wrote that homosexual preference was almost always caused by parental abuse and not considered a "natural" or nature-caused phenomenon. The supposed naturalness of homosexuality was not considered in ancient Rome nor among Middle Eastern cultures of the same eras (where it was often judged a capital crime, especially among Zoroastrians),[109] nor during the rise of Christianity. Ronald Nadler, writing for the Kinsey Institute, notes that homosexual behaviors can be found among many nonhuman primates, and suggests a biological link. But he cautions that what is observed might best be described as same-sex practices rather than true homosexuality. Indeed, "it is more appropriately designated as some form of non-sexual social behavior," inasmuch as it occurs mostly among immature and mutual exploring males, and among females during the estrous phase of the cycle; it occurs most frequently among those in cages, compounds, or corrals.[110] Even if homosexual behavior was found to be a natural (or at least statistically frequent) occurrence among nonhuman species, the implication for Christian ethics would be minimal. Human societies generally do not adopt cannibalism or husband-devouring as acceptable simply because lions and spiders engage in them. Our moral standards derive elsewhere.

A more serious contender for consideration arises from recent studies in genetics and neurophysiology. The phenomena of hermaphroditism (in which a child is born with both male and female genitalia) and transexualism (in which the person born male or female feels trapped in the body of the wrong gender) are thought by some to provide a clue to the biological origin of homosexuality. Many researchers are convinced, however, that biological aspects of gender are independent of the psychological. It has been found that, "not only can intersexed or hermaphroditic children be raised as members of either sex, but children relegated to the wrong category can grow up to be psychologically normal members of the gender to which they were erroneously assigned."[111] Developmentalists note that "homosexuals are never confused about their identity," even when a male adopts the feminine role in sexual relations, and conclude, "There is no evidence to support the hypothesis that homosexuality is biologically based."[112]

Nevertheless, in 1992, Simon LeVay, of the Salk Institute, published his findings that upon examining the brains of nineteen homosexual male cadavers, he determined that a tiny area of the brain thought to control sexual activity was less than half the size in homosexuals than in heterosexuals.[113] LeVay, a homosexual, declared, "This strongly supports the idea that there is a biological basis for the determination of sexual orientation. It's one more nail in the coffin of critics who argue that homosexuality is a choice and thus immoral." Studies of identical twins by Michael Bailey and Richard Pillard show that if one twin is homosexual, the other twin is three times more likely to be homosexual than would be the case with fraternal twins. Here again seems to be strong support for biological origins.[114]

Instead of resolving the issue, however, these findings have been sharply criticized as self-serving and unscientific. John Money, of Johns Hopkins, says, "Of course it [sexual orientation] is in the brain. The real question is when did it get there? Was it prenatal, neonatal, during childhood, puberty? That we do not know."[115] Anne Stirling, a developmental biologist at Brown University, dismisses all three studies as "badly interpreted genetics." A similar fate meets the proponents of the theory that the corpus collosum connecting the hemispheres of the brain is larger in homosexual males, thus establishing a biological link. Kenneth Klivington, assistant to the president of the Salk Institute, notes, "The brain's neural networks configure themselves in response to certain experiences." In other words, it is the homosexual experiences altering the brain's structures, not the structures creating the homosexuality.

If homosexuality is not biologically based, the same may also be true of those who call themselves bisexual, who are satisfied to have sexual relations with either male or female, and may indeed seek them. "I want to experience contact with a man's body," says one forty-year-old bisexual man. "That's just a basic part of who I am."[116] Whether or not this is a basic sexual trait, or simply an orgasmic obsession, bisexuals, like homosexuals, often report having distant, aloof parents, leading some developmentalists to agree with Freud's analysis that they seek nurturance in any human object that has become eroticized.[117] Extensive studies have related lesbianism with the person's having been a victim of incest.[118] John Money compares the acquisition of sexual orientation with learning to speak. "You did not have a native language on the day you were born. But by the age of five you'd got it."[119] Sexual orientation may therefore be neither biologically based nor entirely a matter of choice, but the result of a confluence of conditions. The choice comes in the way one expresses it, leading to a possible distinction between homosexuality, as an established condition, and (to hazard a neologism) homosexualism, as an affirmed and perhaps even an asserted lifestyle as in the often aggressively staged gay pride celebrations in some cities.[120]

Public policy has been slow in removing homosexuality from its roster of crimes. In Britain, in 1957, a parliamentary committee under Sir John Wolfenden's chairmanship recommended that "homosexual behavior between consenting adults in private no longer be a criminal offense." After three years of debate, the recommendation was voted down, but in 1965 it passed the House of Lords and became effective in 1967, when approved by both houses.[121] Change has come more slowly in the United States, with more than half the states maintaining antisodomy laws and some states like Oregon creating 1992 ballot initiatives to outlaw homosexual activity and to deny homosexuals civil rights with reference to public employment.

The official position of most of the churches within Christianity remains one of taking the biblical record at face value, and while there has been a tendency to greater liberalization in attitude toward the treatment of homosexual persons, homosexualism is still almost universally rejected. In some cases, clergy have been dismissed from their positions for opposing the official stand of their denominations.[122] In some churches that require extensive postbaccalaureate training for their clergy, candidates for ordination have been introduced to the theory and practice of modern psychiatry and have employed those insights both in pastoral counseling and in preaching. Among church leaders who have made an intensive study of the nature of love, the older distinction between *eros* (earthly or sexual love, largely governed by natural passions whether heterosexual or otherwise) and *agape* (spiritual love as described in 1 Corinthians 13 and most completely exemplified in God's redemptive love revealed in Christ) has been somewhat mitigated. "Certainly, in Christian ethics today," writes Brian Hebblethwaite, "we shall need to take a much more positive view of 'eros' as part of God's good creation than was taken in earlier Christian centuries. . . . We may agree that less rigid attitudes to homosexuality and to divorce are required in Christian ethics today."[123] Even if homosexualism was judged as misdirected *eros*, we are cautioned that "Christian ethics, like any other ethics, must surely distinguish between promiscuous homosexuality and a stable homosexual relationship."[124]

Given the desire of the Christian ethicist to be fair and understanding, neither bludgeoning the homosexual person with biblical proof texts nor judging him or her with outmoded churchly standards, a question remains: Is there a human deficiency to be faced honestly in the homosexual condition? George Edwards suggests a "trans-genital awareness" by which in effect we ignore gender differences (based presumably on Paul's comment: "In Christ there is neither male nor female") and allow homosexuals to express their love in their own chosen way.[125] This curious use of Paul's effort to establish a full democracy in the spiritual life ignores the biblical injunction that during our terrestrial pilgrimage we are created male and female "in God's image," for the purpose that God is recorded as having ordered in our creation. Our being polar opposites is essential to the continuance of the species. As theologian Emil Brunner expressed it, "This distinction goes down to the very roots of our personal existence, and penetrates into the deepest 'metaphysical grounds' of our personality and destiny."[126] This unique identity is rooted in the image of God that we carry in our very essence, and which can only be damaged when treated as if it were not part of our authentic selfhood.

Erich Fromm expressed this same insight from a psychiatric perspective: "The male-female polarity is the basis for interpersonal creativity. This is obvious biologically, in the fact that the union of sperm and ovum is the basis for the birth of a child." But in the purely psychic realm it is not different; in the love between man and woman, each of them is reborn. "The homosexual deviation is a failure to attain this polarized union, and thus the homosexual suffers from the pain of never-resolved separateness, a failure which he shares with the average heterosexual who cannot love."[127]

It is this pain of separateness that the Christian ethicist must recognize and seek to address redemptively. In the growing acceptance of homosexuality as an alternate lifestyle, many homosexual persons have come out of the closet to try to escape the loneliness they thought was wholly the fault of an unforgiving society. The sense of estrangement still is felt among many of the homosexuals who have expressed themselves. For some it has arisen from the sheer burden of guilt and fear, occasioned by the emergence of diseases associated with unsafe sexual behaviors, especially AIDS.[128]

An interview with a biochemistry professor who has suffered the pain of separateness, as well as the guilt and dread of sexual disease, is illuminating:

> I resisted Christianity because of the injunctions against homosexuality. But greater struggles elicit greater grace, and Christ does, after all, promise new life. The most important thing that's happened is that I finally believe God loves and

accepts me. I'm beginning to accept the reality of solitude. I have a hope that I will one day have a heterosexual orientation, or meet a woman who will help me find one. (Otherwise) the future for me will consist of celibacy. [129]

This remarkable self-disclosure, without either self-reproach or self-justification, may provide something of a paradigm for a new appraisal of the homosexual situation.

Just as there are many homosexuals who are adamantly determined to remain as they are, there are others who seek therapy to adjust to a heterosexual life. For those who feel that a commitment to Christianity requires a heterosexual orientation, there are literally scores of books available written by former homosexuals and lesbians that offer encouragement and practical guidelines. [130] Where such persons and Christian ethicists (who may be in some cases one and the same) can find common ground for dialogue, some kind of societal policy of rapprochement may be possible. Increasing numbers of churches across the nation are providing physical accommodations and time on their agenda for meetings, conversation, and worship. It may be hoped that understanding and dialogue can take the place of vilification and punitive legislation.

Human sexuality is not simply a matter of libidinal expression but, as noted at the beginning of the chapter, is seen by most religious persons and communities as a gift of the Creator by which we share in the creation of new life and new personalities. The fact that this gift is sometimes distorted through mutual exploitation and even violence, as daily newspapers reveal with headlines of rape and love nest homicides, reminds us that here, in the confusion of love with lust, our sinful nature is perhaps most poignantly exposed. The call to love, and to establish families for which our gender differences uniquely fit us, will always be a focus of concern for Christian ethics.

CHAPTER SEVEN

The Family in Transition

The relationship between love and marriage as portrayed in Western art and literature is of more recent origin and is more tenuous than many participants are prepared to believe. Parentally arranged marriages without the children's consent have been more prevalent in history than wedlock for the fulfillment of affection. It is true that ancient Hebrew poets romanticized "the ways of a man with a maid" (Proverbs 30:19), but it is primarily since the Middle Ages that the demand for emotional and sexual fulfillment for both partners has taken center stage. Few would question that the romantic element has enriched the relationship which was earlier more functional in terms of economic and social stability (not to mention political advantage in many cases). Yet within our own century a disturbing phenomenon has emerged. Despite the personal fulfillment theme, we are being inundated with warnings that the family is in critical danger of disintegration, and with it society's foundations.[1]

A common theme in books and conferences on marriage and family life has three components: The family is the key to any culture's survival; the family today is rent by child abuse, abandonment, and delinquency; unless we recover traditional family values, civilization as we know it is doomed.

Where these observations are publicized by religious organizations, the pre-scription is predictable: "Get back to the Bible," and "Families that pray to-gether stay together."

We must ask whether in fact the traditional family (by which is usually meant the nuclear family, with father, mother, and one or more offspring maintaining a close-knit and self-sufficient unit) has been the key to any so-ciety's maintenance; whether the situation today is one of deterioration or sim-ply of transition to some new forms; and whether upon examination the Bible and Church tradition support the family structure and functions as the advo-cates claim.

Following loosely the format we have used in earlier chapters, we examine the historic record, including the biblical and later institutional accounts of what characterized the family in the past, consider the nature of the much publi-cized crisis in marriage and family life, and then examine the implications of these conditions for Christian ethics.

THE HISTORICAL AND BIBLICAL RECORD

Neither anthropologists, sociobiologists, nor social historians are in agreement as to when or why the human family structure began. Seeking to know what is natural in human behavior, some posit that creating families is just something humans do the way birds build nests and bears seek dens; the behavior is species-specific. Others suggest that creating family units was more a conscious survival technique as, a relatively weak species, humans sought mutual protection.[2] A variation on the nature-nurture interaction theory suggests that provision for food and shelter for females during pregnancy, labor, and nursing created an economic rationale for establishing families. "Natural selection doubtless operated to kill off those stocks in which the male refused this pro-tection and care, and to 'select' those for survival in which it was rendered."[3]

Tempting as these speculations are, it has also been noted that natural selection did not operate to kill off countless species where the adult male re-fused protection and care among such social creatures as are found in the insect or amphibian worlds. The female lion continues to hunt during pregnancy, the male providing little or no support. Among apes, the social aggregate is greater than the biological family, which in time disperses with no lasting bonds. Hu-man families, on the other hand, grow emotionally closer as years pass, often with great affection and even reverence expressed between generations. "The study of primates provides no reason to suppose that human beings [would be] divided into family groups."[4] Jane Goodall, in her famous research among chimpanzees, notes that the male adult, apart from his function as sire in con-ception, actually plays no further part in the offspring's development. "This exclusion of the male from familial responsibilities is perhaps one of the major differences between human and chimpanzee societies."[5]

The human family structure and function is at once so complex and so unique that simplistic analogies with other species prove unhelpful. As a single example, if humans, like some birds and mammals, are monogamous, and this is contended to be a natural result of genetic and social promptings, the question arises why the structure is so often violated among humans (as it is not among Canadian geese, swans, cranes, and deer), that in every culture known, laws have been created to secure the family against adultery. This situation prevails even where polygamy is acceptable.[6]

The biblical writers, lacking the tools of anthropology and sociology (perhaps they would not have been impressed even if such had been available), straightforwardly asserted that marriage was the natural estate for humankind, intended so by the Creator. This does not conflict with theories about biological evolution; it simply bypasses them.[7] Their concern was to express an ontological foundation for the bond of marriage in the love that creates a new possibility: "that these two shall be made one in this holy estate." This new possibility becomes a new reality in "one flesh,"[8] as God intended (Matthew 19:4–6).

The importance of the ontological aspect of marriage is hard to overstress because it is central not only to family security, but underscores the biblical understanding of the tragedy of its dissolution. When Jesus made the point ". . . so they are no longer two but one," and followed with the injunction "What therefore God has joined together, let no man put asunder," he was challenged by a group of Pharisees, as to why Moses permitted divorce. Surely there was biblical precedent for dissolving the union. Jesus' retort was blunt: "For your hardness of heart Moses allowed you to divorce your wives—but from the beginning it was not so" (Matthew 19:8).

Yet it is impossible to identify a single biblical view of the family. Harvey Cox makes a special issue of this in decrying the current sentimentalism about National Family Week, and the countless sermons and Sunday school lessons delivered on returning to some supposedly biblical basis for family life. "If there is one common creedal thread running through the popular piety of America, it has to do with the 'sacredness' of the family. Consequently Christian Family Sunday becomes for most people a festival of nostalgia and hypocrisy. [But] the charade becomes even more puzzling when we notice that what is being celebrated as 'family' has almost nothing to do with families pictured in the Bible."[9]

The Hebrew Scriptures do not present arguments for the nuclear family, defined by its self-contained structure with a father and mother dutifully nurturing a close-knit brood of children. Among the Hebrews the family was distinctly patriarchal. The husband had virtual lordship over his wives and children, with his authority passing to the eldest son upon the father's disability or death. The word most often used for family (*Bayit*) meant household, and was inclusive of wives, concubines, children, and servants. Curiously, the counting of family members sometimes omitted the women, as in the description of Jacob's family (Genesis 46:26). The father's authority extended to killing any or all family members who might entice him from the faith (Deuteronomy 13:6–10). Women, though sometimes praised for their virtues (Proverbs 31), were required to eat separately from the men, and even worship apart from them.

The role of the family takes on a new meaning in the New Testament, especially with regard to women. At the outset we notice God sending a messenger to Mary (not to Joseph) to announce the advent of Jesus' birth (Luke 1:26–33). Women are given a more important role in the New Testament church than would have been allowed in the synagogue. The apostle Paul specifically addresses greetings to Priscilla and Aquila, who had been his companions in Syria (Acts 18:18). These and other women were given positions of leadership after Paul overcame his earlier reluctance conditioned by his Jewish background. Christian congregations often met in private homes, so Paul could write of "the church in their house" (1 Corinthians 16:19).

The family was seen as the closest approximation of the kingdom of God on earth, and the marriage relationship was likened to that between Christ and the Church (Ephesians 5:25–30). It was never to be dissolved except where the pledge of unity was broken by unchastity (Matthew 5:32). The care of family members and their future security was a requirement of faith; anyone who failed to provide was "worse than an infidel" (1 Timothy 5:8).

The early Christians, however, lived in a whirlpool of ideas that made up the Greco-Roman culture, within which were some religious and philosophical groups that held the physical body as evil and sexual desire as corrupt. Despite the Jewish tradition that extolled marriage, and Jesus' support for it in the Gospels, the fact that Jesus was celibate, and Paul seemed to give marriage only condescending support (1 Corinthians 7:25–38), caused many early Christians to consider family life of lesser importance than remaining chaste. Some of the early fathers, like Tertullian, were at best apathetic toward marriage, often denigrating women as tempters in the mold of Eve. By the fourth century, celibacy had become the rule for clergy, and Augustine a century later commented that sexuality was the means by which original sin was transmitted.

Christianity nevertheless provided a powerful antidote for the destructiveness of many Roman customs, denouncing the selling of brides to their husbands by parental arrangement and the practice of infanticide. The official position of Rome was distinctly patriarchal, allowing women little autonomy and giving fathers life and death decisions over their children, including the casting out of unwanted babies.[10] If a child misbehaved, and the father beat the child to death in an effort to chastise, there was no penalty.[11] Polygamy among the Romans was unlawful, but men often took concubines and slaves for their sexual pleasure, without legal interference or any particular social stigma. Roman fathers could have their children married or divorced without the latter's consent.[12]

As Christianity gained in popularity throughout Rome, increasing numbers of Romans accepted these Christian teachings: sexual experience must be confined to marriage; in Christ women were equal with men; childhood is sacred and infanticide must be abolished; concubinage and prostitution were equally to be prohibited; and divorce must be limited to grounds of unchastity.

CHANGING PATTERNS IN CHRISTIANITY

Little writing about marriage and family life has survived from the early centuries of Christendom's expansion east and west. Gregory I ("The Great," c. 540–604 A.D.) complimented the Queen of the Franks on her education and "maternal and laudable care" of her son. It is known that Charlemagne (768–814) had a large family by four wives, and educated both the boys and girls "in every virtuous sentiment."[13] King Alfred was reputed to have been a devoted husband and father.[14] Other records from the medieval period tell us something of family life among the lower classes. A polyptych of the Abbot Irminon (c. 801–820) reveals a startling ratio of 252 men for every 100 women, due perhaps to the high rate of death among women in childbirth. One historian suggests, "We must not rule out the possibility of female infanticide," despite the Church's rigorous prohibition against the practice.[15]

This last prospect points up the fact that although we are accustomed to thinking of the medieval period as one of expanding Christianity, numerical growth is deceptive. Conversions to Christianity where the faith was really understood were few. Whole villages might be baptized en masse by eager missionary, but the outward forms of the new religion were merely enameled over the older superstitions and practices, including infanticide and frequent warfare. Thus even in so-called Christian communities, women were not always considered persons in a legal sense; fathers or brothers represented them in court. "Refractory wives might be sold by their husbands when bodily chastisement failed to accomplish its end."[16] The clergy sought to exercise influence to improve the lot of women, by pointing out the sacred role of the Virgin Mary as a reminder that all women are to be protected. Women were further safeguarded by the Church's uncompromising opposition to divorce, a practice that had been common among Greeks, Romans, Germanics, Teutons, and other cultures.

The sacredness of the marriage bond, more or less marginally acknowledged even among non-Christians, was given its most forceful expression in the writings of Thomas Aquinas. Here the ontological union wherein two people become "one in this holy estate" was reaffirmed. But official recognition of marriage as a sacred bond did not guarantee its popular acceptance. In England at that time, a married woman possessed no personal property. "Even the personal effects, clothing, jewels, money, furniture, etc. which the wife owned before her marriage, became the absolute property of her husband."[17] A particularly pernicious problem of clandestine marriages that were easily disavowed arose in the twelfth century, and was not resolved until the sixteenth.

Peter Lombard had proclaimed that a declaration of espousal *per verba praesenti* (present tense: "I take thee") constituted a binding marriage even though no clergy was present. But a declaration *per verba futuro* (future tense: "I will take thee") was only promissory with no binding power. In the flush of passion, dishonorable men had little trouble luring girls (particularly among their servants) into sexual alliances with the first pledge, then getting friends to testify in court that it had been only the second pledge and therefore not a binding marriage. The Roman Catholic church at the Council of Trent (1536) dealt with this problem by declaring that any marriage not performed in the presence of a priest and two or more witnesses was null and void.[18]

The Protestant Reformation wrought a number of changes in attitudes toward and conditions of marriage and family life in Europe and, through the Puritans, in the New World. Martin Luther, seven years before the Catholic Council of Trent did so, denounced the *per verba praesenti* concept, and declared that all pledges of marriage were legally binding. He further held that every marriage must be registered and regulated by the state, and that it should be declared a criminal offense for a man to use verbal tricks in attempting to defraud a woman.

Another departure from the Roman Catholic tradition was in the Protestant denial that marriage is a sacrament. This had a double effect. First, it removed marriage from the control of ecclesiastical authority. Considering the powerlessness of women during and after the Middle Ages, either to contract their own marriages (which were almost universally arranged by parents for social and economic advantage) or to earn an independent living apart from the marriage, the Church's definition of marriage as a sacrament gave virtual sanction to a condition of bondage. Second, and ironically, denying that marriage is a sacrament actually resulted in greater emphasis on its spiritual quality. Husbands were directed to the biblical injunction: "Love your wives as Christ loved the Church and gave himself up for her" (Ephesians 5:2). Wives were no longer to be regarded as chattel without rights, but were to be cherished as Jesus loved the Church. John Calvin, writing his *Institutes of the Christian Religion* in 1534, pointed out that calling marriage a sacrament had been based on a mistranslation of Scripture.[19] The error is best illustrated in the fact that, while calling marriage a sacrament on the one hand, the Roman church stigmatized the conjugal relation as "impurity, and copulation a carnal defilement," and denied it to the priests.[20]

The effect of the Reformation's achievement in recognizing the equality of men and women in the fullest sense is of particular interest in its influence on secular thought. Such a thoroughgoing secularist as Thomas Hobbes wrote in 1651, "God hath ordained to man a helper, and there always be two that are equally parents . . . and whereas some have attributed dominion to the man only, as being the more excellent sex, they misreckon it."[21] John Locke wrote some forty years later in *Concerning Civil Government*, "We see the positive law of God everywhere joins them together without distinction, when it commands the obedience of the children: 'Honor thy father and thy mother' (Exodus 20:12); 'Children obey your parents' (Ephesians 6:1); etc., is the style of Old and New Testament."[22]

In the New World, family life gained an importance not fully appreciated in the Old.

> The firmly organized hardworking Puritan household was largely responsible for the outcome of the New England enterprise; the seekers of gold and various types of treasure had not inaugurated the successful settlement of the New World. Neither had the missionary priests laid a foundation for developing life. For this the family was demanded, the English family that had thrown off the yoke of church and state authority, and was able to proceed in the fear of God under the immediate guidance of the master of the house.[23]

The "master of the house" was not the patriarchal tyrant of twentieth-century novels and movies, nor was the Puritan cold, repressive, and antisex. In fact, Puritan families were neighborly, and loved with genuine passion as was evidenced by large, well-fed, and well-educated families.[24] Their concern for their children was such that they established schools and made formal education a requirement in every community, as would not be the case in most of England and Europe for the next two hundred years.[25]

The industrial revolution brought about serious dislocations in family life in America as well as abroad, a change for which neither the churches nor other social agencies were prepared. Husbands and fathers of the working class were often unable to stay near home where the family had previously shared much of the work. Now in the gray predawn, they would take a lunch box and walk or ride a cart to the factory where they worked in crowded, unsanitary rooms twelve to fourteen hours daily.[26]

It was soon found that women and children could be hired more cheaply than men, and with no child labor laws to block the way, they were brought into the work force in great numbers. Thousands of men were replaced. Out of work and humiliated, many men turned to drink and crime. "Worse still," wrote one historian, "mothers and fathers in some cases lived on the killing labor of their little children," unable to find an alternative just to eat and stay alive.[27] This killing labor is described in accounts of the time: "The children [of both sexes] were clad in male attire, naked to the waist in canvas trousers, with an iron chain fastened to a belt of leather between their legs. [They] hauled tubs of coal up subterranean roads for twelve to sixteen hours a day. It was not unusual to find children of four or five years of age working in these conditions."[28] The churches were not indifferent to the plight of poor children, as the development of the Sunday school movement in England and America gives evidence.[29] But like the Great Awakening and other evangelical efforts, the Sunday school was addressed primarily to the spiritual needs of the individual, and did nothing to ameliorate working conditions and little to strengthen the family. Considering these conditions, along with the spectacle of slavery that sundered countless thousands of black families, it is easy to disbelieve idyllic portrayals of family life in the eighteenth and nineteenth centuries.

Nevertheless, family life did continue to be sustained either in nuclear or extended form,[30] as novelists and essayists of the time amply testify.[31] A great many events molded and reshaped the households of the period including the women's movement, which may have gotten its first major impetus in a letter from Abigail Adams to her famous husband in 1779.[32] Unexpectedly, the same industrial revolution that damaged so many families provided a shaping influence which was also beneficial. As women entered the work force and gained some measure of economic independence, they brought to marriage a greater sense of confidence in their own worth.[33] Further, the treks westward across the American continent tended to strengthen family ties in the absence of other supports such as churches and schools, hastening more of a partnership role within the home. The creation of church-sponsored women's colleges in the nineteenth century and the opening of coed secondary and higher education further amplified the role of women in the home. Among the better educated women, the growing concern for family planning (spurred in part by the popularity of Thomas Malthus's *Principles of Population*) prompted a demand for efficient methods of birth control. In England, from 1861 to 1900, the number of children per family dropped from 6.16 to 3.3.[34]

What all these changes have to do with Christian ethics becomes clearer when we note that, as we move through the twentieth century, the family, the popularly held foundation of society blessed by God, is still in a state of flux.

THE MODERN FAMILY: IS THE CRISIS REAL?

It has become commonplace to say that many of the problems afflicting modern society reflect a breakdown in the home, and that the family, once regarded the last haven of trust separating and protecting us from our society, is disintegrating. Paradoxically, the family is seen as having provided the best features of social life, but must also serve to safeguard us from the failures of society, for which failures the family must be held responsible: "One of the few issues on which there is consensus today is that the family seems to be going through some kind of crisis . . . divorce statistics, examples of wife and child beating, the rates of delinquency, the demands of women's liberation, and rising sexual immorality are cited as evidence that the family is in deep trouble."[35] It is tempting to accept this account, and equally enticing to join the clamor for a return to traditional values to save our families, and civilization itself, from the acids of modernity.

There is no gainsaying that a great number of alterations have taken place in the family in recent decades, but without minimizing the prospective dangers to its stability wrought by those changes, we must ask whether the term *crisis* is appropriate. Sociologists, when using the term, appear to do so in its etymological sense as "dangerous opportunity," and suggest that most fluctuations in the old patterns are necessary and beneficial.

> Marriage and the family as we have known them in the past, are breaking down and must break down. There is absolutely no possibility that they will survive in the new urban-industrial culture that is taking shape everywhere in the world today. Many people take alarm at this, because they assume that marriage and the family are themselves breaking down. It is very important to stress the fact that this is not so.[36]

One writer points out that in earlier generations the central goal in marriage was that it fulfill such obligations as perpetuating the family line, family inheritance, and tradition. Whether the couple felt personally fulfilled in the relationship was secondary.[37] This situation has certainly changed, with personal satisfactions and creative relationships rating much higher. This has brought with it hazards of its own, in many cases an unwillingness to sustain a relationship that proves unsatisfying. Another sociologist, writing for the U.S. Department of Health and Human Services, acknowledges that this has placed the traditional family at risk. "Endemic to changes in family and household organization and intra-family relationships are a diminished quality of parenting, and increased unpleasantness in the way family members treat one another."[38]

Evidence that many changes have been so detrimental as to appear critical may be identified in terms of increased family violence, countless runaway children, irresponsible sexuality, divorce, and suicide. These must be examined at least briefly if we are to articulate an effective ethic for modern families.

That family violence has been on the increase has been noted in numerous studies. One report revealed that of 47 million couples, some 3 million wives and a quarter of a million husbands experienced severe beatings from their spouses.[39] As many as 62.7 million children under the age of eighteen have at some time been severely abused, exploited, and neglected. The National Task Force on Child Abuse and Neglect reveals that 6,000 to 10,000 children die at their parents' hands every year. Another 50,000 unattended latchkey children are abducted by strangers, and 10 percent of them are found dead.[40]

Runaway children number over 2 million each year according to official records,[41] though the National Center for Health statistics would place that figure six times higher to account for unreported cases. It is predicted that one out of ten youth between the age of ten and seventeen will run away from home at least once.[42] Poor relations with parents, including abuse and neglect, are the chief reasons, causing a National Institute of Health report to conclude, "Running away may be any one of a number of things, ranging from a cry of despair to a victory yell."[43] They are often reacting to severe abuse at the hands of alcoholic or drug addicted parents, and "often the runaways have to turn to crime, prostitution, drug dealing, robbery, and so on, in order to survive."[44]

Given the amount of abuse and neglect they suffered before running away, their lot in life is indeed grim.

Irresponsible sexuality has already been touched on in Chapter 6, but we need to clarify the implications for the family. Before 1915, about 75 percent of brides were virgins, but this dropped to 43 percent in 1980, and it has been verified that people who are sexually active before marriage are twice as prone to commit adultery after marriage as others.[45] Thus sexually active young adults are more likely to have unstable marriages. Further, 20 percent of babies born in the United States are to teenage girls, one-third of whom are unmarried.[46] Of unwed mothers who marry before giving birth, the divorce rate is several times the national average for divorce among other married couples. During the recent decade, the number of youth living together unmarried increased 850 percent, in countless cases bringing unwanted children into the world: "The number of cohabiting adults in 1985 was over 2 million; almost a third of all single women between the ages of 20 and 29 had lived with an unrelated man."[47]

The divorce rate throughout the Western nations began climbing after World War II, and has increased in the United States by 250 percent in just the past two decades. By the year 1990, nearly half of all children had experienced divorce in their families.[48] This figure in the "Christian" West is many times higher than in the Orient where in China, for example, divorce occurs in only 2 percent of marriages.[49]

The effects of divorce are more destructive than was once believed, where the popular sentiment was that "it's better to divorce than have children exposed to conflict." The family is the primary group whose close, intense attachments are crucial as prototypes for subsequent ties. The dissolution of such bonds can be devastating because the family "is the whole world with which [the child] has nothing to compare," and its loss is an amputation.[50] One of the most pervasive and distressing reactions on the part of the child is self-blame: "If they're breaking up, maybe it's my fault."[51] Lower academic achievement, an increase in behavior disorders, and poor moral development are often noted, particularly among older children.[52]

Suicide, especially among the young, appears to be a final desperate alternative to running away from home. At any age it takes many forms, from the slow suicide of alcohol and drugs to the punctuation mark of a bullet. From 1950 to 1970, teen suicides increased 200 percent with the most alarming toll in the more affluent suburbs: There was a 250 percent increase in the decade from 1970 to 1980.[53] Why despair should be so highly correlated with privilege is still unknown. A 1980 study by the American Academy of Child Psychiatry revealed that more than 12,000 children were admitted to psychiatric hospitals nationwide for suicide attempts; one out of four psychiatric hospitalizations of children under the age of fourteen is for attempted suicide.

For the ethicist, the reasons behind self-destruction attempts are most significant: "Divorce of parents, failing a grade [in school], death of a loved one, loss of love, abandonment; these are the kinds of stressful events associated with psychiatric problems in general in children."[54] A physician in the Los Angeles Suicide Prevention Center has stated, "For every teenager who succeeds in killing himself or herself, perhaps fifty others make serious suicide attempts that fail."[55]

Clearly a state of crisis does exist in the relationships within our families, and many studies conclude that the situation is getting worse. Among the complications associated with families in distress, there are persistent underlying themes of alienation, depression, loss of love, hopelessness, and despair. It is tempting to take a simplistic view and blame the conditions on permissiveness in the home, or on humanism and lack of faith, or on the fact that many mothers work outside the home, or on the fading role of the father. All these conditions have been highlighted in articles in popular magazines and in books.[56] None of them adequately accounts for the violent turbulence and despair that exists in so many homes. Nor, on the other hand, does a difference in these conditions seem to account for the heights of creativity and spiritual fulfillment that people sometimes reach in other homes.

TOWARD A CHRISTIAN ETHIC OF FAMILY LIFE

Stanley Hauerwas, in his perceptive and highly original *A Community of Character*, takes a hard look at the realities of the current crisis in family life, and agrees that "the family both as we know and experience it and as many want it to be, is in jeopardy."[57] But his assessment is neither as pessimistic as that of many others, nor as filled with wishful thinking. He does not hold with the notion that the family has lost its significance; rather he contends that other institutions surrounding the family have lost their value to us, and we are thus left with the family as a kind of last refuge in which to find personal and social significance. That situation simply has put too great a burden on the family. It has imposed on the family a task for which it was not created, and our tendency is to give way to disillusionment about the family and a partial abandonment of it.

For one thing, Hauerwas notes, "our modern romantic assumption that love is the necessary condition for marriage and the family is profoundly mistaken. Rather, marriage and the family are the necessary conditions for even understanding what love means."[58] Marriage was not initially intended to be "a fulfilling personal experience," in the way modern jargon expresses it. Marriage has as its major reason for being the embodying of moral and social purposes, which serve to nurture the individual, not for his or her personal satisfaction alone but for serving the wider community.

"Moreover," Hauerwas declares, "the family today is not even seen as the bearer of tradition—whether it be the tradition of a nation, religion, or the family itself. As a result, children are not raised or initiated by the family to be worthy of carrying forward the work of their ancestors, but rather they are raised to be able to make 'intelligent choices' when they are adults."[59] The family is adrift in a sea of competing institutions, most of which are seen as threats to autonomy and personal fulfillment, but against which the family is perceived as impotent.

Indeed, sociological analyses have tended to support the notion of the passivity and powerlessness of the family. Wilson Yates, a sociologist and Christian ethicist, notes that a sample of leading family sociology textbooks reveal "their works presuppose the family to be a passive institution."[60] What is needed, he affirms, is "a positive appreciation of the family's own influence in affecting social change." This respect for the family is enjoined by Ronald Fletcher, in writing about the domestic scene in England:

> The family is a continuing nucleus of shared experiences and behavior, a pooling of individual experiences, through which medium the impressions, attitudes, beliefs, tastes of all its members are interdependently being formed. For example, the child's experience in play groups or at school will be brought back to the family, will give rise to discussion; the child's experiences in church may raise arguments in the home; the [parents'] satisfaction or depression about work, degree of security or insecurity, will be issues for the whole family. Trade union commitments . . . potential views and allegiances, will all enter into and color the experience of the family as a whole. The family therefore is intrinsically bound up with the life of all its members in the wider society.[61]

The family, far from providing a mere introduction to society, or serving only as a training ground for something beyond itself, has a dynamic of its own. It creates the conditions in which its members discover each other even as they are developing their individual identities, and these relationships at their best last a lifetime, during and after the period of years when the members have moved out into society for vocational purposes. They return to find the family ties still profoundly affecting their lives.

Here we may rediscover the ontological importance of the family, totally missed by those who think of marriage as merely a contract and of the family as primarily a biological relationship that can be created and discorporated at will or whim. Each of us knows that our selfhood came into being in the context of a given family, as the issue of one father and one mother. I am who I am because of a unique, and never-to-be-repeated combination of genetic factors and personal interactions with those parents (and in most cases, with siblings sharing many of the same conditions). From the biblical perspective, one's being is established not solely by genetics and nurture, but providentially: "It is He that has made us, and not we ourselves" (Psalm 100:3, 119:73).

To the extent that the Christian can understand that marriage and family life are rooted in God's command, and that one's being is the issue of that unique covenant, one is prepared to develop an ethic for comprehending and resolving the problems now threatening to destroy the family. It is clear that the solutions cannot successfully be imposed from without. They must be exercised within the family. Violence, the problem of runaway children, irresponsible sexuality, divorce, and suicide are family problems inasmuch as the resources for dealing with them must originate within the family, or at least in the character of the persons molded by the family. Society, through legislation, may limit these destructive manifestations of discord, but is incapable of resolving the causes of discord.

But from what wellsprings does the family draw its power to cope with these problems? "If we are to sustain marriage as a Christian institution we will not do it by concentrating on marriage itself. Rather, it will require a community that has a clear sense of itself and its mission, and the place of the family within that mission."[62] The community best able to provide the context and support for the family is the Church. But here it must be emphasized that the Church is not essentially the social community of popular familiarity; we must return here to the concept expressed by Paul: the Church as the body of Christ. Marriage, in this understanding, is not viewed as merely something we do from social habit or religious tradition. It is best understood as a vocation, a calling to a particular kind of life, for the nurturance of its members to know themselves as being part of that body of Christ. It is a calling to which we respond out of love (the realm of bonding) and of fidelity (the realm of will).

The atrocities that afflict so many modern families, the abuses, the irresponsible and sometimes cruel uses of sex, and the running away would be reduced almost to the vanishing point were this understanding achieved. One must say "almost" because even the most devoted Christian knows that love can fade, and the will can be dissuaded.

The problem of sin still plagues us. Yet the Christian who has accepted the *at-one-ment* with Christ has the resources both through personal faith and as a member of the community of faith to assess problems as they arise and to seek the solution in a spirit of love and reconciliation.

Christian ethics finds its voice in such a setting where it is acknowledged that God who blessed the marriage union is also the Lord of the home; that sin may infect any part of the marriage relationship (and ironically, the sexual aspect wherein we come closest to sharing God's gift of life seems also the point at which we are most sorely tempted to deviate); that God's power for restoring betrayed and broken relationships is available because of the mediating work of Christ; and that reconciliation within the family and the Church, and with the community to which the Church reaches out, continues to be the greatest challenge and most fulfilling experience in the Christian life.

When Marriage Fails

The indissolubility of marriage has been advocated as fundamental in most cultures around the world. Even those that seem to make it relatively easy to obtain a divorce (as in Islam, where traditionally the husband has only to say "I divorce thee" three times) have never overtly sanctioned the practice.[63] Jesus admitted that Moses permitted divorce "because of the hardness of your hearts" but made it clear it was contrary to God's will.

If we accept the ontological basis of marriage as expressed in the statement, "These two shall be made one," it would seem that indissolubility can justifiably be made into an ethical rule. But there is a real sense in which marriage should be recognized as a process rather than an unalterable fact, in which case rigid rules are inappropriate. Daniel Maguire makes this a key point in his discussion on marriage.

> Though it would produce wonderment in a world held by static paradigms, there are many possible answers to the question: 'Are you married?' The reply might be 'Somewhat.' Or 'Very much.' Or 'More than ever.' Or 'Scarcely.' People are not so much married as marrying. They are not married people (as though the process were complete and done with): they are marrying people.[64]

Our traditional stress on indissolubility was the product of organized religion's penchant for modeling its regulations after legal structures that are inevitably either-or propositions. In such a view one is either one who obeys the law or breaks the law; either a property owner or not; either married or not married. When the churches sought a way to circumvent the rules, they found it necessary to appeal to the "Mosaic exception" or to the "Pauline privilege."[65] In both cases legalism generally prevailed.

A major problem with the indissolubility idea is that it rests on the assumption that the marriage ceremony establishes the ontological union as a fait accompli. Perhaps in heaven this would be the case,[66] or in an earthly utopia. But marriages are not made in heaven or in utopia. They begin, for the most part, in an expression of *eros*, which too often fails to mature to the level of real friendship, much less of *agape*. As Maguire points out,

> There are marital unions that cannot endure and do not. The temptation to which the Church succumbed in the past was to turn the ideal [of no divorce] into an absolute . . . juridical rule. This rule was then enforced without mercy or differentiation. Such juridical absolutism may be indulged in some courts of law; it should not be tolerated in the courts of conscience.[67]

It may be argued that divorce is opposed to the will of God, and that a permanent monogamous arrangement is the moral standard. But to transform this norm into an ecclesiastical or civil law prohibiting divorce is not to be faithful to the broader requirements of faith or Scripture. Among the requirements of faith is that justice be sustained, for God who is love and who calls us to a relationship with himself through faith, is also the God of justice. Love, as *agape*, seeks what is best for the other person, and that best can only be understood in the context of justice. Thus "Love is not the only absolute moral principle. . . . Love (*agape*) moves us to seek equal justice for all. The claims of justice extend to the equal rights of both partners within a marriage. However, their respective roles may vary from society to society, and through social change equal rights should invariably be a concern."[68] Where the right to just and loving treatment has been violated so often and persistently as to make life within that marriage intolerable, divorce must be a viable option.

But what of Jesus' explicit teaching against divorce? Do not his words comprise all we need for Christian ethics? Surely nothing could be more definite than "Everyone who divorces his wife, except on the ground of unchastity, makes her an adulteress; and whoever marries a divorced woman commits adultery." (Matthew 5:32). Interestingly, the Gospel writer quotes Jesus later repeating this teaching (Matthew 19:9), but there has remarriage to *any* other woman an act of adultery. Still more significantly, the words "except on the ground of unchastity" do not appear in either Mark or Luke, where the same teachings are presented. In the latter two no exceptions are allowed. This difference, minor though it appears, is of major consequence. Some scholars are persuaded that the words in all three Gospels represent an ethic of perfection that transcends any possibility of legal formulation.[69] They are in the same category as Jesus' impossible obligation that comes only a few verses later: "You therefore must be perfect as your heavenly Father is perfect" (Matthew 5:48). Clearly, Jesus knew that with humans, such perfection is impossible (Matthew 19:26).

For the sake of both justice and love, there are situations in which the only moral thing is to dissolve a marriage that should never have been consummated. Emil Brunner expressed it well:

> Between the maintenance of the idea of marriage as an unbreakable relation of fidelity, and the command to love one's neighbor as oneself, God's Command must be here perceived in a spirit of free decision. Certainly the fact of divorce is a sign of weakness, and is a specially clear indication that we are an "adulterous generation." But cases are possible where not to divorce might be a sign of greater weakness, and might still be a greater offense against the Divine order.[70]

The conviction that marriage is a fixed order or institution, an "estate," is still held among many Christians in virtually all denominations. Perhaps this must be the case if society is to avoid the divorce mentality that places individual contentment above the security of a bond pledged as a lifelong commitment. But a 1966 publication by the Anglican Church, *Putting Asunder,* opposed the tradition of adjudication by the courts to determine if some offense had caused the separation. This led to the divorce Reform Act of 1969, which echoed the contention that marriage should no longer be preserved if the safety and sensibility of one or both partners had been threatened. A subsequent publication recognized that "Just as it is possible for any organism to wither and die before it has grown into its full nature, so too marriage may break down before it has grown into what it should become."[71] This probably represents the view held today in most Protestant churches.

The Roman Catholic church has consistently rejected this development within Protestant Christianity, and so has resorted to the older doctrine of nullity, by which the church courts propose that the marriage was not valid at the outset. This, according to Daniel Maguire, has demonstrated the futility and even cruelty of the church trying to imitate the state. As a Catholic theologian, he states,

> Current Catholic Church practice is tied to static, either/or categories. Hence the inability to say that this marriage, which was, no longer is. Juridical assumptions, not moral and ethical ones, dominate Catholic marriage court "annulment" procedures at this time. This increases the suffering of persons who while bearing the inevitable sorrow of an unravelled marriage, are told they were never even married. It seems a cruel effort to save ecclesiastical face by aggrieving human beings already in pain.[72]

Maguire concludes by asserting that church courts and tribunals are an anachronism, a position in which he is joined by a Roman Catholic colleague, Father Charles Curran.[73]

Perhaps nowhere has the mingling of secular law and religious ethics been so crude and the results so murky as in debates over divorce. Yet it is clear that Christian ethics can never abandon the position that the essence of marriage, whether it be viewed as "process" or "an indissoluble estate," is in fidelity pledged "before God and these witnesses." Marriage is an act of will sustaining a love consecrated by God. If it is to be made secure and to have about it the quality of permanence, it must be maintained through the grace and discipline of mutual faithfulness, and sundered only in extremity of circumstances where to sustain it would be to violate the integrity of the persons involved.

CHAPTER EIGHT

The Christian as Citizen

Societies, functioning in some ways as an extension of the families that comprise them, serve many of the same concerns. At their best they nurture individual growth and foster loyalty to the whole, which takes form as expressions of responsible citizenship. Within their compass, performing for individuals and families what these could not do for themselves, societies provide a broad range of political and economic services, laws, means of defense, and a variety of cultural enterprises like education, science, and the arts.

In Western societies the idea of citizenship has its roots in two sources that are not always compatible. The first is the Bible, with its emphasis on the community of God's people. *Citizenship* is not a biblical term, but its meaning is implied in Hebrew Scripture where loyalty to Israel involved adherence to God's covenant and a readiness to sacrifice (and go to war if necessary) to preserve the land and the Hebrew people. In the New Testament the Church, transcending any given nation, represents the community of all whom God calls: *communio electorum,* the *ecclesia.*

A second source of our understanding of citizenship derives from ancient Greece and Rome. Among the Greeks, citizenship depended on one's ability to trace the family lineage to the founders of the city-state in which one lived.[1] In Rome, where in addition to being born into citizenship by virtue of one's family (regardless of where one actually resided), one might obtain it through a grant by Caesar. In cases like the apostle Paul's, citizenship might be dual. Paul held Roman status because his family belonged to the pro-Roman provincials who had been given citizenship during the days of the Republic, but he was also a Jew with citizenship in Tarsus. Unlike most Romans, Paul's Jewish heritage prompted him to give ultimate loyalty to God, to the God of his people, but more importantly, to the God of all people. The question of choosing "to obey God rather than men" (Acts 5:29) would not have occurred to most Greeks or Romans,[2] especially after the move to make divinities of the Caesars. Yet it remains a problem for many even today who equate God and country. Alan Geyer has noted, "Notwithstanding the separation of church and state in the United States, no modern nation has had a greater tendency to interpret political loyalty as a religious duty."[3] Problems arise when the will of "the God of all people" is perceived as being in conflict with the will of "all the people" or even of just the leaders of those people.

CITIZENSHIP AND ACTS OF FAITH

Patriotism

Patriotism appears to the popular mind as the very essence of good citizenship. The rebel and the revolutionary are often viewed with a mingling of disdain and mistrust. Yet the zeal of revolutionaries is often fueled by a patriotism that sees no other recourse for changing a corrupt government. Sometimes such dissenters have also been deeply religious.

There is biblical precedent for regarding national spirit as an accompaniment of religious loyalty. Faithfulness to God, and to the covenant nation Israel, is a familiar theme throughout Hebrew Scripture. Jesus instructed his listeners to "Render to Caesar the things that are Caesar's," and Paul urged, "Let every person be subject to the governing authorities."[4] Paul even went so far as to declare that God's authority stands behind all earthly authorities. "Therefore he who resists the authorities resists what God has appointed" (Romans 13:1,2).

The Scriptures nevertheless caution against an easy equation of God's sovereignty with that of the nation. This motif is found among nearly all the prophets, who on occasion denounce Israel as a sinful nation (Isaiah 1:4), as a faithless wife turned harlot (Jeremiah 5:7,8), for whose apostasy God will turn against it (Amos, Chapter 31.), and smite it with a curse (Malachi 4:6). John the Baptizer seems to have foreseen the fall of the Jewish people not only as a nation already occupied by Rome, but as a religio-political entity: "Already the axe is laid at the root of the trees" (Matthew 3:10). John scorned the idea of a pride in nationhood based simply on the idea that the people could trace their roots to Abraham: "You brood of vipers . . . God is able from these stones to raise up children to Abraham" (Luke 3:7,8).

The tension between faith and patriotism is clearly not a recent problem. Despite Paul's urging obedience to the authorities, he and the other disciples were often at odds with the regulations of their native land and in violation of the laws of Rome. Unquestioning patriotism was not seen as a virtue when it was blind to injustices perpetrated by the government. The apostles often became martyrs because of their civil disobedience.

The theme can be noted in the writings of Augustine and Aquinas, where God's sovereignty is seen in conflict with earthly powers. After Charlemagne, the power of the medieval papacy grew to the point where the issue was not so much nation versus faith as loyalty to king versus obedience to the Church. Later, Shakespeare would have a character intone, "Let all the ends thou aim'st at be thy country's, thy God's and Truth's."[5] The mood of the Renaissance was, at least briefly, to expand loyalty to embrace not just one's country, but humanity. In Jonathan Swift's *A Voyage to Houyhnhnms*, the supremely rational creatures affirmed their allegiance to all their kind everywhere. The demand for fealty to king or country was increasingly viewed, as in Samuel Johnson's definition of patriotism, "the last refuge of scoundrels." The Age of Enlightenment fostered a wish to transcend the provincial outlook; Benjamin Franklin stated his wish that "a thorough knowledge of the rights of man may pervade all the nations of the earth, so that a philosopher may set his feet anywhere on its surface and say: 'This is my country.' "[6]

This spirit of universal citizenship was probably not widely shared even in Franklin's time, however. With the rise of nation-states in the seventeenth and eighteenth centuries, nationalism emerged as a kind of second religion, with the transnational emphasis of the Gospel (Matthew 28:19; Acts 10:33) having little impact. The commitment of the individual citizen to God and country became increasingly the hallmark of one's ethics and character. To be accused of a lack of patriotism was worse than an insult. Not all went to the extreme of Nicolas Chauvin, the Bonapartist who made patriotism a holy obligation (and from whose name *chauvinism* derived), yet the proud boast of a nineteenth-century American naval officer, Stephen Decatur, can still be heard: "Our country, right or wrong."[7]

Doubtless the most vigorous intellectual argument enjoining patriotism as a religious duty came from George Friedrich Hegel. For him, the Absolute Spirit was supremely discernible in the Holy Roman Empire, which provided the two dominant forces in civilized life: church and state. The contest between the two continues the necessary dialectic out of which emerges the synthesis of apparent opposites: absolute monarchy and individual rights; national solidarity and personal freedom. The synthesis, according to Hegel, had never been better manifest than in the German state. "If religion be religion of a genuine kind, it does not run counter to the state in a negative or problematical way. It rather recognizes the state and upholds it."[8]

There are numerous obvious benefits of patriotism, both to the individual who needs a sense of belonging and the sharing of a common heritage, and to the nation that requires a reservoir of loyal members with diverse talents to ensure a creative and secure future. These should not be minimized. But there are dangers that also must not be overlooked because they have profound implications for the shaping of both individuals and nations, and also for the distortion and even destruction of them.

From the biblical point of view, the clearest danger is that of idolatry. The First Commandment imposes a strict boundary between our obedience to God and all other allegiances. In times of war or other stress, it is sometimes difficult for the patriot to discern that boundary; giving priority to one's government in the name of national security makes an idol of the state. Further, it tends to blind the individual to what may be grievous faults in the state's claims. Reinhold Niebuhr made a telling point of this in his *Moral Man in Immoral Society,* where he noted that the devotion and generosity of the citizen that affords great moral satisfaction tend to excuse his country's most evident sins, its ambition, it greed, and its will to power. "There is an ethical paradox in patriotism. . . . Patriotism transmutes individual unselfishness into national egotism. Loyalty to the nation is a high form of altruism. . . . The unqualified character of this devotion is the very basis of the nation's power and of the freedom to use the power without moral restraint."[9]

National anthems, valuable as they are in summarizing the virtues of a people and reminding them of their debt to history, also tend to romanticize the land itself, making a fetish of it for which people are willing to shed blood. Tens of thousands of lives have been lost in our generation over the possession of "holy" land. America's anthem presupposes righteousness in all situations: "Then conquer we must, for our cause it is just. . . ." John C. Bennett reminds us, "The capacity of a nation for self-deception is endless. Its claims to righteousness are used to clothe any actions to which it may be led. In an age of ideology, this tendency is exaggerated. And insofar as there is an element of truth in a nation's moral claims . . . in times of crisis the moral problem created by such self-deception is compounded."[10] He notes the destructive effects of national self-righteousness in which each combatant contends the other is wicked and seizes on any shred of evidence to justify a deepening hatred and military preparedness to defeat it.

Unreasoning patriotism often creates an exclusivism that demonizes citizens of other nations, particularly where there has been a history of conflict. Insulting jargon turns vicious as their people are called dagos, kikes, Huns, little brown devils; their homelands are "the Evil Empire" and "the Great Satan," and so on. Nationalism becomes the excuse for perpetuating distortions that make realistic appraisals and subsequent peace efforts more difficult. It is precisely the understanding of this phenomenon, familiar to anyone who can read today's newspapers, that prompted the writer of the New

Testament Book of Revelation to denounce the state which uses such invective (12:3).

Civil Disobedience

But if patriotism can spawn such problems in international affairs, what
is its relation to civil disobedience? Surely the two are opposed to each other?

In countries where there are political parties, polarization often occurs
in which each faction claims to be the true standard bearer for the principles
that should guide the nation. This gives rise to the "us versus them" syndrome,
fostering animosities that involve efforts to discredit and finally silence the
opposition.[11] For the most stark cases in modern history we have only to recall
the Nazi purges of Hitler's Germany, the death squads of the ruling party in
Perón's Argentina, Batista's Cuba, Marcos's Philippines, Somoza's Nicaragua,
and the ongoing tragedies in El Salvador, South Africa . . . the list continues
to grow.

Indeed it seems inevitable, given the sinful human condition, that patriotism will sponsor both oppression *and* revolution. Both sides claim love of
country and/or love of an ideal (not infrequently utopian) that must be
achieved. The problem, as Edmund Burke pointed out, is that for revolutionaries launching their assaults against existing evils, in their impatience "they
make of it not the last bitter medicine of the state, but its daily bread."

Christian theologians have not been indifferent to the problems of civil
disobedience. Martin Luther roundly condemned it. He held that "The office
of both princes and officials is divine and proper, [even though] those who hold
such offices are mostly of the devil."[12] He acknowledged that the abuse of
power is never justified, but sternly rejected the right of people to rise up
against the rulers, affirming that God, in his own good time, will mete out
appropriate judgment. "We are not to resist the *Obrigheit* with force, but only
with our confession of the truth. If it accepts our witness, well and good; if it
rejects it you are excused and you then suffer wrong for God's sake."[13]

John Calvin, by contrast, while concurring that individual Christians
must obey even unjust rulers, found opportunity through the Estates General as
representatives of constitutional order to oppose and even depose tyrants. Here
he made a clear distinction between the private citizen and the delegated authorities: "There is no more illustrious deed even among philosophers than to
free one's own country from tyranny, and yet the private individual who stabs
the tyrant is openly condemned by the voice of the heavenly Judge."[14]

Among the Reformers, John Knox was the first to provide a theologically
grounded justification for civil disobedience and revolution. "Kings have not
an absolute power in their regiment to do what pleases them; but their power
is limited by God's word."[15] To do otherwise than rebel against a tyrant who
rules contrary to the Bible, would be to rebel against God. In this position,

Knox was joined by Samuel Rutherford, a lesser known figure today but a powerful commissioner to the Westminster Assembly in London (1643), who was condemned to death for proclaiming (in his *Lex Rex*) that neither the king or parliament is sovereign, but the law; if either disobey the law, they are to be disobeyed.[16]

Given the Protestant background of most of the signers of America's Declaration of Independence, it is not surprising that the nation was born in revolution. John Locke took much of Rutherford's *Lex Rex* and gave it a secular setting. The concept of inalienable rights "endowed by their Creator"; government "by consent of the governed"; separation of powers; and the right to resist unlawful authority all contain the Reformer's advocacy. Here there is tacit reiteration of some underlying themes in Christian ethics: God's sovereignty makes the state a possibility; the sinfulness of humankind justifies the sometimes coercive nature of government (Calvin believed coercion and restraints were a necessary function of government precisely because of humankind's proclivity to sin), but also prompts the abuses of power to which rulers are tempted.

But what of the theme of reconciliation in Christian ethics? Can civil disobedience ever be accommodated? Wherever rulers or judges have institutionalized injustice, creating laws to sanctify injustice and exploitation (as was done on behalf of factory owners in industrial England and slave owners in America's southern states in the early nineteenth century, with their Jim Crow laws), many Christians have felt compelled to oppose the rulers and challenge the laws. It is only because men like Wycliffe, Huss, and Tyndale defied laws which prevented access to the Bible that we have the Bible today. Only because Jefferson, Franklin, Adams, Hancock, and others challenged and defied the laws that held the colonies in thrall could America become an independent nation. "Law is not God," as Eugene Carson Blake noted after becoming general secretary for the World Council of Churches. "It has always from the first been a basic Christian conviction that there are times when a Christian ought to break the law."

There are at least four courses of action that can be taken, beyond simple acquiescence in unjust situations. The first of these is a petition to have the injustice remedied, and failing that to resist its implementation by nonviolent demonstration. John Howard Yoder provides a captivating example from the time of Christ, when Pontius Pilate brought effigies of Caesar into Jerusalem, in clear defiance of Jewish law against setting up graven images. Drawing from the writing of Josephus, he notes how the Jews petitioned for the removal of the effigies; then, when threatened with execution if they failed to withdraw and go to their homes, the Jews threw themselves to the ground, bared their necks, and said they would accept death rather than dishonor their tradition. Pilate was so astonished, he ordered the statues carted away. There is much of the Gandhi spirit in this approach, but as Yoder points out, "It did not set up a repeatable pattern; for the next effort of protest, this time against Pilate's confiscation of the consecrated temple treasure to build an aqueduct, was put down bloodily."[17]

A second form of action, also nonviolent, is to abide by the laws, however unjust, (or accept the situation however oppressive), and work to effect changes by legal means. This is perhaps the most popular rejoinder: "If you don't like the laws change them," which is only slightly better than "vote with your feet" or "America, love it or leave it." This second course is generally acceptable if the grievances are not too great, and the matter of time not urgent. But anyone who has tried to get a law changed, or to introduce legislation to alter an unfair condition or civic blight, knows the frustration and pardonable outrage against "the oppressor's wrong . . . the law's delay, the insolence of office,"[18] and seeks another way.

A third option would be to disobey the law, while seeking to effect reform, thus putting one's career or even life at risk as a witness to the seriousness of the situation. This, too, is a nonviolent alternative (except perhaps for the extent of the punishment one accepts). This is also called passive resistance, and has perhaps the longest history, having characterized the actions of the early Christian martyrs, the recent demonstrators against racial segregation in America's deep South, and numerous antiwar protestors. This is what many Christians take to be the meaning of Jesus' words "take up [your] cross, and follow me" (Matthew 10:38, 16:24). It has been most powerfully expressed in South Africa, among the followers of Bishop Tutu and others in the struggle against apartheid.

Fortunately, this third position is given at least tacit recognition in most democratic nations, where hospitality to dissent is considered an essential ingredient in the political process. But the protestor is not to count on it. Samuel Johnson once observed that while little progress can be expected where people lack the courage to rebel against injustice, nevertheless the rebel must never ask or expect quarter; if order is to be maintained, rebellion must be punished. In this view, Jesus himself deserved to die, and significantly Jesus stood before his accusers in silence.

The fourth alternative, open revolt, is the most dramatic. Harold Titus has noted, "Societies that frankly recognize the right of revolution seldom experience revolutions, whereas those that deny such rights are more likely to experience violent upheavals."[19] The American Declaration of Independence is explicit in support of this method where extreme situations warrant: "When a long train of abuses and usurpations, pursuing invariably the same Object, evinces a design to reduce them under absolute Despotism, it is their right, it is their duty, to throw off such Government, and to provide new Guards for their future security." If liberty is to be secured, a country is indeed blessed when, as in England in 1688 and in the United States in 1776, its revolution is carried forward by reasonable and moderate leadership.

The Christian rationale for disobedience must never become so generalized as to become modus operandi, a pattern for living. Always there must be the recognition that, "Every State represents human sin on the large scale,"[20] so efforts to correct injustices must avoid using the sinful methods of those guilty of the injustices. The reformers must acknowledge their own sinful pro- clivities. It is this recognition that gives special meaning to the work of liber- ation theology today.

We have already discussed liberation theology at some length, but a spe- cial word deserves to be added. Despite the emphasis in the popular press on certain militant aspects of the liberation movement, we noted in Chapter 4 the efforts in Korea and in other parts of the Orient to disavow the uses of violence. In Latin America, too, the motivation of love and the motif of laying down one's life for the brethren plays a key part.

> Perhaps it is a testimony to the Christian presence within such movements; per- haps it is the age-old Christian tradition asserting itself—in a diffused way—even among non-Christians. In the peoples' movements, in the base communities, there is a movement to find one's identity, the ground of one's subjecthood, in one's brother, with whom and for whom I live, struggle, and am ready to lay down my life. Grace and love thus flow into one another: I affirm God in my brothers and sisters, and I affirm them in God.[21]

Civil disobedience and rebellion have their place within the framework of patriotism because they have their wider place in the context of love. José Bonino quotes with approval a line from Nietzsche: "Your virtue is worth noth- ing if it cannot become indignant," for when injustice and oppression crush lives, virtue requires counteraction. But Bonino further notes Paul Lehman's translation of Karl Barth's *Epistle to the Romans*: "Love is man's existential standing before God, man's being established as a person. . . . The protest against the course of this world should be made through mutual love and not be abandoned."[22]

Perhaps no form of civil disobedience has recently captured public atten- tion, in America at least, as forcefully as the sanctuary movement. The effort here has been to provide, in clear opposition to the law of the land, asylum for refugees from the bloody strife in Central America, especially from El Salvador. "Defying a national policy of tight limits on immigration from Central Amer- ica, Sanctuary workers have smuggled refugees into the United States and har- bored them in churches, religious houses, and private homes."[23] Despite the illegality of the action, which in 1986 resulted in the arrest and conviction of a number of Christian clergy and laypeople, the program has been endorsed by national organizations affiliated with a wide variety of churches: the American Friends (Quakers), the conservative wing of Judaism, United Presbyterians, United Methodists, and the northern wing of the Baptists. "Considering that much of the leadership of the movement consists of clergy and other devout believers, it is not surprising that the illegal actions taken have been defended in the name of moral and ethical premises derived from religious teaching."[24]

It is also not surprising that most of those violating the law consider themselves patriots in the best tradition.[25]

LOVE, JUSTICE, AND THE LAW

Edwin Markham's famous dictum, "In love is all the law you need,"[26] is a twentieth-century echo of Paul's "Love is the fulfilling of the law" (Romans 13:10). Inasmuch as a major function of government is making and enforcing laws, one might hope that in a Christian society the confident assertions of Paul and Markham would vindicate José Bonino's optimism: "Love is the inner meaning of politics, just as politics is the outward form of love."[27]

The problem here is at least twofold. First, one cannot with confidence point to any society or government that can be called Christian.[28] Many political scientists, even among Christian political theorists, would find Bonino's assertion unacceptable, given the multitude of wholly secular enterprises and cartels characterizing the modern state. Second, even if such were found, Reinhold Niebuhr's caveat is still pertinent:

> The whole question about the relation of love to law in Christian thought is really contained in the question *how* love is the fulfilling of law. Law is distinguished by some form of restraint or coercion. The population may be the force and prestige of the mores and customs of a community, persuading or compelling an individual to act contrary to his inclinations.[29]

Such compulsion would seem contrary to love, which must be free. The rejoinder that, if people truly love they will do what is right and lawful without compulsion, is met by a counterargument known to every Christian who has encountered Jim Crow laws or apartheid: There are circumstances in which it is impossible to exercise Christian love without breaking current laws.

The relation of love and law, then, seems at best paradoxical. Yet from the biblical point of view, a resolution may be found in the juxtaposition of justice and righteousness that lay behind the Hebrew concept of law as the gift of a loving God for the ordering of human society.

The words of Amos, "Let justice roll down like waters, and righteousness like an ever flowing stream" (Amos 5:24), place the terms together in something more than poetic parallelism. Justice has to do with giving each person his due, however or by whomever that owed amount is determined. Righteousness is a covenant concept that envisions going beyond whatever is due by going the extra mile, and as Jesus admonished, "If anyone asks for your coat give him your cloak also; never refuse anyone in need" (Matthew 5:39–42). The idea of justice as expressed here is in keeping with legal tradition from Aristotle to Aquinas, to Blackstone and most modern jurists. In righteousness one not only grants what the law requires, but fulfills all that is implied by the covenant relationship between God and Israel, doing what is right in a spirit of generosity, "not reluctantly or under compulsion" (2 Corinthians 9:7; Philemon 14). Among the ancient Hebrews, the law served primarily as a guide for life within the covenant community. But it also extended beyond the society of Israel. The command to "love thy neighbor as thyself" (Leviticus 19:18) embraced as well "the stranger who sojourns with you . . . you shall love him as yourself" (Leviticus 19:34).

Justice is grounded in the recognition of the other person's worth. "We show what we think persons are worth by what we ultimately concede is due them. If we deny persons justice, we have declared them worthless!"[30] But how is a person's worth determined, so we can know what is due? In contract law, the court may be required to determine when a wage settlement has been violated, and an injustice must be rectified. But in the absence of a clear contract, only love can guarantee that the full measure of a person's worth has been recognized and rewarded.

But is this not utopian? Is such a thing possible except in a theocratic state where the messianic hope has been fulfilled: "The government will be upon his shoulder, and his name will be called Wonderful, Counselor, Mighty God, Everlasting Father, Prince of Peace" (Isaiah 9:6)? Certainly the idea is uniquely biblical, always relating justice and the law to God's *hesed*: God's loving kindness toward his people.[31] But it is a forensic term, implying judgment as well as grace. It also requires that we divest ourselves of the popular but inaccurate opinion that Hebrew Scriptures are legalistic, presenting us with a God of wrathful judgment in contrast to the New Testament showing us a God of love. "There is no verse in the O.T. in which God's righteousness is equated with his vengeance on the sinner, and not even Isaiah 5:16, or 10:22 should be understood in such a manner."[32] The whole intent of God, as perceived in both Hebrew and Christian Scriptures is that of restoration of sinners to the covenant relationship.[33]

Righteous persons are those who, like God himself, are engaged in acts of reconciliation, restoration, and love. The often tragic plight of righteous people, however, is found in an accompanying theme in Scripture: the reality of sin. From the time of the Hebrews' enslavement in Egypt, the innocent have often been seen to suffer.

But what can be the relation of this biblical concept of *Hesed* to contemporary law as practiced in the courts? Surely righteous persons, inspired by God's loving kindness, will seek to engage in acts of reconciliation, restoration, and love. But in the absence of a self-conscious covenant community, can such altruism be implemented by way of law? The issue lies in understanding the nature of law, the task of which is to settle things according to rules. There can be no reliable law that discriminates in favor of certain persons, no matter how loving the judge or how deserving the individual whose case is being decided. "In every case the law says, 'This happens to many.' Law brings, if not all, at any rate a large number under the same rule, and treats those brought under the same rule as equals."[34] Law also, at least theoretically, transcends time just as it transcends persons, so that what has been standardized by law will be the same tomorrow as it was yesterday and today. It thus yields predictability, which is the reason jurisprudence is often referred to as a science.

Yet realistically, anyone familiar with how laws are formed knows there are vagaries and change in law, as witness the fact that the U.S. Supreme Court, in the nineteenth century, concluded that black people do not have their rights infringed by being segregated, and approved the "separate but equal" ruling for purposes of racial separateness. It reversed itself in 1954, declaring those earlier judgments unconstitutional.[35]

Is it only an illusion that behind the changing laws there stands "The Law" to which all codes and contracts relate in some way? There are several theories about the origin of law as practiced in our courts. Some contend that it is a body of rules based on the natural order; others maintain it is no more than a collection of socially contrived rules and standards, confirmed by courts, by which individuals and groups can be coerced into living together with a minimum of abrasion. Still others argue that our laws are the civil formulation of commandments received from God by way of inspiration and revelation.

Here we have an apparent trichotomy: law is either natural, contrived, or inspired. It is useful to examine these three theoretical foundations for the laws and see whether they are necessarily mutually exclusive.

Natural Law

Natural law is based on the premise that there is a moral order and purpose resident in the natural order that can be discovered by reason. Natural law theories (which sometimes include intuition, with reason as a means for discovering the order and purpose), may or may not be religious in character, but all hold that we have a duty to seek what is right and to establish rules to ensure that right will be done.

It is in postprimitive thought that we first encounter the idea that justice and right are grounded in *lex naturae*. Ancient tribal life was probably not reflective enough to consider law as rooted in anything higher than authority of the chief. To the Greeks of the classical period, for whom the word *cosmos* implied universal and perfect order, there appeared a necessary connection between natural law and the naturally just. Pythagoreans affirmed a cosmic harmony and distinguished between justice as perceived in the cosmic mind and that meted out by human laws. Aristotle, too, noted the difference between "the naturally just" (*fusai dikaion*) and human legality (*nomikon*). The Stoic philosophers led a kind of back to nature movement that impressed scholars in the new Roman republic. "Stoic philosophers found numerous followers in Rome, among them Cicero, who did much to popularize Greek philosophy in his country."[36] Later Roman jurists identified the law of nature (*jus naturale*) with the philosophical concept of the laws of the nations (*jus gentium*) on the ground that "the universality of a given rule [was] taken as an indication of its naturalness."[37] The second-century jurist Gaius further stressed the common ground of *jus gentium* and "natural reason," which made possible the comparative study of national constitutions.

A lack of legal precision prevented natural law from being taken with complete seriousness by the Romans, who could point to the fact that while slavery was common and supported by the *jus gentium*, it could not be justified by *jus naturale*, inasmuch as, according to Stoic philosophy, all men are born free.[38] The early Christian church also scorned the concept of natural law until Thomas Aquinas melded it with scholastic theology in the thirteenth century. Aquinas declared that God establishes all law as *lex naturae*, in which all things participate. Political and natural law were seen as having a common denominator in the will of God, and because the Church posed as the sole rightful interpreter of this Divine source, it is not surprising that the Church assumed the privilege of ultimate moral judgment. It was the abuse of this prerogative that led, in large part, to the Reformation.

Most commonly associated as the father of natural law in the seventeenth century, Hugo Grotius (1583–1645) held that human reason is consonant with nature's processes, though he bowed to the still formidable influence of the Church in affirming that both reason and nature are under God's sway. Yet he declared that the moral law that reason perceives in nature is as axiomatic as mathematical propositions, which even God cannot negate (or would not, as a rational deity). He thus made natural law ultimately independent of God (see his *De Jure Praedae* and *De Jure Belli ac Pacis*, which became the basis of international law).

The theory gained considerable ground during the Age of Reason, becoming amalgamated with the moral idealism popular among leading thinkers like Voltaire and Rousseau in France, Locke in England, and Paine and Jefferson in America. But not until the nineteenth century did a thoroughgoing philosophy of natural law arrive in the writing of jurist Rudolf Stammler, who based his axiological position on the critical system of Immanuel Kant. Fidelity to reason and conscience have been the hallmark of the new trends that have had their impact on twentieth-century evaluations of the rights of the individual and of civil rights in general with or without religious sanction.

The problems with the natural law theory, as anticipated by Aristotle, have to do with lack of precision and with a tendency to be cavalier with established law. Aristotle first noted a vagueness that could allow for the brute to triumph over the weaker but more virtuous individual. Where are the models in nature for human ethics? Certainly one does not learn proper behavior toward one's children from the crocodile nor toward one's spouse from the black widow spider. Aristotle struggled with the problem, but could only offer reason as a means of keeping nature's laws in balance. Depending on one's definition of nature and reason, one might justify both the burning of heretics and condemnation of the practice; the keeping of slaves or the liberation of them; the absolute right of the state or the natural rights of the individual. This kind of rationalization accounted later for Martin Luther's scornful charge: "Reason is a whore." Perhaps even more disturbing is the way Adolf Hitler employed the natural law theory in support of his fascist program in Nazi Germany. He wrote, "The whole of nature is a continuous struggle between strength and weakness, an eternal victory of the strong over the weak. All nature would be full of decay if it were otherwise."[39]

A second deficiency with the natural law theory was pointed out by Felix Cohen in his *Ethical Systems and Legal Ideals*, where he notes that proponents would move outside of nature to make their evaluations without acknowledging the frame of reference for such judgments. "They failed to make explicit the positive premise involved in every step from the heaven of ethical axioms to the terrestrial fields of law administration."[40] The quasi-religious idealism that seems inherent in natural law theories continues to attract adherents, but appears to be unable to provide an effective bulwark against recurring tyrannies.

Contrived Law

Law as socially contrived is a popular concept with countless supporters today, indeed perhaps the largest number for any theory. Many insist that law is no more than a system of political rules: self-contained, analytical, positive, and independent of morality. They generally are sympathetic with Oliver Wendell Holmes's comment: "I hate justice. When a man talks about justice I know he has stopped thinking in legal ways." But there is no single frame of reference for thinking in legal ways. There is disagreement whether law originates in social tradition, in the state, or in the courts; there is only agreement that they are the product of social strategies.

Many anthropologists, psychologists, and social philosophers have insisted that people make decisions in terms of the customs in which they are conditioned. Auguste Comte, the eighteenth-century father of sociology, tried to apply the methods of the natural sciences to the study of society, and he, too, concluded that values and the laws that safeguard them arise from custom and tradition. But it was the late Roscoe Pond who expressed it most explicitly: "In stating claims or demands in general terms as social interests, attempt is made more or less consciously to secure as much as possible of the whole scheme of social interests with the least sacrifice." This, as Felix Cohen observes, "is the familiar Pragmatist position stated in a socio-legal framework."[41]

There are, of course, ambiguities in social custom, and while legislators occasionally bow to its force, most seek clearer guidelines for establishing laws. They look to the state, or its leaders, or to the courts. Here, too, there are risks. In every generation there have been political leaders who wanted to *be* the state, and to leave after them a structure that would, as in Hitler's dream, "endure a thousand years."

Nearly five centuries ago, Machiavelli attempted to provide a rationale for permitting the control by political rulers of citizens as if the latter were unruly beasts, while at the same time urging the virtues of patriotism to ensure their obedience. Few political leaders have stated so openly their aspiration for such authority, but most would concur that values important to the state should be issued in pronouncements and laws that can be promulgated through whatever media are at hand, including the curriculum of the schools. Law, according to Hobbes, Nietzsche, Hitler, and Carl Schmitt, is a tool created by the state, for the state. For Schmitt, the "crown jurist" of the Nazi party, politics was a gladiatorial arena in which each contender accepts a fight to the death. Social custom for such people is too vague to guide the people; traditions about right and wrong mean nothing unless they have been consciously fabricated by the leaders, and then enforced. "History," wrote Hitler, "shows that the right as such does not mean a thing, unless it is backed up by great power."[42]

To avoid the tendency for popular custom and folk wisdom to be absorbed and domesticated by the state, the ancient Stoics produced what is sometimes erroneously thought to have originated in English common law: the concept of *equity*. This was a method of balancing statute law with a combination of custom and natural law. It entertains a constant tension between positive or statute law and the ideals of society. In our own recent history, it was often invoked by Justice Holmes, who despite his denial that law is a system of reason or deduction from the axioms of natural law (insisting that "law is what the courts will do in fact, and nothing more pretentious"), nevertheless sought always to probe for a sounder insight into justice than statute books alone could provide. Holmes's characteristic position became epitomized in his frequent objections: "Justice Holmes dissents."

Many students of jurisprudence who have acknowledged the ambiguities of natural law, and who have recognized the danger in assuming that justice and law are synonymous, especially when both are defined by the unchallengeable dictate of the state, seek the foundations of morality, justice, and law elsewhere. Many find it in religious tradition.

Inspired Law

Law and the will of God have long been seen by prophets and by many scholars to be so closely related as to be virtually inseparable. From Hammurabi and Moses to Augustine, Aquinas, Luther, Calvin, and to many of the architects of the United Nations, there has been a tradition of "God seekers." These would concur that we have been endowed by God with a knowledge of deity, and that that knowledge has issued in an understanding of what God demands of us: "He has showed you, O man, what is good; and what does the Lord require of you but to do justice, and to love kindness [*hesed*], and to walk humbly with your God" (Micah 6:8).

From the biblical worldview, ours is not a realm that operates according to its own natural, rational, or moral laws, but the creation of God wherein everything serves his purposes. We are not autonomous beings, but creatures whose very humanity rests on the fact that we are created in his image, and that God visits and cares for us. As a consequence, "ethics is not based on a scheme of moral principles or human values, but upon obedience to him whose deeds of justice and mercy have shown men what is good."[43] Hence the close relation between religious ethics and the law.

To be sure there are those who object that religious leaders have often used the will of God to justify ungodly behavior. In Morris Cohen's now classic book *Reason and Law*, we find,

> It is hardly necessary to show that hatred, pugnacity and brutality have not only been human traits at all times, but have been glorified in religion and literature. Consider the command in Deuteronomy to exterminate all the inhabitants of a conquered city, or the ferocious ending of the touching psalm [137] "By the Rivers of Babylon," not to mention the obvious delight in wholesale slaughter in the Book of Esther.[44]

It should be remembered, however, that the Bible is not a single, monolithic production from a solo writer of one historic period, but a collection of writings from many hands over hundreds of years, revealing a maturing understanding of God's purposes. Few biblical scholars today make the claim for the Bible that Muslims traditionally make for the Qur'an, that it was dictated word for word from on high. Rather it is understood that, as sinful creatures who received God's message, their proclivity to hear what they wanted to hear, and to record whatever seemed to justify their plans prompted the scribes to write that God ordered the activities which served their religious or national interest. Other examples beyond Cohen's would include the supposed instructions of God for Israel's feast days, fast days, new moon festivals, prayers, the burning of incense, and so on, that are found in Exodus, Leviticus, Numbers, and elsewhere.[45] They are presented as commanded by God. Yet a few centuries later, Isaiah is found denouncing these same observances in the name of God: "Your new moons and your appointed feasts my soul hates; they have become a burden to me" (Isaiah 1:14, 15). God is presented elsewhere forbidding marriage outside the covenant community, and commanding circumcision as a condition for membership in the covenant community (and thus a condition of salvation). Yet we know that Naomi married outside the faith, and her daughter-in-law Ruth, an outsider, married Boaz, to become the ancestor of Jesus. Circumcision was dismissed by Paul as having no spiritual significance (1 Corinthians 7:19). Hatred of enemies is approved in much of Hebrew Scripture: "Do I not hate them that hate Thee? I hate them with perfect hatred" (Psalm 139:21–22). Such an attitude is denounced in the New Testament (see Matthew 5:44; Romans 12:17–21; Titus 3:3–4; 1 John 3:15).

Justice Benjamin Cardozo, in discussing how all laws, including religious laws, arise and then are replaced, notes, "There is not a creed which is not shaken, not an accredited dogma which is not shown to be questionable, not a received tradition that does not threaten to dissolve."[46] Even laws perceived by faith undergo change.[47]

With the advent of Christianity, the way in which the love of God was perceived as extending to all humankind began to make a significant impact on the way laws were written. The Hebrew prophets had anticipated this: "Are you not like the Ethiopians to me, O people of Israel?" (Amos 9:7). But the cultural and religious exclusiveness of the Jewish people with their aversion to Gentiles (*goi*, "outsiders"), made fellowship with non-Jews difficult. Indeed this was one of the earliest causes of their rejection of Jesus; he spoke freely with Gentiles and ate with sinners. He declared his mission was to the whole world, and his followers declared Gentiles "fellow heirs" of the kingdom (Ephesians 3:1–6; 1 Timothy 2:5–7).

Recalling the way in which emphasis on the sovereignty of God motivated the early Christians to declare they must sometimes choose the will of God over the laws of men (Acts 5:29), note how laws have been gradually modified to acknowledge the need to correct injustice in much human legislation. This can be traced from Magna Charta, to the Bill of Rights, to the Emancipation Proclamation and the freedom of conscientious objectors to reject military service.

In a curious manner the doctrine of sin has also influenced legislation, and not only in the obvious way of prompting laws to curb violent and lustful behavior. Augustine declared that sinful pride and self-love prevent people from loving their neighbors as themselves, and consequently from serving their neighbors' needs except as law requires it. Welfare laws thus arise from an acknowledgment of our sinful resistance to doing what ought to be done; we place ourselves under obligation knowing things will not otherwise improve. In similar fashion, democracy is created because without the checks and balances it provides, our sinful condition would enable tyranny to flourish, and make rebellion and revolution inevitable. John Bennett notes,

> It is realized by Christians that unless suffrage is open to all classes and races great injustice is usually done to people who have no voice; that a nation that does not encourage wide participation in political life fails to develop its human resources; that unless there are constitutional protections for individuals and minorities a nation can easily slide towards tyranny . . . and the State become an idol.[48]

It is, however, in the influence of the Christian concept of love that we find the closest approximation to what might be termed the Christianization of law. The place to see it in clearest contrast to what came before is in the realm of *distributive justice*. Aristotle noted a distinction between *simple* justice (which accords the same reward and punishments to each person) and *distributive* justice, which recognizes that in some cases giving the same to each person may not be just at all. Providing exactly the same food ration to a very small child and a very large man would be one example. Distributive justice seeks a more fair distribution to different people. But on what grounds? Greek distributive justice denied the benefits of citizenship to slaves and foreigners. But within the early Christian community, because all people were loved as being equally children of God, "There was not a needy person among them, for . . . distribution was made to each as any had need" (Acts 4:34–35). Attention to the needs of people, rather than to their social status, eventually worked its way into secular law wherever Christians lived and exercised their influence. Needs were identified not only in terms of survival, but eventually included education, health, police and fire protection, and other entitlements, in addition to freedom of speech, freedom of worship, and even freedom for "the pursuit of happiness." This last one comes as a surprise to many who have misunderstood the Puritan spirit, for it arose out of that Puritan ideal which influenced the authors of the Bill of Rights.

The biblical concept of humankind being created in God's image has raised the common citizen to a dignity never before acknowledged or enjoyed. The imperative "Thou shalt love thy neighbor" has put an edge on the law that never existed before. These facts have had practical and far-reaching implications for the governance of society, and represent what Reinhold Niebuhr modestly called "the relevance of Christian love to the problems of society."[49]

THE CHRISTIAN AND THE ECONOMIC ORDER

Because a civilization, like the communities that comprise it, is the product of labor, intelligent purpose and cooperative planning are required. These demand that ethical decisions be made to prevent the waste of labor and exploitation of the laborers. From the biblical perspective, life in community implies life in mutual service and stands in opposition to any effort of persons or groups to abuse other persons or groups by demanding services without just and adequate compensation. The Bible thus places economic concerns at the center of our attention (Malachi 3:5), and Jesus made some of his most telling points in terms of property (Luke 12:16–21), hard work, and generous wages (Matthew 20:1–15). Emil Brunner insists that "an ethic which ignores economic problems has no right to call itself either a Christian or a Scriptural ethic."[50]

The sense of being a chosen people had a powerful influence on the Hebrews' sense of the proper use of land, tools, and distribution of goods. Meyer Waxman notes, "Since the Jews were chosen from among all the other nations to be a morally distinguished people, it follows that their social relations must be conducted on high ethical levels."[51] Being unfair in business was considered theft: "The harsh term of robbery (*Gesel* or *Geselah*) is used . . . indicating not only the limited form of taking things away from a fellow man by force, but also for forms of unfairness in business dealings."[52] To underpay a laborer was the same as stealing from him.

On the positive side, the insistence of the prophets on justice for the poor, for widows and orphans, is a natural outgrowth of the fact that chosenness is reflected in the lives of all the people of God. "Because each individual's identity is inextricably rooted in the covenant between Israel and the Lord, no individual can live a righteous and full life without addressing the needs of all of God's people."[53]

This theme carries over into the New Testament as we note in the parable of Dives and Lazarus (Luke 16:20f.) and in the definition of pure religion "as caring for orphans and widows in their affliction" (James 1:27). Among many of the early fathers like Ambrose, John of Chrysostom, and Gregory the Great, such care was never to be a source of self-congratulation, as if one had done something virtuous. Gregory declared, "When we minister the necessities of life to those who are in want, we are returning to them their own, not being bountiful with what is ours."[54]

Ownership

The notion of what is ours confronts us with the question of property and its uses, which is at the very heart of the economic issue. In Hebrew Scriptures, the right of property ownership is taken for granted, but the Psalmist's declaration, "The earth is the Lord's and the fullness thereof" (Psalm 24:1) was a reminder that ultimately we are only temporary occupiers with a responsibility for stewardship. In Deuteronomy, special instructions are given to allow some of the bounty of the land to be used by the poor and sojourning strangers (Deuteronomy 24:19–22), a practice reflected in Ruth's gleaning in Boaz's field (Ruth 2:2). The reminder that this was to recall the Hebrews' days of bondage in Egypt, when such consideration would have been most welcome, may also underlie the Golden Rule of Jesus.

In the early Church, as has been previously noted, the sharing of property became the rule: "No one said that any of the things which he possessed was his own, but they had everything in common" (Acts 4:32). That this was a local and temporary situation seems obvious, but it does reveal a basic concern in Christian ethics for taking full responsibility for the well-being of all.

Acquisition of property was common with Christians during the Middle Ages among those who could afford it, and laid the groundwork for the feudal system. It should be remembered, however, that many of those acquiring land and building their little kingdoms were not Christians, but thoroughgoing pagans who merely adopted (or were baptized into) Christianity for whatever reasons seemed expedient. It was not until Thomas Aquinas wrote his *Summa Theologica* in the thirteenth century (II–II q. 66, a.2) that a theological rationale for ownership came into being. His urging that economic activities should be controlled by ethics, and subordinated to spiritual ends, was generally not heeded, albeit widely discussed in the fledgling universities.[55]

The Protestant Reformation had a profound effect on Christian thinking about property ownership and mercantile practices, when large numbers of the rising middle class (as well as many princes) began siding with the reformers against the church of Rome. The latter had vast land holdings, exercised various forms of taxation, tended to support kings and aristocracy, and had generally forbid lending money at interest. Martin Luther was suspicious of the new capitalism, which he felt contributed to a spirit of rebellion against authority. But John Calvin favored initiative and enterprise, and supported the charging of reasonable interest as a means of improving one's business. God had commanded that we earn our bread by the sweat of our brow, and if we are diligent and prosper, it may be evidence that we are working with God rather than against him. Calvin preached responsibility in the uses of property, and actively sought to persuade the merchants of Geneva not to seek monopolies on essential goods or to retail them at high prices. Trade and industry were to be used for God's glory and the service of humanity. His identification of self-denial as the "summary of the Christian life"[56] seems almost quaint in our age noted for its materialism, corporate takeovers, and executive greed.[57]

It was John Locke, in the eighteenth century, who nudged the new capitalism in the direction of almost radical individualism, contending that owning property and making all legitimate profit is a natural right, supported by the theory of natural law. His only qualifications were that one should not acquire more property than one could actually use, and should be sure "there was still enough and as good left" for others to gain and use.[58] It has been argued that Locke and the Puritan movement prepared the way for the nineteenth-century laissez-faire economics of the Manchester School in England, and its less formal gospel of wealth counterpart in America.[59]

Discussion of property rights must be broad enough to include not only real estate and tangible goods, but also noncommodities like clean water and unpolluted air, and such services as medical, educational, sales, and even entertainment. Beyond these, economics is also concerned with employment and the relation of unemployment to inflation. All these influence the quality of life in society and clearly have ethical implications that cannot be ignored. To be sure there are Christians who, while not denying the importance of these concerns, contend that churches should not become involved. This is usually on the grounds that neither the state nor the churches should interfere with the free market, and that the churches' agenda should be confined to spiritual matters. The latter argument is often reinforced with "Let the church be the church."

The problem with the slogan becomes apparent when we recall that the issue of human need was at the very heart of the early Christian church's view of economic justice. The church in the Book of Acts (4:35) was certainly being the church when it distributed property and goods "to each as any had need." It is significant that the Christian community did not leave such matters up to the individual conscience, but made such sharing a requirement. When Ananias and Sapphira secretly tried to withhold proceeds of a sale that should have been used for the whole community, they "fell down dead," upon being discovered in their deception (Acts 5:1–11). It should be noted that they were not struck down by the community, but by the compelling force of conscience.

Controls and Freedom

In our contemporary social and economic systems where individualism and corporate strategy often vie for supremacy, we cannot count on altruism or conscience to provide for basic needs. The churches, for good reasons, can no longer impose requirements, but governments can and often do impose a variety of controls.

Price controls represent one example of the effort to prevent exploitation in the marketplace, and make it possible for at least most citizens to provide for their families. This remains a thorny issue, even among some Christian ethicists. In 1973 when OPEC raised oil prices and cut back supplies, there were not only long lines of irritated customers at the filling stations, but frightened and distressed people in the lower economic classes who were unable to heat their homes. The federal government in the United States then imposed price controls. "This was a blessing for consumers—and the poor in particular. For the eighty-five-year-old widow living without luxuries and on a meager diet already, controls on the price of home heating oil are immensely significant."[60]

A rebuttal to the advocacy of economic controls has been proffered by Milton and Rose Friedman in their book *Free to Choose*. With reference to that 1973–74 oil crisis, the Friedmans blame the long lines at the filling stations on "one reason and one reason only: because legislation administered by a government agency did not permit the price system to function. . . . Supplies were allocated to different areas of the country by command, rather than in response to the pressures of demand as reflected in price."[61]

The Friedman position, popular with a great many economic conservatives, has a history at least as old as John Locke, who noted that while property does not exist in the original "state of nature," it is created when people impose their own creative ideas on nature, modifying it with their efforts. Respect for persons and the property they create forms the basis of the ethic of property rights, and includes the prospect of trading or selling such property at one's own discretion, and for whatever price one wishes to attach.[62] The contribution of Locke to the shaping of laissez-faire in the rising individualism of the eighteenth century lent support to the free enterprise system that created enormous wealth during the industrial revolution. Economist Karl Polanyi stresses this in his history *The Great Transformation*,[63] noting the free market's success in breaking up feudalism and stimulating a vast amount of production.

But Polanyi also notes that the consequences in human terms were often appalling. In country after country where the new capitalism was entrenched with its free market ideology, it was found necessary to intervene with government planning and price controls to protect the wage earners and the stability of society in general. "The concept of self-regulating market," he notes, "was utopian, and its progress stopped by the realistic self-protection of society." One can trace many modern reforms to the realization of the dehumanizing effects potential in the free market system.

> The outpouring of legislation in the Progressive and New Deal eras of twentieth century America came in direct response to human need and social pressure. The exploitation of child labor . . . hazardous working conditions, dehumanizing long hours of work, low wages, periodic times of depression with high unemployment, shoddy and dangerous products, ruin of the natural environment, racial, religious and gender discrimination all evoked social exposé, popular outcry, and governmental intervention. It was as though society instinctively rebelled against the triumph of instrumental economic values over intrinsic social ones.[64]

There is no gainsaying the fact that a free market economy can boast of a certain efficiency in production and distribution, and certainly in profit making. But Philip Wogaman notes that it often makes for great social inefficiency, irresponsibility, and waste. In his book *Economics and Ethics,* he observes that while the free market performs well in providing food, clothing, shelter, and entertainment, "It is an awkward mechanism for providing community-wide facilities in education and recreation and communication. It is a virtually impossible mechanism for providing highways and national defense."[65] In fact, however, the market, where free from any significant restraint, does not provide even the benefits named. Karen Lebacqz, after detailing the plight of workers in South Africa and the Philippines, points out

> . . . in the United States . . . farm workers are often not protected by laws that provide minimum wages or other protections for factory employees. Most migrant farm workers are paid, not by standards of a minimum wage per hour, but by the quantity of produce picked. They work as families but are registered as individuals; thus four or more people may work without getting separate pay. Wages are often withheld until the harvest is over, thus forcing borrowing and paying back of interest.[66]

Another problem relates to the fact that in free market competition, there is a considerable incentive to cut production costs in ways that are damaging to people and to the community. Theoretically, this should correct itself as companies that produce shoddy goods are edged out by those that do not cut costs in such fashion. But we may consider one of the hidden but more treacherous aspects: "The cheapest way to dispose of waste products is generally to dump them into the nearest stream or landfill or to let them belch forth into the skies without using expensive filtering devices or transporting them to safer places."[67] Further, it costs a great deal of money to install safety devices and to cover medical expenses for employees. Companies that evade such costs may increase their competitive edge over companies that offer such benefits.

> The market thus provides an incentive to irresponsible behavior when it saves money to be irresponsible. Somehow the rules of the game have to be structured in such a way that all participants are rewarded for good, not for irresponsible behavior. But that requires priority-setting from some vantage point outside the market mechanism itself.[68]

Priorities and Power

What vantage point might we achieve for priority setting? One approach might be to turn to an elite group of people who by their proven success have demonstrated their qualifications to set the standards. Certainly there have been individuals like Cyrus McCormick, Andrew Carnegie, and Andrew Mellon who viewed their wealth as a social responsibility and endowed schools, libraries, hospitals, and numerous philanthropic foundations. But these seem to have been exceptional persons. The skills and habits of mind entailed in amassing a fortune may not lend themselves to the broader service of human good; the record, at any rate, does not encourage us to rely on the wealthy elite. Carnegie, in particular, despite his visible philanthropies, paid notoriously low wages.

A second strategy might be to involve major corporations in this role. Mobil, Exxon, and others have been conspicuous in their support of cultural programs enriching the lives of countless people. But the enhancing of the quality of life for the educated populace in these ways has not yet addressed the problems of poverty, health care for the elderly, adequate housing, environmental protection, and others that haunt us.

Further, in our relatively democratic structure, room has been provided for corporations to expand, take over other companies, link with like organizations in other countries, and become multinational structures that do not merely set priorities, but exercise vast power. It is ironic that while emerging third world countries are struggling to achieve democratic nationhood, the established democratic societies have created the conditions for the rise of supercorporations that could conceivably transcend all political structures and actually oppose democratic processes. At the start of the 1980s there were 500 such corporations, the United States being home to 42 percent of them, controlling nearly 75 percent of all the world's manufacturing assets.[69] These are not democratic organizations, but actually feudal in their management, viewing stockholders not as citizens of the company but part of the inventory. Laws against monopoly appear to be ineffective against them. "Through price fixing and calculated limitation of production to raise prices and profits, the corporation achieves 'taxation without representation.' Corporations have no discernible center of loyalty."[70] They can be aloof to any governmental system, functioning almost as colonial overlords. If they dislike the government or the standards in a host country they can subvert it (as was alleged of ITT in Chile). This gives them an awesome power, with virtually no restraints.

In such a situation, predicts Kenneth Galbraith, we may witness the rise of a new class of ruler, the "group personality." A vast number of specialists is obviously needed. But, "when power is exercised by [such] a group, not only does it pass into the organization but it passes irrevocably. Group decision, unless acted upon by another group, tends to be absolute."[71] When one considers that one such "group person" as Exxon had in one year gross revenues three times the revenue of New York State (a hundred times that of Nevada) and nearly one-sixth of the total receipts of the U.S. federal government, something of the magnitude of its power can be recognized.[72]

It is not difficult to envision the power that five hundred such group persons might exercise over the world, when they control so great a measure of its industrial and agricultural power. A handful of such corporations, if they proceeded to merge across national boundaries, could seriously influence or even control a host nation's political structure.[73] On the other hand, if competition among such superpersons led to mutual distrust and hostility, they could override their host nation, or break with other nations and call on the armed forces of the host nation to defend them. Nations might thus be drawn into war irrespective of political and diplomatic efforts, to protect the vested interests of the multinational corporations that have provided the nation its economic benefits. Here the Christian doctrine of sin warns that, being narcissistic, the majority of people can be seduced into going to war rather than relinquish their cherished standard of living.

There is another problem with economic democracy that is often overlooked. This is an underlying assumption that the majority will always know what is best for the majority. "This opinion," Emil Brunner declared, "is based simply on the individualistic, optimistic idea of the Enlightenment: that rational self-love will lead to the 'greatest happiness of the greatest number.' "[74] Given the way mass advertising, promotion, and marketing are free to carry out the manipulating of public taste and desire, this optimism appears unwarranted. It is just as easy in a democratic society as in a totalitarian one to be swept up in the spirit of me first, the spirit of mammon, of sheer materialism. The apostle's warning here is especially pertinent: "Be not conformed to his world" (Romans 12:2), with its alluring profits and the seductive tendency to put personal (or corporate) gain above the well-being of the community. Economic democracy offers nothing to discourage acquisition and conformity; indeed it almost invites them.

It is instructive to compare the Gospel ethic of "Do not lay up for yourselves treasures on earth" (Matthew 6:19) and "Do not be anxious about your life . . . about tomorrow . . ." (Matthew 6:25, 34) with the modern economic spirit (whether capitalist or communist) of acquisitiveness, competition, and crippling anxieties about tomorrow. The aim of all economic activity, and certainly within the capitalist framework, is profit that can easily be expressed in mathematical terms. It tends thus to become quantitative and mechanical, rather than qualitative and human service oriented. Further, it tends to dominate both the legal and political spheres, requiring legislation (and legislators) to protect private enterprise favoring the gathering of greater and greater power for large companies. This leads to an economic rationalism, which manages business in terms of formalized and standardized practices that look only to "bottom line" accounting, an attitude that often treats those who produce goods with less respect than the products themselves. In this increasing abstract world of economics, the working person becomes impersonal, numerical. Practically, personal considerations disappear.[75] Such a system is clearly at odds with the Christian concern for service to one's fellow beings. It tends to debase humans and to become irresponsible. Emil Brunner called it "irresponsibility developed into a system."[76]

Nevertheless, it remains true that in a democratic framework, there are possibilities for abuses to be corrected, for wrongs to be redressed. There is no Christian economics per se, but within the democratic system, the individual person who has been granted the gift of faith, and from whom a life of faith and love is required, can exercise responsibility and love. Such a person will recall that a primary purpose of any economic system is to provide for the sustenance of people and the preservation of a balanced environment. For love's sake, and in obedience to the sovereign God, the Christian will seek every means to achieve an equitable distribution of essential products that satisfy real needs and to achieve full employment. Nothing could be more contrary to the spirit of Christian ethics than the creation of artificial needs, overproduction, underemployment, and the devastation of the environment for short-range profit.

Having said that there is no distinctly Christian economic system, can it be required that a Christian conduct business according to the Golden Rule? At least three problems confound such a plan: *interest, wealth,* and *luxury.* Realistically, "the present economic system is absolutely unthinkable without interest . . . the recompense for the loan of an economic good which is to be used for productive ends."[77] Wealth represents a problem because so often it has no real relation to work or achievement. This is especially true after the second or third generation when the heirs simply inherit the benefits. Jesus clearly saw the dangers of wealth, and declared it easier for a camel to go through the eye of a needle than for a rich man to enter the kingdom of God (Matthew 19:24). It would be tempting to dismiss this as poetic hyperbole, but it is consistent with his deep concern for the danger of false self-confidence engendered by worldly goods, which also blunts one's capacity to respond to or even notice the needs of others. He also confronted the "rich young ruler" with the challenge to divest himself of his wealth in order to become a disciple (Luke 16:18–23).

Luxury easily goes beyond wealth into the realm of extravagance and self-indulgence. This remains a perennial lure in any economic system, but one which the Christian will always find offensive, remembering the biblical injunction against vanity and Jesus' warning about mammon (Matthew 6:24).

The Christian transformation of the economic order will come about not by proclaiming a Christian economic order, which would be utopian at best and a paralyzing set of regulations at worst, but by creating conditions in which obedience to God and service to one's fellows leads to human fulfillment: "I came that they may have life, and have it abundantly" (John 10:10).

To create such conditions, the Christian has available a number of strategies. The first is to be absolutely clear that the focus for the whole effort is to be the Gospel proclamation of God's sovereignty, and Christ's work of reconciliation and redemption. No social gospel will succeed if this primary center is omitted or even minimized. The second will include the concept and acts of service. Jesus's command to Peter, "Feed my sheep," and his own example of tireless service, sets the tone for the economic venture in a Christian context. Third, there must be a candid appraisal and confession of the failure of Christians across the centuries to carry out the injunction of Christ to care for the poor and fatherless. There is an appalling contrast between the Gospel challenge and the actual economic conditions in our society where so many millions live below the poverty level and death from starvation is commonplace. Confession must lead to repentance, which is a hollow word unless implemented by restitution for the violence, indifference, and neglect we have allowed to characterize our world.[78] Finally the Christian, individually and as a member of society, must exemplify a lifestyle that is not ordinarily in keeping with the image of corporate success. Competition and acquisitiveness are not compatible with the kind of love that so astonished the ancient Romans ("See how these Christians love each other!") with its willingness to sacrifice personal advantages so that all might "eat their bread with joy" (Acts 2:46). But it is certain that Christianity will be judged in future generations by the degree to which it inspired these qualities in the economic and political spheres that are vitally important to the life of the entire culture.

Caveats abound that cannot be ignored or shrugged aside. Capitalism, especially where its primary emphasis is on free enterprise and financial incentives, has a built-in temptation to acquisitiveness and greed. Socialized economies, on the other hand, have built-in temptations to centralize both political and economic power, power that too often exemplifies Lord Acton's aphorism: "Power tends to corrupt, and absolute power corrupts absolutely," a phenomenon no less characteristic of social bureaucracies than of dictatorships and monarchies. Within each there are those who, when they think of taxation, emphasize human needs such as health and housing. There are also those who would minimize taxes in order to have more to invest so that the benefits of profit may "trickle down" to those less fortunate. There are Christians in both camps, justifying their positions in the name of freedom; meanwhile the weak and the poor continue to suffer. It may be that in the final analysis, the ultimate value will be seen to have been not freedom, but responsibility.

Responsibility for Justice

The responsible citizen becomes a primary focus in a highly original contribution by Karen Lebacqz, who notes that all discussion of justice and law must finally emerge from the abstract to consider the injustices perpetrated by irresponsible people. The Aristotelian dictum of "giving each his due" lends itself to competition among contenders as to what is due, because due is arbitrarily based on need, or merit, or prior contributions that deserve the due as reward or compensation, market demands, equality, and so on.[79] She suggests that concentrating on correcting concrete injustices provides a more fruitful starting place than the usual philosophical straining for definitions. On the other hand, she observes that the correcting process must have a standard of some kind, a "plumb line," to use Amos's term.

That plumb line must be first of all what the Hebrews called *sedaqah*, righteousness, which is perfection in goodness, mercy, benevolence, compassion for the poor, forbearance, the capacity for giving joy, and in short all those qualities for which God is called righteous. Secondly, Lebacqz insists that justice will reside in responsibilities to others, not in rights that can be codified. Thirdly, because injustice invariably involves exploitation, domination, and exploitation that violate relationships within the human family, the process of correction takes shape in rescue and reparation.

> God's justice for the oppressor consists in rebuke and requisition. Those responsible for injustice have the duty of redress—of making amends, setting things right. This includes not only ending the exploitation or oppression but making reparations for the harms caused by past injustices. Both together participate in the restoration of the proper order of relationships in which exploitation and domination would not exist.[80]

To be sure any such justice will be incomplete; justice requires liberation from all past impositions, and that is never entirely possible in a mortal world. But the Christian, who knows that responsibility itself must be based on love, will have no illusions about all injustices being conquered entirely. But neither will the Christian despair. God is known in loving and in the doing of justice.

CHAPTER NINE

Culture and the Ethics of the Kingdom

Every culture has its own set of givens, its conventional requirements according to which, if one complies, all will be well. Because cultures generally include religious practices, it is usually assumed that civil and religious observances should be inculcated and that the arts, education, and whatever aspects of science and technology are present will reflect the uniqueness of the culture in question. With the advent of Christianity, a serious disjunction appears between the faith and its cultural settings, raising important questions for the implementation of its ethics.

The situation is not entirely without precedent. It is well understood that the Jewish faith looks to the time when Abraham received a call from God to break from the cultural tradition of his past, and begin a radically new venture, with all manner of risks to be encountered. What Jesus did, however, was not simply to break from the Greco-Roman culture in which Judaism found itself, but, with his focus on the kingdom of God, to break with the givens, the conventional wisdom of the Judaic tradition as well (yet without violating one "jot or tittle" of God's law), and to challenge the whole notion of the sovereignty of culture in human life. As the taken-for-granted set of a culture's understandings, conventional wisdom had always functioned as sovereign in people's lives, providing direction, security, and identity. Recent studies of Jesus' teaching emphasize that he sharply undermined his culture's conventional wisdom. "His parables imaged a very different understanding of reality. He criticized his people's preoccupation with the traditional concerns . . . family, possessions, righteousness. In like fashion, Jesus' proclamation of God's kingship subverts the conventional wisdom of our culture."[1]

To be sure, definitions of culture abound, as do definitions of Christianity, complicating the problem of their relationship. We may argue for a preferred designation, for example, whether culture is to be understood in narrow terms or so broadly as to include all the patterns and products of learned behavior; whether Christianity is devoted solely to saving souls or to reforming a corrupt world. We might then question with the ancient Tertullian: "What has Athens to do with Jerusalem?" and declare culture to be the fountain of evil.[2] Or we might follow the late Emil Brunner's argument denying that the relationship of Christian faith to culture is even an appropriate theme for Christian ethics. He declared it to be a topic "only for a universal Christian philosophy."[3] Richard Niebuhr sought to clarify the relationship, insisting that "it is not necessarily a problem of Christianity and culture, but Christ and culture." He held that the individual Christian's identification with Christ, rather than "joining" Christianity's churches is the starting place for Christian ethics. "Christianity, whether defined as church, creed, ethics or movement of thought, itself moves between the poles of Christ and culture. The relation of these two authorities constitutes its problem."[4]

Every Christian knows that certain activities are expected by these two authorities, and that all conduct is ethical in nature, subject to judgment from both Christ and one's culture. The special dilemma of the Christian arises from the discovery that the churches themselves participate in the culture's conventional wisdom, and many Christians resist the idea that Christ may in fact stand against both Church and culture. "Much of contemporary Christianity is 'enculturated religion,' radically adapted to culture and domesticated within it. We live in a Babylon often declared to be Zion. We in the church need to hear once again the message of God's kingship."[5]

Jesus' message of the kingdom calls us to reexamine the meaning of God's sovereignty, humankind's proclivity to sin, God's reconciling love and power expressed through Christ, and the implications of these for fraternal love in the context of culture. Jesus' proclamation of the kingdom calls us to create an alternative to the usual understanding and practice of the arts, of education, science and technology, so we can proclaim, "The kingdom of the world has become the kingdom of our Lord, and of His Christ" (Revelation 11:15).

THE ARTS: REFLECTION AND RESPONSIBILITY

It would be gratuitous to rehearse the age-long partnership between religion and the fine arts. Every student of the humanities and the history of religion is aware of the way in which music, painting, poetry, theater, and other art forms have evolved in relationship with religious faith and practices. The affinity can be found in almost any setting whether Jewish, Christian, Hindu, Buddhist, or even Islamic where pictorial arts are traditionally forbidden. It is tempting to concur with Goethe, that "he who possesses science and art has religion." Beethoven's enthusiasm for his art form carried him to the extent of declaring, "Music is a higher form of revelation than all wisdom and philosophy." More modestly in our own time, Albert Einstein wrote, "All religions, arts and sciences are branches of the same tree."[6]

Certainly it is true that it would be difficult to imagine Western art apart from Judaism and Christianity. But the worship of God, which characterizes the life of faith, cannot always be said to have motivated the arts, even when their themes have been religious in nature. Each art form has its own set of disciplines, and the independence and perfection of those have not infrequently become so precious to both artists and their public as to create a rivalry for religious devotion, indeed a substitute religion, and in some instances a temptation to idolatry.

Because the arts, like religion, involve specific behaviors, and all conduct is subject to ethical evaluation, this relationship has important implications for our study. Perhaps the place to start is with the recognition that art, except where it merely imitates nature, seeks to transcend reality in quest of the ideal. "Art is always the child of the longing for something else. It shapes something which is not present, for and through the imagination, because that which is present does not satisfy."[7] In this sense art appears to offer a redemptive service, providing a vision of what may yet be amid the fractured and distorted realities of daily experience.

Herein lies a major problem for ethics. In seeking and objectifying an unrealized and unrealizable perfection, we burden the arts with greater expectations than they can fulfill. American artist Robert Henri states, "There are moments in our lives when we see beyond the usual. Such are moments of our greatest wisdom. It was in this hope that the arts were invented. . . . There is nothing so important as art in the world, nothing so constructive, so life-sustaining."[8] The role for art is here seen as the role was once for religion. Because of this there has always existed in Christianity a certain uneasiness in the presence of art in any form, even though it clearly offers a valuable service. "There have been periods of synthesis, of immediate connection and mutual influence, and there have been periods of disastrous hostile separation. But never have Christianity and culture reached a state of complete fusion."[9]

The issue of art as subversive to faith is of course not new, as we noted in the earlier quotation from Tertullian, who reinforced his hostility by condemning certain arts in particular, notably literature, music, and above all theater with its levity and brutality. There is little in Christian history to match his vehemence until we reach the sixteenth-century Puritans or the seventeenth-century Mennonites.[10] A large measure of the charge against the arts lies in the lure of an aestheticism that creates the demand for "moods," which must be sustained at all costs. In the religious life this is a familiar phenomenon where having just the right music, stained glass windows, elaborate rituals, and costly vestments deflect the worshipper from concern about feeding the hungry, ministering to the sick, and seeking justice for the oppressed. "The man who is entangled in the net of aestheticism feels no responsibility for his fellowmen. . . . He is an aristocrat, he is self-sufficient; he flees from the world of practical action where there is so much to disturb his inner repose and upset his balance."[11]

The claim that the very act of creating religious art ennobles both artist and worshipper has little basis in fact. Of the thousands of carvings and paintings from the Middle Ages, many are little more than pedestrian. "Not a few are mere routine work ground out by large workshops in endless repetition of the same arrangements, and can boast of little more than decorative value. Some of the most famous Masters were at best 'fringe' Christians, and painted religious subjects simply to earn their livelihood."[12] Their private lives seem remarkably untouched by the spiritual themes they were paid to portray. Raphael, for example, was a notorious womanizer, who did not hesitate to plagiarize ideas from others.[13] One of his most famous paintings, *Death of the Virgin*, was at first rejected; "The fathers were shocked because the Madonna was bare legged and resembled a courtesan."[14] Bernini's sensuous *St. Teresa in Ecstasy* reflects his private life of romantic involvements. Carravaggio, founder of the naturalist school in Rome, was a flagrant wanton. "Many artists of the period saw only the technical, rather than the spiritual side of the art they engaged in producing."[15]

Because so much of art is born in the realm between aspiration and reality, the artist sometimes finds it difficult to live harmoniously among the very people for whom the artistic creations are supposedly intended. The charge of artistic temperament is then leveled at the artist, who finds alienation as a reward for what may have begun as a serious effort to ennoble and inspire. No one, Beethoven lamented, could appreciate properly the vision of perfection he strove to share. On the night of the first performance of his Ninth, or Choral Symphony, wherein he proclaimed, *"Seid umschlungen millionen, Diesen kuss der ganzen Welt"* (Be embraced ye millions, here's a kiss for all the world), he left the concert hall in a towering rage, believing he had been underpaid. "For most artists," writes psychoanalyst Daniel Schneider, "the tendency to wrap himself in a cloak of narcissistic self-love because his art is a transformation of himself . . . is a very powerful one."[16] This self-love contains a mixture of masochism and of hostility toward all who fail to respond to the work, and thus threatens an essential bond between art and the community. The artist who rejects such a bond in the name of independence and self-expression may have already succumbed to the self-induced illness of narcissism.

The escapist element in art has served both the hedonist and those who cannot withstand the forces of the world of nature or politics. In his famous essay *L'Art Pour L'Art*, Friedrich Nietzsche lamented that we must turn to art "in order that we may not perish through the truth." Art, he declared, must exist for its own sake and not serve any other purpose. "The struggle against purpose in art is always the struggle against its being subordinated to morality." This view of art has appealed to many artists who seek freedom from all conventions and restraints. It was particularly championed by the American painter James Whistler, whose personal moral excesses shocked even such free thinkers as Oscar Wilde.[17] The disavowal of purpose in art, however, presents us with a contradiction. Seldom is anything done for its own sake, but for some purpose or benefit such as pleasure or escape from pain. "The slogan 'art for art's sake' " wrote George Buttrick, "has about as much wisdom as roads for roads' sake."[18] Art, like roads, may facilitate escape; that, too, is a purpose.

The most ancient caution against art, that of the danger of idolatry, is seldom heard today except among certain Fundamentalists (found among both Christians and Muslims) who apply the Second Commandment literally to any and all forms of naturalistic representation. Given the human proclivity to worship the works of our own hands, it is not only works of art that are idolized, but products of our technology as well (as we note later). But sculptures and paintings meant as aids to worship often become direct objects of worship. Thus we witness millions of Christians around the world venerating wood and stone carvings, and crawling on hands and knees to kiss the feet of plaster images. The fact that the artistic impulse springs from ontological roots, in which the artist seeks to externalize an inward experience of the Divine, makes the enticement to identify the object with the Ultimate Being all the more seductive. In this way idolatry has been rationalized for countless generations.

But having said all these things by way of a caveat against the abuses of art in religion, it must yet be acknowledged that the two have functioned powerfully together to unite the physical and spiritual natures of humankind. This is not to suggest a body-spirit dualism in the ancient Greek sense, but to affirm that we belong as whole beings to both the natural and spiritual realms, and as such have created both art and religion as means of responding to the challenge of being human, of belonging to both the world of nature and to the kingdom of God.

The gifts of art to faith are many, but three deserve special attention. First, it communicates the experience of faith so that those groping for understanding can realize, sometimes with a sense of sudden awareness: "Yes . . . here is what I have felt and known only dimly, now disclosed with a new power." Art is the externalizing of inwardness, and provides a buttoning-on place for the private experiences of one person with another, creating a new ethos between them, and new ways of relating and behaving. It is the yearning for such sharing that brings crowds of people to a sanctuary or to a concert hall, where their comportment is noticeably different from what we find at a prizefight, soccer game, or rock concert. Here they respond to familiar hymns or oratorios, or stand together in awe before a Pietà, or a Rembrandt painting of the Christ.

Second, art affords an experience of confession. This is not simply through showing us an idealized world that evokes admission that our real world is shabby by comparison. A painting such as Picasso's *Guernica,* or Philip Evergood's *The New Lazarus* convicts us of the horrors we have allowed to inflict our world through warfare and the disfiguring of life through lynchings, poverty, and crime. Such works hold before us a needed indictment of ourselves, and rebuke those who seek through art only esthetic pleasure. Art need not be beautiful to qualify as worthy, nor need it be religious thematically to have an impact on the Christian conscience. Paul Tillich called *Guernica* "a great Protestant painting . . . perhaps the outstanding artistic expression of the human predicament in our period."[19]

Finally, and paradoxically, the gift of the arts is to release us from the enchantment of art itself, as they point to the reality beyond themselves. Here Jesus' focus on the kingdom of God holds a special message for the artist who tries to convey something that brings out the best in both him or herself and those who witness the work: "Seek ye first the Kingdom of God, and all the rest shall be added unto you." As the poetry and prose on the pages of Scripture reveal the invisible but powerfully present Word, so the productions of the artist's mind and skills convey us to a point from which we can view our world as it is, and the kingdom that encompasses it.

Michelangelo, who probably did more than any artist to aid the faithful in achieving such a perspective from his Sistine Chapel ceiling, wrote in a rare poetic effort:

> Now know I well that fond fantasy
> Which made my soul the worshipper and thrall
> Of earthly art, is vain;
> Painting nor sculpture now can lull to rest
> My soul that turns to His great love on high,
> Whose arms to clasp us on the cross were spread.

The arts can be powerful agents to inspire sharing, confession, and exaltation. Then like the Herald Angels, they must stand aside "that the King of Glory may come in." This is their ethos.

EDUCATION AND COMMITMENT

Background

Education is of particular importance for Christian ethics because few other human endeavors have so great a potential for shaping successive generations. The wisdom literature of Hebrew Scriptures contain many such injunctions like "Wisdom is the principal thing: therefore get wisdom: and with all thy getting get understanding" (Proverbs 4:7). The Jewish tradition of education was part of the Christian heritage, for nearly every town in the Palestine of Jesus' day possessed a school where attendance was compulsory for all children over the age of six.[20] The early Church followed the Jewish tradition. By 438 A.D., a century after Constantine had liberated Christendom from Roman persecution, the emperor Theodosius mandated a state license for all teachers, and made the license available only to Christians. Education then became the ward of the Church, and that single fact may well have kept the Dark Ages from being a time of total eclipse. Europe was soon overrun by migratory barbarians whose devastations all but destroyed civilization. Only the monasteries kept alight the lamp of learning. Charlemagne and Alfred the Great stand forth as exceptional rulers who created schools in specific response to urgings from the religious leaders. "The Church was, beyond question, the greatest civilizing force in medieval European history."[21]

The great universities of the Middle Ages, beginning with Bologna, Oxford, and the University of Paris, were all products of Christian commitment to education. With the Reformation, Martin Luther declared that schools must serve the double function of enabling people to read the Word of God and of preparing them for responsible citizenship. He further believed that education should be state supported and compulsory. John Calvin was the first to make tax-supported public education workable, and within a generation schools of the type he set up in Geneva in 1559 were established throughout Switzerland, France, Germany, the Netherlands, and through the work of the Puritans in the next generation, in the New World. The role of organized Christianity was important in the founding of eight of the nine prerevolutionary colleges (Harvard, William and Mary, Yale, etc.). "Only the College of Philadelphia was not at first specifically under church control, and it soon came under the dominance of the Anglicans. In addition, the purpose of training students for the Christian ministry is specified in all colonial college charters with the single exception, again, of the College of Philadelphia" (now the University of Pennsylvania).[22]

The industrial revolution witnessed profound changes in the concept of education's function. The Christian conception of the requirements of God and of the predicament of humankind as sinful beings had had a powerful influence on the laws governing education, as witness the Old Deluder Satan Act of 1647 in Massachusetts, mandating the establishment of schools and school attendance. But now the utilitarian philosophies of Jeremy Bentham, William Hamilton, and John Stuart Mill wrought sweeping changes. Training in skills was deemed more important than education in ethics, religion, and social values. In Europe, Pestalozzi retained religion in the curriculum (and was personally a committed Christian), but placed greater emphasis on biology, arithmetic, reading, and in the upper forms, technology and geometry. In 1826, Friedrich Froebel proposed a theory of organic evolution in which nature was conceived as a spiritual organism. Education was seen as the process by which the cosmic mind (no longer the God of the Bible) grows and expands in the mind of the pupil. This was echoed in the writings of Johann Herbart, often called "the father of modern psychiatry," and had considerable influence on the shape of the school curriculum. Gone was the idea of sin; evil was simply the product of faulty education. Religion was considered by Herbart, and later by John Dewey, as only instrumental in providing general ethical guidelines. Indeed for John Dewey, Christian ethics seemed to threaten the very essence of genuine education because it always points to definite aims, values, and goals. "It is nonsense to talk about the aims of education or any other undertaking," he wrote in 1916, "where conditions do not permit of foresight and results."[23] Some three decades later he reiterated the position and added, "I believe that all education proceeds by participation of the individual in the social consciousness of the race."[24]

Critics of Dewey, and of his followers in the progressive education movement, were quick to note that he had not clarified what could *not* qualify as "participation in the social consciousness of the race" from the perpetuation of isolationism and racial supremacy to expansionism and manifest destiny. Who should decide the merits of group morality if "the social consciousness of the race" is the standard? If the group itself must decide, who should (or could) arbitrate among competing factions and from what moral vantage point?

The need to answer such questions gained an unprecedented urgency in the wake of World War II, when it seemed our civilization had barely escaped destruction. Actually, warnings of impending disaster had already appeared as early as 1917, in Oswald Spengler's *The Decline of the West* and in some early theological writings of Karl Barth. The fact that so much of the tragedy was blamed on the educational systems of the time was a new phenomenon. Ortega y Gasset described as barbaric a large proportion of the intelligentsia of the Western world. In his book *The Revolt of the Masses,* he lay the blame squarely on the schools for teaching only techniques for living in a machine-oriented civilization without providing education in moral values, which alone could prevent our misusing those machines for mutual destruction.[25] Frederic Lilge, in *The Abuse of Learning,* charged that specialization in the sciences and technology has encouraged people to develop expertise in the skills of social manipulation apart from moral considerations. The most monumentally tragic illustration was the rise of Naziism in Germany, the nation with the highest cultural heritage in the world.[26] "The most frightening aspect of our present world," wrote Erich Kahler, reflecting on the fall of the Nazi regime, "is not the horrors in themselves, the atrocities, the technological exterminations; but the one fact at the root of it all: the fading away of any human criterion."[27] Lewis Mumford charged that "A third of our student population may, for all intents and purposes, be considered moral imbeciles . . . potential if not actual delinquents." This may have seemed overly harsh when he wrote it in 1951.[28] But that was the generation of students which now runs our schools, businesses, and government agencies. It was perhaps this that prompted former U.N. Ambassador Jeane Kirkpatrick to blame America's public schools (as well as the

State Department and the marines), for the alleged betrayal of military secrets at the embassy in Moscow in April of 1987. President Reagan chose to place the blame entirely on the schools.[29]

The Search for an Educational Philosophy

Efforts to respond to the apparent crisis in social morality, and to the role of education in addressing it, began even while progressive education was at the height of its popularity in the 1940s and 1950s. Walter Lippman excoriated the progressive, or "modernist" education: "Modern education is based on the denial that it is necessary or desirable for schools and colleges to transmit from generation to generation the religious and classical culture of the Western world."[30] His solution was to turn from the many forms of naturalistic philosophies, which viewed humankind as simply an extension of the animal world, and which in the field of education translate into a curriculum that merely trains in skills for survival. Instead, he advocated going back to an earlier idealism (which appears in a variety of forms in educational philosophy as essentialism, Neo-Thomism, perennialism), which promoted the seeking of eternal values, truths, and basic disciplines. Following Lippman's lead, educators like Arthur Bestor, William Bagley, and Canon Bernard Iddings Bell published books with titles such as *Educational Wastelands, How Red the Little Red School House,* and *American Education: A National Failure.*[31] Proposals ranged from the simplistic back to basics to the radical deschooling proposals of Ivan Illich and Paul Goodman, who urge that public schools should be abolished except for the truly motivated youth, allowing the rest simply to drop out and find jobs.[32]

A cornerstone in idealist thought, which appeals to many religious educators, is that there are certain ideas and values that are a priori eternally valid and self-authenticating. The socratic contention was that these are resident in the very nature of things, including the mind of the student. They need only to be drawn out by a competent teacher (the world *education* presumably came from *educare,* "to draw forth"). To Emil Brunner, it seems clear that "This idea of education is far higher than that of Naturalism, as is evident in the very fact that the use of the word 'education,' implies the antithesis between what is and what ought to be."[33] Brunner notes, however, that idealism by itself is inadequate and misleading, if not balanced by the emphasis in naturalism on training in skills needed for living in the world of practical demands. "Naturalism points out rightly that a system of education which is so exclusively oriented 'from within,' does not place man within reality, but separates him from it, that it places its abstractions (which are remote from life and hostile to life) between man and reality."[34]

From the vantage point of Christian ethics, neither naturalism nor idealism provides an adequate foundation on which to build an educational system. The sovereignty of God is the primary tenet for Christian thought, and while this theme cannot and should not intrude on every academic discussion, a commitment to God's sovereignty will create specific assumptions about the teaching of the many disciplines, and especially about the uses to which the products of those subjects are directed. In contrast, even those naturalists and idealists who believe in God (or gods) make nature or ideals the primary frame of reference. Both philosophies make God subject to powers and values that are "above" God. Further, these forces and ideals are defined by human agencies: philosophers, theologians, scientists, and so on, so in a real sense God is no longer sovereign but subject to our humanly contrived formulas. Thus one might say, "God wouldn't do so-and-so because it wouldn't be right." What is "right" has been decided by human logic that places us over against God, whose sovereignty is thus effectively denied.

Further, neither naturalism nor idealism take seriously the "fallen" state of humankind, our ontological apartness from God, our sinful nature. It has often been noted that underlying all educational philosophy is a particular view of human nature.

> If man is conceived as merely a high order of animal, destined to snarl and fight his way to such advantages as he can attain; as a canny, somewhat intelligent but strangely selfish and often vicious organism to be controlled and if possible exploited; then the various aspects of a society reflect those conceptions. Education, law, economics, government, religion—the varied means of organized life—are built in terms of the way man is conceived.[35]

If, on the other hand, humans are conceived dualistically, comprised in idealist terms as traced from Plato, having a mental or spiritual nature which is good, and a physical nature which is base and evil, education is generally designed to save us from our baser selves through enlightenment of the mind. This theme, which runs through educational philosophies from Plato to Hegel and much of contemporary conservative literature, is often mistaken to be advocating something very like Christian thought. It is not. Nowhere does the Bible treat of our physical nature as evil, since God created all things and saw that they were good (Genesis 1:31). When Paul writes in the New Testament of "sinful flesh"(Romans 8:3, 6; 1 Corinthians 3:1; Galatians 5:19), he refers not to our physical or animal nature, but to the human proclivity for godless behavior.[36]

A Christian Proposal

What the Christian ethicist has to suggest is that whether training in finite skills for social efficiency (a naturalist goal, perfectly acceptable to the Christian for as far as it goes) or probing for eternal truths (an idealist goal), any education designed to help us achieve our fullest potential must begin with an acknowledgment of God's sovereignty and humankind's ontological estrangement.

But surely this does not belong to the tasks of education in a nonsectarian, pluralistic society. Even in the palace school of Charlemagne, in the later medieval universities of Christendom, and in the schools established by Luther, Calvin, and the Puritans, it was recognized that necessary worldly disciplines such as the seven liberal arts (logic, mathematics, astronomy, and the rest) held autonomous rules for instruction and testing that were independent of theological consideration. It is true that there was much of what Paul Tillich called "inducting education" going on, through the religious traditions and symbols in the very atmosphere in which these disciplines were taught.[37] But the humanist influence of the sixteenth and seventeenth centuries changed much of this. William Penn, an ardent Christian, advocated that education must be dedicated to the creation of an enlightened electorate, and that such could not be achieved in a doctrinaire school environment.

Among leading philosophers of education who have understood both the necessary functions of educational institutions and the elements of Christian commitment, the late Robert Hutchins wrote, "A sound philosophy in general suggests that men are rational, moral and spiritual beings and that the improvement of men means the fullest development of their rational, moral and spiritual powers. Man is by nature free, and he is by nature social. To use his freedom rightly he needs discipline. To live in society, he needs the moral virtues."[38] Hutchins acknowledges that education, in the sense of schooling, cannot do it all.

> Education deals with the development of the intellectual powers; moral and spiritual powers are the sphere of the family and the church. All three agencies must work in harmony; for though a man has three aspects, he is still one man. The schools cannot take over the role of the family and the church without promoting the atrophy of those institutions and failing in the task that is proper to the schools.[39]

What of the development of self-consciously Christian schools? As an alternative to public schools where Christian teaching is (presumably) absent, these have been proliferating in the United States for the past several decades, but especially since the civil rights movement in the 1960s. Many people regard them as a means of putting God back into education and fulfilling the biblical injunction, "Train up a child in the way he should go, and when he is old he will not depart from it" (Proverbs 22:6). Others have seen the schools as a way to avoid participating in social actions of which they disapprove. There have been almost countless examples of both, with an uneven record of academic strength. Some have been accused of perpetuating regional biases through indoctrination in a single point of view, fostering religious, racial, and political bigotry.

At their best, Christian schools encourage a devotion to learning and create a spirit of place that is exemplary. It has often been noted that the long history of college and university education began in the Christian churches of Europe, and that the earliest colleges in America were almost all established by the Christian denominations across the frontier.[40] But it was at the level of the elementary schools that the religious influence was most effective historically, beginning with those of Puritan New England in the seventeenth century.

The argument that values are more effectively inculcated in a Christian environment during the earliest years has kept alive a certain adversarial relation between public and private religious schools. Recent highly publicized studies support the contention that the latter provide a safer and more orderly environment, require more homework, have better attendance, and foster higher academic achievement than the former. Advocates of public schools argue that these phenomena merely reflect the fact that private schools are more selective, appeal to financially secure families, and are elitist and college oriented.[41] Furthermore, they insist, the very essence of the democratic life is in the sharing of a common heritage so all may participate in elections and other public processes from the basis of commonly held insights. They recall James Madison, who wrote, "A popular government without popular information, or the means of acquiring it, is but a prologue to a farce or tragedy, or perhaps both." The task of building an education system to serve the new republic led from the Puritan schools of the seventeenth century to the Common School during the nineteenth, under the careful but energetic guidance of Horace Mann. Mann, a Unitarian Christian, insisted that the most ethical way to provide for an enlightened electorate was to provide common experiences in a common language. This meant that subjects would be taught in English, without religious messages, to children from all backgrounds regardless of spoken language, religious beliefs, or economic status. In addition it would be compulsory, and free in the sense of being supported by taxes collected from everyone.[42]

The decision of Christian parents to take their children out of the mainstream of public education should be done, according to Emil Brunner, only with greatest reluctance if at all. Beside the obvious strain of private expenditure, there is the consideration that religious schools tend to pull students away from the community as a whole, and may thus limit the child's social experiences and fail to develop a sense of community responsibility. Furthermore "the Christian spirit, which is all that matters, is not in the least guaranteed by the obligation to accept a special Christian creed or by emphasis on Christian religious instruction."[43] The parochial experience may, ultimately, prove counterproductive.

The situation with religiously sponsored higher education may present significantly different prospects. Here students, free from parental and social influences previously beyond their control, may select the college or university that provides a religious context for their studies quite by intent. We have already noted the fact that historically, higher education began under the sponsorship of the Christian church. A Danforth Foundation study done in 1965 revealed that Christian colleges provided an exceptional atmosphere of intellectual ferment and, all out of proportion to their size, were sending more undergraduates into graduate and professional schools than secular institutions of higher learning. They were also more highly represented in the professions and positions of public leadership.[44]

Writing about that same time, Elton Trueblood noted that the genius of the Christian college or university is that religious commitment does not supplant intellectual rigor, but provides a consistent point of reference according to which all courses may be taught. The very word *university* implies a unity of disciplines that in fact seldom exists on secular campuses where a multitude of often conflicting points of view vie for the students' loyalty. By contrast, "The Christian college is marked not by the mere offer of religious studies, but by giving them centrality and consequent emphasis."[45] To the rebuttal that this implies the imposition of a sectarian, theological emphasis, which would be inherently unethical, Trueblood replies,

> In actuality, theology cannot be avoided. If it is not taught in one way it will be taught in another, because it deals with questions which students ask. [Cardinal] Newman clarified this point: "Supposing theology be not taught, its province will not simply be neglected, but will be actually usurped by other sciences, which will teach without warrant conclusions of their own in a subject matter which needs its own proper principles for its due formation and disposition."[46]

What is at stake in education is a recovery of concern for understanding the nature of human beings and for our prospective destiny. Whether this can best be achieved in secular tax-supported schools or in avowedly Christian institutions will continue to be debated among educators and ethicists.

Meanwhile there are those, particularly vocal in the past decade, who deny any advantage at all to liberal arts education, including that which is religiously oriented. "Liberal education has always been backward looking. In America, the liberal arts college was imbued with Christian influences and precepts, but these too had the effect of making liberal education *retardataire*." The author of that statement then concludes that only the research ethic is relevant to modern society. "In fact, from the perspective of the research ethic, liberal education is not 'higher' education at all and therefore should be prevented from spilling over into universities and research institutes. It should be confined to institutions approximating what Europeans used to call the 'upper secondary school.' "[47]

This point of view, which has its roots in the pragmatic philosophy of John Dewey and his followers, gained increasing popularity in the 1960s and 1970s under the banner of relevance in education. Its greatest exemplar was Cornell University, according to Allan Bloom, and led to "the closing of the American mind" (the title of his book). Cornell offered a six-year Ph.D. program to promising high school students who had already made "a firm career choice" and was designed to rush the students past all the old traditional liberal arts, religious, and humanist courses to the start of their careers. Yet, "nothing was done to guide or inform their energy, and the result was merely to add multilife-styles to multidisciplines, the diversity of perversity to the diversity of specialization."[48] There was no recognition that the college or university years represent a small but all-important corridor of time in a person's life between the intellectual desert of earlier youth and the often dreary professional life ahead, a brief time when, if ever, the youth may be exposed to the greatest ideas and ideals of the human race. Nor was there evidence of understanding on the part of faculty or administration of "the undeniable fact that students who enter are uncivilized, and that the universities have some responsibility for civilizing them."[49] It would be difficult, Bloom wrote, to discover anything more contrary to the spirit of even secular ethics than to rob education of a conscientiously devised ethical rationale.

That some kind of ethical framework is urgently needed for the kinds of problems encountered in our schools at all levels has been urged in almost countless articles blaming schools for their failure to equip youth to decide issues ranging from cheating on examinations to delinquency, drug abuse, sexual promiscuity, and murder. The Texas-based Institute for Character Education, in an effort to address the problem, has developed a brief curriculum based on a set of principles like citizenship, tolerance, and kindness, which is now being used in more than 33,000 elementary classrooms in 45 states.[50] For those who agree with President James Laney of Emory University that such an approach is "a mere Band-Aid," the American Constitution and Declaration of Independence, John Locke's natural rights, and John Calvin's ultimate rights of mankind seem to provide all the principles we need. Colgate philosopher Huntington Terrell agrees: "We don't have to be converted. It's what we have in common."[51] A sobering rejoinder, however, might be that such principles have not afforded the specific guidance needed by students and faculty who are enticed by large defense contracts to do secret research, which the government forbids to be published, in clear violation of academic freedom. Or, even if that dilemma was "purportedly resolved" by appeals to national security, other questions remain, (for example, on the basis of what ethical principles can a university justify doing research that would lead to the militarizing of outer space, or threaten the quality of life on earth through environmental mismanagement for immediate financial gain in an economy whose bottom line is always and only profit?

Christian ethics proposes that among the goals of education might well be to challenge students with an imaginative consideration of God's will for their lives; to equip them for creative fulfillment of their potentials as conceived within that context; and to envision forms of service to enhance human life. The question for modern education, whether public or private, becomes as the late President Howard Jefferson of Clark University expressed it, ". . . not whether religion and liberal education are compatible, but whether an education which excludes religion can be truly liberal."[52] Christian educators are not called upon to impose their convictions on their students, but as Swarthmore's President Courtney Smith wrote, if we demur about what we value, "Students will graduate from school feeling that values don't count for much. They'll balk at religious, moral, or ethical, or political commitment, or stake everything on getting ahead which will always be viewed in a materialistic way."[53] The Christian's ethical responsibility is to become involved in helping guide the educational process at the local level, and where possible in higher places of authority so that students are challenged to make moral judgments where human values are at stake. The Christian educator, whether in a secular or religious institution, will always seek opportunities for ethical issues to be clearly presented and moral commitment encouraged. The urgency of the task is evident when we realize that the drug pusher in a Los Angeles gang, the military officer who lied to Congress, and the insider trader on Wall Street all attended schools that presumably provided an education, but one deficient in ethical training. Richard Mouw said it well: "I don't think I would be a teacher if I did not want to change people's attitudes. A certain kind of ignorance and dullness of mind and moral blindness afflict people, and it is an important part of my task to do what I can to eliminate that."[54]

SCIENCE AND TECHNOLOGY

The biblical injunction for humankind to "have dominion . . . over all the earth" (Genesis 1:26) reflects a presupposition that we are not immersed in the world of nature as are other animals. We have a measure of transcendence over it: We can study it, reduce its patterns to equations and laws, and use these to fulfill our own purposes. Our science and our technology reveal our uniqueness, perhaps even something of our spiritual nature: "like unto God." Our misuse of these powers reveals our arrogance, our unlikeness to God, indeed our opposition to God, our sinful nature. It exposes our deepest ethical and spiritual dilemma. If we are to understand this, we must adopt not an anthropocentric view of God, but a theocentric view of humankind, a point made powerfully by James Gustafson.[55] Humankind gains its spiritual identity and freedom, as Emil Brunner earlier noted, not by technical mastery alone, but through theoretical knowledge that also reveals human uniqueness and is indispensable to science. "Even the animal has a certain technical ability, but he never has any science, or knowledge for its own sake."[56] Science and technology are keys to our spiritual nature, and are not antithetical to it as some would have us believe.

Spiritual freedom, science, and technology are thus linked in biblical perspective, and because each of them has profound implications for human behavior, each has its ethical aspect that is appropriate for our consideration. "The hour when science was born was an important date in the history of human freedom; at the same time it was also the beginning of a dangerous development."[57] The dangerous features of both science and technology have been accorded so much attention in recent years that to reiterate the charges would be both tedious and redundant. There may be some value, however, in reminding ourselves of Robert Oppenheimer's expression of dismay over the first use of atomic energy in America's bombing of civilian populations in Hiroshima and Nagasaki: "Science has known sin, and this is a knowledge we dare not lose." This came at a time when science was widely held to be morally neutral. C. P. Snow, in his "two cultures" concept, later declared that science cannot claim moral neutrality, and certainly not moral indifference.[58] Albert Einstein affirmed in one of his last writings that science can benefit from the insights of religion to direct its powers.[59] A new attitude of openness for dialogue between scientists and religious leaders began to appear in the 1950s and 1960s, which had no precedent in modern history. Charles Townes, after winning the Nobel Prize for his work on lasers and masers, addressed this concern in an article entitled "The Convergence of Science and Religion," in which he stated, "They both represent man's efforts to understand his universe, and must be dealing with the same substance." The fact that both are so intimately related to mankind's decision making in every area of private and public life makes their cooperation all the more urgent: "Converge they must, and through this should come new strength for both."[60]

In an effort to understand the relation of science, technology, and religion, it is helpful to clarify their distinctive features, the history of the much publicized conflict among them, and the way in which critical features of Christian ethics can foster greater cooperation among them for the benefit of us all.

A Question of Relationship

Albert Einstein's observation that "all religions, arts, and sciences are branches of the same tree"[61] has also been suggested by scholars in other fields.[62] It seems probable that primitive peoples have always regarded their world as being governed by some sort of wondrous power. Not all tribes or individuals agreed as to the nature of this power, some regarding it as personal, others as impersonal; some as unchangeable and reliable, others as capricious. But it was a power; it was responsible for the weather, the seasons, the universe. "Thus the 'science' of the primitive was one with his religion. Many of the myths and legends of early times have come to us as great literature; for example, the story of how mankind came to possess fire is found in the myth of Prometheus in Greek religion. In Sumerian mythology the origin of the arts of civilization is connected with an act of the gods.[63] The two distinct stories of the creation of heaven and earth found in the first two chapters of Genesis are attributed by many biblical scholars to the adaptation of a Canaanite version of a Babylonian myth.[64] To read the two Genesis accounts as science we would have to overlook the obvious contradiction between them, wherein according to the first account (Genesis 1:1–2:4a), Adam was created *after* the creation of plants and other animals; according to the second story (Genesis 2:4b–25), Adam was created first, *before* the trees, animals, and so on.

Science is not opposed to religion per se, but when religious people try to oppose their story accounts of natural or historic events to scientific data, a certain disjunction is inevitable. Nobel laureate Arthur H. Compton (physicist and Presbyterian elder) expressed it well: "Science can have no quarrel with a religion that postulates a God to whom men are as his children . . . with free, intelligent wills, capable of learning nature's laws, of seeing dimly God's purpose in nature, and of working with him to make that purpose effective."[65]

Science and religion have different functions. Perhaps Albert Einstein put it too simply, yet nonetheless helpfully:

> Science can only ascertain what is, but not what should be, and outside of its domain judgements of all kinds remain necessary. . . . Religion is the age old endeavor of mankind to become clearly and completely conscious of these values and goals. If one conceives of religion and science according to these definitions then a conflict between them appears impossible.[66]

Science can be described in a variety of ways: It is a body of knowledge that can be exhibited in an array of equations; it is a method of discovery and knowing; it is characterized by a certain attitude: "It is given to the open, unfettered quest for truth. It is a potent force for good in the world (as witness its contributions to curing diseases, improving agriculture, fighting ignorance and superstition)."[67] On the other hand, similar descriptions can be applied to religion. It, too, is an organized body of knowledge; an area of experience; a way of knowing and thinking; it, too, has made its contributions to good in the world, having fostered the building of hospitals, created the first great universities in the Western world, and sponsored the first free public schools. It, too, has fought superstition, and, in fact, as geologist Frank Rhodes points out, religion provided the opportunities for science in the first place: "The original dependence of science on Christian theology is seen most clearly if we remind ourselves of the presuppositions of modern science. These are a belief in an orderly, regular, rational universe, a belief that this orderliness is intelligible, and a belief in a broad principle of causality. . . . It was the philosophy, theology, and outlook of a whole Christian civilization that provided the cradle of modern science."[68]

The differences between science and religion are not insignificant; they ask different kinds of questions and employ their own epistemologies, their own ways of seeking data and interpreting their experiences. Science asks questions like, What is the chemical composition of this object? How long, or heavy, or soft, or magnetic is it? By what sequence does one event follow another? What theories can be constructed to correlate the various particular bodies of data and of natural law for explanatory or predictive purposes? The concern here is for information about phenomena and processes.[69] Biologist Jacob Bronowski, however, points out that the concern is not merely for information, but for ways to relate such data in meaningful relationships: "All science is the search for unity in hidden likeness. The scientist looks for order in the appearances of nature by exploring such likenesses."[70]

Religious questions arise in an effort to understand the why, the whence, and the whither of things; what life is in terms of its meaning and destiny; whether death is the end of all life; and in between birth and death how we should relate to each other and our environment. Religion incorporates questions about required behaviors for the good life and the meaning of "good." Above all it seeks to know whether there is a transcendent or immanent power creating and guiding the patterns of nature, and if it is personal so we can relate with such a power or being in prayer and meditation. Is such a deity to be worshipped, and will it provide us moral guidance in this life and a welcome in the next?

It is clear that science and religion are distinct; neither is equipped to answer the questions of the other, and for either to intrude on the domain of the other is unwarranted. Yet the two are not unrelated. The people who work within their domains must often ask questions of both. If a scientist is asked by his or her government to use scientific means to achieve something the scientist considers immoral, the sense of the action's immorality does not arise from science per se, but from a value system outside the scientific realm. Hence Robert Oppenheimer's exclamation that "science has known sin." But that knowledge came from nonscientific origins. This also underlay Einstein's declaration that "Science without religion is lame, religion without science is blind."[71] The blindness may be illustrated by Harold Schilling's observation that from a purely objective point of view there was no scientific reason to oppose the experiments on human beings by Nazi physicians, however cruel and inhuman they might seem to the socially concerned.[72]

Conflict and Dialogue

If there is some agreement about the reciprocal benefits of science and religion, why have there been times of such apparent hostility between them, and just how old is the antagonism? Some would trace the conflict to the nineteenth-century opposition of religious leaders to Darwin's evolutionary hypothesis. Others find it earlier, in the seventeenth-century controversy between Galileo and the Roman Catholic church, over whether the sun moved around the earth or vice versa.[73] Still others would point to Roger Bacon's struggles with the scholastic theologians in the thirteenth century, who distrusted his scientific inquiries and imprisoned him for them. Some would hark back to Lucretius's denunciation of organized religion about 60 B.C. in his *De Rerum Natura* while promoting the mechanistic naturalism of Epicurus. Actually the conflict is at least as ancient as Aristotle's rejection of Democritus's atomic theory three centuries before that. It is interesting to speculate what might have occurred in the relation of science and religion had the church fathers followed the atomists instead of Aristotle. In adopting the latter as their authority on natural science, they imported a nonbiblical metaphysics that viewed nature and God as virtually equivalent, denying the radical transcendence of God, which is basic to the biblical view. In Aristotle's philosophy, nature itself was virtually divine, with "final causes" built into each element calling it toward fulfillment. "It was a self-explanatory system. In impregnating nature with final causes . . . Aristotle was in effect substituting nature for God."[74]

The Christian belief that God transcends nature, and is "wholly Other," to use Karl Barth's phrase, is directly opposed to the notion of an all-pervading immanent deity, or one whose existence can be deduced from observations of nature. This is why Francis Bacon and Descartes rejected Aristotle's efforts to "prove" God's existence (as Aristotle tried to do in the last book of *Physics*), arguing from the phenomena of motion and change to an "unmoved mover." Science, they insisted, must be free from presuppositions based on deduction, and become inductive and experimental. It is significant that the men who renounced Aquinas's Aristotelianism and pointed the way to a mechanistic conception of the cosmos (asserting that God's nature cannot be deduced, but known only through his self-disclosure), were men of science as well as devout Christians. Copernicus, for example, was a canon of the Roman Catholic church; Galileo was convinced (despite accusations of heresy against him) that his science glorified God; Kepler was called "the God seeker" by his associates; Robert Boyle devoted much of his time to translating the Bible; Michael Faraday and John Dalton were men conspicuous for their Christian piety.

Today, religious thinkers who are free from the obsession to defend creedal anachronisms by attacking scientific evidence with biblical proof texts are expressing not only concurrence with, but gratitude for the work of science. The latter has liberated from pious nonsense, studies ranging from human development to cosmology. John Polkinghorne, a former professor of mathematical physics at Cambridge and an ordained priest in the Church of England, describes the feel of the worldview offered by science, and notes its similarity with that held by most Christians. "Firstly, the world is intelligible. This is so familiar a fact that we take it for granted. It creates the possibility of science."[75] It is intelligibility that makes possible the expression of natural phenomena in mathematic terms, which are not only universally usable but that make possible the prediction of new phenomena and theories. Einstein's general relativity and the modern theory of gravitation are examples. Mathematics is the creation of the human mind, which enabled Isaac Newton to insist that with his mathematics he was "simply thinking God's thoughts after him." "If it is true," says Polkinghorne, "that intelligibility is the ground on which fundamental science ultimately makes its claim to be dealing with the way the world is, then it gives science a strong comradeship with theology, which is engaged in the similar, if more difficult, search for an understanding of God's ways with men."[76]

A second aspect of the world as viewed by science, according to Polkinghorne, is the dependence of the world processes on an interplay of chance and necessity. "Without contingent chance, new things would not happen. Without lawful necessity to preserve them in an environment whose reliability permits competitive selection, they would vanish away as soon as they were made." Polkinghorne sees in this something like a rehabilitation of the old argument from design. Providence is never static nor whimsical; things are designed to make novelty possible without giving way to irrationality.[77]

A third aspect noted by Polkinghorne is that there is a delicate and intricate balance in nature, necessary for the emergence of life. Some kind of planning appears to suggest itself. "For example, suppose things had been a little different in those crucial first three minutes. . . ." [referring to the big bang theory of the universe's origin] ". . . when the gross nuclear structure of the world got fixed as a quarter helium and three-quarters hydrogen. If things had gone a little faster, all would have been helium; and without hydrogen how could water [vital to life] have been able to form?" A fourth point is one that the biblical Psalmist made, and with which every scientist can agree. Namely, we inhabit a seemingly insignificant planet circling an undistinguished star in a third-rate galaxy. "If there is a purpose in the universe, as I believe there is, it is perhaps not exhausted by what happens in our solar system. . . . The universe has to be as big as it is to give a reasonable chance of life developing."[78] Our planet now seems not so insignificant after all.

Finally, Polkinghorne notes that the world as described by science[79] contains highly complicated metastable systems with the power of reproducing themselves, but it does not have any people in it. "There is scale and mechanism and structure, but where is the appreciation of the grandeur of that scale, the intricacy of that mechanism, the beauty of that structure? The experience of wonder . . . is an authentic part of the scientist's experience. But where does wonder find its lodgement in the world as described by science? It is missing, as are our experiences of goodness, beauty and obligation."[80] As a human endeavor, science cannot go it alone, but needs the complementary gifts of religious insight. In tandem, science and religion are vital to our understanding of the way the world is.

Evaluating Uses

Welcome as may be the suggestion that science and religion need not be in conflict, the greater problem remains evaluating the uses to which scientific discoveries are employed. The most threadbare of clichés is that morality has not kept pace with technical progress, yet the platitude is useful in bringing into relief that developments may in fact have accelerated too fast for our ethical controls. William Barrett, in his trenchant book *The Illusion of Technique*, reminds us that modern science, which we are prone to hyphenate as science-technology, has only been on the scene three hundred years. Before that, science, such as it was, maintained an immediate bond between humankind and nature, and sought not so much for "facts" as for theoretical models that could be expressed mathematically and would enable us to envision nature as a whole. Facts were only then sought to verify the theory.[81] The shift in emphasis from intellectual models to the demand for facts by which to establish laws and strategies for standing away from and controlling nature, "is nothing less than a change in the being of man himself. Henceforth he stands very differently within Being, and in a different relation to beings that encompass him. The authentic history of our epoch has to be grasped at the level of Being rather than ideas."[82] The ethical resources for guiding our science-technology, must, according to Barrett, be found in the ontological realm, in that relationship with being, the source of our human nature that has produced both science and technology and all the blessings and dangers they offer.

Is science itself capable of revealing the moral resources? Sociobiologist Edward O. Wilson believes so, and offers sociobiology as, if not a substitute for religion, at least its primary guide: "Ethical philosophers intuit the deontological canons of morality by consulting the emotive centers of their own hypothalmic-limbic system. Only by interpreting the activity of the emotive centers as a biological adaptation can the meaning of the canons be deciphered."[83] Extrapolating from this point, Wilson later declared unequivocally that ". . . innate censors and motivators exist in the brain that deeply and unconsciously affect our ethical premises; from these roots morality evolved as an instinct."[84] "Understanding the brain, especially the limbic system, that complex array of neurons and hormone-secreting cells located just beneath the 'thinking' portion of the cerebral cortex . . . will enable us to reconstruct the evolutionary history of the mind, and of the moral self."[85]

An Aristotelian might find in Wilson's premise a suggestion of teleological import. If the moral sense is part of the given structure of the organism, it may well have been implanted there by the Creator, that is, humankind was preprogrammed for moral behavior. Doubtless most sociobiologists would object to such an intrusion of metaphysics, but if so they have yet to offer an explanation for the source of the standards by which the organism evaluates and identifies the best behavior as opposed to alternatives. Philip Hefner notes that some of the more philosophically oriented people in the scientific community have sought to solve this problem by relating the "good" with basic human needs that supply their own inherent "ought" by way of ethical compulsion. He quotes R. M. Hare's *Language of Morals* and Philippa Foot's *Essays in Moral Concepts* to epitomize this argument that "the practical implication of the use of moral terms, is that virtues of oughts actually turn out to be needs."[86] Hefner, while acknowledging the common sense of such an approach, sees essential flaws in it, particularly in the careless confusion of such terms as *needs* and *wants* and the uncritical movement to link them with *oughts.* Indeed, he urges that carefully articulated theology can only conclude that science and religion are both essential to comprehending the whole truth about what is and about what ought to be.

> The power of the scientific description irresistibly moves the discussion of *is* and *ought* into the arena of survival and nonsurvival. Theology therefore has no alternative today but to speak its truth about what is and what ought to be in terms relevant to survival. The concepts and vocabulary of survival must be transvalued, given new meanings. They are the meanings that relate all of earthly existence to God and his will.[87]

Survival takes on more than biological significance.

Reciprocal Benefits

The reciprocal benefits of the science-religion dialogue and their implications for ethics can be illustrated in different ways. For example, science has forced religion to consider a new worldview, at variance with the old Ptolemaic cosmology and with the apparent three-storied universe of the Bible. At the same time religion has provided science with an enhanced view of the world (a *weltanschauung,* or comprehensive philosophy regarding the cosmos, as an alternative to the *weltbild,* or mere world picture of science), a vision of ends for which humankind and the world were intended. Hugh Montefiore insists that the Christian eschatology is essential in approaching the ethical implications of technology. "If there is no perspective of eternity, man is bound to exploit this world to the full."[88] Such exploitation can lead to ecological disaster.

Richard Jones suggests another gift that religion can bring to science and technology: a direction toward emancipation from political coercion. "Science is made to serve a political purpose. It is set to work to attain goals determined by 'politics' in the widest sense—by politicians, by commerce and industry, and the hope of being able to meet some popular need which may have simply welled up into people's expectations. This is where ethical scrutiny and assessment become relevant."[89] It was, after all, a political decision to employ engineers and spend billions of dollars on military programs instead of using such resources for research on better food-growing techniques to feed the starving millions on our planet, clean up toxic waste dumps, and rebuild our decaying inner cities.

How shall Christian ethicists bring such a gift to the scientific-technological communities? It must be recognized first of all that science and technology, like politics, do not exist or function in a vacuum. Their practitioners are people who belong to communities where values are maintained, discussed, and implemented however imperfectly. Christian ethicists, perhaps lacking expertise in science, technology, and politics (though there are some who do have such skills and insights), can enter into dialogue with the specialists, and explore with them the meaning of such terms as the good, the humane, the just, the fair. The moral life is profoundly social, and as Richard Jones points out, the quality of human life is high on any list of priorities. "An engineer may be quite unaware of the wider implications of what he proposes, as when a fertilizer is proposed for farming purposes and the consultant has no concern about what happens to the rivers into which it will later be swilled."[90] Engineers may be enticed into doing something beneficial but unprecedented because of pressures from the political and business communities. The Christian ethicist, with a *weltanschauung* and an *eschatology* biblically informed, may stimulate discussion of the long-range implications of the many developments. Concern for the quality of life, and for living in obedience to the will of God, are powerful incentives for people in the scientific-technical-political world to reevaluate what they are about. "The quality-of-life discussion is inextricably linked with discussion about population, resources, ecology. Man and the earth have a common history; such an holistic vision is needed if we are to face the challenges of the future."[91]

This holistic vision must include not only the quality of life for the future of our own generation; it must stimulate responsible thinking about the well-being of generations in the far distant future. It is now well known that improperly disposed nuclear waste can endanger life on our planet thousands of years hence. But the danger is not limited to anything so dramatic as nuclear waste; commonly used herbicides and pesticides, as well as carcinogenic by-products of decomposing plastics, put us all at risk. "The possible result of the combined effects of the quantity and complexity of modern wastes could be the destruction of the ecosphere, the web of natural processes which make life on earth possible."[92]

The Christian ethicist has another gift for the scientific community, but one which may be vigorously resisted in many quarters, and that is the concept of sin. This is not to raise the melodramatic specter of the evil scientist, because it is clear that people of science are no more sinful than any others in the population. It is rather to remind ourselves of that human trait to put self-interest and community or national interest (to say nothing of the profit motive) ahead of the humane values. While some people still cling to the illusion of humankind's essential goodness, we have vast evidence to the contrary. Scientific technology seems particularly vulnerable to the charge of amorality, as a 1980 discussion of the growing popular hostility toward it at a Massachusetts Institute of Technology conference attests. Someone there even suggested that freedom of science and technology be severely limited.[93] The suggestion failed to gain much support because it was not accompanied with a clear proposal as to who would regulate them. If it were the military establishment, for example, would this mean the diversion of the majority of research and development funds toward the military? It is already the case that "Military Research and Development accounts for more financial and intellectual resources than are devoted to research and development of health, food production, energy, and environmental protection combined."[94] While many would resent the term *sin* being applied to this situation, the fact is that while 24 percent of the world's investments are for military expansion, only 3 percent is allocated to agriculture, and millions of people literally die of starvation annually. If "The earth is the Lord's and the fulness thereof . . . and they that dwell therein" as the Scriptures teach, we must face the facts of our defilement of God's domain and of God's people which, though not caused by scientific technology per se, has certainly been made more efficient by it.

Christian ethics can help reorient scientists and technologists, as well as politicians. No human endeavor has a holy mandate to fulfill itself at any cost. The future need not be an Orwellian or technophiliac nightmare. A more optimistic view is held by physicist-theologian Ian Barbour, who urges,

> A greater emphasis is needed on technologies related to survival, health and minimal material welfare. Technology as an instrument of justice must reduce rather than increase the gaps between rich and poor. Technologies of agriculture, public health, and low-cost housing—along with schools, hospitals and public transportation—are relevant to developing nations as well as to low-income groups in industrial nations.[95]

Barbour admits that moral exhortation seldom inspires adequate reform, and laments that even the churches tend to support the status quo. Yet, "Biblical images still have a latent power to evoke response," and Christian ethics imposes a sacred obligation to care for the poor and downtrodden of the earth. "Today, as in ancient Israel, the sharing of resources is a demand for justice, not an act of charity."[96]

The prophetic view of the created order; of the proclivity of humans to sin against each other as well as against God; of God's redeeming love in Christ; and the commandment to serve the needs of our fellow mortals are all pertinent to any discussion of Christian ethics. Our use of nature's powers and our employment of techniques for living that may either limit or enhance our earthly life are all subject matter for Christian ethics. They are also appropriate topics for dialogue among Christians and those engaged in the pursuit of scientific and technological endeavors.

CHAPTER TEN

Christians in a Non-Christian World

In Chapter 5 we discussed the role of the individual Christian who lives and moves among non-Christians, and the necessity to relate creatively with them. Now we must consider the way in which Christianity as a whole engages alternative belief systems and policies in a world where ideologies and economic and political actions anywhere take on global significance, and where the ease of travel makes interaction almost inescapable.

This is not an altogether novel situation. Christianity has for centuries been involved in mission enterprises, communicating with societies amid changing cultural and religious environments. Sometimes, as we noted in the first two chapters, Christianity has appropriated non-Christian elements into its own tradition, especially in adopting forms of worship (e.g., the prayer beads and votive candles of Islam), importing festival elements (Christmas trees, Easter eggs, Halloween icons), and adapting the concept of natural law.

An uneasiness has always existed among some Christians whether Christianity risks loss of its identity through interaction with non-Christians. On the other hand, there are Christian ethicists who declare that the uniqueness of the Christian faith makes any form of interaction with other traditions questionable at best: "The Christian ethics," states Heinrich Kraemer, "is entirely incommensurate with all other ethics in the world."[1] Erling Jostad, noting the rise of the New Christian Right, observes that from their point of view moralism posits only one correct moral answer to any ethical problem, and bases its criteria on the absolute authority of the Bible."[2]

There are still other Christians who insist that Christianity, though unique as a religion offering salvation, has no special form of ethics to offer to other cultures at all. Lucien Richard describes a group among contemporary Roman Catholic writers (for whom) "There is one single ground of ethics for Christians as for others. At the level of the ground of ethics, the morality of revelation is the morality of reason." Where reason prevails, all ethics are basically alike, Christian or otherwise.[3] He quotes several holding this opinion, including Richard McCormick who declares, "There is existentially only one *essential* morality common to all men. Christian morality is, in its concreteness and materiality, *human morality.*"[4]

Complicating the situation further is a suspicion among some advocates of Christianity that many who call themselves Christian are, in belief and practice, not truly Christian at all. Among the contentions that divide them, civil rights, the uses of power, and justification of violence in capital punishment and war remain a few of the thorniest. But if they are at odds with each other, and consider their divisions ethically and morally defensible, how shall they relate to those completely outside the Christian fold? Most denominations have abandoned the belief that they must convert the Jews, for example. Yet there remains in many places a latent anti-Semitism, the residue of an earlier anti-Jewish sentiment that was once considered by many Christians to be a normal expression of their loyalty to Christ. What of the prospects, then, for dealing creatively and fraternally with those traditions like Islam, Hinduism, and Buddhism that are even more remote from the biblical faiths we trace to Abraham? A brief overview of these problems may prepare us for a somewhat more detailed exploration.

Facing Issues

The dynamics of Hebrew religious and national life in the ancient world, from which Christianity emerged, was powered by the perception of and response to the will of God. Their social creativity, sense of justice, and capacity for self-criticism were expressions of this spirituality. When they neglected the spiritual discipline, their religion declined into a sacramental system that many of the prophets denounced as a prelude to their failure as a nation,[5] and to a legalism which Jesus would later reject as binding "heavy burdens, hard to bear" (Matthew 23:4).

Christianity initially offered freedom from such burdens and stressed, instead of a system of rituals and laws by which to be saved, that Christ was himself the way of salvation (John 14:6; Romans 3:20–26, 8:1–11). Jesus did impose a requirement for the life of faith: that it issue in love for the brethren as "a new commandment" (John 13:34). Not only so, it must include love for the enemy (Matthew 5:44; Luke 6:28f.). This was in fact the core of its ethics, and when Christianity began to deemphasize this message, and to withdraw into itself as a pietistic, salvation-oriented religion multiplying its rules and rituals, it, as Israel before, lost much of its dynamic power.

Much of Christianity today is imbedded in the non-Christian world and, as we noted, is greatly influenced by it. We witness a wide array of decisions being made by church organizations with reference to everything from real estate acquisition and arguments to retain tax exemptions to supporting national military ventures made without any reference to Christian principles. Judged in the light of Jesus' command to love the enemy, writes one critic, "The most popular forms of Christianity today stand condemned."[6] Paul Tillich warned almost three decades ago, out of his experience with the Christian churches in Nazi Germany, that it is dangerously easy when churches want to remain popular and avoid controversy to "shape themselves into the image of those who attack them."[7]

In an effort to understand the issues facing Christians in a non-Christian world, we must first examine at least briefly but candidly the degree to which Christians are unwittingly embedded in and identified with non-Christian and even anti-Christian agencies and biases within the Christian world.

Secondly, we address the persistent question of the uses of force in our world, with specific reference to capital punishment and war.

Finally, we seek to explore ways in which Christians can engage in creative dialogue with members of other religious traditions. In a shrinking planetary community, the encounters are inevitable (in the southern California community where I teach, every major religious tradition in the world is represented, and more than sixty different languages are spoken in which these religions are expressed). Whether the experience will be creative or disruptive depends in large measure on the willingness of the Christians involved to accept these others as part of God's family. Not all representatives of the different religious traditions have been schooled to such openness, and even with Christendom there are those whose exclusivism prompts them to reject every effort at interaction. The need to make the effort is growing urgent in the face of militant politics; time may be running out.

NON-CHRISTIAN CHRISTIANITY

The most conspicuous non-Christian element in the early Church to draw the ire of the apostle Paul was the backward drag of its Jewish conservative membership. A major emphasis in his Letter to the Romans is on releasing their dependence on the old laws by which they thought salvation could be achieved, and accepting God's gift of victory over sin and death extended in Christ Jesus. Elsewhere, however, he and other New Testament writers reemphasize a religious theme held in common by Jews and Christians, that of translating faith into practical deeds: feeding the hungry, caring for widows and the fatherless, and "keeping oneself unspotted from the world" (James 1:27). Above all is the key to everything else: the expression of faith in unqualified love for all and especially for our enemies.

> The more [Jesus] has been studied, the more the conclusion has emerged that what he taught about loving enemies is fundamental, not peripheral, to the church and its understanding of its own existence. Indeed it is fundamental to the survival of the human race. Unless humans learn to live with their enemies, indeed unless we learn to love our enemies, our days on this earth are numbered.[8]

This is a message not simply overlooked, but actively rejected by many Christians. It is for this reason that William Klassen is so critical of the Moral Majority, which along with similar groups makes its appeal to some 60 million television viewers every month.[9] "Since loving the enemy is conspicuously absent in its 'gospel' it has to be termed as false, and those who proclaim it designated as false prophets. In the Bible the true prophets soon found themselves expelled from the presence of the king, for they refused to ally themselves with the king or tell him what he wanted to hear."[10] Klassen also insists,

> Every popular form of Christianity must be tested by this standard: What are the elements of Christian faith which run counter to popular morality? How is the truly human aspect of Christianity being expressed? There were denominations in the United States who refused to listen to the State Department when it raised objections to their efforts to help Cuba in a hurricane aftermath; there were Christians in the United States who insisted on helping the North Vietnamese even while the United States foreign policy dictated that Christians in the United States could not love their enemies![11]

Acting on Christian love as proclaimed in the Gospels was denounced as tantamount to treason. How does it happen that the teachings of Jesus are so often rejected by the very people who proclaim their faith in him so fervently? It would be tempting to attribute it to hypocrisy, but also grossly unfair in most cases. Several possibilities suggest themselves.

First, while it may seem almost too obvious and hackneyed an excuse, most of us feel insecure in the presence of a truly prophetic or pioneering spirit, or when presented with a new idea. We are, after all, raised to embrace the beliefs and customs of the family, tribe, religion, and nation. Stanley Hauerwas notes that we are all members of some particular "story-formed community," and gain our sense of identity, character, and virtue from being faithful to that "narrative." To introduce a new "story" risks rejection from the outset, which is doubtless why the apostle Paul and the writer of Matthew's Gospel strove so hard to demonstrate that Christ was the fulfillment of, not a rival to, their messianic expectation.[12]

A second reason for some Christians, particularly converts on the mission field, clinging to non-Christian ways of thinking and behaving is that they fear reprisal from family and friends who have not become Christians with them. Paul suffered severe persecution from former Jewish colleagues when he accepted Christ's lordship (2 Corinthians 11:24–28). He knew the temptation to placate them by retaining some pre-Christian Jewish habits and traditions.[13] The history of Christian missions is replete with stories of new converts retaining customs, celebrations, and philosophical points of view associated with the religion they presumably left behind. In some cases this was out of habit, but not infrequently it was to minimize resentment and hostility.

A third cause may lie in the actual misunderstanding of what Christianity stands for. A sizable percentage of people who join the church have had inadequate instruction in the meaning of the Christian faith, and bring many of their prejudices and non-Christian points of view with them. When such people become popular within the church and assume roles of leadership, they may assume their attitudes and beliefs to be quite in conformity with Christian ethics and teach them to others.

A more serious aspect of this problem has been raised by a New Testament scholar, who writes that portions of the Bible may have been purposely mistranslated by those in the hire of King James to counsel passivity in the face of injustice.[14] If this is the case, surely those who hold to non-Christian points of view that they thought were biblical can hardly be blamed.

A fourth reason derives from the fact that even the most sincere Christian, well schooled and dedicated, may be so identified with the secular culture that loyalty to the faith and to the culture are viewed as virtually synonymous. This is not a matter of conscious accommodation, but of confused allegiances that fail to discern discrepancies. Paul Tillich cites the case of nationalism that tends to consecrate thoroughly secular values.

> Nationalism is ultimately rooted in the natural and necessary self-affirmation of every social group, analogous to that of every living being. This self-affirmation has nothing to do with selfishness (though it may be distorted into selfishness). Nationalism . . . can only appear when secular criticisms have dissolved the identity of religious consecration and group self-affirmation, and the consecrating religion is pushed aside and the empty space filled by the national idea as a matter of ultimate concern.[15]

Loyalty to God and country, virtuous as such allegiances may appear, often leads to the equation of the two, with potentially idolatrous results. In defense of the American way, or British sovereignty, South African white supremacy, capitalistic free enterprise, or some other cluster of secular values, Christians can be drawn into taking positions contrary to the ways of love and reconciliation. When choices are forced, the non-Christian values are often accorded higher priority.

There are those who feel that Christianity has become so much a part of the Western culture, it really has no distinctive ethic to offer. Western civilization is viewed as Christian, by virtue of the latter's being the dominant religion; at the very least it can be termed Judeo-Christian. But as Stanley Hauerwas has emphasized, the Christian ethic is unique, and distinct from the naturalistic-idealist ethic of secular society, and we are in error to assume that the values and purposes of secular society are identical with God's purposes.

> Isn't it possible that Christians, because of the ethos peculiar to their community, might find themselves in deep discontinuity with the ethos of a particular society? By virtue of the distinctive narrative that forms their community, Christians are distinct from the world. They are called to be nothing less than a sanctified people of peace . . . faithful to God's calling of them as a foretaste of the Kingdom. In this sense sanctification is a life of service and sacrifice that the world cannot account for on its own terms.[16]

The Radical Right

Yet another source of non-Christian elements within Christianity, and potentially the most dangerous of all, is the mind-set called the radical right. Historically, groups which could be so identified have adhered to ideologies that have been amalgams of religion and nationalism. Both of these phenomena are powered by self-affirmations as power structures having rules and regulations by which to shape the lives and behaviors of their adherents. Both have a consciousness of a calling, the sense of a sacred obligation to be fulfilled. This was clearly the case with ancient Israel, and to a degree with modern Israel, which was and is both a nation and a faith; it is also the case with Islam in many parts of the Near and Middle East today. Paul Tillich noted similar situations in medieval Germany's *Corpus Christianum*, in France's and Great Britain's divine right, and in America's manifest destiny.[17] When these elements become the total preoccupation of groups within a national or religious movement, a right-wing fundamentalism emerges that permits of no alternatives, and justifies virtually any action that secures its success.

The radical right is composed of ideologues whose spiritual ancestors are those who defended the national and religious establishment of ancient Israel against the prophets who sought to correct its abuses. We may recall Amaziah, the institutional conservative, who attacked Amos: "Never again prophesy at Bethel, for it is the King's sanctuary, and a temple of the kingdom" (Amos 7:13). The same mind-set is found among those who crucified Jesus; in the conservative Jewish faction who persecuted the apostle Paul; among the reactionaries who jailed Roger Bacon and Galileo, burned Hus and Tyndale, and sought to halt the Reformation; and among those Protestants who in their turn persecuted the Roman Catholics. We find clergy of the eighteenth century, like T. R. Malthus, William Paley, and J. B. Sumner, who ostensibly, on religious grounds, preached that poverty and inequality are inevitable (partially for reasons that populations increase faster than resources), and a necessary state of affairs "under Providence." Thus while Leviticus and Deuteronomy made aid to the poor mandatory, and Jesus warned that "as you did it not to one of the least of these, you did it not to me" (Matthew 25:45), the religious right was proclaiming the folly of embodying benevolence in the law, specifically opposing England's poor laws, and declaring that the poor have no legal right to subsistence.[18]

In Chapter 2, we noted how the social gospel at the turn of our century sought to restore the early Church's program of care for the poor and disabled, not only within the churches but in public life, often against opposition from entrenched business interests. Ronald Preston, of the University of Manchester, relates how this emphasis influenced the economic and political life of England up through the 1960s. But, he notes, "there has been a cultural backlash. Now simple theories and moral absolutes are more in favor. The USA has seen the same tendency." Preston then adds a remarkable observation: "One feature that is common to both countries is that a number of exponents of the new right were formerly of the old left."[19]

We might seek to account for the shift from left to right in terms of fatigue, disillusionment with unfulfilled expectation, or a generation gap. Clinton Morrison notes that among the benefits of the pioneer spirit is that it fosters a creative idealism that is socially altruistic, often antiestablishment and prophetically forward looking. It is often seen as left wing. "But what is more the teaching of history than that the children of the generation of the Spirit prove to be the generation of uninspired mandarins."[20]

Whatever the case, the mandarins of the New Right, if uninspired, are not lacking in zeal. In fact, they take their ideology from an interpretation of Scripture that reduces the Bible to a crystal ball foretelling vast social unrest and a nuclear Armageddon to accompany the imminent Second Coming of Christ. Hal Lindsay's popular book *The Late Great Planet Earth* (which has purportedly sold 20 million copies) lays out a scenario in which God presumably decreed a "dispensational" division of history: We are to witness a climactic seven years of "end time" with the Beast of Revelation appearing; the return of Jews to the homeland; vast "tribulation" followed by the coming of Christ with his avenging legions to wage the cosmic war to end all wars. Lindsay enthuses, "Imagine, cities like London, Paris, Tokyo, New York, Los Angeles, Chicago—obliterated."[21] Characteristically, there is no note of grief for the victims or doubt about the militarism of Christ in such portrayals. Indeed, among many who identify with the New Right, like Jerry Falwell, Tim LaHaye, and (until their exposure in 1987 for immorality and fiscal abuses) Jim Bakker and Jimmy Swaggart, God is presented as a warrior deity, and Christian nations are urged to be armed to the limit to fight evil. Falwell has nothing but contempt for talk about strategic arms limitations; he regards "peaceful intentions" as "stupidity."[22]

What many observers, including the Christic Institute of Washington, D.C., find disturbing about the New Right, or "Radical Right," is not simply that they proclaim a message contrary to the Gospel of the Prince of Peace, but that they are

> organizing for political power: power in Congress, in the armed forces, in state governments, in city councils, in school boards throughout America. The Religious Right claims to control the Republican Party organizations in several states, and has learned how to use the court system to advance its political ideology. In Alabama (March 1986), a federal judge banned 40 textbooks used in schools because they allegedly promote ideas—including environmentalism, feminism, and internationalism—that are offensive to Fundamentalist parents.[23]

How far from the Christian Gospel the Religious Right has moved was reflected in an observation by Daniel Maguire: "When Jesus came the first time, he came as a lamb, willing to die to take away the sins of the world. Apparently Jesus had enough of being portrayed as a lamb. Next time he will come as a lion. And what a lion! His weapons are now earthquakes and thermonuclear blasts."[24] Perhaps members of the Religious Right, which makes so great an issue of the "antichrist" and the "Beast" of Revelation, have neglected to note the warning of the apostle Paul: "If [any] should preach a gospel contrary to that which we preached to you, let him be accursed" (Galatians 1:8). The danger of distorting the faith that undergirds the ethical decisions of Christians, and by which Christianity itself is judged by the rest of the world, cannot be taken lightly. The Antichrist may be found among those who misrepresent the very Gospel they so fervently proclaim.

THE ISSUES OF VIOLENCE

If Jesus' injunction to "turn the other cheek" and "love your enemies" were taken at face value by all Christians, it would seem that pacifism should be universally acknowledged among them; arguments about capital punishment would give way to developing strategies for rehabilitation of criminals; and disarmament would be a major theme in any discussion of international conflict. Yet, as we have seen, no consensus exists among Christians on these issues, as on many others, and for reasons that have their roots deep in history. Perhaps no unanimity of judgment is possible. At the very least, we can make an effort to understand why the issue of violence is so complex, and not merely made difficult by theological nit-picking.

Relatively protected white Americans and other white Westerners are prone to think of violence in terms of overt action that causes pain and/or injury. Robert McAfee Brown points out, however, that one root of the term is the Latin *violare*, which has many meanings: to infringe upon, to disregard, to abuse, or to deny. Thus many in our society who have known discrimination, particularly minority groups, have experienced violence whether it involved physical harm or not. "The basic overall definition of violence would then become violation of personhood. Personhood can be violated or denied in subtle ways that are not obvious at all except to the victim. In broadest terms, an act that depersonalized would be an act of violence, since it transforms a person into a thing."[25] To deprive a person access to a drinking fountain by posting a sign WHITES ONLY, to pay so meager a wage as to deny a worker a decent standard of living; to make medical care prohibitive because of high fees; to provide inadequate education for the needs of youth—all can be termed acts of violence. All these are clearly ethical issues to which a Christian must address a response.

More obviously, of course, to deny a person life or liberty is a violent act, and this is where Christian ethics faces its most difficult challenge. Yet we must note that criminal acts, which invoke discussions of punishment by violent means (from handcuffing, to jailing, to executing) often have their roots in seemingly less strident forms of violence. A society that tolerates violence against youth by curtailing needed funds for education, that winks at inadequate wages, allows exploitive rents and mortgages, and provides insufficient health care so that America has, for example, the poorest health care of seventeen major nations in the world[26] may find itself burdened with revolt and anarchy, to which it then, characteristically, responds with overt violence.

But how should we deal with violent lawbreakers, even conceding that their actions may have been prompted by a sense of outrage at real injustice? Their deeds have violated the personhood of others, perhaps even brought about their death, the ultimate violation.

Capital Punishment

Appeals to the Bible reveal that in the Hebrew Scriptures the Mosaic law included a detailed penal code, and the death penalty was not uncommon.[27] Access to capital punishment was denied the Jewish courts shortly before the Christian era, though capital trials and executions without Roman intervention are still on record, and Paul attests to the high priest's authority to carry out such a sentence (Acts 26:10).

Nowhere in the New Testament is capital punishment advocated. "We cannot argue from biblical precedent for capital punishment. We can also not simply say that antiquity had no alternative forms of punishment; in addition to actual restitution, the Mosaic code provided for flogging and exile. Instead biblical history exhibits a developmental pattern in its handling of social evils and abuses of authority."[28]

It is known that the early Christians abhorred violence, and it is not clear just when the practice of executions was first reintroduced to Christian communities. It is recorded that heresy judgments were often accompanied by rough handling even as early as the second century. Constantine, who was not a baptized Christian until on his death bed, commanded the death penalty for disobedience to the decision of the Council of Nicaea.[29] There was little Christian charity shown to criminals or heretics by the fathers of the medieval church, and by the time of the Inquisition, the Church assumed the power of life and death over all its subjects. "Medieval Europe adopted the Oriental practices of flaying, impaling, or breaking over the wheel. Later came the gallows . . . beheading was reserved for the nobility."[30] By the fifteenth century there were 17 crimes in England for which the death penalty could be used; the number gradually increased, so that during the 38-year reign of Henry VIII, 72,000 executions were carried out. At the start of the nineteenth century, English law listed 250 capital crimes, including damaging a fishpond, picking pockets, or associating with Gypsies.[31]

Movements to abolish capital punishment have a fitful history. The Puritans, who are often accused of repressive attitudes, actually began to reduce the number of capital crimes, and the Quakers succeeded briefly from 1682 to 1718 in limiting capital punishment to first degree murder in Pennsylvania. Benjamin Franklin is credited with the first movement to abolish the death penalty altogether, in 1787. But the history of the matter is one of ebbs and flows, with every incident of murder or other major crime changing ordinarily rational people into vengeful furies.

Opponents of capital punishment often cite the commandment against killing and New Testament references to mercy, forgiveness, and reconciliation. On the other side of the argument are those who quote the ancient Hebrew *lex talionis*, "an eye for an eye," and Mosaic examples of the death penalty. Their antagonists counter that the Gospel set aside many Old Testament laws and practices (regarding circumcision, for example, and rigid Sabbath laws), and nowhere advocates punishment by death.

The most frequent argument given by proponents of capital punishment is that it deters crime, and eliminating it would result in an increase of homicides. Studies over the past half century among the major Western nations, however, have refuted this claim. The British Royal Commission, concluding a long study of the problem in many lands, reported in 1953: "The general conclusion that we have reached is that there is no clear evidence in any of the figures we have examined that the abolition of capital punishment has led to an increase in the homicide rate, or that its reintroduction has led to its fall."[32] A 1960 study among the states showed a *lesser* rate of homicides in states that had abolished capital punishment than in neighboring states that retained the death penalty.[33] Warden Lewis E. Lawes, formerly of Sing Sing Prison, once declared that of the 150 men he led to the electric chair, not one would say he had given any thought to the possible penalty when he committed murder.

One argument heard for those who favor the death penalty, even while admitting it may not be a deterrent, is that "at least it will prevent that killer from killing again." But many judges have observed that murderers are the least likely to be repeat criminals; homicides are usually enacted in a momentary heat of passion. It is the embezzlers, thieves, and white collar criminals who are the most frequent repeaters. Further, "the death penalty often prevents convictions for murder because it is repugnant to jurors."[34] It may actually result in criminals going free, rather than being removed from society.

Another concern is that the death penalty puts the arresting officers at greater risk. "After several killings of policemen, Austrian police claimed that the presence of the death penalty in the law offered such a threat to certain types of offenders that they should go to the extreme in attempting to avoid capture, and that if the death penalty were removed there would be less danger of the police. The death penalty was abolished."[35]

Again, there is the problem of juries having been given inadequate evidence on which to determine guilt or innocence, and whether a person convicted of a crime deserves the extreme penalty. In a 1989 case in Alabama, for example, a juror declared she would never have voted for the death penalty if the defense attorney (twice dismissed from the courtroom for drunkenness) had revealed evidence of the condemned man's mental retardation. The convict was executed.[36]

Yet another concern is the number of actually innocent people who have been mistakenly convicted and executed, only to be exonerated too late by later evidence. An early study by Professor Edwin Borchard, of Yale University, detailed 65 such cases, and Judge Jerome Frank declares, "No one knows how many innocent men, erroneously convicted of murder, have been put to death by American governments. For, once a convicted man is dead, all interest in vindicating him generally evaporates."[37]

There are alternatives to the death penalty, including longer periods of incarceration up to life imprisonment without possibility of parole. But stopping there is far from adequate. One major objection to those opposing capital punishment has been that they are bleeding hearts who care more for the criminal than for the victim. Actually the opposite may be the case; the vengeful spirit that clamors for the death penalty has seldom bothered to seek restitution or compensation for the victim. Michael Endres, professor of criminal justice at Xavier University, notes,

> We have ignored the value of holding the offender directly accountable to his victim or his victim's kin in modern justice systems. Material amends for an awful crime by no means offer a perfect solution. On the other hand, the taking of another life offers no compensation at all. Under the present circumstances, victims and their survivors are twice victimized. First, directly by the offender, and second, indirectly by the state, which ignores any responsibility toward the victims incurred by the offender.[38]

In this light, Christian ethics clearly has something to offer that secular ethics has not, or at least has neglected in the past. Compassion both for the victim and the perpetrator of crime proves in the long run to be more practical as well as more humane than pragmatic or substantive jurisprudence. The convicted criminal, in making restitution, would use whatever skills or training he or she has to earn the means to support the injured party. Most prisons already have well-equipped metal and wood shops, libraries, and other facilities for gainful employment. If a man kills the father of a family, he becomes in that case the provider for that family for the rest of his life, whether the death sentence now becomes a life sentence without parole or a limited sentence with parole. This is a far more creative solution than the base satisfaction derived from revenge or the life-devaluing eye-for-an-eye form of justice.

In the final analysis, as Endres points out,

> the issue of the death penalty is linked to the fundamental matter of the kind of society in which we wish to live. It is all too easy to kill—the trees for another concrete roadway; the animal for its pelt; the enemy, the fetus, the aged, the defective—and the killer himself. We ought to guard against the growth of a mentality which sees the destruction of life as the solution to any problem including that of violence itself.[39]

Violence tends to beget violence, and most nations in the Western world have renounced the death penalty. Indeed, with the abolition of the death penalty in France in 1981, the United States is virtually the only Western democracy to retain it.

War

In one sense war is an extrapolation of the death penalty to the international scale: "Those who have afflicted us, must be afflicted." The analogy breaks down when we recognize that in the case of war, many innocent people are killed, not just the criminals. Further, war and the preparations for war have always had about them a certain business-and-profit aspect that has a massive effect on the economy. Cartels and international agreements are often involved that bear little if any resemblance to the seeking and punishing of some criminal or even a syndicate of criminals.

Nevertheless, historically vendettas and border clashes are usually justified as legitimate forms of retaliation for a prior assault. Even when the ancient Israelites took possession of the Promised Land after their exodus from Egypt, and the inhabitants fought back, the warfare was excused on the grounds of the barbaric practices of the enemy. The slaughter of such a community was advocated as a command from the Lord: ". . . put all its males to the sword, but the women and the little ones, the cattle and everything else in the city, all its spoil, you shall take as booty to yourselves; and you shall enjoy the spoil of your enemies"(Deuteronomy 20:13–14). In the case of besieging very remote lands: "You shall utterly destroy them, the Hittites and the Amorites, the Canaanites and the Perizzites, as the Lord your God has commanded . . . save nothing alive that breathes" (verses 16–17).

Wars of aggression were such a constant with the peoples of Israel and Judah that they nearly bankrupted themselves, and the prophets pleaded in despair, "Your country lies desolate, your cities are burned with fire." When the people retorted that God would continue to favor them, Isaiah charged that God could no longer abide their religious pretenses: "Even though you make many prayers, I will not listen; your hands are full of blood" (Isaiah 1:7, 15). The conflict between those we now call prophets, and the false prophets who sided with the kings' military ambitions is of course well recorded; indeed the words of Isaiah, Jeremiah, Amos, Zephanish, and Zechariah were so caustic that today they might be considered anti-Semitic. But their plea to beat swords into plowshares, and spears into pruning hooks (Isaiah 2:4; Joel 3:10; Hosea 2:18) went largely unheeded until the days of their occupation, when they became moot.

Warfare was as abhorrent to the early Christians as were all other forms of violence. Many in the first two centuries chose death rather than serve in the Roman army. Rome might be the occupying country, but patriotism was not a priority; they would "render unto Caesar" any taxes due, but they would not kill for him. Yet even before the fourth century, when Constantine liberated Christianity from persecution, the attitude toward defending the Roman Empire by military means had begun to change.

The concept of a *just war* came into circulation during the declining years of the empire, when some Christians proposed that though warfare is an evidence of sin, the securing of peace and unity might require military action as a necessary evil. Augustine (354–430) grudgingly admitted this possibility in *The City of God* (Book XIX, Chapter 7) but added, "This is true; but how many wars, how much slaughter and bloodshed have provided this unity?" He denied that warfare is natural to the human condition, but insisted it reveals our sinfulness, which has placed us below the "lower animals" who, though devoid of rational will "live more peaceably with their kind than men."

During Charlemagne's ninth-century efforts to restore the empire (which had fallen in 476 A.D.) as the Holy Roman Empire, military might became a virtue. By the time the Crusades reached their height in the twelfth century, the armies of Christendom were an accepted fact.

Thomas Aquinas (1225–1274) may or may not have been familiar with pre-Christian arguments against war in Euripides and Aristophanes, but was certainly aware of Augustine's opposition. He agreed essentially with Augustine's definition of peace as "well-ordered concord," except for the caveat that while peace produces concord, the reverse is not necessarily true. Concord may be at the expense of freedom, as in the *Pax Romana*, where there was indeed enforced concord, but not peace worth having. Jesus had said, "My peace I give to you; [but] not as the world gives . . ." (John 14:27), and noted that his peace would be a cause of conflict (Matthew 10:34). Aquinas thus wrote that as conflict may be inevitable, there may be such a thing as a just war. In his *Summa Theologica* (Part II, Q.40, Article I) he wrote his *apologia* containing certain provisions: (1) Such wars must be waged by constituted authority; (2) The cause must be just; (3) There must be intention of establishing good or correcting some evil.

In the centuries between Aquinas and the Protestant Reformation, no serious critique of his position on war was proffered, and the armies of the popes grew in strength as conflicts grew in number. The Reformers themselves did little to alter the contention that warfare might be acceptable on some occasions, although John Calvin did urge the French Huguenots not to take arms against the Catholics: "It is better that we all perish than to cause such a scandal to the cause of Christ." The Saint Bartholomew's Day massacre of several thousand Protestants in Paris (August 1572) hardened Protestant determination, and warfare became a common tragedy among so-called Christian nations throughout Europe in the next century. Marginal Christian writers like Rabelais, Swift, and Montaigne would lament the atrocities; others like Hobbes and Malthus would refer to war as a kind of purgative for overpopulated nations. Hegel even inferred that warfare was a necessary part of the dialectic of history, cleansing nations from the corrosive effects of too much peace and of the luxury that often accompanies it.

Christian churches have often been enlisted in the process of blessing armies and war efforts in general. Many nations today have official anthems that are military in character; the U.S. national anthem, in particular, contains a strong endorsement for military action: "Then conquer we must, when our cause it is just . . ." with the added sanctification: "And this be our motto: 'In God is our trust.' "[40]

In an essay asserting that "The 'Just War' justifies too much," Donald Wells observes that in the Middle Ages the objection to war seems to have been based less on the fact of the killing involved than on the reasons given. By implication, a carefully wrought rationale favoring a particular military engagement could weigh more heavily than an argument concerning the pain and death of its victims. Taking Aquinas's three major points, Wells points out that Hitler, Mussolini, and Tito were "just as much constituted authorities" as President Roosevelt and the Queen of England. Secondly, the justness of the causes of World War II could not be subjected to an impartial, international judge; all constituted parties claimed to be justified for reasons of their own. Third, Hitler set forth eloquent arguments he deemed valid for prosecuting a war that would establish good and correct some evil, and persuaded millions of his fellow Germans of the rightness of his cause. Aquinas's prescription for a just war, Wells concludes, gives no guidance at all, but actually provides excuses for war.[41] He notes further the addendum to Aquinas's arguments by Franciscus de Victoria (1480–1546) that would assert a just war must use only those means "proportional to the ends." This remains too vague to be useful. How do we determine that just this much violence is acceptable, but no more?

This forces us beyond the consideration that war is an extrapolation of the death sentence, justifying the execution of a known criminal. In war, more than the guilty are the targets of annihilation. Even the enemy soldiers, fighting on behalf of some evil empire are not the only ones subject to the death sentence of war. It is a painful fact that while the Allies, early in World War II, were opposed to saturation bombing on humanitarian grounds, as well as on the proportionality principle, the atomic bombing of the undefended cities of Hiroshima and Nagasaki and the near obliteration of Dresden brought that discussion to an end. More than eighty wars have occurred since World War II, with over 25 million casualties.[42] Conventional weaponry has often been tragically inaccurate, devastating civilian populations along with military targets. To be sure, recent technology has produced impressive improvements toward pinpoint bombing, with so-called smart bombs employed in the 1991 Persian Gulf war. But even these did not prevent the destruction of a civilian shelter, killing more than two hundred men, women, and children. The total death toll of that war was in the tens of thousands, while it left the dictator, Hussein, in full control.

The proportionality idea, that war might be justified if the effort expended were proportional to the wrong being redressed, is an argument that still has appeal to many, as Father John Courtney Murray's proposal before the 1959 Council of Religion and International Affairs attests. He advocated that communism is an evil so vast that any means for destroying it is acceptable, pleading only that large numbers of people ought not be slaughtered needlessly.[43] But we must ask how many needless deaths make an acceptable limit just short of large numbers. When President Reagan secretly ordered an air attack against "that mad dog" Muammar al-Qadaffy's Libya, to punish Qadaffy for allegedly training terrorists in April 1986 (four days before his Assistant Secretary of State John Whitehead assured the world on television that America would not attack), Qadaffy himself was not killed, but a hundred innocent people were, including Qadaffy's adopted child. The number of deaths from Reagan's bombing far exceeded the number killed by Qadaffy's terrorists. We may ask if that was proportional, or a large enough number to qualify for Father Murray's "large number . . . slaughtered needlessly."

Even more problematic for the just war theorists is the estimated 100,000 people killed in the 1991 Persian Gulf war. At least half of these were civilians who had already suffered for years under Saddam Hussein's brutal reign, while Hussein was left in power to perpetrate further horrors on the Kurds, driving them over the mountains to die of starvation and cold. It would appear that the proportionality aspect of the just war theory in modern warfare is rendered improbable if not obsolete. This is especially true if nuclear weapons are in our future. The U.S. Catholic Bishops' Pastoral Letter asserted, "A nuclear war could never be a Just War because a nuclear exchange would produce massive or total annihilation."[44]

Our problem is further exacerbated by the realization that much of the just war debate is still based on a romantic conception of war in medieval terms, as if we were only concerned with sword thrusts now replaced with bullets. This toys-in-the-attic imagery is obsolete in the days of automated battlefields and the prospect of megadeath from arsenals containing bombs with a hundred times the destructive power as the one dropped on Hiroshima. The superpower stockpiles are in such numbers that the entire planet could be incinerated in a matter of minutes. But even without the use of the thousands of such bombs now in storage, it is sobering to realize how technological advances enabled the United States during the Vietnam War to drop more conventional bombs on the city of Hanoi in the six days of the Christmas bombing than were dropped by Nazis on all of Great Britain in six years of World War II.[45] Much of the world struggles under the burden of old-fashioned warfare, which has become increasingly violent.

The advent of nuclear weapons as already noted dwarfs the destructive capacities of the past. The emphasis on military technology now requires some 70 percent of America's research and development monies, taking a heavy toll on other kinds of research that could improve the quality of life. As we inaugurate what one former navy officer calls the "warfare state," the U.S. military budget is projected by *World News Digest* to rise from $269.3 in 1990 to an unprecedented $309.2 billion in 1992. Meanwhile the United States ranks seventeenth among Western nations in doctor-patient ratio, twenty-first in infant survival, eighteenth in life expectancy. "Our inner cities decay and our infrastructure deteriorates. As these resources are diverted nationally, they also reflect a global diversion of $600 billion from the needs of a suffering world."[46]

With so much of our economy and research capability being absorbed by the military-industrial complex, what we may be witnessing is a subverting of the military by militarism. This is not a mere play on words. Militarism is a mind-set that justifies all military action in the name of national security, and promotes it with a technology that provides almost limitless power for destruction. Military personnel are by no means all militarists. Quite often in fact, the most outspoken militarists are civilian politicians and sometimes clergy, as we noted earlier. Militarism is demonic in its readiness to excuse the most flagrant abuses of human rights and life in the name of national interest.

Militarism may become a philosophy, or even a theology unto itself. Alan Geyer, writing on technology as theology, notes the ascendency of technical values and commitments that have subverted what he calls Incarnational Truth.

> Our obsessions are not with the Center and Goal of Creation, with the love which would redeem and reorder all our material existence; they have become fixated on the stuff to be redeemed. We have become tools of our tools. Thus we

are imbued with a trained incapacity to cope critically with the most demonic of all the grossest forms of materialism: the idolatry of military technology. It has perverted economic and energy priorities . . . generated a vicious weapons-petroleum complex, and subverted civil liberties and educational institutions. Will this generation of weapons forfeit future generations of human beings?[47]

The answer need not be one of despair. While there are some in our society, perhaps even a large number, who are willing to divert resources from the poor, from the elderly and infirm, and from education and science and the arts, not all agree.

Alan Geyer's is not a call for unilaterally throwing away all our military capability; this would be sheer folly in a predatory world. But he advocates that a beginning must be made to eliminate the conditions that make their presence seem mandatory. This will not be achieved by our present posture of mutual belligerence which, as Carl Sagan has expressed it, has fostered an arms buildup "so bloated, so grossly in excess of what's needed [for the nations] to dissuade each other, that if it weren't so tragic it would be laughable."[48] We do not make the world safer by making it more dangerous.

It was the hope of George Washington, after America's declaration of independence, that the army might be disbanded so the fledgling republic would not be known for its military prowess, but rather for its enhancement of human rights and dignity. This hope was born of a thoroughly grounded Christian faith. Its ethical implications are profound and far reaching. But across the decades that followed, few shared that vision. Militarism, with its pomp and winsome power fueled by a zeal to be the most economically prosperous of all nations, has had seductive appeal. It has become unpatriotic not to be military minded. Yet the late John F. Kennedy, himself a decorated war hero, once said that there will always be wars until the status of the conscientious objector is as honored as that of the warrior.

Beyond conscientious objection to war, some Christian ethicists seek direction for specific action to create conditions for peace. Violence, as Daniel Maguire notes, minimizes conditions for rationality, is inherently escalatory, tends to bypass efforts at social and cultural restructuring (which must take place if the causes of conflict are to be resolved), and makes community building and harmony hard to achieve in the postviolent period.[49] Alan Geyer adds, "The first requisite of a faithful Christian theology for our time and for all time, is to learn again and again how little we know about our faith itself unless, and until we do the things that make for peace."[50] The first step, he insists, is learning to speak the truth. "As the Quakers have always told us, speaking the truth to power is the very first step in peacemaking."[51] If Americans learned nothing else from the Iran-contra scandal that shook America's governing administration for years after 1986, we should have learned that deception and violations of public trust can only lead to ever more grave threats to peace.

A second step toward securing peace is what Geyer calls *futuring,* the "imaginative opening to better historical possibilities in the face of enemies, cynics, scoffers, even liars—that is the minimal requirement of peacemaking."[52]

A third step is that envisioned by Rodrigo Carazo, former president of Costa Rica, who with the support of the United Nations has created a University of Peace. In Costa Rica, he has built an institution to which students, already equipped with college degrees in every discipline from agriculture to medicine to zoology, study and develop techniques for creating harmonious conditions for international understanding. "We have for so long prided ourselves on our war colleges and military academies where we study war. Why not a university for peace studies? Christian missionaries have studied and developed strategies for peaceful relationships for centuries. The models are already at hand."[53]

Overarching and undergirding these requisites to peacemaking, and addressing the perennial issue of war, the Christian believes that an ontological identification with Christ, the Prince of Peace, must be effected. The "world's" peace, as we noted, is always a version of *Pax Romana,* steel tipped and iron shod. A "theological centralism" or "humanism of the Incarnation," as Alan Geyer expresses it, may yet prove to be the most practical road to peace and the end of war.

CHRISTIAN ETHICS AND OTHER RELIGIONS

When the apostles first went forth, as Jesus had urged, to "make disciples of all nations," it was not to proclaim a superior ethic or even to make converts, but to proclaim God's forgiving and redeeming love extended through Christ. Jesus had insisted that the comportment of his disciples should be a cut above that of nonbelievers; when it came to love and generosity, ". . . what more are you doing than others? Do not even the Gentiles do the same?" (Matthew 5:46). But Jesus' primary concern was not with the superiority or inferiority of their moral code; he wanted people to love each other and to seek the kingdom together. All else would follow including, presumably, a better ethical life (Matthew 6:33).

Yet it is true, as Brian Hebblethwaite reminds us, "Until relatively recently, the superiority of Christianity as an ethical system was assumed by Christians . . . the ethical content of other faiths was overlooked and Christianity held to bring not only the gospel but morality as well to the heathen."[54] Translations of the sacred Scriptures of other religions by missionaries began to erode this confidence, and during the late nineteenth and early twentieth century, when the comparative study of the religions of the world was gradually introduced into theological seminaries, and then into colleges and universities, the fact of other ethical systems of high order could not be denied. To be sure, Friedrich Schliermacher (1768–1834) had already discussed other religious traditions, but having argued that monotheism was superior to any form of polytheism[55], he further charged that among monotheistic traditions, the Islamic faith is too fatalistic to provide a genuine ethic, and Judaism depends too much on a reward-and-punishment system to foster ethical judgment. In similar fashion Ernst Troeltsch (1865–1923) dismissed polytheisms, and held that the dependence of Judaism and Islam on the law (a point familiar to students of Paul, though of course Paul could know nothing yet of Islam) made them inferior to Christianity, which offers a personal relationship to a loving, redeeming Father.

Among the popular books on the world's religions in the 1920s, Robert Hume's *The World's Living Religions* urged an open and liberal acceptance of all faiths. "Every religion is itself an attempt to compare and conserve the higher values in human life through connection with the Supreme." He then added that "an intelligent, friendly, and fair" approach to the study required "the making of careful scientific and evaluating comparisons."[56] Hume was a conscientious scholar and gifted translator whose book sharply outlined each of the eleven major religions, and contained more citings of original texts than any book of its kind at the time. But his methodology of "scientific and evaluating comparisons" was rendered questionable by a decidedly Christian bias of which Hume was probably unaware. It is impossible to make evaluating comparisons without a predetermined gauge or pattern by which to make the judgments. At the close of each chapter in which a particular religion was discussed he included a section on strengths and weaknesses, which are always drawn with reference to Christian Ideals.[57] In discussing Christianity, Hume found no weaknesses except that individual Christians often fail to live up to its high standards.

Enthusiasm for the study of the world's major religions, spurred in part by increased emphasis on world missions in the churches and by opportunities for travel among young people, led to a demand for comparative religion classes in higher education. This evoked a spate of books that encouraged an open and tolerant view. In some cases the eagerness to avoid any semblance of bigotry led to minimizing the differences among the religions. It became commonplace to hear that all religions are basically alike, offering the Fatherhood of God, the brotherhood of man, and some version of the Golden Rule. As recently as 1981, one of the most popular university texts included a heading "Let the Best Faith Win. . . ." "The most adequate faith or best faith is that which takes fullest account of reality in all its aspects. Who is to be the judge of adequacy? Obviously each person must judge for himself."[58]

We may question the easy assumption that all religions are alike, when we discover that they do not all teach the Fatherhood of God, for example. Buddhism does not, nor does Taoism. The caste system of the Hindu religion implicitly denies the brotherhood of humankind leaving some people out as "untouchable." As for the Golden Rule, it is true that an obverse form of it (e.g., "Do nothing to others you would not have them do to you") can be found in many religions.[59] But the mere avoidance of injury to others is a far cry from the self-sacrificing performance of positive service, like taking food and medical aid to some remote population, which characterizes the practical ethics of the Golden Rule (and is a common practice in Christian missions); such service is seldom found where the obverse form is proffered.

A major difficulty for Christians today, if Arnold Toynbee is correct, is that we live in an "ex-Christian civilization," and Christians are seen by non-Christians to be representatives of a wholly secular culture.

> Our late modern secular way of life is still a Christian one in many ways, and many members are still consciously trying to lead a Christian life. But the surviving features of the Christian way of life are now, I should say, no longer our civilization's distinctive features. They are not its distinctive features in the eyes of us Westerners ourselves, and, what is a good deal more important, they are not its distinctive features in the eyes of the non-Western majority of the human race.[60]

But Toynbee urges that we not despair. The fact remains, he insists, that

> there is emancipation in the sense of the ideal of Western liberalism: the emancipation of slaves, the emancipation of women, the emancipation of industrial workers, the emancipation of the subject colonial peoples of Asia and Africa. The Western ideal of emancipation for individuals, though it has been secularized and though many of those who care for it today have lost the memory of its religious origin, is nevertheless truly a legacy from Christianity to a post-Christian secular Western civilization.[61]

Actually, each religion has something to offer humankind, and Toynbee sounds a note of urgency for their coming together to share their gifts. "All the living higher religions ought to subordinate their traditional rivalries and make a new approach towards one another in the face of a fearful common adversary: a revival of the worship of collective human power, armed with new weapons both material and spiritual." In a statement rare for an academic historian, he adds, "If the great religions of the world are to approach one another, they must find common ground. . . . This permanent common ground is human nature, especially the self-centeredness which is Original Sin in human nature."[62]

Those familiar with Toynbee's thesis found in his other writings will recall his observation that the world's great living religions all came into existence independently, but apparently in response to a common set of crises, within the space of a few generations. "They all made their appearance," he reminds us, "after Original Sin had shown its power by causing the downfall of one or two generations of secular civilizations . . . when Mankind had received surprising and humiliating setbacks in its endeavors."[63] Our world is now in jeopardy to a greater degree than ever before because of technological powers never before available. And because human nature is uniform, we can expect little more than ultimate disaster unless the benefits of the best of the religions can be made available, and people of goodwill can overcome the destructive forces of human self-worship. The cooperation of the great religions is not simply a good idea, but an imperative if the human race is to survive. The greatest contribution to the venture that Christianity can make, Toynbee believes, is in its "vision of God as loving His creatures, so greatly that He has sacrificed Himself for their salvation [and] a conviction that human beings ought to follow the example that God has set them in His incarnation and crucifixion."[64] In short, we are to be the means of making God's incarnation visible to the world in practical deeds of love and reconciliation.

While Toynbee points to a "common ground" in original sin, which challenges the many different religions to address their concern in harmony, John Bennett proposes a "common ground morality," which may provide the means for responding. "I think it would be accurate to think of several traditions, Christian, Jewish, humanistic, or perhaps some other religious tradition, with their own sources of illumination and inspiration in a pluralistic society, interacting and actually overlapping in certain conclusions. To some extent this area of overlap is where we find the moral convictions most important to our society."[65] This is not to suggest the least common denominator theme of those who fail to recognize the very real differences among the religious traditions. "It is a mistake to isolate the area of moral overlap and reduce it to a few moral propositions. Rather, we should encourage our various religious traditions . . . to be themselves and depend upon their own sources of inspiration, and we should thank God that they do, at some points of great importance for social ethics, overlap."[66]

Bennett notes some specific points at which the relationships between Christian ethics and the common ground morality (or the overlap) becomes particularly clear. First is the worship of God, who transcends all human authorities and powers and expression of the ideal. There is a great deal of self-worship in our culture, where every element of human-created goods becomes idolatrously cherished and sought after. Even our devotion to freedom, as defined and secured by our laws and our murderous wars, becomes idolatrous.

Second, the specifically Christian contribution to the dialogue and shared insights is seen in "the love expressed in Christ's life and death and commanded by Him; love that is outgoing to all neighbors, to the stranger within the gates, to the enemy and adversary at home and abroad."[67] This love is not an ideal known to philosophy or human reason. It does not belong to any common ground morality known outside Christianity; it is unique. Yet it does inspire humaneness, which makes its special contribution to common ground morality.

A third Christian contribution that Bennett emphasizes is in its teaching about human nature, teaching that acknowledges original sin, but guards against cynicism by its emphasis on God's image within us.

The emphasis upon the universality of sin and imperfection is, after all, the second thing to say about humanity, not the first thing. The first thing is a positive affirmation that we are made in the image of God, and God has come to us and identified himself with us in Christ. And today, perhaps it is this divine "yes" to humanity that may often be the most important thing for the Christian to say to the world.[68]

The fact that there are many rich insights available to Christians from non-Christian sources, as encounters with people of other faiths has often revealed, should occasion nothing but rejoicing. As Bennett affirms,

If Christians had a monopoly on the most important principles of justice, there would be little hope of making them operative in society. It is enough for them, for Christians, to do their part in nourishing the sources of social insight which belong to their tradition and their community and then to cooperate gladly, ungrudgingly, with others who share their objectives.[69]

The question of strategy for Christian interaction with other religions remains for many a stumbling block. Some fifty years ago, the missionary E. Stanley Jones proposed a theme, "Christ at the Round Table," as a vehicle for drawing the many religious leaders on the mission fields of the world into dialogue. Advocating an openness to all traditions, he did not propose that Christians stop being Christians (or that Buddhists or Muslims must convert to Christianity), but that we learn from each other. Individual missionaries often attempted such dialogue, but there was little popular support. The creation of the National Council of Christians and Jews in America provided much opportunity for fellowship. The Academy of Jewish, Christian and Islamic Studies on the West Coast has created trialogues in which representatives of each faith speak about a given topic, like the sovereignty of God, social justice, war and peace, and so forth; these events have been sponsored on more than a hundred university campuses, and have been presented on Vatican Radio, and at the World Council of Churches in Vancouver in 1984. Books like Philip Ashby's *The Conflict of Religions* and James and Marti Hefley's *Arabs, Christians, Jews* are becoming more common. Pope John Paul II took the initiative in 1986 to invite the leaders of many non-Christian religions to meet for discussion on how they might cooperate for the achievement of world peace.

The opportunities are available, and more so now than ever as people from all areas of the globe are on the move. In some regions, as in many of our major cities, we can find all the major religions represented and expressed in every major language. This offers an unprecedented set of circumstances favorable for such engagement and mutual helpfulness. In such settings, God's love for his creatures and for the whole of creation sets for us the standard for our relationships to each other. This acknowledgment is at the very heart of what we may strive to do and to become. Ronald Preston, of Manchester, has underscored this most helpfully in his *The Future of Christian Ethics*, where he reminds us of the great advantages of living in an ecumenical age. "We need to work ecumenically," he notes, to accommodate a wide spectrum of views and to help each other "to cope more adequately with social change." Secondly, "We must not constantly be searching for something so distinctly Christian as to say that no one else could have arrived at it." This requires a greater modesty in working with other Christians, but also with non-Christians of goodwill. Finally, "Group work is indispensable."[70] We need to recover the grace of clear and helpful communication and of dissemination of the benefits to "build up the body of saints."

As Christian churches of the many denominations continue to fulfill the "great commission" of Jesus to his disciples (Matthew 28:19f.), it may be doubted they will be successful in "making disciples of all nations," at least in any near future. Yet certainly creative interaction with people of other faiths can introduce them to "the way" of Christ, and whether they accept him as savior may have to await the will and work of God's spirit. Meanwhile, the ethics of Christianity provides a buttoning-on place as we work with people around the globe to achieve peace, not alone through reducing conflict but through creating the conditions that enhance life: freedom from want and fear, from disease and injustice. Jesus outlined his own earthly agenda and ours as bringing good news to the poor, liberty to captives, recovery of sight, and freedom from oppression (Luke 4:18f.). These are not platitudes; they require risk taking and vigorous action.

Since the days of Constantine, Christianity in some form has enjoyed a more or less official status in the Western world. "There are," as Ninian Smart points out, "many differences in ethical stance, e.g., over abortion, but somewhat at the margin. Martin Luther King, Jr., John Paul II, Mother Teresa, Allan Boesak, Archbishop Runcie of Canterbury, although of quite different historic pasts, gain wide Christian recognition in this ecumenical age."[71] They have also impressed the non-Christian world with their good work, the expression of their deep faith translated into ethical action. It may be anticipated that others will catch the vision and follow.

That vision is not necessarily of a universal, exclusive Christianity in the historically envisioned concept of Christendom. Nor is it a simple nod to the new pluralism that calls for "a frank affirmation that major religions are independent ways to what Christians call salvation, that the Qur'an or the eight-membered path are divine revelation and action every bit as much as any in the biblical tradition."[72] It is rather the Christ's own vision of the kingdom of God. Jesus always subordinated himself to God and to the coming kingdom, admitting that there were some things that even he, the Son, could not know about it but which were known to the Father (Matthew 24:36). Yet it is significant that it was Jesus' "great commission" (Matthew 28:19) which has initiated ecumenical dialogue with other religions, to make effective an exchange of insights and cooperation in humanitarian ventures across ethnic and national boundaries. "In the end," as Michael Keeling observes, "ethics is the undertaking of a discipline to change the self and the world. The Christian faith is that only co-operation in the Kingdom of God can count as an achievement for the individual. In the Kingdom we learn to bear one another's burdens, until [and here he quotes Charles Williams] 'each and every person is incorporated into the life of one community.' "[73]

In this sense, the dream of Matthew Fox's "Cosmic Christ," despite Fox's flirtation with a mysticism many would find uncomfortable,[74] may be a viable aspect of the vision for drawing humankind together in quest of a spiritual ethos. "The earth is the Lord's," instructed the Psalmist. Indeed, the universe is the Lord's. The coming century may require Christians to fashion an ethic suitable for more vast ventures than ever dreamed of before. God's kingdom is vast.

Meanwhile, en route to that new century, Christians may find preparatory changes imperative, invoked by Jesus' call to repentance. As Chung Hyun-Kyung reminded the World Council of Churches' delegates at Canberra in 1991,

> Genuine repentance means a radical change of direction in our individual and communal life. The first is from *anthropocentrism* to *life centrism*, to learn how to live with the earth. Human beings are a very small part of nature, not above it. The second change is from *dualism* to *interconnection*. Women and men, black and white, poor and rich: we forget that we all come from the same source of life, God, and all the webs of our lives are interconnected. The third is from the *culture of death* to the *culture of life*. The Persian Gulf War is the best example of the culture of death; the way the conflict is solved is through killing.[75]

Chung Hyun-Kyung's call to repentance is not a sentimental, religious summons, just as Jesus' initial call was not when he warned that the kingdom is at hand (Matthew 3:2). The challenge is for a radical, almost wrenching alteration of Christians' lifestyles and life's direction. Only then will Christians be able to divest themselves of their selves, and be able, as Paul commands, to "put on Christ" (Romans 13:14; Galatians 3:27), acquire a new nature (Ephesians 4:24), which identifies with the mind of Christ (1 Corinthians 2:16) and that alone makes possible the creation of a genuine Christian ethic.

NOTES

CHAPTER ONE

1. Johnson, Oliver, *Ethics*, New York: Holt, Rinehart and Winston, 1965, p. 123.

2. Ramsey, Paul, *Basic Christian Ethics*, New York: Charles Scribner's Sons, 1953, p. 73.

3. Trepp, Leo, *Judaism, Development and Life*, Belmont, Calif.: Dickenson, 1966, p. 120.

4. Waxman, Meyer, *Judaism, Religion and Ethics*, New York: Thomas Joseloff, 1967. Waxman observes, "Since men are usually prone to take advantage of the weak, the Bible attaches a warning: 'Thou shalt fear the Lord thy God.' Honesty is thus the *prima factor* in determining the future state of man. 'One who deals honestly in business . . . is considered as if he observed all the commandments of the Torah' " (see pp. 342–343).

5. Ibid., p. 216.

6. Ibid., p. 14.

7. Ibid.

8. Trepp, *Judaism*, p. 19.

9. Ibid.

10. Baeck, Leo, *The Essence of Judaism*, New York: Schocken, 1967, p. 84.

11. Rotenstreich, Nathan, *Jewish Philosophy in Modern Times*, New York: Holt, Rinehart and Winston, 1968, pp. 135–136.

12. Baeck, *Essence*, p. 26.

13. Klausner, Joseph, *Jesus of Nazareth,* Boston: Beacon Press, 1964, p. 384.

14. Durant, Will, *Caesar and Christ,* New York: Simon & Schuster, 1944, p. 667.

15. Trepp, *Judaism,* p. 20.

16. Neusner, Jacob, *From Politics to Piety: The Emergence of Pharisaic Judaism,* Englewood Cliffs, N.J.: Prentice-Hall, 1973, p. 4.

17. Ibid., pp. 9–10.

18. Ramsey, *Christian Ethics,* p. 59. Rabbi David Novak makes a telling point: "Christians saw Christ as having fulfilled and transcended the law and as having brought the Church, as the body of Christ, along with him. Jews saw Jesus and his followers as having usurped the Law's proper power and authority for themselves." He also notes, however, that after the work of Schweitzer, Harnack, and others, Jesus has been seen by many Jews and Christians as possibly opening up the prospect of union among all people, held together not by legal ordinance but by the rule of love. See Novak, David, *Jewish-Christian Dialogue,* New York: Oxford University Press, 1989, pp. 73f.

19. "The stranger that sojourns with you . . . you shall love him as yourself" (Leviticus 19:34). Waxman points out that the Torah makes it unlawful even to charge interest on a loan to such a person; he must be treated as a brother, that is, a fellow Jew (see Waxman, *Judaism,* p. 345).

20. Bultmann, Rudolph, *Theology of the New Testament,* Vol. I, trans. Kendrick Grobel, New York: Charles Scribner's Sons, 1955, pp. 28, 49.

21. Plato's *Apology* contains the lengthy discourse of Socrates on his condemnation, which contrasts remarkably with the relative silence of Jesus, when the latter stood before the court. One parallel of particular interest is Socrates's statement: "I am called wise . . . but the truth is, only God is wise," and Jesus' comment: "Why do you call me good? None is good, save one, that is God" (Luke 18:19).

22. The seriousness with which the concept of sin is presented in Hebrew thought is revealed in the fact that these three words most commonly found, *Chet,* "failure"; *chataah,* "great transgression"; and *chattah,* "wickedness" all have the same root. In Exodus 32, *chata* is translated as the "great sin" three times (see 2 Kings 17:21). The more general term for lurking wickedness, *chattah,* is found in Genesis 4:7, "If you do not do well, sin lies at the door" (a favorite warning against idleness among the Puritans, often quoted in the primers of early colonial schools). The word appears more than 160 times in the Old Testament (cf. *pesha,* "violation" more common to Talmudic use). The most commonly used Greek term is *hamartia,* which means simply "error." Sin understood as offense or trespass, *paraptoma,* is employed by Paul in Colossians 2:13, ". . . being dead in your sins."

23. Tillich, Paul, *Systematic Theology,* Vol. 1, Chicago: University of Chicago Press, 1950, p. 218.

24. Houlden, J. L., *Ethics and the New Testament,* Harmondsworth, Middlesex, England: 1973, p. 32.

25. See *The Protestant Era,* University of Chicago Press, 1948, pp. 35f.; *Systematic Theology,* Vol. II, University of Chicago Press, 1957, pp. 118f.; *Political Expectations* (ed. James Luther Adams), Harper & Row, 1971, especially the *Essays on Christianity and Marxism* and *The Political Meaning of utopia.*

26. Brunner, Emil, in *Contemporary Thinking About Jesus,* an anthology compiled by Thomas Kepler, Nashville: Abingdon Press, 1944, p. 253.

27. Quanbeck, W. A., "Forgiveness," in *The Interpreter's Dictionary of the Bible,* Vol. 2, New York: Abingdon Press, 1962, p. 316.

28. The Hebrew *kaphar* is clearly related to blood sacrifices in Exodus 29:36, Leviticus 4:20, 16:19, and elsewhere, but in Exodus 30:16, money can be used to atone for sins; in Proverbs 16:6, sins may be atoned for by loyalty and faithfulness. It is of crucial importance to note, however, that in all these cases atonement was not simply something mankind devised to appease God; it was God who established these acts as acceptable to himself, providing mankind a means of being reassured of God's willingness to forgive. In the New Testament, God is shown as entering directly into the atoning act by sending Christ to identify with mankind even to the extent of accepting our mortality, and being subject to the particularly cruel kind of death we inflict on each other.

29. Ramsey, *Christian Ethics,* p. 5.

30. It was Origen (c. 185–254 A.D.) who first formulated the theory that the word *ransom* must imply a recipient, and that this must logically have meant "The Evil One." Gregory the Great (540–604 A.D.) suggested that God's strategy included trickery; the Evil One was the Leviathan of the Old Testament, whom God caught on "the hook" of Christ's divinity, with Jesus' flesh as bait. Leviathan tried to swallow the hook and was thus forever overcome. Not to be outdone by such wild metaphors, Peter Lombard (1100–1160 A.D.) went so far as to declare that "The cross was a mousetrap to catch the devil, baited with the blood of Christ."

31. Major, H. D. A., in *The Mission and Message of Jesus,* co-authored by T. W. Manson and C. J. Wright, New York: E. P. Dutton, 1938, p. 135.

32. Bultmann, Rudolf, *Theology of the New Testament,* Vol. II, trans. Kendrick Grobel, New York: Charles Scribner's Sons, 1955, p. 54.

33. A. B. Bruce in the classic *Expositor's Greek New Testament* suggests that the best clue to Jesus' meaning is found in Matthew 17:27, in his word concerning the temple tax, where the *didrachmon* was the *lutron,* or temple fee (or tax) required. Christ's life is thus given as the price of our admission, in a sense, into the Holy of Holies. See Bruce, A. B., *Expositor's Greek New Testament,* Vol. I, Grand Rapids: Wm. B. Eerdmans (no date), p. 259.

34. Barclay, William, *The Gospel of Mark,* Philadelphia: Westminster Press, 1956, p. 269.

35. Tillich, Paul, *Systematic Theology,* Vol. II, Chicago: University of Chicago Press, 1957, p. 174.

36. Arias, Mortimer, "Evangelism and Social Ethics," in *Perkins Journal,* Vol. Dallas, Tex.: Southern Methodist University Press, 1982, p. 39.

37. Pannenberg, Wolfhart, "The Kingdom of God and the Foundation of Ethics," in *Theology and the Kingdom of God,* ed. Richard John Neuhaus, Philadelphia: Westminster Press, 1969, pp. 102–126.

38. Braaten, Carl E., *Eschatology and Ethics,* Minneapolis: Augsburg, 1974.

39. Manson, T. W., *Ethics and the Gospel,* New York: Charles Scribner's Sons, 1960, p. 65. This point has been reemphasised by Truz Remdtorff in *Ethics,* Vol. 1, Philadelphia: Fortress Press, 1980, pp. 182–188. More recently Stanley Hauerwas and William Willimon asserted the same message: "How meager is our righteousness when set next to this vision of God's Kingdom." With Hauerwas and Willimon, the somewhat facile equation of the Kingdom with the Church as "the story, the whole story of what God has revealed himself to be in Christ" tends to weaken the argument, but they

stop short of making the two identical. Indeed the point they make is that the living fellowship, "the coloby [of Heaven] is the vessel that carries us there" (*Resident Aliens*, Nashville: Abingdon Press, 1989, pp. 90–91).

40. Matthew 5:13, 14, and 10:16.

41. Ellul, Jacques, *The Presence of the Kingdom*, trans. Olive Wyon, Philadelphia: Westminster Press, 1951, p. 9.

42. Borg, Marcus, "Jesus and the Kingdom of God," in *The Christian Century*, April 22, 1987, p. 380.

43. Ibid.

44. Ramsey, *Christian Ethics*, p. 25.

45. Cox, Harvey, *The Secular City*, New York: Macmillan, 1965. "Secularization as the liberation of man from religious and metaphysical tutelage . . . is the legitimate consequence of the impact of biblical faith on history" (p. 17). Cox's position has often been misrepresented as a preference for the secular over the sacred. What he affirmed was that the Bible itself reflects a desacrilizing of nature, politics, and philosophical values which had already been falsely endowed with a sanctity of their own. Having declared in favor of retaining the concept of a transcendent God, however, Cox is faulted for not having clarified how his secularized world proves a better place to experience God and to share his love.

46. Curran, Charles, E., *Themes in Fundamental Moral Theology*, Notre Dame, Ind.: University of Notre Dame Press, 1977, p. 146.

47. Hauerwas, Stanley, *Vision and Virtue*, Notre Dame, Ind.: University of Notre Dame Press, 1974, pp. 112–113.

48. Taylor, Charles R., *World War III and the Destiny of America*, Nashville: Sceptre Books, 1979, p. 161.

49. Meshek (Psalm 120) refers to a country whose inhabitants were called *Mushki*. The first appears in the Assyrian texts of Tiglath Pilezer, around 1100 B.C., and have no relation whatever to Moscow, the present Russian city. Gog was the chief prince of Meshek. Cf. G. G. Howie, in *The Interpreter's Bible*, Vol. 2, New York: Abingdon Press, 1962, pp. 436–437.

Chapter Two

1. Meeks, Wayne A., *The First Urban Christians*, New Haven, Conn.: Yale University Press, 1983, p. 32.

2. Houlden, J. L., *Ethics and the New Testament*, Middlesex, England: Penguin Books, 1973, p. 4.

3. Manschreck, Clyde L., *A History of Christianity*, Englewood Cliffs, N.J.: Prentice-Hall, 1974, p. 15.

4. Gadamer, Hans-Georg, *Philosophical Hermeneutics*, trans. David Linge, Berkeley: University of California Press, 1977, p. 58.

5. Latourette, Kenneth Scott, *A History of Christianity*, New York: Harper & Brothers, 1953, p. 122.

6. Houlden, *Ethics*, p. 35.

7. Robinson, James M., *The Nag Hammadi Library*, San Francisco: Harper & Row, 1977, p. 4.

8. Ibid., p. 10

9. The Nicene Creed (325 A.D.) had declared that Christ is one substance with the Father. Arius (256–336) objected because the word *homoousion* used to express this is not a biblical word, so he substituted *homoiousion* (note the *i* making *homoi* instead of *homo*), making Christ only similar or "like unto" the Father. Among several factions of Arius's followers, one continues to have influence even today. The Unitarian Universalist church tends to follow this position, emphasizing the humanity of Jesus and therefore his "un-likeness" to the Father (*anamoios*).

10. Marshall, George N., *Challenge of a Liberal Faith*, Boston: Unitarian Universalist Association, 1970, p. 236–238.

11. Clark, Elizabeth A., *Clement's Use of Aristotle*, Lewiston, N.Y.: Edwin Mellen Press, 1977. For an excellent introduction to the major fathers of the early Church, see *The Early Church Fathers*, ed. and trans. Henry Betenson, London: University of Oxford Press, 1969.

12. This should not be taken to infer that those whose primary concern seemed to be doctrinal were quarrelsome pedants or mere office seekers. The fact is they were vigorous scholars who often carried their debate into the highest courts of Rome. "Be diligent. Be God's athlete," wrote Ignatius, and he paid for his courage, torn apart by wild beasts in the Flavian amphitheater. Polycarp was burned at the stake in Smyrna.

13. Hatch, Edwin, *The Influences of Greek Ideas on Christianity*, New York: Harper, Cloister Library, 1957, p. 167.

14. Ibid., p. 169.

15. Ibid., pp. 169–170.

16. Cochrane, Charles Norris, *Christianity and Classical Culture*, London: Oxford University Press, 1972, p. 374.

17. Ibid.

18. Payne, Robert, *The Fathers of the Western Church*, New York: Viking Press, 1951, p. 79.

19. Deansley, Margaret, *A History of Early Medieval Europe*, London: Methuen, 1969, p. 91.

20. Averroës's *Commentary on Plato* is available in a splendid translation by E. I. J. Rosenthal, Cambridge University Press, 1969.

21. Walker, Williston, *A History of the Christian Church*, New York: Charles Scribner's Sons, 1959, p. 255.

22. Aquinas, Thomas, *Summa Theologica*, Part I of Second Part Q 94 A 5, "The possession of all things in common is said to be of the natural law." In *Great Books of the Western World*, Vol. 2, trans. Fathers of the English Dominican Province, Chicago: University of Chicago Press, 1952, p. 225.

23. Ibid., pp. 316–318.

24. Ibid., p. 577.

25. Garrison, W. E., and Hutchinson, Paul, *Twenty Centuries of Christianity*, New York: Harcourt, Brace, 1959, pp. 176–177.

26. Duvernoy, Jean, *Le Registre d'Inquisition de Jacques Fournier*, 3 vols., Oxford: Parkers.

27. One striking ethical consequence of Luther's literal interpretation of Paul's Letter to the Romans (Chapter 13) was the blunting of criticism of the Nazi movement in Germany in the early 1930s. It should be noted, however, that the Roman Catholic church made a similar error, actually signing a Concordat with Hitler in 1933, agreeing not to interfere. In 1934 a group of Evangelical Christians, led by Karl Barth, signed

The Barmen Confession, openly denouncing Hitler, while the Roman Catholic church (of which Hitler was a baptized member) failed to excommunicate him or denounce him in such harsh official terms.

28. Meuller, William, *Church and State in Luther and Calvin*, Nashville: Broadman Press, 1954, pp. 74–75.

29. Bancroft, George, *The History of the United States of America*, Volume II, New York: Appleton and Company, 1883, pp. 405f.

30. The German sociologist Max Weber wrote in *The Protestant Ethic and the Spirit of Capitalism* (1904) that the Calvinist emphasis on hard work as a response to God's commands and Christ's redemption of those elected for salvation was the dynamic underlying the economic success of Protestant communities. In 1926, Richard H. Tawney published a refutation of Weber's thesis in *Religion and the Rise of Capitalism*. Tawney insisted the theology was only incidental; the social conditions of the times, combined with the growing emphasis on individualism and self-reliance, were the key factors in capitalist success.

31. Brunner, Emil, *Christianity and Civilization*, New York: Charles Scribner's Sons, 1949, p. 99.

32. Cousins, Norman, *In God We Trust*, New York: Harper & Brothers, 1958, p. 5.

33. Ibid., p. 8.

34. Tillich, Paul, *Political Expectations*, ed. James Luther Adams, New York: Harper & Row, 1971. It is important to note the two kinds of criticism in Tillich's thought. The first employs a standard or ideal by which things (even other standards) can be measured. The second possesses no objective standard but "combines an unconditioned No with an unconditioned Yes." Thus while a social act or an institution can be measured against the first ideal, the whole social organization may be brought into question by "what lies beyond all social organizations, by what is boundless (by an infinite justice) as over against the actual life of justice." See pp. 10ff.

35. Whitehead, Alfred North, *Science and the Modern World*, New York: Macmillan, 1946, p. 275.

36. Hershey, Gerald, and Lugo, James, *Human Development*, New York: Macmillan, 1979, p. 25.

37. Bainton, Roland, *Christendom*, Vol. 2, New York: Harper & Row, 1966, p. 159.

38. Manschreck, *History of Christianity*, p. 344.

39. Ibid.

40. Rauschenbusch, Walter, *Christianity and the Social Crisis*, New York: Macmillan, 1912, p. 287.

41. Ibid.

42. Curran, *Themes*, Ind. p. 17.

43. Among natural law theorists there has always existed opposing interpretations as to the relation of individuals to each other and to society as a whole. Ethical questions hang in the balance. Medieval ecclesiastics, for example, tended to favor centralism in both church and state, by which divine right rulers might (as Louis XV did) define their role as having absolute power invested in themselves. On the other hand, like with Locke, Rousseau, and Spinoza, natural law was invoked in order to overthrow absolutism in favor of popular sovereignty. In neither case was a future, an *eschaton* of holiness and righteousness envisioned that could serve as a corrective.

The term *persona moralis* was indeed used in the eighteenth century to suggest either a monarch or a "collective personality" (the state), but "in the end the origin of the adjective 'moral' passed entirely into oblivion, and its real sense was forgotten." Gierke, Otto, *Natural Law and the Theory of Society*, trans. Ernest Barker, Boston: Beacon Press, 1957, p. 121.

44. Curran, *Themes*, p. 29.

CHAPTER THREE

1. Wand, J. W. C., *A History of the Modern Church: 1500 to the Present*, London: Methuen, 1971, p. 230.

2. Herron, George Davis, *The Christian Society*, New York: Johnson Reprint, 1969, p. v.

3. Hebblethwaite, Brian, *Christian Ethics in the Modern Age*, Philadelphia: Westminster Press, 1982, pp. 14f.

4. Hume, David, *A Treatise of Human Nature* (first published in 1739), in *Ethics*, ed. Oliver A. Johnson, New York: Holt, Rinehart and Winston, 1965, p. 165.

5. Kant, Immanuel, *Fundamental Principles of the Metaphysics of Morals*, in *Great Books of the Western World*, Vol. 42, trans. Thomas Kingsmill Abbott, Chicago: University of Chicago Press: 1952, p. 254.

6. Kant, Immanuel, "Preface to the Metaphysical Elements of Ethics," in *Great Books of the Western World*, Vol. 42, trans. Thomas Kingsmill Abbott, Chicago: Encyclopedia Britannica, 1971, p. 365.

7. Hebblethwaite, *Christian Ethics*, p. 17.

8. Hegel, Georg Wilhelm Friedrich, *The Philosophy of Right*, trans. T. M. Knox, in *Great Books of the Western World*, Vol. 46, Chicago: University of Chicago, 1952, p. 12.

9. Ibid., p. 19.

10. Ibid., p. 47.

11. A foe of Roman Catholicism for its perpetuation of feudalism, Marx reserved even greater scorn for "the 'Spirit' of Protestantism in England, where the estates of the church were to a large extent given away to rapacious royal favorites." In Scotland, " 'the republican remedy' for the large number of beggars was to propose re-introducing slavery." Marx, Karl, *Capital*, in *Great Books of the Western World*, Vol. 50, Chicago: University of Chicago, 1952, p. 358.

12. Marx, Karl, *Manifesto of the Communist Party*, in *Great Books of the Western World*, Vol. 50, Chicago: University of Chicago Press, 1952, p. 434.

13. Nietzsche, Friedrich, "The Anti-Christ," trans. Walter Kaufman, in *The Portable Nietzsche*, New York: Viking Press, 1969, p. 571.

14. Freud, Sigmund, "New Introductory Lectures on Psychoanalysis" in *The Major Works of Sigmund Freud*, in *Great Books of the Western World*, Vol. 54, Chicago: University of Chicago Press, 1952, p. 876.

15. Ibid., p. 875.

16. See Barbour, Ian, *Issues in Science and Religion*, New York: Harper & Row, 1966, pp. 256f.

17. Comte, Auguste, "Character of the Positive Philosophy," in *The Age of Ideology*, ed. Henry Aiken, New York: Mentor Books, 1956, p. 128.

18. Clifford, William C., "The Ethics of Belief," in *Religion from Tolstoy to Camus*, ed. Walter Kaufmann, New York: Harper & Brothers, 1961, p. 206.

19. Ayer, A. J., *Language, Truth and Logic*, New York: Dover, 1936, pp. 108–109.

20. James, William, *The Will to Believe, and Other Essays*, New York: David McKay, 1927, pp. 24–25.

21. Dewey, John, *Democracy and Education*, New York: Free Press, 1966, pp. 357–358.

22. Dewey, John, *A Common Faith*, New Haven, Conn.: Yale University Press, 1934. See Chapter 2, especially pp. 43–53.

23. Bayles, Ernest E., *Pragmatism in Education*, New York: Harper & Row, 1966, p. 59.

24. Ibid.

25. Morris, Van Cleve, and Pai, Young, *Philosophy and the American School*, Boston: Houghton Mifflin, 1976, p. 250.

26. Conot, Robert, "When Inhumanity Was Tried in Court," *Los Angeles Times*, November 17, 1985, Part IV, p. 3.

27. Ibid. Conot points out that while the United States has condemned interference in other nations' affairs by the Soviet Union, and even by staunch allies like England, France, and Israel, it has allowed the CIA to attempt to destabilize regimes in Iran and Central America, and to still lend support to the murderous Pol Pot regime in Cambodia, a regime that exterminated 20 percent of its own population.

28. Watson was the first to receive a doctoral degree in psychology from the University of Chicago (1903). His first published explication of behaviorism appeared in 1913: "Psychology as the Behaviorist Views it," in *Psychological View*, Vol. 20, pp. 158–177. His "Image and Affection" soon followed in the *Journal of Philosophy, Psychology and Scientific Method* (1913), Vol. 19, pp. 421–428. His book *Behaviorism* was published in 1930 by W. W. Norton.

29. Skinner, B. F., *The Technology of Teaching*, New York: Appleton-Century-Crofts, 1968, p. 62.

30. Allport, Gordon W., *Becoming: Basic Considerations for a Psychology of Personality*, New Haven, Conn.: Yale University Press, 1955, p. 100.

31. Skinner, B. F., *Science and Human Behavior*, New York: Macmillan, 1953, p. 447.

32. Hebblethwaite, *Christian Ethics*, p. 28.

33. Heidegger, Martin, *Existence and Being*, trans. Werner Brock, Chicago: Henry Regnery, 1949, p. 370.

34. Arthur Cochrane suggests that Heidegger misunderstands the doctrine of Creation as expressed in *creatio ex nihilo*. The biblical concept of God as the highest uncreated being does not imply that "nothing" is co-eternal with God, or that from that "nothing" the universe was created. The Hebrew word *bara*, in Genesis 1, means "fashioned," but the biblical writer does not speculate from what. The message is simply that we have been created by God with a nature distinct from his. See Cochrane, *The Existentialists and God*, Philadelphia: Westminster Press, 1956, pp. 141–142.

35. Heidegger, Martin, *Platons Lehre von der Wahrheit; mit einem Brief über den "Humanismus."* Bern, Switzerland: A. Frank, Verlag A. G., 1947, p. 53.

36. Sartre, Jean-Paul, *Existentialism and Humanism*, trans. Philip Mairet, London: Methuen, 1948, p. 18.

37. Ibid.

38. Jaspers, Karl, *Philosophy of Existence*, trans. Richard Grabau, Philadelphia: University of Pennsylvania Press, 1971, p. 96.

39. Leaky, L. S. B., and Goodall, Vanne Morris, *Unveiling Man's Origins*, Cambridge, Mass.: Schenken, 1969, p. 27. The date 4004 B.C. was established by Archbishop James Ussher in 1653, by tracing recorded dates of biblical events backward to what seemed (taking each date as historical fact) the necessary starting point. This date is still printed as a footnote to Genesis 1 in many Bibles. See *The Holy Bible*, Nashville: Dove, 1973.

40. In 1968, the U.S. Supreme Court ruled that such antievolution laws are unconstitutional. Yet the battle continues across America. An antievolution program with a regularly published *Creation Research Society Quarterly* is well financed by a group of business and science-oriented professionals. A similar program in California publishes a journal called *Origins*, urging legislators to require the teaching of creationism in public schools. Laws to this effect have been proposed in nineteen American states, though in 1982, a federal judge in Arkansas ruled such legislation unconstitutional.

41. Hordern, William, *A Layman's Guide to Protestant Theology*, New York: Macmillan, 1956, p. 61.

42. Ibid.

43. Waterman, Leroy, *The Religion of Jesus*, New York: Harper & Brothers, 1952, pp. 238f. Waterman rejected the Christ of theology, in favor of the Jesus of human history, and insisted that Jesus' statement "the kingdom of God is within you" (Luke 17:31) meant that it is already at hand for us to grasp, albeit with God's help.

44. Duchene, Francois, *The Endless Crisis*, New York: Simon & Schuster, 1970. This book is not about Christian ethics per se, but its sixty contributors, including scholars, ambassadors, and other professionals like John Kenneth Galbraith, Henry Kissinger, and Arthur Schlesinger present so compelling a case for the mounting crisis in Western culture as to command the attention of everyone serious about the Christian's response.

45. Fosdick, Harry Emerson, "Beyond Modernism" in *The Christian Century*, December 4, 1935, pp. 1549–1552. Fosdick concluded that modernism had "lost its ethical standing ground and its power of moral attack."

46. Barth, Karl, *The Epistle to the Romans*, trans. Sir Edwyn Hoskins, London: Oxford University Press, 1959, p. 36.

47. Barth, Karl, *The Word of God and the Word of Man*, trans. Douglas Horton, New York: Harper Torchbooks, 1957, p. 140.

48. Barth, Karl, *Dogmatics in Outline*, trans. G. T. Thompson, New York: Philosophical Library, 1947, p. 37.

49. A meeting of German Protestant leaders, Lutheran, Reformed, and United churches, at Barmen, in 1934, adopted six articles that defined Christian opposition to the national socialism of Hitler. While Pastor Martin Niemöller had been the leader of the Pastor's Emergency League, the primary resistance movement against Naziism, it was Karl Barth who provided the major theological structure and content of the Barmen Declaration.

50. Barth, *Word of God*, p. 146.

51. Barth, *Epistle*, p. 479.

52. Barth, Karl, *Church Dogmatics*, III, Edinburgh: T. & T. Clark, 1960.

53. Brunner, Emil, *The Divine Imperative*, trans. Olive Wyon, Philadelphia: Westminster Press, 1947, p. 58.

54. Ibid., p. 82.

55. Ibid., p. 83.

56. Ibid., p. 84.

57. Brunner, Emil, *Man in Revolt*, trans. Olive Wyon, Philadelphia: Westminster Press, 1947, pp. 68f.

58. Ibid., p. 130.

59. Ibid., pp. 130–131.

60. Brunner, Emil, *The Divine-Human Encounter*, trans. Amandus Loos, Philadelphia: Westminster Press, 1943, p. 129.

61. Ibid.

62. Ibid., p. 139.

63. Ibid., p. 141.

64. Ibid., p. 139.

65. Brunner, *Divine Imperative*, p. 291.

66. Ibid., pp. 566–567. See also notes on p. 569f.

67. Niebuhr, Reinhold, *Moral Man and Immoral Society*, New York: Charles Scribner's Sons, 1932, pp. 88f.

68. Niebuhr, Reinhold, *An Interpretation of Christian Ethics*, New York: Harper & Brothers, 1935, pp. 7f.

69. Niebuhr, Reinhold, *Does Civilization Need Religion?* New York: Macmillan, 1941, pp. 22–23.

70. Niebuhr, Reinhold, *The Nature and Destiny of Man*, New York: Charles Scribner's Sons, 1947, Part II, p. 1.

71. *Ibid.* Part 1, p. 186.

72. Ibid., p. 193.

73. Ibid., p. 208.

74. Niebuhr, Reinhold, "The Christian Witness in the Social and National Order," quoted in his book *Christian Realism and Political Problems*, New York: Charles Scribner's Sons, 1953, p. 109. It is significant that Emil Brunner delivered a similar charge at the World Council: "The Christian Church is not entitled . . . to pass judgement on the process of secularization and de-Christianization, without confessing at the same time its own share of responsibility for this development." *Man's Disorder and God's Design*, Vol. 3, New York: Harper & Brothers, 1948, p. 178.

75. Ibid., pp. 114–115.

76. Machen, J. Gresham, *Christianity and Liberalism*, Grand Rapids, Mich.: Eerdmans, 1946, pp. 20f.

77. Lippman, Walter, *A Preface to Morals*, New York: Macmillan, 1929, p. 33.

78. Potter, Charles, *Humanism, a New Religion*, New York: Simon & Schuster, 1930, pp. 96–97.

79. Tillich, Paul, *Systematic Theology I*, Chicago: University of Chicago Press, 1951, p. 14.

80. Tillich, Paul, *Dynamics of Faith*, New York: Harper & Row, 1957, pp. 1–2.

81. Tillich, Paul, *Systematic Theology II*, Chicago: University of Chicago Press, 1957, p. 33.

82. Tillich, Paul, *Morality and Beyond*, New York: Harper Torchbooks, 1963, p. 83.

83. Ibid., p. 85.

84. Ibid., p. 88.

85. Bonhoeffer, Dietrich, *Prisoner for God*, New York: Macmillan, 1954, p. 163.

86. Ibid., p. 179.

87. Bonhoeffer, Dietrich, *The Cost of Discipleship*, trans. R. H. Fuller, New York: Macmillan, 1960, p. 45.

88. Cox, Harvey, *The Secular City*, New York: Macmillan, 1965, p. 63.

89. Cox, Harvey, *The Seduction of the Spirit*, New York: Simon & Schuster, 1973, p. 62.

90. Ibid.

91. Ibid., p. 77.

92. Fletcher, Joseph, *Situation Ethics*, Philadelphia, Westminster Press, 1966, p. 18.

93. Ibid., p. 23.

94. From an address given by Joseph Fletcher at the University of Houston; printed in the Spring issue of *Extra*, 1966.

95. Lehmann, Paul, *Ethics in a Christian Context*, New York: Harper & Row, 1963, p. 65.

96. Hebblethwaite, *Christian Ethics*, pp. 87–88.

97. Ibid., p. 90.

CHAPTER FOUR

1. Niebuhr, H. Richard, "The Disorder of Man in the Church of God," in *Man's Disorder and God's Design*, New York: Harper & Brothers, 1948, p. 79.

2. Bonhoeffer, *Cost of Discipleship*, p. 45.

3. Rauscher, The Reverend Canon William V., *Church in Frenzy*, New York: St. Martin's Press, 1980, pp. 6–15.

4. Oldham, J. H., *Life Is Commitment*, New York: Association Press, 1959, p. 8.

5. Kelley, Robert A., "The Suffering Church: A Study of Luther's Theological Crisis," delivered at California State University, Fullerton, November 9, 1983.

6. Calvin, John, *Institutes of the Christian Religion*, trans. John Allen, Philadelphia: Westminster Press, Book IV, Chapter I.

7. Brunner, *Divine Imperative*, pp. 524–525.

8. Ibid., pp. 526–527.

9. Barth, Karl, *Dogmatics in Outline*, trans. G. T. Thompson, New York: Philosophical Library, 1947, p. 142.

10. Bonhoeffer, Dietrich, *Ethics*, trans. Neville Horton Smith, New York: Macmillan, 1955, p. 21.

11. De Dietrich, Suzanne, *The Witnessing Community*, Philadelphia: Westminster Press, 1958, p. 169.

12. Birch, Bruce C., and Rassmussen, Larry L., *The Bible and Ethics in the Christian Life*, Minneapolis: Augsburg, 1976, pp. 132–133.

13. Sayres, Dorothy, *Creed or Chaos?* New York: Harcourt, Brace, 1949 (from collection of earlier essays), pp. 26–27. Interestingly, D. Elton Trueblood, writing at the same time in America, observed precisely the same phenomenon in his then widely read *The Predicament of Modern Man*, New York: Harper & Brothers, 1944, p. 64.

14. Sayres, Dorothy I., *The Mind of the Maker*, New York: Meridian Books, 1956, p. 13.

15. Lehmann, Paul L., *Ethics in a Christian Context*, New York: Harper & Row, 1963, p. 46.

16. Birch and Rassmussen, *Bible and Ethics*, p. 127.

17. Ibid., p. 129.

18. Hauerwas, Stanley, *A Community of Character*, Notre Dame, Ind.: University of Notre Dame Press, 1981, p. 9. The need for direct instruction lies, as Hauerwas points out, in the fact that, "The ability to provide an adequate account of our existence is the primary test of the truthfulness of a social ethic. No society can be just or good that is built on falsehood. The first task of Christian social ethics, therefore, is not to make the 'world' better or more just, but to help Christian people form their community consistent with their conviction that the story of Christ is a truthful account of our existence. For . . . only when we know 'what is going on' do we know 'what we should do' " (p. 10).

19. Walter, Howard Arnold (1883–1918), "I Would Be True," published in *The Hymnal for Youth*, Philadelphia: Westminster Press, 1941, p. 180.

20. Hauerwas, *Community of Character*, p. 11.

21. Yule, George S., "The Incarnation and the Unity of the Church," in *The Reformed World*, Vol. 37, No. 5, Geneva, Switzerland: World Council of Churches, 1983.

22. The Roman Catholic church holds the following to have been fully ecumenical: Lateran I, 1124; Lateran II, 1139; Lateran III, 1179; Lateran IV, 1215; Lyons I, 1245; Lyons II, 1274; Vienne, 1311–1313; Constance, 1414–1418; Basle-Ferrara-Florence, 1431–1439; Lateran V, 1512–1563; Vatican I, 1870 (adjourned unfinished); Vatican II, 1962.

23. *Man's Disorder and God's Design*, New York: Harper & Brothers, 1948, is a one-volume edition actually containing four books: *The Universal Church in God's Design*, *The Church's Witness to God's Design*, *The Church and the Disorder of Society*, and *The Church and International Disorder*. It is perhaps the best single source for introducing the reader to the greatest theological writers of the Protestant world in the first half of our century.

24. Hauerwas, *Community of Character*, p. 49.

25. Stromberg, Jean, *Mission and Evangelism: An Ecumenical Affirmation*, New York: World Council of Churches NCCC/DOM, 1983, p. 19.

26. *Los Angeles Times*, February 3, 1986, pp. 1, 17.

27. Cox, *Seduction of the Spirit*, pp. 243, 251.

28. Hebblethwaite, *Christian Ethics*, p. 113. Swiss-born theologian Hans Kung insists that our growing global ecumenical consciousness is the most important single phenomenon of our time, for there can be no world peace without religious peace: "The ecumenical dialogue is anything but the specialty of a few starry-eyed religious peaceniks. For the first time in history, it has taken on the character of a urgent desideratum for world politics. It can help make our earth more livable, by making it more peaceful and more reconciled." Kung, Hans, *Christianity and the World Religions*, New York: Doubleday, 1986, p. 443.

29. Cox, *Seduction of the Spirit*, p. 152.

30. Leviticus 25:9f. proclaims a year of jubilee liberating people from debt and from labor, but doing so as an expression of spiritual release: "it shall be holy unto you." Isaiah 61:1, "proclaim liberty to the captives," was given its fullest spiritual interpretation by Jesus in Luke 4:18.

31. Note *Luke 4:18*, in which Jesus identifies himself with Isaiah 61:1. See also Romans 8:21, " . . . the glorious liberty [*eleutherian*] of the children of God"; Galatians 5:1f.: "For freedom did Christ set us free." Note also 2 Corinthians 3:17; James 1:25.

32. Shaull, Richard, *Heralds of a New Reformation*, Maryknoll, N.Y.: Orbis Books, 1984. "These theologians present us with a different perspective from which to reinterpret the Christian story as a whole. Martin Luther [and] John Calvin did the same thing" (pp. 5, 6).

33. Cardinal Ratzinger, of the Sacred Congregation for the Doctrine of the Faith, quoted in *Woodstock Report*, Woodstock Theological Center, Georgetown University, Washington, D.C., October 1984, No. 5, p. 1.

34. Hebblethwaite, *Christian Ethics*, p. 91. First published in England under the title *The Adequacy of Christian Ethics*.

35. Ibid., p. 93.

36. Long, Edward LeRoy, Jr., *A Survey of Recent Christian Ethics*, New York: Oxford University Press, 1982, p. 158.

37. Gutierrez, Gustavo, *A Theology of Liberation*, trans. and ed. Sister Caridad Inda and John Eagleson, Maryknoll, N.Y.: Orbis Books, 1973, p. 4. See my discussion of this in *The World of Philosophy*, Chicago: Nelson-Hall, 1983, pp. 76–77.

38. Hanks, Thomas D., *God So Loved the Third World*, trans. James C. Dekker, Maryknoll, N.Y.: Orbis Books, 1984, p. 4.

39. Ibid., p. 13.

40. Hanks lists five additional words relating to oppression, including *tsar* (enmity), which occurs 70 times in the Old Testament; its cognate *tsarar* (to impoverish), 46 times; *tsuq* (to besiege), 11 times; *lahats* (to squeeze), 31 times; and *ratsats* (to grind or pound), 20 times. See pp. 10–25.

41. Gutierrez, *Theology of Liberation*, p. 4.

42. Moon, Cyris Hee-Suk, "Minjung Theology: An Introduction," *Pacific Theological Review*, San Francisco: San Francisco Theological Seminary, Winter 1985, p. 7.

43. Ogden, Shubert M., *Faith and Freedom*, Nashville: Abingdon, 1979, pp. 37f.

44. Koyama, Kosuke, *Waterbuffalo Theology*, Maryknoll, N.Y.: Orbis Books, 1981, pp. viii–ix.

45. Cone, James H., *Black Theology and Black Power*, New York: Seabury Press, 1969, p. 117.

46. Cone, James H., *A Black Theology of Liberation*, Philadelphia: J. B. Lippincott, 1970, p. 21.

47. Ibid., p. 80.

48. Long, Charles, quoted in *Black Theology: A Documentary History 1966–1979*, eds. Gayraud S. Wilmore and James S. Cone, Maryknoll, N.Y.: Orbis Books, 1979, pp. 619f.

49. Boesak, Allan Aubrey, *Farewell to Innocence*, Maryknoll, N.Y.: Orbis Books, 1977, p. 56.

50. Ibid., p. 126.

51. Ibid., p. 144.

52. Moon, "Minjung Theology," p. 7.

53. Ibid., pp. 10–11.

54. Park, A. Sung, "Minjung Theology," *Pacific Theological Review*, San Francisco: San Francisco Theological Seminary, Winter 1985, p. 14.

55. Ibid.
56. Gutierrez, Gustavo, *The Power of the Poor in History*, trans. Robert Barr, Maryknoll, N.Y.: Orbis Books, pp. 136–137.
57. Shaull, *Heralds of a New Reformation*, p. 2.
58. Bell, Wesley, "A Woman's Work Is Never Done," *Symbiosis*, Scottsdale, Ariz.: Food for the Hungry, Inc., June 1985, p. 4.
59. A careful analysis of biblical language by Anne McGrew Bennett reveals an astonishing array of feminisms, which raises the question how Hebrew society could have evolved into such masculine domination. See Bennett, Anne McGrew, *From Woman-Pain to Woman-Vision*, Minneapolis: Fortress Press, 1989, Chapter 8.
60. Deen, Edyth, *Great Women of the Christian Faith*, New York: Harper & Brothers, 1959, p. 5.
61. Russell, Letty M., *The Future of Partnership*, Philadelphia: Westminster Press, 1979, pp. 159f.
62. Cullmann, Oscar, *The Christology of the New Testament*, trans. Shirley C. Guthrie, and Charles A. M. Hall, Philadelphia: Westminster Press, 1963, p. 14.
63. Gutierrez, *Theology of Liberation*, p. 13.
64. Park, A. Sung, "Minjung Theology," p. 20.
65. Ibid.
66. Brown, Robert McAfee, *Religion and Violence*, Philadelphia: Westminster Press, 1973, p. 75.
67. The qualifying phrase "in some measure" is not just a hedge, but a reminder that "the capitalist system" is not a single, monolithic entity. The form that Marx attacked in the nineteenth century, and which even he admitted was a corrective to feudalism, is not in operation today. The form in use in many third world countries, and which truly exploits the poor is one that actually bolsters, rather than corrects, a persistent kind of feudalism in which a few families control most of the land and resources. It is this situation with its intentionally limited crop production that keeps the few landowners wealthy, the poor workers in poverty, and from which the dominant nations prosper through special trade agreements.
68. Arias, Esther, and Arias, Mortimer, *The Cry of My People*, New York: Friendship Press, 1980, pp. 133f. To be sure, similar criticism could be made of socialist and communist systems, Dr. Jan Womer, formerly principal of Mansfield College, Oxford, notes: "We must admit that any economic or political system is based upon humans and human nature. Unless that nature is challenged, controlled or changed, any system can bring pain and injustice to people beneath those who control the system (from an unpublished letter, quoted by permission).
69. Ellul, Jacques, *The Subversion of Christianity*, trans. Geoffrey W. Bromily, Grand Rapids, Mich.: Wm. B. Eerdmans, 1986, p. 18.
70. Ibid.
71. Ibid., p. 204.
72. Pottenger, John R., *The Political Theory of Liberation Theology*, New York: State University of New York Press, 1989, p. 163.
73. Radner, Ephraim, "From Liberation to Exile: A New Image for Church Mission," *The Christian Century*, October 18, 1989, p. 931.
74. Ibid.
75. Ibid., p. 934.

76. Long, John D., "Mainstream Cased Study," *Progressions*, Indianapolis, Ind.: The Lilly Endowment, January 1990, pp. 7f.

77. O'Donovan, Oliver, *Resurrection and Moral Order*, Grand Rapids, Mich.: Wm. B. Eerdmans, 1986, p. 246.

78. Ibid.

79. Wogaman, J. Philip, *Christian Moral Judgement*, Louisville, Ky: Westminster/ John Knox Press, 1989, p. 133.

CHAPTER FIVE

1. Lehmann, Paul L., *Ethics in a Christian Context*, New York: Harper & Row, 1963, p. 117.

2. Wilson, Edmund O., *Sociobiology*, Cambridge, Mass.: Harvard University Press, 1975.

3. Oiserman, Theodore, "The Human, the Specifically Human," in *The Problem of Man in Philosophy*, Moscow: "Social Sciences Today" Editorial Board, 1988, p. 66. See also Fedoseyev, Pyotr, "Man in the Modern World," ibid., pp. 36f. and the antireductionist argument of Nina Yulima, in "Man in Philosophy of Physicalism," ibid., pp. 85–101. These papers were presented at the conference held in Brighton, England, August 21–27, 1988.

4. Niebuhr, *Nature and Destiny of Man*, p. 5.

5. I have attempted to deal with this a bit more in depth in the opening chapter of my book, *The World of Philosophy*, Chicago: Nelson-Hall, 1983, pp. 1–4.

6. King, Winston, *Introduction to Religion*, New York: Harper & Brothers, 1954, p. 80. The same point was made by Frank Rhodes, in *Christianity in a Mechanistic Universe*, London: Intervarsity Fellowship, 1965.

7. Stumpf, Samuel Enoch, *Philosophy: History and Problems*, New York: McGraw-Hill, 1971, p. 4.

8. Einstein, Albert, *Out of My Later Years*, New York: Philosophical Library, 1950, p. 9.

9. Lons, Veronica, *Egyptian Mythology*, Middlesex, England: Hamlyn, 1968, p. 24.

10. In the *Phaedrus*, Plato becomes more poetic, describing how mankind, composed of both soul and body, is likened to a charioteer driving two horses: one white, gallant and gentle, with its eyes on celestial glories, the other dark and wild, plunging downward with lusty passion.

11. Lucretius, *De Rerum Natura*, trans. W. E. Leonard, New York: E. P. Dutton, 1921. Note particularly pp. 6 and 23. Angered by religious myths that kept people in terror of death, Lucretius contended that if they could understand we are composed of lifeless atoms ceaselessly connecting and disjoining and reconnecting, the fear of death would be alleviated. Life and death are simply the way of things.

12. Bronowski, Jacob, *The Ascent of Man*, Boston: Little, Brown, 1973, p. 41. Bronowski was well aware, as a practicing Jew as well as a ranking scientist, that when we speak of "man" in the biblical sense we are confined to *Homo sapiens*.

13. Haselden, Kyle, "One Adam or Many?" in *The Christian Century*, August 3, 1966, p. 951. In a more recent study, *In Search of Ourselves* (Minneapolis: Burgess, 1981), Frank Poirer raises again the question of how many evolutionary lines there

might be for early humans, noting that Neanderthal fossils have been "traced from Near Eastern, African, Asian and European sites" (p. 332). See also Philip Stein and Bruce Rowe, *Physical Anthropology*, New York: McGraw-Hill, 1982, pp. 429f.

14. Brunner, Emil, *Man in Revolt*, Philadelphia: Westminster Press, 1947, pp. 398f.

15. Ibid.

16. Eccles, Sir John, and Robinson, Daniel N., *The Wonder of Being Human*, London: New Science Library, 1985, p. 67.

17. Spencer, Herbert, *The Data of Ethics*, New York: Lovell, 1879, p. 86.

18. Danto, Arthur C., in *The Encyclopedia of Philosophy*, Vol. 5, New York: Macmillan, 1972, pp. 448–449. Danto credits Ernest Nagel with having provided the best summary of the naturalist position, and excerpts this list from his "Naturalism Reconsidered" (1954).

19. Montague, Ashley, *The Humanization of Man*, New York: Grove Press, 1962, p. 16.

20. Ibid., p. 27.

21. Ibid., p. 38.

22. Ibid., p. 41.

23. Freud, Sigmund, "General Introduction to Psychoanalysis," trans. John Rivere, in *The Major Works of Sigmund Freud*, in *Great Books of the Western World*, Vol. 54, Chicago: University of Chicago Press, 1952.

24. Freud, Sigmund, "Instincts and Their Vicissitudes," ibid., pp. 413–414.

25. Freud, Sigmund, "The Ego and the Id," ibid., p. 707.

26. Erikson, Erik, "Identity and the Life Cycle," *Monograph Psychological Issues*, Vol. I, New York: International Universities Press, 1959.

27. Vander Zanden, James W., *Human Development*, New York: Knopf, 1985, p. 40. See also Hopkins, J. Roy, *Adolescence*, New York: Academic Press, 1983, pp. 80f.

28. "Erikson's theory does not clearly specify the kinds of experiences that people must have in order to cope with and resolve various psychological crises. His theory is a descriptive overview . . . that does not do a very good job of explaining how or why this development takes place." Shaffer, David R., *Developmental Psychology*, Monterey, Calif.: Brooks/Cole, 1985, pp. 51–52.

29. Piaget, Jean, *The Development of Thought*, New York: Viking Press, 1977.

30. Kohlberg, Lawrence, "Moral Stages and Moralization," in *Moral Development and Behavior*, ed. T. Lickona, New York: Holt, Rinehart and Winston, 1976.

31. From a conversation with Dr. Kohlberg during a conference in San Francisco. In 1984, I was interested to hear him lament the fact that he had not yet actually met a representative of stage 6, and wondered whether, "Maybe they all died out with Gandhi and Martin Luther King, Jr." Yet he was willing to entertain the prospect for a stage 7. He died before having the opportunity to complete his research for it.

32. Vander Zanden, *Human Development*, p. 310.

33. Gilligan, Carol, "Why Should a Woman Be More Like a Man?" *Psychology Today*, June 1982, pp. 68–77.

34. Wilson, *Sociobiology*. See also Wilson, Edward O., *On Human Nature*, Cambridge, Mass.: Harvard University Press, 1978. "Innate censors and motivators exist in the brain that deeply and unconsciously affect our ethical premises; from these roots, morality evolved as instinct" (p. 5). Wilson places great faith in the concept of instinct, an idea seriously questioned by great numbers of psychologists for half a century.

But to put his idea "in starkest form," Wilson persists, "Human beings are guided by an instinct based on genes" (p. 38).

35. Batten, Mary, "Sociobiology, A New View of Human Nature," in *Human Development*, Guilford, Conn.: Dushkin, 1983, p. 5.

36. Schell, Robert, and Hall, Elizabeth, *Developmental Psychology Today*, (4th ed.), New York: Random House, 1983, p. 65.

37. Wogaman, *Christian Moral Judgement*, p. 37.

38. Ibid.

39. In Chapter 1, God is presented as creating Adam at the end of the sixth day, *after* the fish, birds, land animals, and plant life had been established. In Chapter 2, verses 4–7 explicitly state that the first individual person was created *before*: "when no plant of the field was yet in the earth." Many scholars have concluded that the first account is of *priestly* origin (called a P source); the second came from a different group of writers identified as J (because they always employed the name *Jehovah*, JHVH, for God). Other writers used different names. The two chapters were written at different times and were joined when the Book of Genesis was being compiled. See Simpson, Cuthbert A., "The Growth of the Hexateuch," in *The Interpreter's Bible*, Vol. I, New York: Abingdon-Cokebury, 1952, pp. 185f.

40. The phrase "Let us make man in our image" employs the plural in the manner of monarchs using the royal "we" for first-person singular, though it is also suggested that a primitive concept of a heavenly court of angels or subdeities may account for the plural *Elohim*, used for God. See Porteous, N. W., "Man, Nature of, in the Old Testament," in *The Interpreter's Dictionary of the Bible*, Vol. 2, New York: Abingdon Press, 1962, p. 243.

41. I owe this phrase to Dr. Lenn Goodman of the University of Hawaii. "Creation and Evolution: Another Round in an Ancient Struggle," *Zygon, A Journal of Religion and Science*, Vol. 18, No. 1, March 1983, p. 29.

42. Ibid.

43. Eccles and Robinson, *Wonder of Being Human*, pp. 70–71. Eccles's research in neurophysiology and animal psychology has led him to state, ". . . human reasoning is capable of framing universal propositions in such a way as to arrive at universally true conclusions. There is simply not a shred of evidence to suggest that nonhuman animals do likewise. The facts of human morality and ethics are clearly at variance with a theory that explains all behavior in terms of self-preservation and the preservation of the species."

44. The words *tselem*, and *demuth* (Genesis 1:26, 27) are usually translated "image" and "likeness," respectively. The first word appears seventeen times in the Old Testament, having such meanings as model, picture, or even a dream. The second is more abstract, and may simply connote similarity.

45. Adam's acquiescence has given rise to a centuries-old tradition, found among certain Christian and even Islamic sects, to make Eve the author of sin and thus to justify keeping women in subjection. There is no biblical warrant for this; it is simply a product of masculine enculturation.

46. Becker, Ernest, *The Denial of Death*, New York: Free Press, 1973, p. 5.

47. See Buttrick, George, *Christ and Man's Dilemma*, Nashville: Abingdon Press, 1946, pp. 15–24.

48. Elliot, T. S., "The Rock," *Collected Poems 1909–1935*, New York: Harcourt, Brace, 1936.

49. Hauerwas, *Vision and Virtue*, p. 115.

50. Tillich, Paul, *The New Being*, New York: Charles Scribner's Sons, 1955, p. 16.

51. Justification "in the Pauline sense" reveals a contrast between the Old Testament view of *tsadaq* (to make or declare right) which was achieved by way of obedience to laws or by expiation for sins, and Paul's use of *dikaioo* as deliverance from the whole complexity of human involvement in sin. It is effected by an act of grace, freely bestowed by God through Christ. Paul's insistence that "a man is not justified by works" (i.e., obedience to laws and ceremonial requirements) is accompanied by his assurance that we are justified by faith (e.g., our spiritual bond with Christ and in Christ). See Romans 3:20, 24, 5:1, 9, 8:30 and Galatians 2:16, 3:11, 24. James's declaration that "a man is justified by works" (2:24), and that faith without works is dead (2:20) caused Martin Luther to complain that James's letter is "an epistle of straw." But what James seems to be saying is that faith, if genuine, will issue in good deeds.

52. Fowler, James W., *Becoming Adult, Becoming Christian*, New York: Harper & Row, 1984, p. 53.

53. Ibid., p. 55. Many of us who teach and do research among children can also attest that at this stage children often make genuine efforts at prayer, often imitative at first, but nevertheless earnest and seeking.

54. Ibid., p. 67.

55. Ibid., p. 70.

56. Ibid., p. 140.

57. Hebblethwaite, *Christian Ethics*, pp. 101–102.

58. Wood, James E., Jr., ed., *Jewish-Christian Relations in Today's World*, Waco, Tex.: Baylor University Press, 1971, pp. 20–21.

59. Visser t'Hooft, W. A., ed., *The First Assembly of the World Council of Churches*, Amsterdam, N.Y.: Harper & Brothers, 1949, p. 161. I am particularly indebted to Dr. George Grose, president of the Academy of Judaic, Christian, and Islamic Studies, for this reference in his "Foundations for Dialogue," which he presented at the World Council of Churches during its meeting in Vancouver, August 1983.

60. Serious students of the major religions are aware, for example, that "the Fatherhood of God and the brotherhood of man" are not really a common denominator, as has sometimes been proclaimed. Confucius did not believe in a personal God, nor apparently did Lao Tse or the Gautama Buddha. The Hindu caste system renders "brotherhood of man" virtually impossible to actualize, and this was one of the reasons for Mohandas Gandhi's rejection of it.

61. Brown, Robert McAfee, *Making Peace in the Global Village*, Philadelphia: Westminster Press, 1981, p. 88.

62. Moltmann, Jurgen, *On Human Dignity*, trans. M. Douglas Meeks, Philadelphia: Fortress Press, 1984, p. 6.

63. Ibid., p. 15.

64. Tillich, Paul, *The New Being*, New York: Charles Scribner's Sons, 1955, p. 23.

CHAPTER SIX

1. The *Adam* of Genesis 1:26 is rendered *Ish* in Genesis 2:23 and thereafter where an individual man or husband is indicated, and *zakar*, where "male" is being contrasted with "woman" (*ishshah*), or with "female" in general (*neqebah*).

2. Cox, Harvey, *The Seduction of the Spirit*, New York: Simon & Schuster Touchstone Books, 1973, p. 228.

3. Gustafson, James M., *Ethics from a Theocentric Perspective*, quoted in Post, Stephen G., *A Theory of Agape*, Lewisburg: Bucknell University Press, 1990, pp. 91f.

4. Brunner, Emil. *Divine Imperative*, p. 341.

5. Anne McGrew Bennett points out that not only is God not exclusively referred to as masculine in Scripture, but sometimes as distinctly feminine. Indeed: ". . . the core ideas about God are weighted in favor of words of the feminine gender. In addition to Torah, Shekinah, and Chokmah we find the following:

Ruach	the Spirit of God; feminine gender
Bat Kol	the voice of God; actually the "daughter of the voice"; double feminine
Binah	understanding; feminine gender
Rehem	mercy; feminine gender

Bennett, Anne McGrew, *From Woman-Pain to Woman-Vision*, Minneapolis: Fortress Press, 1989, p. 93.

6. It may be argued that the employment of artificial means of birth control is not a private sexual act inasmuch as the Roman Catholic church condemns it while those who advocate population reduction favor it. In this sense it is a public concern. Yet as a part of sexual activity, the selection and use of birth control methods is still very much a private choice.

7. Such a lament was chronicled in ancient Greece, when Socrates decried the waywardness of youth and their disrespect for their elders. It is echoed in the plaint of the old lady in Dickens's tale: "Ah, Mr. Pickwick, young people was very different when I was a girl." Pickwick's reply was no less characteristic: "No doubt of that, Ma'am . . . and that's the reason I would make much of the few that have any traces of the old stock." *The Pickwick Papers*, Thomas Nelson (no date), Chapter 28, p. 402.

8. Vander Zanden, *Human Development*, pp. 390–391.

9. Vander Zanden, *Human Development*, p. 400.

10. Christenson, Reo M., "How to Put Pre-Marital Sex on Hold" in *Christianity Today*, February 19, 1982, p. 18.

11. Zigler, Edward T., and Stevenson, Matia Finn, *Children in a Changing World*, Pacific Grove, Calif.: Brooks Cole, 1993, p. 508. See also Vander Zanden, *Human Development*, p. 400.

12. Hopkins, J. Roy, *Adolescence*, New York: Academic Press, 1983, p. 259.

13. Ibid., p. 260. See also Vander Zanden, *Human Development*, p. 398.

14. Peplau, L. A., Rubin, S., and Hill, C. T., "Sexual Intimacy in Dating Relationships," *Journal of Social Issues*, 1977, 33(2), pp. 86–109. See also Schuster, Clara Shaw, and Ashburn, Shirley Smith, *The Process of Human Development*, New York: J. B. Lippincott, 1992, p. 632.

15. *Time*, July 4, 1983, p. 51.

16. Pear, Robert, New York Times News Service, quoted in *Los Angeles Herald Examiner*, June 13, 1986, A2, p. 1. The *Los Angeles Times*, May 31, 1991, quoted Dr. Michael Gottlieb: "AIDS has changed us forever. It has brought out the best in us, and the worst." See also Kimball, Ann Marie, "AIDS, the Global Epidemic," *Christianity and Crisis*, September 21, 1992, p. 298.

17. Kinsey, A. C., Pomeroy, W. B., and Martin, C. E., *Sexual Behavior in the Human Male*, Philadelphia: W. B. Saunders, 1948, p. 379.

18. Reiss, I. L., "The Sexual Renaissance," *Journal of Social Issues*, 1966, 22(2), pp. 123–137.

19. Hopkins, *Adolescence*, p. 269.

20. Hopkins, quoting the study by R. W. Libby, in the *Journal of Marriage and the Family*, 1978, 40, pp. 79–92. See also Schuster and Asburn, *The Process of Human Development*, 1992: "Religious affiliation does not appear to make a significant difference in sexual behavior; however, the individual's degree of devotedness to a concept of God and participation in religious activities is highly correlated."

21. McLaren, Robert B., "Sex, Violence and Films," in *Los Angeles Times*, January 1, 1982, pp. 12–13.

22. This was a major theme of Unwin's book *Sex and Culture* published in 1934, and to which he returned in *Sexual Regulations and Cultural Behavior* in 1935. In 1936, before he died at Cambridge University, he was completing work on his final book, in which he described the methods of observation he had used in studying primitive culture to establish whether a relation between sexual restraint and cultural progress could be verified. Unwin, J. D., *The Sexual and Economic Foundations of a New Society*, London: George Allen and Unwin, 1940, pp. 92–104.

23. In the late 1930s, sociologist Pitrim Sorokin produced his monumental four-volume *Social and Cultural Dynamics* in which he traced "the disintegration of the sensate culture," noting among other things the progressive decline in cultural values where eroticism prevailed. This theme was echoed in his 1944 *The Crisis of Our Age* (New York: E. P. Dutton, Chapter IX) and again in his 1948 *The Reconstruction of Humanity* (Boston: Beacon Press), in which he discusses "what is pathological in the main compartments of our culture" is its assumption that "true reality value is sensory, and that there is no supersensory reality value." Sexual gratification, wealth, power, popularity, and hedonic values are the only goals. Art, literature, and even law and ethics reflect the gradual diminution of concern for humane and altruistic endeavors, without which no culture can survive (Chapters IV, VII, and VIII).

24. *Acta Apostolicae Sedis*, 68 (1976), par. n. 8, cited by Charles Curran, *Issues in Sexual and Medical Ethics*, Notre Dame, Ind.: University of Notre Dame Press, 1978, p. 31.

25. Thorpe, Louis P., *The Psychology of Mental Health* (2nd ed.), New York: Ronald Press, 1969, p. 460. See also Schuster, Cara, and Ashburn, Shirley, *The Process of Human Development*, Boston: Little, Brown, 1986, pp. 248–514.

26. Curran, Charles, *Issues in Sexual and Medical Ethics*, p. 50.

27. Mayo, Mary Ann, *Parents' Guide to Sex Education*, Grand Rapids, Mich.: Zondervan, 1986, p. 179.

28. Moore, Mary Lou, *Realities in Childbearing*, Philadelphia: W. B. Saunders, 1978, p. 120.

29. *Proceedings of the 1958 Lambeth Conference*, London: Bishops of the Anglican Communion.

30. Brunner, *Divine Imperative*, p. 654. Brunner, a Swiss Protestant, wrote this in response to the pope's *Encyclia Connibi*.

31. Burtchael, James T., "Human Life and Human Love," *Commonweal*, November 15, 1968.

32. Fromm, Erich, *The Art of Loving*, New York: Harper Torchbooks, 1956, pp. 33–34.

33. Kollar, Armin, *The Foundation of Jewish Ethics*, New York: Macmillan, 1929, p. 211.

34. Qualben, Lars, *A History of the Christian Church*, New York: Thomas Nelson, 1942, p. 188.

35. Calvin also pointed out the fallacy in calling marriage a sacrament at all, placing it on a par with baptism and Holy Communion. The Greek word *musterion*, which is always translated "mystery" elsewhere in the Bible, was mistakenly rendered "sacrament" in the one reference to marriage in Ephesians 5:32.

36. Barclay, William, *The Letters to the Galatians and the Ephesians*, Philadelphia: Westminster Press, 1958, p. 35.

37. Bell, Wesley, "A Woman's Work Is Never Done," *Symbiosis*, Vol. 4, No. 3, June 1985, p. 4.

38. Hole, Judith, and Levinim, Ellen, "The First Feminists" in *Radical Feminism*, New York: Quadrangle Books, 1973, p. 7.

39. Goldsmith, Judith, *National Organization for Women*, Washington, D.C., 1984.

40. O'Hare, Padraic, "To Each (Her) Due" in *Women and Religion*, ed. Regina Coll, Mahwah, N.J.: Paulist Press, 1982, p. 16.

41. Ibid., p. 18.

42. Miller, Jeremy, O. P., "A Note on Aquinas and the Ordination of Women," *New Blackfriars*, 1981, 61 (719), p. 190.

43. Ibid.

44. O'Hare, "To Each," p. 21.

45. Vatican II, *Declaration on the Church in the Modern World*, 1965, n. 29.

46. The shame of nakedness appears in the story of Adam and Eve, in the cursing of the sons of Noah, in threatenings against apostasy from God ("I will show the nations thy nakedness," Nahum 3:5), in numerous Old and New Testament passages, and even to Revelation 17:16, where "the harlot" is to be made "desolate and naked."

47. Janson, H. W., *History of Art*, New York: Abrams, 1969, p. 21.

48. Byrne, Donn, and Kelley, Kathryn, "Pornography and Sex Research," in *Pornography and Sexual Aggression*, ed. Neil Malamuth and Edward Donnerstein, New York: Academic Press, 1984, p. 2.

49. Ibid., p. 3. It is of interest that the Protestant churches never created anything comparable to the Catholic "Index of Forbidden Books" (*Index Librorum Prohibitorum*), following instead the Reform principle of granting freedom of conscience under the discipline of the Holy Spirit. It is of more than passing interest, however, to note that in 1643, England's then Presbyterian Parliament employed numerous arbitrary rulings of censorship reminiscent of the Star-Chamber proceedings they had just abolished, inspiring John Milton to write his *Areopagitica* (1644) protesting censorship in any form. For the Puritans, the "community of the faithful" became the context for such discipline, assuming the Holy Spirit was always present to guide moral choice. It is possible that this concept has motivated American courts to rely on "prevailing community standards" for definitions of obscenity and pornography, apparently trusting that a nascent puritanism may still serve as a moral guide. As for the Roman Catholic *Index*, it was formally abandoned by the church in June 1966.

50. Kronhausen, Eberhard, and Kronhausen, Phyllis, *Pornography and the Law*, New York: Ballantine Books, 1964, pp. 56–57.

51. Ibid., p. 67.

52. Rushoony, Rousas, *The Politics of Pornography*, New Rochelle, N.Y.: Arlington, 1974, p. 9.

53. *Codex Juris Canonici 403* et. seq. (1917). Cf. Burke, Redmond, *What Is the Index?* St. Paul: Bruce, 1917, for a full explication of these canons.

54. Kronhausen and Kronhausen, *Pornography*, pp. 25–26. The Kronhausens do not make the distinction that I have made here between sensual idealism and erotic realism, apparently content to accept all sexual references under the second category. Thus they include the *Venus of Milo* in the same category with the intercourse scenes on the walls of Pompeian villas and the erotic writings of Ovid as "traces of reaction against anti-erotic cultural trends . . . a breakthrough."

55. Baron, Larry, and Straus, Murray A., "Sexual Stratification, Pornography, and Rape in the United States," in *Pornography and Sexual Aggression*, p. 196.

56. Court, John H., "Sex and Violence: A Ripple Effect" in *Pornography and Sexual Aggression*, p. 150. See also "How Harmful Is Pornography?" in *Christianity Today*, July 11, 1986, p. 86, and Ross, Mary Ellen, "Censorship or Education?" in *The Christian Century*, March 7, 1990, p. 244.

57. Kirk, Jerry, quoted in *Christianity Today*, July 11, 1986, p. 27.

58. Court, "Sex and Violence," p. 162. See Bandura, A., *Aggression: A Social Learning Analysis*, Englewood Cliffs, N.J.: Prentice-Hall, 1973; Berkowitz, L. "Sex and Violence: We Can't Have It Both Ways," *Psychology Today*, December 1971, pp. 14–23; Brownmiller, S., *Against Our Will: Men, Women and Rape*, New York: Simon & Schuster, 1975; Court, J. H., "Pornography and Sex Crimes: A Re-evaluation in the Light of Recent Trends Around the World," *International Journal of Criminology and Penology*, 5, pp. 129–157.

59. Ostrow, Ronald J., "Meese Panel Asks Porn Crackdown," *Los Angeles Times*, July 10, 1986, pp. 1, 16, 17.

60. Quoted in *Time*, July 21, 1986, p. 15.

61. Ibid., p. 22.

62. Lederer, Laura J., "Pornography Is a Social Carcinogen," *Los Angeles Times*, July 6, 1986, Part V, p. 5. "The question that we must ask is not whether pornography causes sexual violence; we should ask if pornographic media contribute, even in small measure, to the sexual abuse, molestation, rape, battery and sexually oriented kidnappings and murders of women and children." A more extensive study can be found in Malamuth, Neil, and Donnerstein, Edward, eds., *Pornography and Sexual Aggression*, New York: Academic Press, 1984, Chapter 2. See also Gubar, Susan, and Huff, Joan, *For Adult Users Only: The Dilemma of Violent Pornography*, Indianapolis: Indiana University Press, 1989.

63. Vander Zanden, *Human Development*, p. 500.

64. *Time*, July 21, 1986, p. 18.

65. Quoted from an address to the Morality in Media conference in St. Louis, in the *Journal of the National Federation for Decency*, August 1986, p. 12.

66. Newton, Lisa H., "The Irrelevance of Religion in the Abortion Debate," *Hastings Center Report*, New York: Hastings-on-Hudson, August 1978. Quoted in *Abortion: The Moral Issues*, ed. Edward Batchelor, New York: Pilgrim Press, 1982, pp. 3f.

67. Mead goes further to ask whether "the commotion made by the mass media and politicians over abortion is not a cover for unwillingness to face the mass murder of innocents in other parts of the world," contending that the state should not have the power of life and death over citizens of any age or condition. Mead, Margaret, "Rights to Life," *Christianity and Crisis*, January 8, 1973, quoted in *Abortion: The Moral Issues*, pp. 13–14.

68. Barth, Karl, *Church Dogmatics*, Part III, Vol. 4, pp. 415–422, Edinburgh: T. & T. Clark, quoted in Batchelor, *Abortion*, pp. 92f.

69. *Los Angeles Times*, October 8, 1992, pp. A1, A32.

70. Tertullian, in *De Pudicitis, XII*, declared idolatry, adultery, and homicide as irremissible sins, based on Acts 15:20. It is important to note, however, that the writer of Acts did not make them irremissible; he simply urged Gentile converts to "refrain" from them.

71. The popularity of natural law as a frame of reference, not only in Roman Catholicism but in Protestantism as well, has been noted with some misgiving by Robin Gill of Edinburgh. He points out that even if it could be established that procreation is the obvious function of sexuality, "It is far from clear that it should be the only or indispensable function. To derive an exclusive moral prescription from an empirical observation of function was to commit an extraordinary category error." *A Textbook of Christian Ethics*, Edinburgh: T. & T. Clark, 1985, p. 456.

72. Quoted from Karl Barth, in *Abortion: The Moral Issues*, p. 94.

73. In her book *Culture and Commitment*, Mead describes a variety of cultures that have transmitted rules, sanctions, and other bases for ethical decisions in different ways to successive generations. What she observes to be disturbingly characteristic of our generation is the sense among youth that "old rules are now meaningless," and that "there are no adults anywhere in the world from whom they can learn what the next steps should be" (New York: Doubleday, 1970, p. 87).

74. Mead, "Rights to Life," p. 11.

75. Draper, Elinor, "Birth Control," *Encyclopedia Britannica*, Chicago: Helen Hemingway Benton, 1974, Macropedia, Vol. 2, p. 1069. See also Boykin, John, "Which Life? Whose Choice?" in *Stanford*, Palo Alto: Stanford University Press, December 1989, p. 32. *Roe vs. Wade* allows for abortion in all three trimesters, though it imposes stricter criteria in the third.

76. Maguire, Daniel C., *The Moral Choice*, New York: Winston Press, 1979, pp. 151–152.

77. Le Jeune, Jerome, "Is There a Natural Morality?" address delivered at the John Paul II Institute, Washington, D.C., June 20, 1989.

78. *Time*, April 6, 1981, p. 21.

79. MacIver, Marylou, "The Church and Abortion," *Presbyterian Survey*, May 1985, p. 28.

80. Diamond, James D., "Abortion, Animation, Hominization," *Theological Studies*, Vol. 36, No. 2, June 1975, p. 311. In fact only 30 percent actually survive and develop full term.

81. Calahan, Daniel, "Abortion Decisions: Personal Morality," quoted in *Biomedical Ethics*, ed. Thomas Mappes and Jane Zembarty, New York: McGraw-Hill, 1981, p. 424. It should be noted that since this publication, Calahan has moved closer to the prochoice position.

82. Fanning, Marilyn, "The Church and Abortion," *Presbyterian Survey*, May 1985, p. 28.

83. Barth, *Church Dogmatics*, p. 95.

84. Ibid., p. 97.

85. Ibid., p. 98. In Volume III:4, pp. 415–423, Barth says abortion may be forgiven in certain critical situations, but the initial "No" prevails.

86. Gustafson, James, "A Protestant Ethical Approach," in *Abortion*, p. 208.

87. Ibid., p. 208.

88. Weddington, Sarah Ragle, "The Woman's Right of Privacy," in *Abortion*, p. 15.

89. Traducianism actually went further, to affirm that the personality of the individual is inherited from the parents along with physical characteristics. This was supposed to account for family traits being passed along, but more importantly, it gave support for the hope that one's line would be continued, and each of us would live on in our children.

90. Moore, Mary Lou, *Realities in Childbearing*, p. 163.

91. Gaffney, James, *Matters of Faith and Morals*, Kansas City: Sheed and Ward, 1987, pp. 196–197.

92. Muntzel, Philip A., "National Dialogue on Abortion Issues," *Church and Society*, Louisville, Ky.: Social Justice and Peacemaking Unit, Presbyterian Church (U.S.A.), January/February 1990, 124 pp.

93. *The Christian Century*, Chicago: Christian Century Foundation, April 29, 1992, pp. 448, 449.

94. *The Christian Century*, May 20–27, 1992, p. 536.

95. *The Christian Century*, June 17–24, 1992, p. 608.

96. *The Christian Century*, August 12–19, 1992, p. 738.

97. *The Christian Century*, April 8, 1992, p. 358.

98. *The Christian Century*, July 1–8, 1992, p. 641.

99. Bailey's 1955 *Homosexuality and the Western Christian Tradition*, has been widely quoted, and is used as a key reference in the Westminster *Dictionary of Christian Ethics*, 1967, p. 153. Nevertheless, Edwards, even while seeking every possible support for a more accepting attitude toward homosexuality, rejects Bailey's interpretation. See also Edwards, George R., *Gay/Lesbian Liberation*, New York: Pilgrim Press, 1984, p. 33.

100. Boswell, John, *Christianity, Social Tolerance, and Homosexuality*, Chicago: University of Chicago Press, 1980, pp. 106–107.

101. Aquinas, Thomas, *Summa Theologica*, Part II, 2nd section, pp. 152–154; *Summa Contra Gentiles*, XI, pp. 10–11, 18–22, 29.

102. Curran, Charles, *Issues in Sexual and Medical Ethics*, Notre Dame, Ind.: University of Notre Dame Press, 1978, p. 48.

103. Overholser, Winfred, "Homosexuality: Sin or Disease?" in *Contemporary Religious Issues*, ed. Donald Hartsock, Belmont, Calif.: Wadsworth, 1968, p. 261.

104. Kinsey, Alfred C., Pomeroy, W. B., and Martin, C. E., *Sexual Behavior in the Human Male*, Philadelphia: W. B. Saunders, 1948, pp. 650f.

105. Freud, Sigmund, *Three Essays on the Theory of Sexuality*, trans. James Strachey, London: Hogarth, 1974, pp. 2f.

106. Lewes, Kenneth, *The Psychoanalytic Theory of Male Homosexuality*, New York: Simon & Schuster, 1988, p. 52.

107. Overholser, "Homosexuality," p. 262. He concedes, however, that evi-

dence is not strong for homosexuality being traceable to a natural "error" of the endocrine system: "Endocrine imbalance probably does not account for the aberrations of more than a small fraction of the whole group."

108. Spitzer, Robert L., "A Proposal About Homosexuality and the APA Nomenclature: Homosexuality as One Form of Sexual Behavior and Sexual Orientation Disturbance as a Psychiatric Disorder," June 7, 1973. This paper was included in a press release of the *American Psychiatric Association*, December 15, of that same year.

109. Greenberg, David, *The Construction of Homosexuality*, Chicago: University of Chicago Press, 1992. Greenberg suggests that during the Babylonian exile, Israel was influenced by the extreme antipathy to homosexuality in Zoroastrianism. It was during this time that the priestly Leviticus codes were being formulated.

110. Nedler, Ronald D., "Homosexual Behavior in Nonhuman Primates," in *Homosexuality/Heterosexuality*, The Kinsey Institute Series, New York: Oxford University Press, 1990, pp. 139f.

111. Skolnick, Arlene S., *The Psychology of Human Development*, San Diego: Harcourt, Brace, Jovanovich, 1986, p. 334.

112. Schuster, Clara, and Ashburn, Shirley, *The Process of Human Development*, Philadelphia: J. B. Lippincott, 1992, p. 306. See also Bell, A. P., Weinberg, M. S., and Hammersmith, S. K., *Sexual Preference: Its Development in Men and Women*, Bloomington: Indiana University Press, 1981.

113. *Newsweek*, February 24, 1992, p. 46.

114. Ibid., p. 47.

115. Ibid., p. 48.

116. *Time*, August 17, 1992, pp. 50–51.

117. Ibid., p. 51.

118. Herman, Judith, *Father-Daughter Incest*, Cambridge: Harvard University Press, 1981; Hart, John, *The Theory and Practice of Homosexuality*, London: Routledge & Kegan Paul, 1981; Mayer, Adele, *Sexual Abuse: Causes, Consequences and Treatment of Incestuous and Pedophilic Acts*, Holmes Beach, Fl.: Learning Publications, 1985; Peters, David, *A Betrayal of Innocence*, Waco, Tex.: Word, 1986.

119. *Time*, August 17, 1992, p. 51.

120. A distinction is commonly made between *femininity*, as a fact of gender, and *feminism*, as a point of view vis-à-vis gender rights. One might make a similar case for the distinction between nationality and nationalism; science and scientism. It is usually homosexualism, rather than homosexuality, to which some of the public reacts with hostility, as when confronted with flamboyant gay pride parades or the insistence that public school libraries include books approving of the gay lifestyle, an act seen (for example, in New York and Oregon in 1992) as not simply presenting homosexuality as a fact, but as active recruitment of children.

121. As an ironic footnote to history, the vote to repeal a nineteenth-century law making homosexualism a crime was cast by the Marquess of Queensbury, the great-grandson of the prosecutor who secured a two-year prison sentence for Oscar Wilde on the charge of sodomy.

122. Professor Daniel Maguire, commenting on these events and others (like the excommunication of a woman for her work in Planned Parenthood, rejection of a fifteen-year-old girl's application for confirmation because she spoke positively on the abortion issue, ordering a Catholic sociologist to burn his research on divided issues among bishops over celibacy and ordination of women) charges: "the issue is power." The Vatican, he writes, has been losing control over the way Catholics must think

since Vatican II, and is struggling to regain it. "Sexual and reproductive ethics is the chosen ground for this struggle. It need not have been so. The pelvic zone is not the focus of biblical morality and religion. In Galileo's time, the chosen ground was physics and astronomy, but the issue was the same: power." *Los Angeles Times*, August 24, 1986, Part V, p. 5; September 6, Part I, p. 2.

123. Hebblethwaite, Brian, *Christian Ethics*, pp. 89–90.

124. Ibid., p. 99.

125. Edwards, *Gay/Lesbian*, pp. 123f.

126. Brunner, *Man in Revolt*, p. 345.

127. Fromm, *The Art of Loving*, pp. 33–34.

128. *Time*, August 3, 1992. Nearly a decade earlier, July 4, 1983, a *Time* article noted that the outbreak of AIDS was highly correlated with homosexual intercourse, the average perpetrator having had sixty different sexual partners in a twelve-month period.

129. Malgrem, Dallin, "The Homosexual Christian," *Presbyterian Survey*, Atlanta: Presbyterian Publishing House, November/December 1983, Vol. 73, No. 10, p. 24.

130. For those who seek such information: Jeanette Howard's *Out of Egypt* (Monarch Publications, England, 1991); Earl Wilson's *Counseling and Homosexuality* (Word, 1991); John White's *Parents in Pain* (Intervarsity, 1979) are suggestive, and a small part of a reading list from Exodus International, in San Raphael, California.

CHAPTER SEVEN

1. Even during the industrial revolution, when families were being disrupted by vast changes in the workplace, books on ethics did not treat the institution of marriage as a problem. But after World War II theologian Emil Brunner warned that "the crisis in marriage presents the Christian ethic with the most serious and the most difficult problem with which it has to deal." *The Divine Imperative*, p. 341.

2. Victor, Joan, and Sander, Joelle, *The Family: The Evolution of Our Oldest Human Institution*, Indianapolis: Bobbs-Merrill, 1978, pp. 10f.

3. Goodsell, Willystine, *A History of Marriage and the Family*, New York: AMS Press, 1974, p. 304.

4. Steward, Julian, "The Economic and Social Basis of Primitive Bands," in *Essays in Anthropology*, Berkeley: University of California Press, 1938, pp. 332f.

5. Goodall, Jane van Lawick, *In the Shadow of Man*, Boston: Houghton Mifflin, 1971, p. 185.

6. In the Chinese language, a humorous play on words is discovered in the fact that the word symbol for peace is "one woman under one roof," while the word for treachery includes three women with the roof symbol sometimes omitted:

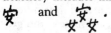

7. As noted in an earlier chapter, both Protestant and Roman Catholic theologians, Emil Brunner and Pierre Chardin among them, have affirmed that humankind emerged only after eons of evolutionary development, such development being guided to the point where humans became aware cognitively and spiritually of their Creator's requirements.

8. The writer of Matthew uses a derivative of the word *sarkos* for flesh, which is employed extensively in the New Testament for "worldly," with carnal undertones (see Paul's warning about flesh serving the law of sin), when the more gentle term *soma*

was available, meaning simply "the body." Thus *oste ouketi eisin duo, alla sarx mia*. Note, however, that John uses the term in declaring, "The Word became flesh (*sarx*) and dwelt among us" (John 1:14), reflecting the fact that *sarkos* is not limited to mere biological flesh. It is characteristic of Hebrew thought that flesh represents the whole person, as the ideal unity of marriage covers the whole nature. "It is a unity of soul as well as body: of sympathy, interest, purpose. They are no longer two but one flesh, one spirit, one person." See Bruce, Alexander Balmain, *The Expositor's Greek Testament*, Grand Rapids, Mich.: Wm. B. Eerdmans, (no date) p. 246.

9. Cox, *Seduction of the Spirit*, p. 227.

10. Durant, Will, *The Story of Civilization*, Vol. III, New York: Simon & Schuster, 1944, p. 56.

11. Nass, Gilbert, and McDonald, Gerald, *Marriage and the Family* (2nd ed.), Menlo Park, Calif.: Addison Wesley, 1982, pp. 19–20.

12. Ibid., p. 20.

13. Einhard, *The Life of Charlemagne* (first written between 817 and 830), Ann Arbor, Mich.: University of Michigan Press, 1969, p. 48. Translator unknown. Charlemagne can hardly be described as a model Christian parent. Despite being a doting father (he was so careful in the training of his sons and daughters that "he never took his meals without them when he was at home, and never made a journey without them," according to Einhard), his philandering became notorious. Perhaps in remorse for this behavior, he refused to allow his daughters to marry. Rebelling, the girls engaged in affairs with men at the court, and one of his sons, Pepin, plotted against him in an episode reminiscent of Absolom's treachery against King David.

14. Ducket, Eleanor Shipley, *Alfred the Great*, Chicago: University of Chicago Press, 1958, pp. 189f.

15. Coleman, Emily R., "Medieval Marriage Characteristics" in *The Family in History*, ed. Theodore Rabb and Robert Rothberg, New York: Harper Torchbooks, 1973, p. 5.

16. Goodsell, *History of Marriage*, p. 198.

17. Cleveland, Arthur R., *Women Under the English Law*, London: Hunrst and Blackett, 1896, p. 173.

18. Zimmerman, Carle, *Family and Civilization*, New York: Harper & Brothers, 1947, p. 517.

19. Calvin demonstrated that the Greek word *musterion*, which is everywhere else in the Bible translated as "mystery," was written as "sacrament" only in this one passage, Ephesians 5:32.

20. Calvin, John, *Institutes of the Christian Religion*, 1535 (published in final form in 1559), trans. John Allen, Philadelphia: Presbyterian Board of Christian Education, 7th American ed., 1936, Book IV, Chapter 19, pp. 768f.

21. Hobbes, Thomas, *Leviathan*, in *Great Books of the Western World*, Vol. 23, Chicago: University of Chicago Press, 1952, p. 109.

22. Locke, John, *Concerning Civil Government*, in *Great Books of the Western World*, Vol. 35, Chicago: University of Chicago Press, 1952, p. 36.

23. Messer, Mary Burt, *The Family in the Making*, New York: G. P. Putnam's Sons, 1928, p. 258.

24. Historians have noted that the colonists, presumably in response to the biblical injunction "Be fruitful and multiply" usually had large families. Benjamin Franklin was one of seventeen children, and families of twenty to twenty-five were not unknown.

The first governor of Massachusetts, Sir William Phipps, was one of twenty-seven. However, the average number born to those married between 1700 and 1710 was 7.5. See James, Henrietta, "Morphology of New England Society" in *The Family in History*, ed. T. K. Rabb, New York: Harper & Row, 1971, p. 202.

25. It is remarkable to consider that the Pilgrims landed in Plymouth in 1620, and established Harvard only fifteen years later. The settlers in Massachusetts passed a law that every village of fifty or more families must build a public school; attendance was required, with fines levied against parents who failed to comply.

26. The replacement of handwork by machines not only reduced personal pride in workmanship, but often created work of inferior quality that could be marketed faster and cheaper. As the multiplication of machines increased, countless displaced workers were thrown out of work, and a devastating toll of poverty followed. One example with its ramifications may illustrate. In 1806, Manchester had only one loom. By 1818, there were two thousand. Scores, then hundreds of workers were laid off. In desperation, a band of them attacked the factories and smashed the looms. Parliament retaliated by establishing a death penalty for anyone breaking a machine or loom, and soon executions were reducing the already starving populations. Factory owners refused to believe there could be poverty in England when they themselves were growing rich. See Inglis, Brian, *Poverty and the Industrial Revolution*, London: Hodder and Stoughton, 1971, p. 100.

27. Gibbins, Henry D., *Industry in England, Historical Outlines*, New York: Scribner's, 1914, p. 392.

28. Quoted in Hershey, Gerald, and Lugo, James, *Human Development*, New York: Macmillan, 1979, pp. 24–25. The authors added the editorial comment: ". . . conditions so terrible that criminals today would certainly choose the death penalty rather than be forced to endure them."

29. The Sunday school movement was actually begun by Robert Raikes in England in the 1780s, but soon spread to the United States, providing not only religious instruction but also basic reading and writing skills for working class children (including children of slaves in America's southern states, despite the illegality of it). By 1824, there were 723 such schools in America.

30. Nuclear and extended forms of family life are usually distinguished by their economic structure, with the father or mother as the essential support of the family unit characterizing the nuclear form. In the extended family three or more generations of family members share the work and resources. It is not always the case, however, that all share equally; among Hopi Indians it is the wife who owns the land, livestock, and water rights, and these are not "joint property." See Lamanna, Mary, and Riedmann, Agnes, *Marriages and Families*, Belmont, Calif.: Wadsworth, 1985, pp. 10–11.

31. One has only to consider the writings of Mulcaster and Pestalozzi, Austin, Dickens, Thackeray, Alcott, and Twain to be impressed with the great amount of sentiment and loyalty that existed with regard to the family.

32. Abigail wrote just before the signing of the Declaration of Independence: "I long to hear that you have declared Independence and, by the way . . . if particular care and attention are not paid to the ladies, we are determined to foment a rebellion."

33. One historian noted that the population of one factory town in Massachusetts was comprised 80 percent of women aged 16 to 25 who had left their homes from elsewhere to work there, and not always from economic necessity. See Messer, Mary Burt, *The Family in the Making*, New York: G. P. Putnam's Sons, 1982, p. 26.

34. Crouzet, Francois, *The Victorian Economy*, New York: Columbia University Press, 1982, p. 26.

35. Hauerwas, *Community of Character*, p. 155.

36. Mace, David R., "Contemporary Issues in Marriage" in *Marriage and the Family: Coping with Change*, ed. Leonard Cargan, Belmont, Calif.: Wadsworth, 1985, p. 6.

37. Ibid.

38. Sussman, Marvin, "The Family Today," p. 21.

39. Ibid.

40. Biwerman, John, "Their Mission: Help Find Thousands of Missing Children," *The Boston Globe*, January 1, 1983.

41. Craig, Grace, *Human Development* (4th ed.), Englewood Cliffs, N.J.: Prentice-Hall, 1986, p. 403.

42. Justice, Blair, and Duncan, David F., "Running Away: An Epidemic Problem of Adolescence," *Adolescence*, Fall 1976, p. 365.

43. Surface, Bill, "The Case of the Runaway Teenager," *Reader's Digest*, May 1970, p. 145.

44. Craig, *Human Development*, p. 403.

45. Vander Zanden, *Human Development* (2nd ed.), p. 460.

46. Rogers, Dorothy, *Adolescence and Youth*, Englewood Cliffs, N.J.: Prentice-Hall, 1981, p. 202. Los Angeles Mayor Tom Bradley declared in the summer of 1986 that fully one-third of births in Los Angeles County were illegitimate.

47. Berger, Kathleen, *The Developing Person Through the Life Span*, New York: Worth Publishers, Inc., 1988. See also Schuster, Carol, and Ashburn Shirley, *The Process of Human Development*, Boston: Little Brown, 1980, p. 622, and Second Edition, 1986, p. 617.

48. Lefrancois, Guy R., *Of Children*, Belmont, Calif.: Wadsworth, 1989. "In 1948, one child in 14 was raised in a single parent family; at the present somewhere close to half of all children spend an average of six years in a one parent family" (p. 13). Diane Papilia's 1990 *A Child's World* supports the contention (New York: McGraw-Hill, p. 480f.); Michael and Sheila Cole's *The Development of Children* (New York: W. H. Freeman, Scientific American Books, 1989) puts the figure of children of divorce at 42 percent, but notes also that 27 percent of children had parents who were never married at all (p. 386).

49. Nass, Gilbert D., and McDonald, Gerald W., *Marriage and the Family*, Reading, Mass.: Addison Wesley, 1982, p. 453.

50. Elkins, Frederick, *The Child and Society*, New York: Random House, 1960, p. 46.

51. Levinger, George K., *Divorce and Separation*, New York: Basic Books, 1979, p. 300.

52. Duncan, T. Roger, *You're Divorced But Your Children Aren't*, Englewood Cliffs, N.J.: Prentice-Hall, 1979, p. 299.

53. *Time*, September 1, 1980, p. 56.

54. Marsh, Ellen Surrey, "Depression, Suicide Join List of Childhood Diseases," *Los Angeles Times*, September 6, 1983, Part V, p. 1.

55. Hart, Nancy, and Keidel, Gladys, "The Suicidal Adolescent," *American Journal of Nursing*, January 1979, p. 80.

56. Families in which the mother has too dominant a role or is the only parental figure seem to deprive children of a male-female balance for role modeling and a general

sense of security. "The vanishing father is perhaps the central fact of the changing American family structure today." Perry, John, and Perry, Erna, *Pairing and Parenthood*, San Francisco: Canfield Press, 1977, p. 91.

57. Hauerwas, *Community of Character*, p. 167.

58. Ibid., p. 168.

59. Ibid., p. 169.

60. Yates, Wilson, "The Family and Power," *The Annual of the Society of Christian Ethics*, 1981, p. 123.

61. Fletcher, Ronald, *The Family and Marriage in Britain* (3rd ed.), New York: Penguin, 1973. Quoted by Yates in "The Family and Power," p. 150.

62. Hauerwas, *Community of Character*, p. 174.

63. In the Qur'an, Surah II, 227, God seems to accept a firm intention to divorce; Abdullah Yusuf Ali points out in his commentary: "Reconciliation is recommended, but if they are really determined against reconciliation, it is unfair to keep them tied indefinitely. Divorce is the only fair and equitable course, though, as the Apostle has declared, of all things permitted, divorce is the most hateful in the sight of God." *The Holy Qur'an*, copyrighted by Khalil Al-Rawaf, 1946, p. 89.

64. Maguire, Daniel C., *The Moral Revolution*, San Francisco: Harper & Row, 1986, p. 78.

65. In Matthew 5:32, Jesus refers to adultery as the grounds provided by Moses for allowing divorce. In 1 Corinthians 7:15 Paul says that in the case of one of the partners being an unbeliever: "If the unbelieving partner desires to separate, let it be so."

66. One cannot avoid the rejoinder here, however, that Jesus pointed out that in heaven, where the biological need for procreation no longer prevails, "They neither marry nor are given in marriage." The fact that this appears in all three synoptic Gospels deserves attention because it opens a new understanding of the love that binds all people without exclusive claims such as here separate us and limit our expressions of mutual affection. See also Matthew 22:30, Mark 12:25, and Luke 20:35.

67. Maguire, *Moral Revolution*, p. 79.

68. Holmes, Arthur F., *Ethics: Approaching Moral Decisions*, Downers Grove, Ill.: Inter-Varsity Press, 1984, p. 113.

69. Ramsey, *Christian Ethics*, p. 73. This point was often made by Reinhold Niebuhr and Emil Brunner.

70. Brunner, *Divine Imperative*, p. 362.

71. Jones, Richard G., *Groundwork of Christian Ethics*, London: Epworth Press, 1984, p. 126.

72. Maguire, *Moral Revolution*, p. 79.

73. Curran, Charles, *Transition and Tradition in Moral Theology*, Notre Dame, Ind.: Notre Dame University Press, 1979, p. 52.

CHAPTER EIGHT

1. In ancient Greece, three kinds of people inhabited the city-states: *citizens*, whose direct ancestors established the city-state where one resided: Athens, Corinth, Sparta, and so on; *metics*, whose movements from city to city deprived them of citi-

zenship in any city but that of their origin, and even that might be forfeit; and *slaves*, who enjoyed few privileges and virtually no rights.

2. An exception would be in Sophocles's drama *Antigone*, where the heroine appealed to "the unwritten laws of God that know not change," in opposing the dictates of King Creon. Note Antostrophe II, lines 484–491.

3. Geyer, Alan, *Piety and Politics*, Richmond, Va.: John Knox Press, 1963, p. 39.

4. See Deuteronomy 7:6; Psalms 33:12; Proverbs 14:34; Isaiah 49:7; Matthew 22:21; Romans 13:1.

5. Cardinal Wolsey's speech in *King Henry VIII*, Act 3, Scene 2.

6. Quoted in Norman Cousin's *In God We Trust*, New York: Harper & Brothers, 1958, p. 43.

7. Decatur's toast after successfully terminating America's tribute to Algeria, in 1815, was, "Our country! In her intercourse with foreign nations may she always be in the right, but our country, right or wrong."

8. Hegel saw a reciprocal responsibility between state and church: "Since religion is an integrating factor in the state, implanting a sense of unity in the depths of men's minds, the state should even require all its citizens to belong to a church." *The Philosophy of Right*, in *Great Books of the Western World*, Vol. 46, Chicago: University of Chicago Press, 1952, p. 86.

9. Niebuhr, Reinhold, *Moral Man and Immoral Society*, New York: Charles Scribner's Sons, 1932, p. 91.

10. Bennett, John C., *Foreign Policy in Christian Perspective*, New York: Charles Scribner's Sons, 1966, p. 13.

11. See Reich, Robert, *Tales of a New America*, New York: Times Books, 1987.

12. *Weimar Ausgabe*, LI, 254.

13. Ibid., XI, 277.

14. *Institutes*, II, Sec. III, p. 298.

15. In *Works*, Vol. 6, New York: AMS Press, 1968, p. 236.

16. The only reason Rutherford escaped execution is that he died first of natural causes.

17. Yoder, John Howard, *The Politics of Jesus*, Grand Rapids, Mich.: William B. Eerdmans, 1972, p. 91.

18. Ibid., p. 92.

19. *Hamlet*, Act III, Scene I.

20. Titus, Harold H., and Keeton, Morris, *Ethics for Today*, New York: American Book Company, 1966, p. 489.

21. Brunner, *Divine Imperative*, p. 445. Brunner observes that from a theological point of view, the state is a God-given order of sinful reality. "In history, in the growth of every State the most brutal, anti-divine forces have taken a share, to an extent unheard of in individual life, save in that of some prominent criminals. In the State we human beings see our own sin magnified a thousand times. The State is the product of collective sin." Yet the state, perhaps paradoxically, must also educate for morality, and does so through law and, hopefully, through public schools.

22. Bonino, José Miguez, *Toward a Christian Political Ethics*, Philadelphia: Fortress Press, 1983, pp. 112–113.

23. Ibid., p. 113. Lehman is quoted, adding his own commentary to Barth: "Love frees the revolution for the practice of truth in its cause."

24. Wald, Kenneth D., *Religion and Politics in the United States*, New York: St. Martin's Press, 1987, p. 145.

25. Ibid. It is also perhaps not surprising that the secular international organization called Greenpeace, dedicated to nonviolent confrontation with whaling ships, seal hunters, and other ecological despoilers, bases its philosophy on an aspect of Christian ethics, specifically on "what the Quakers call bearing witness." Greenpeace, Box 3720, Washington, DC 20007.

26. The theme of violating the law in order to fulfill the role of true patriot has been the theme of numerous books published by the Fellowship of Reconciliation: *International Civil Disobedience: Theory and Practice*, 1982, containing essays by Martin Luther King, Jr., Noam Chomsky, Paul Goodman, and others edited by H. A. Bedau, 282 pp.; *Politics of Non-Violent Action* by Gene Sharp, 1973, 990 pp. (3 vols.); *Strength to Love* by Martin Luther King, Jr., edited by Coretta Scott King, 1981, 155 pp.; *Roots of Resistance* by William Watley, 1985, 159 pp.

27. Edwin Markham (1852–1940) wrote,

> Here is the truth in a little creed,
> Enough for all the roads we go;
> In love is all the law we need,
> In Christ is all the God we know.

No sentimentalist about the law, however, he also wrote:

> The laws are the secret avengers,
> And they rule above all lands;
> They come on wool-soft sandals,
> But they strike with iron hands.

First published by Doubleday, 1920; See *Modern American Poetry*, ed. Louis Untermeyer, New York: Harcourt, Brace, 1942, pp. 110f.

28. An exception to this might be one of the self-conscious Christian sects, like the Amish, or a monastic community like on Iona, which are virtually laws unto themselves.

29. Niebuhr, Reinhold, *Christian Realism and Political Problems*, New York: Charles Scribner's Sons, 1953, p. 147.

30. Maguire, Daniel C., *The Moral Revolution*, San Francisco: Harper & Row, 1986, p. 4.

31. There is no adequate translation for *hesed*. It means more than loving kindness, though this is the most popular usage in English. It includes forgiveness and redemption, as in the case of Hosea's relation to his profligate wife (an analogue of Israel's waywardness). It means steadfastness against all discouragement or even betrayal, represented in the covenant that God initiates, which God will never forsake even though we forsake him. Jesus elaborates this in his comment on the "unforgivable sin," in which he declares that all sins against God and the Christ will be forgiven because of God's loving kindness and grace. "Only blasphemy against the Spirit will not be forgiven" (Matthew 12:31). That is to say, breaking the bond with God by rejecting the mediation of the Spirit is the only fracture that cannot be healed; if we absolutely refuse forgiveness, we have made forgiveness impossible and are like the elder brother in the prodigal son story, who was left in the outer darkness because "he was angry and refused to go in" (Luke 15:28).

32. Achtemeier, E. R., "Righteousness in the Old Testament" in *The Interpreter's Dictionary of the Bible*, Vol. 4, New York: Abington Press, 1962, p. 83.

33. Judgment is an integral part of the restoration process, but it is meted out in love: "Blessed is the man whom Thou dost chasten" (Psalm 94:12). This understanding is carried over into the New Testament: "The Lord disciplines him whom he loves, and chastises every son whom he receives" (Hebrews 12:6).

34. Brunner, Emil, *Justice and the Social Order*, trans. Mary Hottinger, New York: Harper & Brothers, 1945, p. 22.

35. One could argue that the Supreme Court did not in fact reverse itself, because none of its members who made the earlier judgments were even alive in 1954. But it has been popularly assumed that the continuity of the Court is a concomitant of the continuity and integrity of the law. Clearly this can no longer be assumed; jurisprudence is by no means an exact science.

36. Nussbaum, Arthur, *A Concise History of the Law of Nations*, New York: Macmillan, 1962, p. 15.

37. Ibid., p. 16.

38. Allen, D. K., *Law in the Making*, London: Oxford University Press, 1958, pp. 23f.

39. Hitler, Adolf, *Mein Kampf*, trans. R. Manheim, Boston: Houghton Mifflin, 1943, p. 266. Hitler also excoriated philosophers in general for failing to provide "a definite, uniformly acknowledged philosophy." His own proposal for filling the void produced what Winston Churchill called "this hideous epoch in which we dwell."

40. Cohen, Felix, *Ethical Systems and Legal Ideas*, Ithaca, N.Y.: Cornell University Press, 1959, pp. 5f.

41. Ibid.

42. Quoted from *Speeches of Hitler from 1923–43* (ed. G. Prange, Washington, D.C.: Public Affairs Press), in Gould, Truit, *Political Ideologies*, New York: Macmillan, 1973, p. 116.

43. Anderson, B. W., "The Old Testament View of God," in *The Interpreter's Dictionary of the Bible*, Vol. 2, New York: Abingdon Press, 1962, p. 417.

44. Cohen, Morris Raphael, *Reason and Law*, New York: Collier Books, 1950, p. 34.

45. The description of Solomon's plans for the Temple, in 2 Chronicles 2:4, makes references to "show bread, burnt offerings, new moons and the appointed feasts of the Lord . . ." as "ordained forever for Israel."

46. Cardozo, Benjamin N., *The Nature of the Judicial Process*, New Haven, Conn.: Yale University Press, 1957, p. 26.

47. "When an adherent of a faith is brought continuously in touch with influences and exposed to desires inconsistent with that faith, a process of unconscious cerebration may take place. The formulas of the old faith are retained and repeated by force of habit, until one day the realization comes that conduct and sympathies . . . have become so inconsistent with the logical framework that it must be discarded" (Ibid., pp. 178–179).

48. Bennett, John C., "Democracy," in *Dictionary of Christian Ethics*, ed. John Macquarrie, Philadelphia: Westminster Press, 1967, p. 87. See also Barth, Karl, *Against the Stream*, New York: Philosophical Library, 1954, p. 44; Niebuhr, *Nature and Destiny of Man*, Part II, p. 268.

49. Niebuhr, *Interpretation of Christian Ethics*, Chapter IV.

50. Brunner, *Divine Imperative*, p. 395. Brunner notes, "The prophets as well as Jesus and the Apostles, explain the law of love mainly by using illustrations from the economic order."

51. Waxman, *Judaism*, p. 339.

52. Ibid.

53. Pemberton, Prentice L., and Finn, Daniel Rush, *Toward a Christian Economic Ethic*, Minneapolis: Winston Press, 1985, p. 27.

54. Ibid., p. 37. Pemberton and Finn quote with appreciation "Patristic Social Consciousness: The Church and the Poor" in *The Faith That Does Justice*, ed. John C. Haughey, New York: Paulist Press, 1977.

55. See Tawney, R. H., *Religion and the Rise of Capitalism*, New York: Harcourt Brace, 1926, Chapter 1, Sec. II.

56. *Institutes of the Christian Religion*, Book II, Chapter VII.

57. "In 1989 CEOs (corporate executive officers) at Fortune 100 firms made an average 1.2 million in salary . . . more in one week than the average worker does in a year . . . during a period of extensive cost cutting." *USA Today*, April 27, 1990, Section B, p. 1. See also Crystal, Graef, *The Overcompensated Executive*, New York: W. W. Norton, 1990, where the author notes that some top executives receive as much as $50 million yearly while stockholders actually experience a shrinking return on investment and workers are laid off.

58. Locke, John, *Second Treatise on Civil Government*, in *Great Books of the Western World*, Vol. 35, Chicago: University of Chicago Press, 1952, pp. 31–32.

59. Tawney's position on this is well known (see *Religion and the Rise of Capitalism*), having derived in large part from Max Weber and from Ernest Troeltsch. See also Brunner, *Justice and the Social Order*, p. 276.

60. Pemberton and Finn, *Toward a Christian Economic Ethic*, p. 139.

61. Friedman, Milton, and Friedman, Rose, *Free to Choose*, New York: Avon Books, 1979, p. 6. It should be pointed out, the Friedmans to the contrary, that the shortage of petroleum products was not created by the government, and subsequent revelation of oil surpluses at the time has fueled the suspicion that the so-called shortages may indeed have been the creation of the oil companies operating in a marketplace with too few controls. Certainly the crisis was felt in every part of the country before controls were invoked.

62. Locke, *Second Treatise*, Chapter V.

63. Polyanyi, Karl, *The Great Transformation: The Political and Economic Origins of Our Time*, Boston: Beacon Press, 1957, pp. 141f.

64. Wogaman, J. Philip, *Economics and Ethics*, London: SCM Press, 1986, p. 20.

65. Ibid., p. 22.

66. Lebacqz, Karen, *Justice in an Unjust World*, Minneapolis: Augsburg, 1987, p. 27.

67. Wogaman, *Economics and Ethics*, p. 23.

68. Ibid.

69. Kindleberger, Charles P., and Audretch, David B., eds., *The Multinational Corporation in the 1980s*, Cambridge, Mass.: MIT Press, 1983, p. 3.

70. Maguire, Daniel, *The Moral Choice*, New York: Doubleday,/Winston Press, 1978, p. 16.

71. Galbraith, John Kenneth, *The New Industrial State* (3rd ed.), Boston: Houghton Mifflin, 1978, p. 69.

72. Ibid., p. 79.

73. Root, Franklin R., *International Trade and Investment*, Cincinnati: Southwestern, 1984. "Government officials . . . regard the multi-nationals as far more than a business institution . . . threatening the integrity of the national community" (pp. 511f.).

74. Brunner, *Divine Imperative*, p. 414.

75. Ibid., p. 419.

76. Ibid., p. 423.

77. Ibid., p. 434.

78. A major thrust of Robert McAfee's book *Religion and Violence* (Philadelphia: Westminster Press, 1973) is to force recognition that we cannot plead innocence by simply claiming we have not overtly inflicted physical injury. "Whatever 'violates' another, in the sense of infringing upon or disregarding or abusing or denying that other, whether physical harm is involved or not, can be understood as an act of violence. The basic overall definition of violence would then become violation of personhood" (p. 7). In the broadest terms, he notes, any act that depersonalizes, that prevents a healthy fulfillment of life's possibilities (e.g., denying education, health care, and decent chance for a job) is a violent act for which we must repent. Even if we have not done so directly, but have elected officials who have done so, we are guilty.

79. Lebacqz, *Justice in an Unjust World*, pp. 150f.

80. Ibid., p. 155.

CHAPTER NINE

1. Borg, Marcus J., "Jesus and the Kingdom of God," *The Christian Century*, April 22, 1987, p. 380.

2. Many second-century Christian writers held that Christianity is a way of life quite distinct from the prevailing culture: The Shepherd of Hermas, the Epistle of Barnabus, First Epistle of Clement; but Tertullian took the radical view that culture is the purveyor of sin. See *De Spectaculus ii*; Apology XXXIX; *De Corona*; *On Repentance*.

3. Brunner, *Divine Imperative*, pp. 483f. Brunner nevertheless found ample reason for devoting some 30 pages to the ethical implication of many facets of Western culture to Christianity, and his insights have enriched the study of Christian ethics for more than half a century since the book was first written in 1932.

4. Niebuhr, H. Richard, *Christ and Culture*, New York: Harper & Brothers, 1951, p. 11. Niebuhr's book has become a classic in its analysis of the forms that the relationship has taken across the centuries: Christ against culture, the Christ of culture, Christ above culture, Christ and culture in paradox, and Christ the transformer of culture. His conclusion that there can be no specific "Christian" position remains a constant critical challenge.

5. Borg, "Jesus and the Kingdom of God."

6. Einstein, *Out of My Later Years*, p. 9.

7. Brunner, *Divine Imperative*, p. 499.

8. Henri, Robert, *The Art Spirit*, New York: J. B. Lippincott, 1951. Quoted from the flyleaf and p. 136.

9. Holthusen, Han Egon, "What Is Christian in Christian Literature?" in *Christian Faith and the Contemporary Arts*, ed. Finley Eversole, Nashville: Abingdon Press, 1962, p. 92.

10. There were significant exceptions among the Puritans, like John Milton and Jonathan who employed poetry and prose with great power in the service of faith. In the nineteenth century the most vocal critic of literature as subversive of faith was, ironically, Leo Tolstoy, who had already won international acclaim for his novels *War and Peace* and *Anna Karenina.*

11. Brunner, *Divine Imperative*, pp. 500–501.

12. Nathan, Walter L., *Art and the Message of the Church*, Philadelphia: Westminster Press, 1961, p. 157.

13. Having seen Michelangelo's Sistine Chapel ceiling, which was being painted just a few hundred yards from where Raphael was working on his *The School of Athens*, Raphael allegedly copied Michelangelo's style and "stole" one of his human figures. Writes historian Frederick Hartt: "His own style was never again to be quite the same." See Hartt, Frederick, *History of Italian Renaissance Art*, New York: Abrams and Prentice-Hall, 1969, p. 462.

14. Fleming, William, *Art and Ideas*, (3rd ed.), New York: Holt, Rinehart and Winston (no date), p. 329.

15. Huyghe, René, ed., *Larousse Encyclopedia of Renaissance and Baroque Art*, New York: Prometheus Press, 1967, p. 220.

16. Schneider, Daniel, *The Psychoanalyst and the Artist*, New York: Farrar, Strauss, 1949, p. 140.

17. Canady, John, *Mainstreams of Modern Art*, New York: Holt, Rinehart and Winston, 1959, pp. 296f.

18. Buttrick, George, *Faith and Education*, New York: Abingdon Cokesbury, 1952, p. 17.

19. Tillich, Paul, *Theology of Culture*, New York: Oxford University Press, 1959, p. 68.

20. Bouquet, A. C., *Everyday Life in New Testament Times*, New York: Charles Scribner's Sons, 1955, p. 156.

21. Durant, Will, *The Age of Faith*, New York: Simon & Schuster, 1950, p. 818.

22. Brubacher, John S., and Rudy, Willis, *Higher Education in Transition*, New York: Harper & Row, 1968, pp. 7–8.

23. Dewey, John, *Education and Democracy*, New York, Macmillan, 1916, p. 61.

24. Dewey, John, *Education Today*, New York: G. P. Putnam's Sons, 1949, p. 3. Here Dewey was not suggesting anything so mystical as Carl Jung's archetypal racial unconscious, but rather the acknowledged consensus of social standards: the pragmatic dictum, "whatever works" in terms of the needs of the group.

25. Ortega y Gasset, José, *The Revolt of the Masses*, New York: W. W. Norton, 1957, p. 113.

26. Lilge, Frederic, *The Abuse of Learning*, New York: Macmillan, 1948.

27. Kahler, Erich, "Man Without Values," in *Tower and the Abyss*, New York: Braziller, 1957, p. 244.

28. Mumford, Lewis, *The Conduct of Life*, New York: Harcourt, Brace and World, 1951, p. 154.

29. Kirkpatrick, Jeane, "Blame State Department, the Marines, and Lax Teaching of Values," *Los Angeles Times*, April 17, 1987. Predictably, the response from the educational community was swift and caustic, one teacher charging that Kirkpatrick herself had "openly embraced and exchanged gifts with the Argentine military dictator responsible for the reign of terror of the Disappeareds."

30. Lippman, Walter, "Education Versus Western Civilization" in *The American Scholar*, Vol. 10, No. 2, Spring 1941, p. 187.

31. It is impossible to do justice to the many schools or systems of educational thought that have emerged in the past half century. Students interested in their background will find them abundantly documented in John Brubacher's *Modern Philosophies of Education*, New York: McGraw-Hill, 1969; George Kneller's *Foundations of Education* (1971); William F. O'Neill's *Educational Ideologies* (1981); Daniel Selakovich's *Schooling in America* (1984); and George Kneller's *Movements of Thought in Modern Education* (1984).

32. Illich, Ivan, *Deschooling Society*, New York: Harper & Row, 1970; Goodman, Paul, *Compulsory Mis-education*, New York: Vantage Press, 1964. Critics note that neither writer evidences understanding of the job market trends, in which the uneducated will find a rapidly shrinking prospect for employment, or of what happens to societies where there are great numbers of people who are illiterate, unemployed, and living in a cycle of despair and anger. Nor is there evidence that such conditions cause people to return to school, or that, if they do, there will be schools and jobs waiting for them. Once taxes are cut for education, they are hard to restore. Further, the level of sophistication required for jobs in a technological society is such that dropouts fall hopelessly behind. The Founding Fathers showed great insight in advocating universal, compulsory education.

33. Brunner, *Divine Imperative*, p. 505.

34. Ibid., p. 506.

35. Pullias, Earl, *A Search for Understanding*, Dubuque, Iowa: Wm. C. Brown, 1965, p. 11.

36. This is set forth with particular clarity in Karl Barth's *The Epistle to the Romans*, in which he notes that even our religious life, which is supposedly an expression of our spiritual nature, is of the flesh: "Religion neither overcomes human worldliness nor transfigures it; not even the religion of Primitive Christianity or of Isaiah or of the Reformers can rid itself of this limitation. Nor is it merely fortuitous that an odor of death seems, as it were, to hang about the very summits of religion. Since religion is human, utterly human history, it is flesh." Barth, Karl, *The Epistle to the Romans*, London: Oxford University Press, 1950, p. 276.

37. Tillich, Paul, *Theology of Culture*, New York: Oxford University Press, 1959, pp. 146–147.

38. Hutchins, Robert M., *The Conflict in Education*, New York: Harper & Row, 1953, pp. 69–70.

39. Ibid., pp. 70–71.

40. Of the nine colonial colleges founded before 1776, beginning with Harvard (founded in 1635, chartered in 1650), all but the University of Pennsylvania were given their birth by church denominations. "The role of organized Christianity was important in the founding of the pre-Revolutionary Colleges. In addition, the purpose of training students for the Christian ministry is specified in all colonial college charters with the single exception, the College of Philadelphia." Brubacher, John S., and Willis, Rudy, *Higher Education in Transition*, New York: Harper & Row, 1968, p. 7.

41. Ornstein, Allan C., and Levine, Daniel U., *An Introduction to the Foundations of Education*, Boston: Houghton Mifflin, 1985, p. 548.

42. Van Scotter, Richard, Hass, John, Kraft, Richard, and Schott, James, *Social Foundations of Education*, Englewood Cliffs, N.J.: Prentice-Hall, 1985, p. 270.

43. Brunner, *Divine Imperative*, p. 515.

44. Patillo, Manning, and Mackenzie, Donald, *Eight Hundred Colleges Face the Future*, St. Louis, Miss.: Danforth Foundation, 1965, p. 36. Conversations with directors at the Danforth Foundation indicate that no significant study of this kind has been done in more recent years.

45. Trueblood, D. Elton, *The Idea of a College*, New York: Harper & Brothers, 1959, p. 29.

46. Ibid.

47. Rothblatt, Sheldon, "Standing Antagonisms," in *The Future of State Universities*, New Brunswick, N.J.: Rutgers University Press, 1985, p. 46.

48. Bloom, Allan, *The Closing of the American Mind*, New York: Simon & Schuster, 1987, p. 338.

49. Ibid., p. 341.

50. Bowen, Ezra, "Looking to Its Roots," *Time*, May 25, 1987, p. 29.

51. Terrell, Huntington, *Time*, May 25, 1987, p. 29.

52. Quoted in "Education: Christian and Liberal" by Phillip Moulton, *The Christian Century*, April 21, 1954, p. 489.

53. Smith, Courtney C., "Contributions of Quakerism to Education," in *The Westonian*, Vol. 62, No. 3, p. 6.

54. Mouw, Richard, "The Ethics of Teaching Ethics" in *The Annual of the Society of Christian Ethics*, ed. D. M. Yeager and Gilbert Meilander, Georgetown: Georgetown University Press, 1989, p. 273.

55. Gustafson, James M., *Theology from a Theocentric Perspective*, Chicago: University of Chicago Press, 1981, pp. 97–99 and 251f.

56. Brunner, *Divine Imperative*, p. 491.

57. Ibid.

58. Snow, Charles P., "The Moral Un-neutrality of Science" in *Science*, Vol. 133, No. 3448 (January 27, 1961), p. 256.

59. Einstein, *Out of My Later Years*, p. 26.

60. Townes, Charles, "The Convergence of Science and Religion" in *Think*, published by IBM, March 1966, p. 7.

61. Einstein, *Out of My Later Years*, p. 9.

62. See Bertocci, Peter A., *Introduction to the Philosophy of Religion*, Englewood Cliffs, N.J.: Prentice-Hall, 1952, pp. 9f.; King, Winston, I., *Introduction to Religion*, Harper & Brothers, 1954, p. 80; Magee, John B., *Religion and Modern Man*, New York: Harper & Row, 1967; McLaren, Robert B., *The World of Philosophy*, Chicago: Nelson-Hall, 1983, pp. 1–4; Misch, Georg, *The Dawn of Philosophy*, Cambridge, Mass.: Harvard University Press, 1951, pp. 4f.

63. Long, Edward LeRoy, *Science and Christian Faith*, New York: Association Press, 1950, p. 16.

64. Simpson, Cuthbert A., "The Book of Genesis," in *The Interpreter's Bible*, Vol. 1, New York: Abingdon-Cokesbury Press, 1952, p. 445.

65. Compton, Arthur Holly, "A Modern Concept of God," in *Man's Destiny in Eternity*, The Garvin Lecture, Boston: Beacon Press, 1949, p. 19.

66. Einstein, *Out of My Later Years*, p. 25. There are some who object to the "is" versus "ought" dualism utilized by Einstein: "Science can only ascertain what is . . ." and calling this "the naturalistic fallacy." Science, it is declared, may have in fact found the roots of morality in the limbic system of the human brain, where the bridge from

is to ought is logically made. See Hefner, Philip, "Is/Ought: A Risky Relationship Between Theology and Science," in *The Sciences and Theology in the Twentieth Century*, ed. A. R. Peacock, Northumberland, England: Oriel Press (Routledge and Kegan Paul), 1981, pp. 58f.

67. Schilling, Harold K., *Science and Religion*, New York: Charles Scribner's Sons, 1962, p. 15.

68. Rhodes, Frank H. T., in *Christianity in a Mechanistic Universe: A Symposium*, ed. D. B. Mackay, London: Intervarsity Fellowship Press, 1965, p. 18.

69. Schilling, *Science and Religion*, p. 20.

70. Bronowski, Jacob, *Science and Human Values*, New York: Harper & Row, 1965, p. 13.

71. Einstein, *Out of My Later Years*, p. 26.

72. Schilling, *Science and Religion*, p. 19.

73. Long, *Science and Christian Faith*, p. 14.

74. Baillie, John, *Natural Science and the Spiritual Life*, New York: Charles Scribner's Sons, 1952, p. 19.

75. Polkinghorne, John, *The Way the World Is*, London: Triangle SPCK, 1983, p. 9. Polkinghorne is now President of Queen's College, Cambridge.

76. Ibid., p. 11.

77. Einstein made a similar observation to Edwin Boring, of Harvard: "Derr Herr Gott wurfelt nicht," "The Lord God did not gamble." I owe this quote to Dr. Boring, who shared it in a letter some years ago.

78. Ibid., p. 14. It will be noted that Polkinghorne avoids the Fundamentalist presupposition of God having created everything just as it now is my divine fiat. He grants God freedom to be God, and to do things God's own way, which appears to have been the way of probability and evolution.

79. That is to say, by the physical sciences; whether the social sciences are truly "science" must be argued elsewhere.

80. Ibid., p. 16.

81. Barrett, William, *The Illusion of Technique*, Garden City, N.Y.: Anchor Press/Doubleday, 1978, pp. 180f.

82. Ibid., p. 183.

83. Wilson, *Sociobiology*, p. 563.

84. Wilson, Edward O., *On Human Nature*, Cambridge, Mass.: Harvard University Press, p. 5.

85. It is interesting that this bold declaration about the origin of the human moral sense comes not from a neurologist, but from an entomologist, and is based on his observation of insect behavior. One is reminded of the location of the soul, by a mathematician, René Descartes, in the pineal gland behind the third ventricle of the' brain. The gland, found in most vertebrates above the reptile, remains of unknown function, probably does not generate a moral sense, and is not found in insects.

86. Hefner, "Is/Ought," p. 68.

87. Ibid., p. 76.

88. Montefiore, Hugh, *Can Man Survive?* Huntington, N.Y.: Fontana Books, 1970, p. 75.

89. Jones, Richard G., *Groundwork of Christian Ethics*, London: Epworth Press, 1984, p. 206.

90. Ibid.

91. Ibid., p. 208.

92. Braun, Ernest, and Collinridge, David, *Technology and Survival*, London: Butterworths, 1977, p. 11.

93. The proposal was that the government "regulate science as one regulates the railroads." Graham, Loren R., *Between Science and Values*, New York: Columbia University Press, 1981, pp. 291f.

94. Norman, Colin, *The God That Limps: Science and Technology in the Eighties*, New York: W. W. Norton, 1981, p. 71.

95. Barbour, Ian G., *Technology, Environment, and Human Values*, New York: Praeger Scientific Studies, 1980, p. 295.

96. Ibid., p. 311.

CHAPTER TEN

1. Kraemer, Heinrich, *The Christian Message in a Non-Christian World*, Grand Rapids, Mich.: Kregel, 1963, p. 86.

2. Jorstad, Erling, *The Politics of Moralism*, Minneapolis: Augsburg, 1981. This is also quoted in Lucien Richard's *Is There a Christian Ethic?* See n. 3.

3. Richard, Lucien, OMI., *Is There a Christian Ethic?* New York: Paulist Press, 1988, p. 25.

4. McCormick, Richard, "Does Faith Add to Ethical Perception?" in *The Distinctiveness of Christian Ethics*, New York: Paulist Press, 1980, p. 162.

5. See Amos 5:21–24; Isaiah 1:12–23; Ezekiel 45:9; Micah 6:8. The message had been sounded earlier as a warning when the nation was being founded: Exodus 23:17; Deuteronomy 28:15f.

6. Klassen, William, *Love of Enemies*, Philadelphia: Fortress Press, 1984, p. 7. Klassen, writing as dean of the Interfaith Peace Academy in Jerusalem, notes, "The ease with which [the Moral Majority] identifies America with Christianity, and the fact that they do not follow Jesus in teaching release from hate, supports that judgement."

7. Tillich, Paul, *Christianity and the Encounter of the World Religions*, New York: Columbia University Press, 1963, p. 11.

8. Klassen, *Love of Enemies*, pp. 6–7.

9. This figure is quoted in *The Armageddon Report* of the Christic Institute, Washington, D.C., April 1986, p. 3.

10. Klassen, *Love of Enemies*, p. 7.

11. Ibid., p. 8.

12. Hauerwas, *Community of Character.* I have not done justice to the sweep of Hauerwas's contention; he moves quickly beyond this brief point to the fact that Jesus did not come to provide an ethic, but a story of the kingdom. Our efforts to find the "real man" behind the story, or to make the kingdom fit our earthbound ideas of kingdoms (sticking in our own stories without listening to his), have gotten us badly off the track. "Ethicists have found this useful because the notion of the Kingdom sounds like it involves normative guidelines to inform a social ethic. The scriptures can be scavenged for individual sayings that seem to determine the character of such a Kingdom. . . . But this strategy is doomed to failure" (p. 44).

13. It may even be that his early admonition to women to "keep silence in the churches" (1 Corinthians 14:34) was such an accommodation, but one which he

amended later in declaring that in Christ "there is neither male nor female" (Galatians 3:28). He addressed special greetings to women who had become leaders in the churches (Colossians 4:15; 2 Timothy 4:19, and "She who is at Babylon, who is likewise chosen" in 1 Peter 5:13, whom some commentators agree may have been Peter's wife, later martyred.

14. Drawing on original sources, Walter Wink suggests that the injunctions of the Sermon on the Mount, which seem to urge placid inaction, fitted King James's strategy for keeping Christian activists quiet during his tyrannical reign in seventeenth-century England. Tragically, the mistranslation has also been used by advocates of apartheid in modern South Africa. Wink proposes that Jesus offered neither violence nor inaction, but a way of strategic nonviolent resistance. See his *Violence and Non-violence in South Africa: Jesus' Third Way*, Philadelphia: New Society, 1987, published in cooperation with Fellowship of Reconciliation, pp. 12–14.

15. Tillich, *Christianity and the Encounter*, p. 15.

16. Hauerwas, Stanley, *The Peaceable Kingdom*, Notre Dame, Ind.: University of Notre Dame Press, 1983, p. 60.

17. Tillich, *Christianity and the Encounter*, pp. 14f.

18. Preston, Ronald H., *Church and Society in the Late Twentieth Century*, London: SCM Press, 1983, p. 58.

19. Ibid., p. 60.

20. Clinton Morrison is professor of New Testament at Louisville Theological Seminary and author of *An Analytical Concordance to the Revised Standard Version of the New Testament* (Westminster Press, 1979). This comment is from an unpublished letter and is quoted with his permission.

21. Lindsay, Hal, *The Late Great Planet Earth*, Grand Rapids, Mich.: Zondervan Press, 1970, p. 155.

22. Falwell, Jerry, *Listen America!* New York: Doubleday Bantam Books, 1980, pp. 67, 84; see also LaHaye, Tim, *The Battle for the Mind*, Old Tappan, N.J.: Flemming H. Revell, 1980, p. 218.

23. Lang, Andrew, *Armageddon, The Religious Theory of Survivable Nuclear War*, Washington, D.C.: The Christic Institute, April 1986, p. 4.

24. Maguire, Daniel C., *The Moral Revolution*, San Francisco: Harper & Row, 1986, p. 54.

25. Brown, Robert McAfee, *Religion and Violence*, Philadelphia: Westminster Press, 1973, p. 7.

26. Schuster, Clara, and Ashburn, Shirley, *The Process of Human Development*, Boston: Little, Brown, 1986. Quoted from the World Health Organization.

27. The most common form of execution was stoning (Leviticus 24; Deuteronomy 17, 22, 24; 1 Kings 21), though burning alive was prescribed for sexual offenses (Leviticus 20; Deuteronomy 13; Joshua 7) and death by the sword (which was often against whole communities guilty of apostasy, e.g., Exodus 32:27; cf. Deuteronomy 13:15, 1 Kings 18:40, 2 Samuel 3:27) was also employed as were beheading (2 Kings 6:31; 2 Samuel 16:9) and shooting with arrows as a kind of firing squad, for trespassing on sacred ground (Exodus 19:13).

28. Holmes, Arthur F., *Ethics: Approaching Moral Decisions.* Downer's Grove, Ill.: Inter-varsity Press, 1984, pp. 97–98.

29. Latourette, Kenneth Scott, *A History of Christianity*, New York: Harper & Brothers, 1953, p. 157.

30. Block, Eugene, *And May God Have Mercy*, San Francisco, Fearon, 1962, p. 16.

31. Ibid.

32. Ibid., p. 24.

33. Ibid.

34. Ibid., p. 25.

35. Ibid., p. 27.

36. *Los Angeles Times*, May 27, 1990, p. M4.

37. Frank, Jerome, and Frank, Barbara, *Not Guilty*, Garden City, N.Y.: Doubleday, 1957.

38. Endres, Michael E., *The Morality of Capital Punishment*, Mystic, Conn.: Twenty-Third Publications, 1985, p. 131.

39. Ibid., pp. 132–133.

40. Quoted from the *Book of Worship for United States Forces*, Washington, D.C.: U.S. Government Printing Office, 1974, p. 199.

41. Wells, Donald, "How Much Can the 'Just War' Justify?" *Journal of Philosophy*, LXVI, December 1969, pp. 819–829.

42. Smylie, Robert, *War in Slow Motion*, ed. Zelle Andrews, New York: Pilgrim Press, 1985, p. 4.

43. Murray, John Courtney, *Morality and Modern War*, New York: The Council on Religion and International Affairs, 1959, p. 6.

44. Smylie, *War*, p. 5.

45. Brown, Robert McAfee, *Making Peace in the Global Village*, Philadelphia: Westminster Press, 1981, p. 49.

46. Smylie, *War*, p. 7.

47. Geyer, Alan, *The Idea of Disarmament: Thinking the Unthinkable*, Elgin, Ill.: Brethren Press, 1982, p. 205.

48. Carl Sagan spoke these words on a nationally televised debate, and was quoted in the April 1984 issue of *Friends of the Earth* newsletter, eds. Anne and Paul Ehrlich, San Francisco.

49. Maguire, Daniel, *The Moral Revolution*, San Francisco: Harper & Row, 1986, pp. 54–59.

50. Geyer, *Idea of Disarmament*, p. 193.

51. Ibid., p. 195.

52. Ibid., p. 200.

53. It was the author's privilege to serve as president of the Pacific Interfaith Peace Prize Foundation in 1986, and to present Dr. Carazo with its annual award. Dr. Carazo shared these words during the banquet at which the award was given. They were reiterated on October 23, 1990, before The Faculty Lyceum, at California State University, Fullerton.

54. Hebblethwaite, *Christian Ethics*, p. 101.

55. Schliermacher, Friedrich, *The Christian Faith*, Edinburgh: T. & T. Clark, 1928, pp. 34f. The argument was that polytheisms tend to leave us adrift in a sea of naturalisms and competing deities, whereas monotheism draws us into greater dependence on God.

56. Hume, Robert E., *The World's Living Religions*, New York: Charles Scribner's Sons, 1924, Preface.

57. Among the "elements of strength" in Islam, for example, he lists its monotheism and the concept that God is merciful; its "weakness" is due to its reliance on force, its fatalism, its low estimate of women, and the "pathetic weakness of its founder's moral character" (pp. 243–244). In the chapter on Taoism, the "strengths" include returning good for evil (compared directly to Jesus' teaching); its "weakness": the lack of a Supreme Being.

58. Hutchinson, John A., *Paths of Faith*, New York: McGraw-Hill, 1981, pp. 524, 528.

59. Hume, *World's Living Religions*, pp. 276–279.

60. Toynbee, Arnold, *Christianity Among the Religions of the World*, New York: Charles Scribner's Sons, 1957, p. 46.

61. Ibid., p. 52.

62. Ibid., p. 85.

63. Ibid., p. 86.

64. Ibid., p. 106.

65. Bennett, John C., *Christian Ethics and the National Conscience*, Boston: Alexander Graham Bell Lecture (Boston University Alumni Association), 1964, p. 18.

66. Ibid.

67. Ibid., p. 21.

68. Ibid., p. 23.

69. Ibid., p. 24.

70. Preston, Ronald H. *The Future of Christian Ethics*, London: SCM Press, 1987, p. 11.

71. Smart, Ninian, *The World's Religions*, Englewood Cliffs, N.J.: Prentice Hall, 1989, p. 352.

72. Heim, S. Mark, "Reconsidering Religious Pluralism," *The Christian Century*, July 10–17, 1991, p. 688.

73. Keeling, Michael, *The Foundations of Christian Ethics*, Edinburgh, Scotland: T. & T. Clark, 1990, p. 238.

74. Fox, Matthew, *The Cosmic Christ*, San Francisco: Harper & Row, 1988, pp. 129f.

75. Hyun-Kyung, Chung, "Welcome the Spirit," *Christianity and Crisis*, New York: Christianity and Crisis Inc., July 15, 1991, p. 222.

INDEX